Penguin Books

THE TWELVE CAESARS

Not much is known about the life of GAIUS SUETONIUS TRANQUILLUS. He was probably born in A.D. 69 – the famous 'year of the four Emperors' – when his father, a Roman knight, served as a colonel in a regular legion and took part in the Battle of Betriacum. From the letters of Suetonius's close friend Pliny the Younger we learn that he practised briefly at the bar, avoided political life, and became chief secretary to the Emperor Hadrian (A.D. 117–38). He was one of several Palace officials, including the Guards Commander, whom Hadrian dismissed when he returned from Britain for behaving impolitely to the Empress Sabina. Suetonius seems to have lived to a good age and probably died around the year A.D. 140. The titles of his books are recorded as follows: *The Twelve Caesars*; *Royal Biographies*; *Lives of Famous Whores*; *Roman Manners and Customs*; *The Roman Year*; *Roman Festivals*; *Roman Dress*; *Greek Games*; *Offices of State*; *Cicero's Republic*; *The Physical Defects of Mankind*; *Methods of Reckoning Time*; *An Essay on Nature*; *Greek Terms of Abuse*; *Grammatical Problems*; *Critical Signs Used in Books*. But apart from fragments of his *Illustrious Writers*, which include short biographies of Virgil, Horace, and Lucan, the only extant book is *The Twelve Caesars*, the most fascinating and richest of all Latin histories.

ROBERT GRAVES has also translated Lucan's *Pharsalia* and *The Golden Ass* by Apuleius for the Penguin Classics. Born in Wimbledon in 1895, he has made his home in Majorca since 1929, by which time he was already living by writing. He has now published over 120 books; those published in Penguins are the historical novels *I, Claudius*, *Claudius the God*, *Count Belisarius* and *Wife to Mr Milton*; *Collected Short Stories* and *Antigua, Penny, Puce*, both fiction; *Goodbye to All That*, his autobiography; *The Greek Myths*, a modern dictionary of Greek mythology; *The Crowning Privilege*, lectures and essays on poetry; and *Selected Poems*. His principal calling has always been poetry, and from 1961 to 1966 he was Professor of Poetry at Oxford, and became an Honorary Fellow of St John's College, Oxford, in 1971.

MICHAEL GRANT has been successively Chancellor's medallist and fellow of Trinity College, Cambridge, Professor of Humanity at Edinburgh University, first Vice-Chancellor of Khartoum University, and President and Vice-Chancellor of the Queen's University of Belfast. Until 1966 he was President of the Virgil Society, and was President of the Classical Association in 1977–78. He has translated Cicero's *Selected Works*, *Selected Speeches on the Good Life*, and *Murder Trials*, and Tacitus's *Annals of Imperial Rome* for the Penguin Classics: his other books include *The Civilizations of Europe* (1965), *Gladiators* (1967), *Roman Literature* (Pelican), *Latin Literature* and *Greek Literature* (both anthologies in Penguin Classics), *Cleopatra* (1972), *The Jews in the Roman World* (1973), *The Army of the Caesars* (1974), *The Fall of the Roman Empire* (1976), *Cities of Vesuvius* (1976, Penguin), *Saint Paul* (1976), *Jesus* (1977) and *History of Rome* (1978).

Gaius Suetonius Tranquillus
THE TWELVE CAESARS

TRANSLATED BY ROBERT GRAVES
REVISED WITH AN INTRODUCTION BY MICHAEL GRANT

PENGUIN BOOKS

Penguin Books Ltd, Harmondsworth, Middlesex, England
Penguin Books, 625 Madison Avenue, New York, New York 10022, U.S.A.
Penguin Books Australia Ltd, Ringwood, Victoria, Australia
Penguin Books Canada Ltd, 2801 John Street, Markham, Ontario, Canada L3R 1B4
Penguin Books (N.Z.) Ltd, 182–190 Wairau Road, Auckland 10, New Zealand

This translation first published by Penguin Books 1957
This revised and expanded edition first published by Allen Lane 1979
Published in Penguin Books 1980

Picture research, captions and essays by Sabine MacCormack
Maps and genealogical tables drawn by Reginald Piggott

Designed by Gerald Cinamon and Malcolm Farrar
Made and printed in Great Britain by
Butler & Tanner Ltd, Frome and London
Set in Monophoto Ehrhardt

CONTENTS

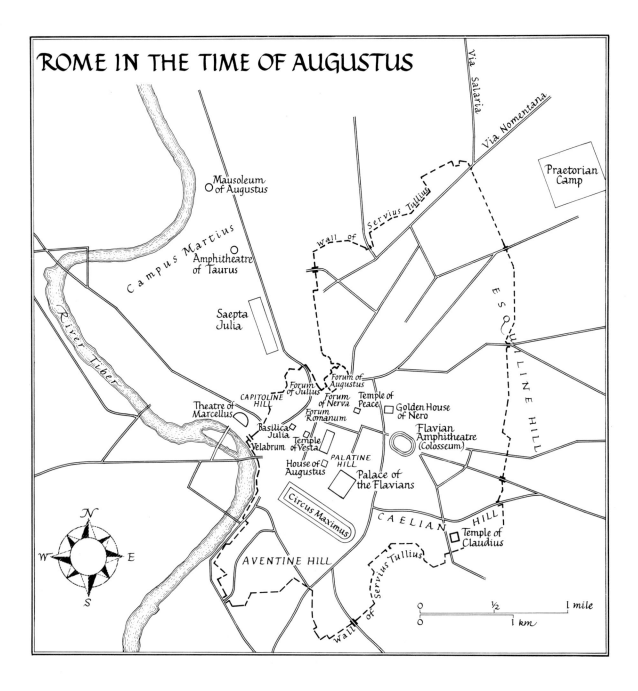

ROME IN THE TIME OF AUGUSTUS

Via Salaria

Via Nomentana

Praetorian Camp

Mausoleum of Augustus

Campus Martius

Amphitheatre of Taurus

Wall of Servius Tullius

Saepta Julia

River Tiber

E S Q U I L I N E   H I L L

Forum of Augustus

Forum of Julius

CAPITOLINE HILL

Forum of Nerva

Temple of Peace

Golden House of Nero

Theatre of Marcellus

Forum Romanum

Basilica Julia

Velabrum

Temple of Vesta

Flavian Amphitheatre (Colosseum)

House of Augustus

PALATINE HILL

Palace of the Flavians

Circus Maximus

CAELIAN   HILL

Temple of Claudius

N
W   E
S

AVENTINE HILL

Wall of Servius Tullius

0 ___ ½ ___ 1 mile
0 ___ 1 km

INTRODUCTION

Gaius Suetonius Tranquillus was born in about A.D. 70. His family probably came from Hippo Regius (Annaba in Algeria). Suetonius may have taught literature at Rome for a time. He also seems to have practised law, and then served on the staff of Pliny the younger, when Pliny was governor, with special powers, of Bithynia-Pontus (northern Asia Minor) in c. A.D. 110–112; Pliny had earlier helped to secure him a small property in Italy.

Subsequently Suetonius, who was a Roman knight (*eques*), occupied a succession of posts at the imperial court. First he held the 'secretaryship of studies' (*a studiis*), of which the precise functions are uncertain. Then he became director of the imperial libraries, and was finally placed in charge of the Emperor's correspondence. Probably he occupied the first two of these three offices under Trajan (98–117); the last and most important appointment dates from Hadrian (117–138). In 122, however, he seems to have been dismissed from his post for disrespectful behaviour towards the empress Sabina. And yet if, as is sometimes suggested, one of his lost treatises, *On Public Offices*, was the last of his works to be written, this choice of subject, made at a time of administrative reforms by Hadrian, suggests that he finally enjoyed at least a partial return to imperial favour. An allusion in his extant writings seems to indicate that he was still alive after 130. Pliny described him as a quiet and studious man, devoted to writing. He was a representative of a new generation of professional scholars who became prominent in this period.

In the reign of Trajan he wrote his first series of biographies, *The Lives of Illustrious Men*. In pursuance of a Greek tradition, these were biographical sketches of Roman literary personalities – grammarians, fifteen orators (*De Grammaticis et Rhetoribus*), thirty-three poets (*De Poetis*), and six historians. Only a few fragments of this work have survived. In the orators' section, a brief abstract of the life of Passienus Crispus, of the time of Augustus, has come down to us. Of the poets, we have Terence, Virgil, Horace and part of Lucan. Brief studies of Tibullus and Persius may also belong to the collection, though it seems likely that they have been edited and abbreviated by later hands. The Lives of the historians have disappeared, except for a fragmentary account of Pliny the elder.

The Lives of the Caesars are biographies of the 'Twelve Caesars', from Julius to Domitian (d. A.D. 96). The work is preserved, except for a few chapters of Julius's life. It was dedicated to Gaius Septicius Clarus, who became prefect of the Praetorian Guard in 119 and was dismissed along with Suetonius himself three years later. Apart from the rather undistinguished Cornelius Nepos (d. 24 B.C.), Suetonius is the first Latin biographer whose works have come down to us. He was aware that he must strike out in a different direction from the writers of history, which was regarded as a different genre. This seemed all the more important for Suetonius because of the overpowering contemporary work of Tacitus, which could not be rivalled. In consequence, he abandoned the chronological method which his Greek fellow-biographer Plutarch tended to favour, and adopted a method – which had occasionally been employed in Greek and Latin before – whereby the straight narrative was interrupted by material classified according to subject-matter, dealing successively with the different characteristics which his personages displayed; in this procedure of classification, it may be possible to detect the expert on grammar and grammarians (whose lives, as we have seen, he narrated).

Suetonius's principal contribution, however, lies in his relatively high degree of objectivity. With him, we have moved away from the traditional eulogistic treatment, and have entered a much more astringent atmosphere, in which the men whom he is describing are looked at with a cooler and more disenchanted eye. Owing to our losses in earlier literature, it is impossible to state with any assurance whether, and to what extent, this had been achieved by previous writers. But at all events Suetonius innovated by selecting the rulers of Rome as targets for this exercise. He gathers together, and lavishly inserts, information both for and against them, usually without adding any personal judgement in one direction or the other, and above all without introducing the moralizations which had so frequently characterized Greek and Roman biography and history alike. Occasionally conflicting statements are weighed. In general, however, the presentation is drily indiscriminate. This has the result – since he loves an entertaining story – that eccentricities rather than virtues remain in the reader's mind. But the author's own opinions are rarely permitted to intrude, and indeed he himself, in collecting all this weird, fascinating material, appears to make little effort to reach a decision about the personalities he is describing, or to build up their characteristics into a coherent account. Perhaps, he may feel, that is how people are: they possess discordant elements which do not add up to a harmonious unity.

The best quality of his work is his power to create rapid, dramatic and often moving narrative, including, at times, impressive set-pieces, among which the death of Nero is especially notable. The stories are generally told in a clear and straightforward manner, though his curiously disjointed and staccato diction can lead to obscurity. An unusual, if not unprecedented, feature is his willingness to quote verbatim from his sources, offering literal citations from imperial letters and public and private records. This documentary material, however, is almost entirely limited to Augustus: so it was probably after writing that emperor's biography (the second of the twelve) that he was dismissed from court, and consequently lost access to the archives.[1] His employment of literary authorities is hard to reconstruct, because, like so many other authors, he is reluctant to cite them by name. He twice quotes Pollio (d. A.D. 4), however, and once Cremutius Cordus (d. A.D. 25), and he echoes the *Acts* of Augustus on at least four occasions.

The period about which Suetonius is writing is one of the most important, critical and formative in the his-

1. Perhaps the last six Lives formed a supplement, published later than the rest.

tory of the western world, and with the exception of the Greek Dio Cassius (who is much later, incomplete, and often anachronistic) Suetonius and Tacitus are our only major literary sources for the epoch. Tacitus, for all his superlative merits, colours and patterns his facts; Suetonius's deadpan method, despite his inadequacies, is often a very valuable corrective, and the personal touches which he so abundantly provides are something we scarcely find in Tacitus at all. Certainly, modern methods are out of sympathy with Suetonius's Caesar-orientated, palace-centred approach; and there is, admittedly, a danger that by accepting it too slavishly we shall forget all the important things that are happening in other parts of the empire. On the other hand, the current reaction against his concentration on imperial personalities has gone too far – so far, indeed, that we have been told that the emperors did not matter very greatly, and that the Roman world would have manifested much the same trends and developments without them. This is, however, highly questionable. Granted that the Republic would still have broken down had Caesar never existed, the autocracy which followed might have assumed a very different form had there not been an Augustus; and Claudius and Vespasian, too, fulfilled highly individual and influential roles. Tacitus, Dio Cassius, inscriptions, coins, and works of art tell us something about them. But it is only from Suetonius that we get a plausible idea of what sort of people they were.

His *Twelve Caesars* provided a model for Einhard's *Charlemagne* in the ninth century, and a source for Petrarch's *Lives of the Illustrious Romans* in the fourteenth. The English translation by Philemon Holland (1606), though diffuse, is spirited and popular. In our own time, Suetonius contributed largely to *I Claudius* (followed by *Claudius the God*), the best-seller and television success of Robert Graves.

It is also Robert Graves whose English rendering is presented in this volume. 'The younger Pliny,' he observed, 'who persuaded the Emperor Trajan to grant Suetonius the immunities usually granted only to a father of three children, though he had none, wrote that the more he knew of Suetonius, the greater his affection for him grew; I have had the same experience.' Indeed, this is clear enough from his version, which makes vivid and compulsive reading and conveys the peculiarities of Suetonius's methods and character better than any other translation. Why, then, have I been asked to 'edit' it? Because Robert Graves (who explicitly refrained from catering for students) did not aim at producing a precise translation – introducing, as he himself points out, sentences of explanation, omitting passages which do not seem to help the sense, and 'turning sentences, and sometimes even groups of sentences, inside-out'. But I feel that Mr Graves has been much too modest in this willingness to exclude from his readership those who want greater verbal exactitude; and indeed time has proved this conjecture right, since admiration for the style of his Suetonius has been great, and does not flag. What I have tried to do, therefore, is to make such adjustments as will bring his version inside the range of what is now generally regarded by readers of the Penguin Classics as a 'translation' – without, I hope, detracting from his excellent and inimitable manner. Maps, a key to terms, a list of reigns, a short list of publications about Suetonius, and an index have also been added.

MICHAEL GRANT
Gattaiola, 1979

I

JULIUS CAESAR

AFTERWARDS DEIFIED

*(The introductory paragraphs on the origins
of Caesar's family are lost in all manuscripts.)*

Gaius Julius Caesar lost his father at the age of fifteen.[1] During the next consulship, after being nominated to the priesthood of Jupiter, he broke an engagement, made for him while he was still a boy, to marry one Cossutia; for, though rich, she came of only equestrian family. Instead, he married Cornelia, daughter of that Cinna who had been Consul four times, and later she bore him a daughter named Julia. The Dictator Sulla tried to make Caesar divorce Cornelia; and when he refused stripped him of the priesthood, his wife's dowry, and his own inheritance, treating him as if he were a member of the opposite party. Caesar disappeared from public view and, though suffering from a virulent attack of quartan fever, was forced to find a new hiding-place almost every night and bribe householders to protect him from Sulla's secret police. Finally he won Sulla's pardon through the intercession of the Vestal Virgins and his near relatives Mamercus Aemilius and Aurelius Cotta. It is well known that, when his most devoted and eminent friends pleaded Caesar's cause and would not let the matter drop, Sulla at last gave way. Whether he was divinely inspired or showed peculiar foresight is an arguable point, but

1. 85–84 B.C.

these were his words: 'Very well then, you win! Take him! But never forget that the man whom you want me to spare will one day prove the ruin of the party

THE CITIZEN AND THE DICTATOR
1 (left). *Portrait head of Caesar found near Tusculum, and probably carved during Caesar's lifetime. It shows an unidealized likeness.* (Turin.)
2 (right). *Portrait head of Caesar wearing an oak wreath, the civic crown, which was traditionally awarded for saving a Roman's life in battle; it is worn here by Caesar as a token that he 'saved the State'. The slight upward glance suggests Caesar's deification.*

ΙΛΙΟΥ ΠΕΡΣΙΣ
ΚΑΤΑ ΣΤΗΣΙΧΟΡΟΝ

ΤΡΩΙΚΟΣ

ΙΛΙΑΣ
ΚΑΤΑ ΟΜΗΡΟΝ
ΑΙΘΙΟΠΙΣ ΚΑΤΑ ΑΡΚΤΙ
ΝΟΝ ΤΟΝ ΜΙΛΗΣΙΟΝ
ΙΛΙΑΣ ΗΜΙΚΤΑΝ
ΓΟΜΕΝΗ ΚΑΤΑ ΠΓΑΙΟ
ΛΟΣ ΑΙΓΙΠΤΙΡΙΟΣ

THE ORIGINS OF ROME. *According to Roman myth, Romulus, the founder of Rome, was descended from refugees from Troy in Asia Minor, who came to Italy after their city had been besieged for ten years and conquered by the Greeks.*

3 (left). *Tabula Iliaca: terracotta relief inscribed with verses from Homer's* Iliad, *showing the city of Troy and the Greek camp with Greek ships on the seashore.* (Rome, Capitoline Museum.)

4 (above). *Roman altar: Aeneas, son of Venus, one of the refugees from Troy and ancestor of Romulus, from whom Julius Caesar claimed descent, escaping from Troy. He carries his father Anchises and leads his son Ascanius by the hand. The story was told in Virgil's* Aeneid *(see Ill. 49).* (First century A.D., Tunis, Bardo Museum.)

which you and I have so long defended. There are many Mariuses[2] in this fellow Caesar.'

2. Caesar first saw military service in Asia, where he went as aide-de-camp to Marcus Thermus, the provincial governor.[3] When Thermus sent Caesar to raise a fleet in Bithynia, he wasted so much time at King Nicomedes' court that a homosexual relationship between them was suspected, and suspicion gave place to scandal when, soon after his return to headquarters, he revisited Bithynia: ostensibly collecting a debt incurred there by one of his freedmen. However, Caesar's reputation improved later in the campaign, when Thermus awarded him the civic crown of oak-leaves, at the storming of Mytilene, for saving a fellow-soldier's life.

3. He also campaigned in Cilicia under Servilius Isauricus, but not for long, because the news of Sulla's death sent him hurrying back to Rome, where a revolt

2. Gaius Marius (157–86 B.C.), the famous enemy of Sulla, was Consul seven times.

3. 81 B.C.

DIS·MAN·CLAVDIAE·T·F·FAB·VLLAE
FLAVIVS·EVPHRANOR·ET·VARIVS·SPLENDO
DIS·PARENTE····PIETA···FECERVNT

ORIGINS OF ROME

5 (above). *Roman funerary plaque: Rhea Silvia reclining
in the centre is approached by Sleep from the right, while
the god Mars, from whom while asleep she will conceive
the twins Romulus and Remus, founders of Rome, waits
on the right.* (Paris, Louvre.)

headed by Marcus Lepidus seemed to offer prospects
of rapid advancement.[4] Nevertheless, though Lepidus
made him very advantageous offers, Caesar turned
them down: he had small confidence in Lepidus's
capacities, and found the political atmosphere less
promising than he had been led to believe.

4. After this revolt was suppressed, Caesar brought
a charge of extortion against Cornelius Dolabella, an
ex-Consul who had once been awarded a triumph, but
failed to secure a sentence; so he decided to visit
Rhodes until the resultant ill-feeling had time to die
down, meanwhile taking a course in rhetoric from
Apollonius Molo, the best living exponent of the art.
Winter had already set in when he sailed for Rhodes
and was captured by pirates off the island of Pharma-
cussa. They kept him prisoner for nearly forty days,
to his intense annoyance; he had with him only a physician and two valets, having sent the rest of his staff away

to borrow the ransom money. As soon as the stipulated
fifty talents arrived (which make 12,000 gold pieces),
and the pirates duly set him ashore, he raised a fleet
and went after them. He had often smilingly sworn,
while still in their power, that he would soon capture
and crucify them; and this is exactly what he did. Then
he continued to Rhodes, but Mithridates was now
ravaging the near-by coast of Asia Minor; so, to avoid
the charge of showing inertia while the allies of Rome
were in danger, he raised a force of irregulars and
drove Mithridates's deputy from the province – which
confirmed the timorous and half-hearted cities of
Asia in their allegiance.

5. On Caesar's return to Rome, the Assembly voted
him the rank of colonel, and he vigorously helped their
leaders to undo Sulla's legislation by restoring the tribunes of the people to their ancient powers. Then one
Plotius introduced a bill for the recall from exile of
Caesar's brother-in-law, Lucius Cinna – who, with
other fellow-conspirators, had escaped to Spain after
Lepidus's death and joined Sertorius. Caesar himself
spoke in support of the bill, which was passed.

6. During his quaestorship[5] he made the customary
funeral speeches from the Rostra in honour of his aunt
Julia and his wife Cornelia; and while eulogizing Julia's

4. 78 B.C.   5. 69 B.C.

maternal and paternal ancestry, did the same for the Caesars too. 'Her mother', he said, 'was a descendant of kings, namely the Marcii Reges, a family founded by the Roman King Ancus Marcius; and her father, of gods – since the Julians (of which we Caesars are a branch) reckon descent from the Goddess Venus. Thus Julia's stock can claim both the sanctity of kings, who reign supreme among mortals, and the reverence due to gods, who hold even kings in their power.'

He next married Pompeia, Quintus Pompeius's daughter, who was also Sulla's grand-daughter, but

THE 'GOOD GODDESS' (*Bona Dea*), *goddess of healing. Her cult was introduced into Rome, probably during the third century* B.C., *from Greek Southern Italy. Her festival, on the night of 4 December, was celebrated exclusively by women. The intrusion of Publius Clodius during this festival, when it was being celebrated at Caesar's house, caused a major scandal.*
6. *Roman altar, early second century* A.D. (Rome, Villa Albani.)

divorced her on a suspicion of adultery with Publius Clodius; indeed, so persistent was the rumour of Clodius's having disguised himself as a woman and seduced her at the Feast of the Good Goddess, from which all men are excluded, that the Senate ordered a judicial inquiry into the alleged desecration of these sacred rites.

7. As quaestor Caesar was appointed to Further Spain, where the governor sent him off on an assize-circuit. At Gades he saw a statue of Alexander the Great in the Temple of Hercules, and was overheard to sigh impatiently: vexed, it seems, that at an age when Alexander had already conquered the whole world, he himself had done nothing in the least epoch-making. Moreover, when on the following night, much to his dismay, he had a dream of raping his own mother, the soothsayers greatly encouraged him by their interpretation of it: namely, that he was destined to conquer the earth, our Universal Mother.

8. At all events, he laid down his quaestorship at once, bent on performing some notable act at the first opportunity that offered. He visited the Latin colonists beyond the Po, who were bitterly demanding the same Roman citizenship as that granted to other townsfolk in Italy; and might have persuaded them to revolt, had not the Consuls realized the danger and garrisoned that district with the legions recently raised for the Cilician campaign.

9. Undiscouraged, Caesar soon made an even more daring attempt at revolution in Rome itself. A few days before taking up his aedileship,[6] he was suspected of plotting with Marcus Crassus, an ex-consul; also with Publius Sulla and Lucius Autronius, who had jointly been elected to the consulship but found guilty of bribery and corruption. These four had agreed to wait until the New Year, and then attack the Senate House, killing as many senators as convenient. Crassus would then proclaim himself Dictator, and Caesar his Master of Horse; the government would be reorganized to suit their pleasure; Sulla and Autronius would be appointed Consuls.

Tanusius Geminus mentions their plot in his *History*; more information is given in Marcus Bibulus's *Edicts* and in the *Orations* of Gaius Curio the Elder. Another reference to it may be detected in Cicero's letter to Axius, where Caesar is said to have 'established in his consulship the monarchy which he had planned while only an aedile'. Tanusius adds that Crassus was

6. 65 B.C.

prevented, either by scruples or by nervousness, from appearing at the appointed hour; and Caesar therefore did not give the agreed signal which, according to Curio, was letting his toga fall and expose the shoulder.

Both Curio and Marcus Actorius Naso state that Caesar also plotted with Gnaeus Piso, a young nobleman suspected of raising a conspiracy in the city and for that reason appointed Governor of Spain, although he had neither solicited nor qualified for the position. Caesar, apparently, was to lead a revolt in Rome as soon as Piso did so in Spain; the Ambrani[7] and the people who lived beyond the Po would have risen simultaneously. But Piso's death cancelled the plan.

10. During his aedileship, Caesar filled the Comitium, the Forum, its adjacent basilicas, and the Capitol itself with a display of the material which he

7. A people of Liguria.

meant to use in his public shows, building temporary colonnades for the purpose. He exhibited wild-beast hunts and stage-plays; some at his own expense, some in co-operation with his colleague, Marcus Bibulus – but took all the credit in either case, so that Bibulus remarked openly: 'The Temple of the Heavenly Twins in the Forum is always simply called "Castor's"; and I always play Pollux to Caesar's Castor when we give a public entertainment together.'

Caesar also put on a gladiatorial show, but had collected so immense a troop of combatants that his terrified political opponents rushed a bill through the House, limiting the number of gladiators that anyone might keep in Rome; consequently far fewer pairs fought than had been advertised.

11. After thus securing the goodwill of the public and their tribunes, Caesar tried to get himself the control of Egypt by popular vote. His excuse for demanding so unusual an appointment was an outcry against

WILD ANIMALS, *in the countryside, and in public displays.*
7 (above). *Fresco in the house of Lucretius Fronto in Pompeii; it reflects a view such as might be enjoyed in the wild-beast park of a wealthy Roman landowner's estate.*

8 (opposite). *In Rome and other cities of the Empire, notables could gain popularity by staging shows in which wild animals were displayed. Roman terracotta plaque with lions, hunters, and spectators in an amphitheatre. (Rome, Terme Museum.)*

the Alexandrians who had just deposed King Ptolemy XII, although the Senate had recognized him as an ally and friend of Rome. However, the aristocratic party opposed the measure; so, as aedile, Caesar took vengeance by replacing the public monuments – destroyed by Sulla many years ago – that had commemorated Marius's victories over Jugurtha, the Cimbri, and the Teutones. Further, as Judge of the Court of Inquiry into Murder, he prosecuted men who had earned public bounties for bringing in the heads of Roman citizens outlawed during the proscriptions; although this rough justice had been expressly sanctioned in the Cornelian Laws.

12. He also bribed a man to bring a charge of high treason against Gaius Rabirius who, some years previously, had earned the Senate's gratitude by checking the seditious activities of Lucius Saturninus, a tribune. Caesar, chosen by lot to try Rabirius, pronounced the sentence with such satisfaction that, when Rabirius appealed to the people, the greatest argument in his favour was the judge's obvious prejudice.

13. Obliged to abandon his ambition of governing Egypt, Caesar stood for the office of Chief Priest, and used the most flagrant bribery to secure it. The story goes that, reckoning up the enormous debts thus contracted, he told his mother, as she kissed him goodbye on the morning of the poll, that if he did not return to her as Chief Priest he would not return at all. However, he defeated his two prominent rivals, both of whom were much older and more distinguished than himself, and the votes he won from their own tribes exceeded those cast for them in the entire poll.

14. When the Catilinarian conspiracy came to light, the whole House, with the sole exception of Caesar, then Praetor-elect, demanded the death penalty for Catiline and his associates. Caesar proposed merely that they should be imprisoned, each in a different town, and their estates confiscated. What was more, he

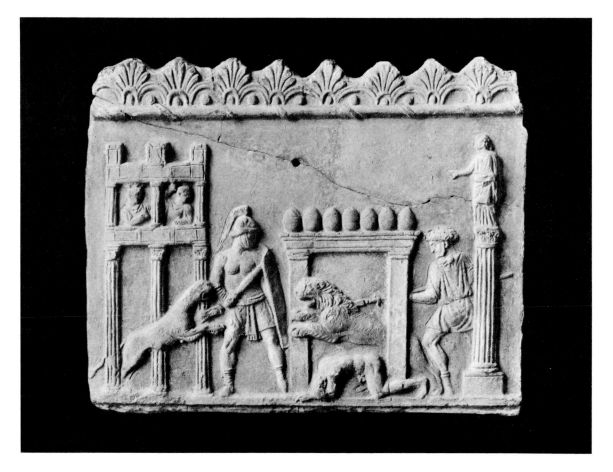

THE CAPITOL AND ITS GODS

9 (opposite). *View of the Capitol from the Forum. The substructures and the arches are Roman. The arches once formed a continuous arcade, and were part of the record office,* tabularium, *which was completed in 78* B.C.

10 (below). *The Capitoline Triad, Jupiter Best and Greatest (Optimus Maximus) in the centre, his consort Juno on the right, and his daughter Minerva on the left. The genealogical connections were imposed on these three originally Italian divinities from Greek mythology. In Rome and elsewhere they, but especially Jupiter, epitomized the Empire and Roman power (see Ill. 98). Roman relief, second century* A.D. *(Trier, Rheinisches Landesmuseum.)*

so browbeat those senators who took a sterner line, by suggesting that the commons would conceive an enduring hatred for them if they persisted in this view, that Decimus Silanus, as Consul-elect, felt obliged to interpret his own proposal – which, however, he could not bring himself to recast – in a more liberal sense, begging Caesar not to misread it so savagely. And Caesar would have gained his point, since many senators (including the Consul Cicero's brother) had been won over to his view, had Marcus Cato not kept the irresolute Senate in line. Caesar continued to block proceedings until a body of Roman knights, serving as a defence force to the House, threatened to kill him unless he ceased his violent opposition. They even unsheathed their swords and made such passes at him that most of his companions fled, and the remainder

huddled around, protecting him with their arms or their gowns. He was sufficiently impressed, not only to leave the House, but to keep away from it for the rest of that year.

15. On the first day of his praetorship,[8] Caesar ordered Quintus Catulus to appear before the Assembly and explain why he had made so little progress with the restoration of the Capitol; demanding that Catulus's commission should be taken from him and entrusted, instead, to another.[9] However, the senators of the aristocratic party, who were escorting the newly-elected Consuls to their inaugural sacrifice in the Capitol, heard what was afoot, and came pouring downhill in a body to offer obstinate resistance. Caesar withdrew his proposal.

16. Caecilius Metellus, a tribune of the people, then defended his colleagues' veto by bringing in some highly inflammatory bills; and Caesar stubbornly championed them on the floor of the House until at last both Metellus and himself were suspended by a Senatorial decree. Nevertheless, he had the effrontery to continue holding his office and his court, until warned that he would be removed by force. Thereupon he dismissed the lictors, took off his praetorian robe, and went quickly home, where he had decided to live in retirement because the times allowed him no other alternative.

On the following day, however, the populace made a spontaneous move towards Caesar's house, riotously offering to put him back in his post; but he restrained their ardour. The Senate, who had hurriedly met to deal with this demonstration, were so surprised by his unexpectedly correct attitude that they sent a deputation of high officials to thank him publicly; then summoned him to the House where, with warm praises, they revoked their decree and confirmed him in his praetorship.

17. The next danger that threatened Caesar was the inclusion of his name in a list of Catilinarian conspirators handed to the Special Commissioner, Novius Niger, by an informer named Lucius Vettius; and also in another list laid before the Senate by Quintus Curius, who had been voted a public bounty as the first person to betray the plot. Curius claimed that this information came directly from Catiline, and Vettius went so far as to declare that he could produce a letter written to Catiline in Caesar's own hand. Caesar would not lie down under this insult, and

appealed to Cicero's own admission that he had voluntarily come forward to warn him about the plot; and that Curius was not therefore entitled to the bounty. As for Vettius, who had been obliged to produce a bond when he made his revelations, this was declared forfeit and his goods seized; the commons, crowding around the Rostra, nearly tore him in pieces. Caesar thereupon sent Vettius off to gaol; and Novius Niger, the Commissioner, as well, for having let a magistrate of superior rank to himself be indicted at his tribunal.

18. The province of Further Spain was now allotted to Caesar. He relieved himself of the creditors who tried to keep him in Rome until he had paid his debts, by providing sureties for their eventual settlement. Then he took the illegal and unprecedented step of hurrying off before the Senate had either formally confirmed his appointment or voted him the necessary funds. He may have been afraid of being impeached while still a private citizen, or he may have been anxious to respond as quickly as possible to the appeals of our Spanish allies for help against aggression. At any rate, on his arrival in Spain he rapidly restored order, and returned to Rome in the following summer with equal haste – not waiting until he had been relieved – to demand a triumph and stand for the consulship. But the day of the consular elections had already been announced. His candidacy could therefore not be admitted unless he entered the city as a civilian; and when a general outcry arose against his intrigues to be exempted from the regulations governing candidatures, he was faced with the alternative of forgoing the triumph or forgoing the consulship.

19. There were two other candidates: Lucius Lucceius and Marcus Bibulus. Caesar now approached Lucceius and suggested that they should join forces; but since Lucceius had more money and Caesar greater influence, it was agreed that Lucceius should finance their joint candidacy by bribing the voters. The aristocratic party got wind of this arrangement and, fearing that if Caesar were elected Consul, with a pliant colleague by his side, he would stop at nothing to gain his own ends, they authorized Marcus Bibulus to bribe the voters as heavily as Lucceius had done. Many aristocrats contributed to Bibulus's campaign funds, and Cato himself admitted that this was an occasion when even bribery might be excused as a legitimate means of preserving the Constitution.

Caesar and Bibulus were elected Consuls, but the aristocrats continued to restrict Caesar's influence by ensuring that, when he and Bibulus had completed their

8. 62 B.C.   9. Gnaeus Pompeius (Pompey).

11. POMPEIUS MAGNUS, *The Great, portrait bust.* (Copenhagen, Ny Carlsberg.)

term, both should govern provinces of the smallest possible importance, designated as 'woods and mountain-pastures'. Infuriated by this slight, Caesar exerted his charm on Pompey, who had quarrelled with the Senate because they were so slow in approving the steps that he had taken to defeat King Mithridates of Pontus. He also succeeded in conciliating Pompey and Marcus Crassus – they were still at odds after their failure to agree on matters of policy while sharing the consulship. Pompey, Caesar, and Crassus now formed a triple pact, jointly swearing to oppose all legislation of which any one of them might disapprove.

20. Caesar's first act as Consul was to rule that a daily record of proceedings in the Senate, and in the People's Court, should be taken and published; he also revived the obsolete custom of having an orderly walk before him, during the months in which his colleague held the rods of office, while the lictors marched behind. Next, he introduced an agrarian law, and when Bibulus delayed its passage through the Senate by announcing that the omens were unfavourable, drove

him from the Forum by force of arms. On the following day Bibulus lodged a complaint in the House, and when nobody dared move a vote of censure, or make any observation on this scandalous event – though decrees condemning minor breaches of the peace had often been passed – he felt so frustrated that he stayed at home for the rest of his term, satisfying his resentment with further announcements about unfavourable omens.

Caesar was thus enabled to govern alone and do very much as he pleased. It became a joke to sign and seal bogus documents: 'Executed during the Consulship of Julius and Caesar', rather than: '... during the Consulship of Bibulus and Caesar'. And this lampoon went the rounds:

> The event occurred, as I recall, when Caesar
> governed Rome –
> Caesar, not Marcus Bibulus, who kept his seat
> at home.

The plain called Stellas had been devoted to public purposes in earlier times; and the Campanian Territory had also been set aside and farmed on behalf of the government. Caesar partitioned both these districts among fathers of three or more children, without casting the customary lots. When the Roman tax-farmers asked for relief, he cancelled one-third of their obligations, but gave them frank warning not to bid too high for their contracts in future. He freely granted all other pleas, whatsoever, and either met with no opposition or intimidated anyone who dared intervene. Marcus Cato once tried to delay proceedings by talking out the debate, but Caesar had him forcibly ejected by a lictor and led off to prison. Lucius Lucullus went a little too far in opposing Caesar's policy, whereupon Caesar so terrified him by threats of prosecution that Lucullus fell on his knees and begged Caesar's pardon. Hearing that Cicero had been making a doleful speech in court about the evils of his times, Caesar at once granted the long-standing plea of Cicero's enemy, Publius Clodius, to be transferred from patrician to plebeian rank; rushing this measure through the House at three o'clock, just before the adjournment. Finally, he began an attack on his aristocratic opponents as a body by bribing an informer, who appeared on the Rostra and announced that some of them had tried to make him assassinate Pompey. As had been arranged, the informer mentioned a few names, but the whole affair raised such strong suspicions of double-dealing that

Caesar, realizing that he had been too hasty, is said to have poisoned his agent.

21. Caesar then married Calpurnia, daughter of Lucius Piso, his successor in the consulship; and at the same time betrothed Julia to Pompey, thus breaking her previous engagement to Servilius Caepio, who had recently given him a great deal of support in the struggle against Bibulus. He now always called on Pompey to open debates in the House, though having hitherto reserved this honour for Crassus; thereby flouting the tradition that a Consul should continue, throughout the year, to preserve the order of precedence established for speakers on New Year's Day.

22. Having thus secured the goodwill of his father-in-law Piso and his son-in-law Pompey, Caesar surveyed the many provinces open to him and chose Gaul as being the likeliest to supply him with wealth and triumphs. True, he was at first appointed Governor only of Cisalpine Gaul and Illyria – the proposal came from Vatinius – but afterwards the Senate added Transalpine Gaul to his jurisdiction, fearing that if this were denied him, the commons would insist that he should have it.

His elation was such that he could not refrain from boasting to a packed House, some days later, that having now gained his dearest wish, to the annoyance and grief of his opponents, he would proceed to 'stamp upon their persons'. When someone interjected with a sneer that a *woman* would not find this an easy feat, he answered amicably: 'Why not? Semiramis was supreme in Syria, and the Amazons once ruled over a large part of Asia.'

23. At the close of his consulship the praetors Gaius Memmius and Lucius Domitius Ahenobarbus demanded an inquiry into his official conduct during the past year. Caesar referred the matter to the Senate, who would not discuss it, so after three days had been wasted in idle recriminations, he left for Gaul. His quaestor was at once charged with various irregularities, as a first step towards his own impeachment. Then Lucius Antistius, a tribune of the people, arraigned Caesar who, however, appealed to the whole college of tribunes, pleading absence on business of national importance; and thus staved off the trial.

To prevent a recurrence of this sort of trouble he made a point of putting the chief magistrates of each new year under some obligation to him, and refusing to support any candidates, or allow them to be elected, unless they promised to defend his cause while he was absent from Rome. He had no hesitation in holding

THE CELTS. *In France, Spain, and Britain the Roman conquerors encountered the Celts, a group of nations of different culture, language, and religion, whom in the end they failed to comprehend.*
12 (above). *Celtic divinity wearing a torque. Bronze statuette, first century* B.C. *or* A.D. (Saint-Germain-en-Laye, Musée des Antiquités Nationales.)
13 (opposite). *Torque of electrum from Norfolk, first century* B.C. (London, British Museum.)

some of them to their promises by an oath, or even a written contract.

24. At last Lucius Domitius Ahenobarbus stood for the consulship and openly threatened that, once elected, he would remove Caesar from his military command, having failed to do this while praetor. So Caesar called upon Pompey and Crassus to visit Luca, which lay in his province, and there persuaded them to prolong his governorship of Gaul for another five years, and to oppose Domitius's candidature.

This success encouraged Caesar to expand his regular army with legions raised at his own expense: one even recruited in Transalpine Gaul and called *Alauda* (Gallic for 'The Crested Lark'), which he trained and equipped in Roman style. Later he made every Alauda legionary a full citizen.

He now lost no opportunity of picking quarrels – however unfair and dangerous – with allies as well as hostile and barbarous tribes, and marching against them. At first the Senate set up a commission of inquiry into the state of the Gallic provinces, and some speakers went so far as to recommend that Caesar should be handed over to the enemy. But the more successful his campaigns, the more frequent the public thanksgivings voted; and the holidays that went with them were longer than any general before him had ever earned.

25. Briefly, his nine years' governorship produced the following results. He reduced to the form of a province the whole of Gaul enclosed by the Pyrenees, the Alps, the Cevennes, the Rhine, and the Rhône – about 640,000 square miles – except for certain allied states

RESULTS OF CONQUEST. *Roman institutions superseded indigenous ones.*

14 (opposite). *Roman theatres and amphitheatres were not merely architectural forms characteristic of Italy: they also implied a particular way of relating to one's equals and one's superiors, and a particular way of spending one's time. Theatres and amphitheatres were built in most major towns in the Roman provinces. Amphitheatre at Arles, France.*

15 (below). *The Maison Carrée at Nîmes, a Roman temple built probably during the lifetime of Augustus, is modelled on temples of the second century B.C. in Italy, while the carved frieze of acanthus reflects the style of the Ara Pacis (Altar of Peace) in Rome (see Ill. 47).*

which had given him useful support; and exacted an annual tribute of 400,000 gold pieces.

Caesar was the first Roman to build a military bridge across the Rhine and cause the Germans on the farther bank heavy losses. He also invaded Britain, a hitherto unknown country, and defeated the natives, from whom he exacted a large sum of money as well as hostages for future good behaviour. He met with only three serious reverses: in Britain, when his fleet was all but destroyed by a gale; in Gaul, when one of his legions was routed at Gergovia among the Auvergne mountains; and on the German frontier, when his generals Titurius and Aurunculeius were ambushed and killed.

26. During these nine years Caesar lost, one after the other, his mother, his daughter, and his grandson. Meanwhile, the assassination of Publius Clodius had caused such an outcry that the Senate voted for the appointment of only a single Consul; naming Pompey as their choice. When the tribunes of the people wanted Caesar to stand as Pompey's colleague, Caesar asked whether they would not persuade the commons to let him do so without visiting Rome; his governorship of Gaul, he wrote, was nearly at an end, and he preferred not to leave until his conquests had been completed.

Their granting of this concession so fired Caesar's ambitions that he neglected no expense in winning popularity, both as a private citizen and as a candidate for his second consulship. He began building a new Forum with the spoils taken in Gaul, and paid more than a million gold pieces for the site alone. Then he announced a gladiatorial show and a public banquet in memory of his daughter Julia – an unprecedented event; and, to create as much excitement among the commons as possible, had the banquet catered for partly by his own household, partly by the market contractors. He also issued an order that any well-known gladiator who failed to win the approval of the Circus should be forcibly rescued from execution and kept alive. New gladiators were also trained, not by the usual professionals in the schools, but in private houses by Roman knights and even senators who happened to be masters-at-arms. Letters of his survive, begging these trainers to give their pupils individual instruction in the art of fighting. He fixed the daily pay of the regular soldiers at double what it had been, for all time. Whenever the granaries were full he would make a lavish distribution to the army, without measuring the amount, and occasionally gave every man a Gallic slave.

27. To preserve Pompey's friendship and renew the family ties dissolved by Julia's death he offered him the hand of his sister's grand-daughter Octavia, though she had already married Gaius Marcellus, and in return asked leave to marry Pompey's daughter, who was betrothed to Faustus Sulla. Having now won all Pompey's friends, and most of the Senate, to his side with loans at a low rate of interest, or interest-free, he endeared himself to persons of less distinction too by handing out valuable presents, whether or not they asked for them. His beneficiaries included the favourite slaves or freedmen of prominent men.

Caesar thus became the one reliable source of help to all who were in legal difficulties, or in debt, or living beyond their means; and refused help only to those whose criminal record was so black, or whose purse so empty, or whose tastes were so expensive, that even he could do nothing for them. He frankly told such people: 'What you need is a civil war.'

28. Caesar took equal pains to win the esteem of kings and provincial authorities by offering them gifts of prisoners, thousands at a time, or lending them troops whenever they asked, and without first obtaining official permission from the Senate or people. He also presented the principal cities of Asia and Greece with magnificent public works, and did the same for those of Italy, Gaul, and Spain. Everyone was amazed by this liberality and wondered what the sequel would be.

At last Marcus Claudius Marcellus, the Consul, announced in the House that he intended to raise a matter of vital public interest; and then proposed that, since the Gallic War had now ended and peace was restored, Caesar should be relieved of his command before his term as Governor-General expired; that a successor should be appointed; and that the armies in Gaul should be disbanded. He further proposed that Caesar should be forbidden to stand for the consulship without appearing at Rome in person, since a decree against irregularities of this sort still appeared on the Statute Book.

Here Marcellus was on firm legal ground. Pompey, when he introduced a bill regulating the privileges of state officials, had omitted to make a special exception for Caesar in the clause debarring absentees from candidacy; or to correct this oversight before the bill had been passed, engraved on a bronze tablet, and registered at the Public Treasury. Nor was Marcellus content to oust Caesar from his command and cancel the privilege already voted him: namely to stand for the consulship *in absentia*. He also asked that the colonists whom Caesar had settled at Novum Comum under the Vatinian Act should lose their citizenship. This award, he said, had been intended to further Caesar's political ambitions and lacked legal sanction.

29. The news infuriated Caesar, but he had often been reported as saying: 'Now that I am the leading Roman of my day, it will be harder to put me down a peg than degrade me to the ranks.' So he resisted stubbornly; persuading the tribunes of the people to veto Marcellus's bills and at the same time enlisting the help of Servius Sulpicius, Marcellus's colleague. When, in the following year, Marcellus was succeeded in office by his cousin Gaius, who adopted a similar policy, Caesar again won over the other Consul – Aemi-

lius Paulus – with a heavy bribe; and also bought Gaius Curio, the most energetic tribune of the people.

Realizing, however, that the opposition had made a determined stand, and that both the new Consuls-elect were unfriendly to him, he appealed to the Senate, begging them in a written address not to cancel a privilege voted him by the commons, without forcing all other governors-general to resign their commands at the same time as he did. But this was read as meaning that he counted on mobilizing his veteran troops sooner than Pompey could his raw levies. Next, Caesar offered to resign his command of eight legions and quit Transalpine Gaul if he might keep two legions and Cisalpine Gaul, or at least Illyricum and one legion, until he became Consul.

30. Since the Senate refused to intervene on his behalf and his opponents insisted that they would accept no compromise in a matter of such national importance, Caesar crossed into Cisalpine Gaul, where he held his regular assizes, and halted at Ravenna. He was resolved to invade Italy if force were used against the tribunes of the people who had vetoed the Senate's decree disbanding his army by a given date. Force was, in effect, used and the tribunes fled towards Cisalpine Gaul; which became Caesar's pretext for launching the Civil War. Additional motives are suspected, however: Pompey's comment was that, because Caesar had insufficient capital to carry out his grandiose schemes or give the people all that they had been encouraged to expect on his return, he chose to create an atmosphere of political confusion.

Another view is that he dreaded having to account for the irregularities of his first consulship, during which he had disregarded auspices and vetoes; for Marcus Cato had often sworn to impeach him as soon as the legions were disbanded. Moreover, people said at the time, frankly enough, that should Caesar return from Gaul as a private citizen he would be tried in a court ringed around with armed men, as Titus Annius Milo had lately been at Pompey's orders.[10] This sounds plausible enough, because Asinius Pollio records in his *History* that when Caesar, at the Battle of Pharsalus, saw his enemies forced to choose between massacre and flight, he said, in these very words: 'They brought it on themselves. They would have condemned me regardless of all my victories – me, Gaius Caesar – had I not appealed to my army for help.' It has also been suggested that constant exercise of power gave Caesar

a love of it; and that, after weighing his enemies' strength against his own, he took this chance of fulfilling his youthful dreams by making a bid for the monarchy. Cicero seems to have come to a similar conclusion: in the third book of his *Essay on Duties*, he records that Caesar quoted the following lines from Euripides's *Phoenician Women* on several occasions:

> Is crime consonant with nobility?
> Then noblest is the crime of tyranny –
> In all things else obey the laws of Heaven.

31. Accordingly, when news reached him that the tribunes' veto had been disallowed, and that they had fled the city, he at once sent a few cohorts ahead with all secrecy, and disarmed suspicion by himself attending a theatrical performance, inspecting the plans of a school for gladiators which he proposed to build, and dining as usual among a crowd of guests. But at dusk he borrowed a pair of mules from a bakery near Headquarters, harnessed them to a gig, and set off quietly with a few of his staff. His lights went out, he lost his way, and the party wandered about aimlessly for some hours; but at dawn found a guide who led them on foot along narrow lanes, until they came to the right road. Caesar overtook his advanced guard at the river Rubicon, which formed the frontier between Gaul and Italy. Well aware how critical a decision confronted him, he turned to his staff, remarking: 'We may still draw back: but, once across that little bridge, we shall have to fight it out.'

32. As he stood, in two minds, an apparition of superhuman size and beauty was seen sitting on the river bank playing a reed pipe. A party of shepherds gathered around to listen and, when some of Caesar's men, including some of the trumpeters, broke ranks to do the same, the apparition snatched a trumpet from one of them, ran down to the river, blew a thunderous blast, and crossed over. Caesar exclaimed: 'Let us accept this as a sign from the Gods, and follow where they beckon, in vengeance on our double-dealing enemies. The die is cast.'

33. He led his army to the farther bank, where he welcomed the tribunes of the people who had fled to him from Rome. Then he tearfully addressed the troops and, ripping open his tunic to expose his breast, begged them to stand faithfully by him. The belief that he then promised to promote every man present to the Equestrian Order is based on a misunderstanding. He had accompanied his pleas with the gesture of pointing to his left hand, as he declared that he would gladly

10. 52 B.C.

reward those who championed his honour with the very seal ring from his thumb; but some soldiers on the fringe of the assembly, who saw him better than they could hear his words, read too much into the gesture. They put it about that Caesar had promised them all the right to wear a knight's gold ring, and the 4,000 gold pieces required to support a knighthood.

34. Here follows a brief account of Caesar's subsequent movements. He occupied Picenum, Umbria, and Etruria; captured Lucius Domitius Ahenobarbus who had been illegally named as his successor in Gaul and was holding Corfinium for the Senate; let him go free; and then marched along the Adriatic coast to Brundusium, where Pompey and the Consuls had fled from Rome on their way to Epirus. When his efforts to prevent their crossing the straits proved ineffective, he marched on Rome, entered it, summoned the Senate to review the political situation, and then hurriedly set off for Spain; Pompey's strongest forces were stationed there under the command of his friends Marcus Petreius, Lucius Afranius, and Marcus Varro. Before leaving, Caesar told his household: 'I am off to meet an army without a leader; when I return I shall meet a leader without an army.' Though delayed by the siege of Massilia, which had shut its gates against him, and by a failure of his commissariat, he won a rapid and overwhelming victory.

35. Caesar returned by way of Rome, crossed the Adriatic and, after blockading Pompey for nearly four months, behind immense containing works,[11] routed him at Pharsalus in Thessaly. Pompey fled to Alexandria; Caesar followed, and when he found that King Ptolemy XIII had murdered Pompey and was planning to murder him as well, declared war. This proved to be a most difficult campaign, awkward both in time

11. At Dyrrhachium in Epirus.

and place, fought during winter within the city walls of a well-equipped and cunning enemy; but though caught off his guard, and without military supplies of any kind, Caesar was victorious. He then handed over the government of Egypt to Queen Cleopatra and her younger brother;[12] fearing that, if made a Roman province, it might one day be held against his fellow-countrymen by some independent-minded governor-general. From Alexandria he proceeded to Syria, and from Syria to Pontus, news having come that Pharnaces, son of the famous Mithridates, had taken advantage of the confused situation and already gained several successes. Five days after his arrival, and four hours after catching sight of Pharnaces, Caesar won a crushing victory; and commented drily on Pompey's good fortune in having built up his reputation for generalship by victories over such poor stuff as this. Then he beat Scipio and King Juba in North Africa, where the remnants of the Pompeian party were being reorganized; and Pompey's two sons in Spain.[13]

36. Throughout the Civil War Caesar was never defeated himself; but, of his generals, Gaius Curio was killed fighting in North Africa; Gaius Antonius was captured off Illyricum; Publius Dolabella lost another fleet off Illyricum; and Gnaeus Domitius Calvinus had his army destroyed in Pontus. Yet, though invariably successful, he twice came close to disaster: at Dyrrhachium, where Pompey broke his blockade and forced him to retreat – Caesar remarked when Pompey failed to pursue him: 'He does not know how to win wars' – and in the final battle, where all seemed lost and he even considered suicide.[14]

37. After defeating Scipio, Caesar celebrated four triumphs in one month with a few days' interval between them; and, after defeating the sons of Pompey, a fifth. These triumphs were the Gallic – the first and most magnificent – the Alexandrian, the Pontic, the African, and lastly the Spanish. Each differed completely from the others in its presentation.

As Caesar rode through the Velabrum on the day of his Gallic triumph, the axle of his triumphal chariot broke, and he nearly took a toss; but afterwards ascended to the Capitol between two lines of elephants, forty in all, which acted as his torch-bearers. In the Pontic triumph one of the decorated wagons, instead

THE APPARITION ON THE RUBICON. *Roman myth peopled the countryside with various divinities who personified aspects of nature. One such was the Greek god Pan, identified with the Roman Faunus, who might be heard in remote places playing reed pipes.*
16 (opposite). *Pan teaches the shepherd Daphnis to play the reed pipes. Roman copy of a Hellenistic original. (Rome, Terme Museum.)*

12. Ptolemy XIV.
13. The three battles were at Zela (Pontus), Thapsus (North Africa), and Munda (Spain).
14. Munda.

of a stage-set representing scenes from the war, like the rest, carried a simple three-word inscription:

I CAME, I SAW, I CONQUERED!

This referred not to the events of the war, like the other inscriptions, but to the speed with which it had been won.

38. Every infantryman of Caesar's veteran legions earned a war-gratuity of 240 gold pieces, in addition to the twenty paid at the outbreak of hostilities, and a farm. These farms could not be grouped together without evicting former owners, but were scattered all over the countryside. Every member of the commons received ten pecks of grain and ten pounds of oil as a bounty, besides the three gold pieces which Caesar had promised at first and now raised to four, by way of interest on the delay in payment. He added a popular banquet and a distribution of meat; also a dinner to celebrate his Spanish victory, but decided that this had not been splendid enough and, five days later, served a second more succulent one.

39. His public shows were of great variety. They included a gladiatorial contest, stage-plays for every Roman ward performed in several languages, chariot-races in the Circus, athletic competitions, and a mock naval battle. At the gladiatorial contest in the Forum, a man named Furius Leptinus, of praetorian family, fought Quintus Calpenus, a barrister and former senator, to the death. The sons of leaders of Asia and Bithynia danced the Pyrrhic sword dance.

One of the plays was written and acted by Decimus Laberius, a Roman knight; after the performance he was given five thousand gold pieces and had his gold ring, the badge of equestrian rank, restored to him – so that he could walk straight from stage to orchestra, where fourteen rows of seats were reserved for his Order. A broad ditch had been dug around the race-course, now extended at either end of the Circus, and the contestants were young noblemen who drove four-horse and two-horse chariots or rode pairs of horses, jumping from back to back. The so-called Troy Game, a sham fight supposedly introduced by Aeneas, was performed by two troops of boys, one younger than the other.

Wild-beast hunts took place five days running, and the entertainment ended with a battle between two armies, each consisting of 500 infantry, twenty ele-phants, and thirty cavalry. To let the camps be pitched facing each other, Caesar removed the central barrier of the Circus, around which the chariots ran. Athletic contests were held in a temporary stadium on the Campus Martius, and lasted for three days.

The naval battle was fought on an artificial lake dug in the Lesser Codeta, between Tyrian and Egyptian ships, with two, three, or four banks of oars, and heavily manned. Such huge numbers of visitors flocked to these shows from all directions that many of them had to sleep in tents pitched along the streets or roads, or on roof tops; and often the pressure of the crowd crushed people to death. The victims included two senators.

40. Caesar next turned his attention to domestic reforms. First he reorganized the Calendar which the College of Priests had allowed to fall into such disorder, by inserting days or months as it suited them, that the harvest and vintage festivals no longer corresponded with the appropriate seasons. He linked the year to the course of the sun by lengthening it to 365 days,[15] abo-lishing the short extra month and adding an entire day every fourth year. But to make the next first of January fall at the right season, he drew out this particular year[16] by two further months, inserted between November and December, so that it consisted of fif-teen, including the short extra one inserted after February in the old style.

41. He brought the Senate up to strength by creat-ing new patricians, and increased the yearly quota of praetors, aediles, and quaestors, as well as of minor officials; reinstating those degraded by the Censors or condemned for corruption by a jury. Also, he arranged with the commons that, apart from the Consul, half the magistrates should be popularly elected and half nominated by himself. Allowing even the sons of pro-scribed men to stand, he circulated brief directions to the voters. For instance: 'Caesar the Dictator to such-and-such a tribe of voters: I recommend So-and-so to you for office.' He limited jury service to knights and senators, disqualifying the Treasury tribunes.[17]

Caesar changed the old method of registering voters: he made the city landlords help him to complete the list, street by street, and reduced from 320,000 to 150,000 the number of householders who might draw free grain. To do away with the nuisance of having to summon everyone for enrolment periodically, he made the praetors keep their register up to date by replacing the names of dead men with those of others not yet listed.

---

15. The year had previously consisted of 355 days.   16. 46 B.C.
17. The property grade next below the knights.

INSTITUTIONS OF THE REPUBLIC
17 (above). *Roman silver denarius c. 106* B.C., *showing on the obverse the helmeted head of the goddess Roma, and, on the reverse, a voting scene.* (London, British Museum.)

42. Since the population of Rome had been considerably diminished by the transfer of 80,000 men to overseas colonies, he forbade any citizen between the ages of twenty and forty, who was not serving in the army, to absent himself from Italy for more than three years in succession. Nor might any senator's son travel abroad unless as a member of some magistrate's household or staff; and at least a third of the cattlemen employed by graziers had to be free-born. Caesar also granted the citizenship to all medical practitioners and professors of liberal arts resident in Rome, thus inducing them to remain and tempting others to follow suit.

He disappointed popular agitators by cancelling no debts, but in the end decreed that every debtor should have his property assessed according to pre-war valuation and, after deducting the interest already paid directly, or by way of a banker's guarantee, should satisfy his creditors with whatever sum that might represent. This left debtors with perhaps a fourth part of their property. Caesar dissolved all workers' guilds except the ancient ones, and increased the penalties for crime; and since wealthy men had less compunction

about committing major offences, because the worst that could happen to them was a sentence of exile, he punished murderers of fellow-citizens (as Cicero records) by the seizure of either their entire property, or half of it.

43. In his administration of justice he was both conscientious and severe, and went so far as to degrade senators found guilty of extortion. Once, when an ex-praetor married a woman on the day after her divorce from another man, he annulled the union, although adultery between them was not suspected.

He imposed a tariff on foreign manufactures; forbade the use, except on stated occasions, of litters and the wearing of either scarlet robes or pearls by those below a certain rank and age. To implement his laws against luxury he placed inspectors in different parts of the market to seize delicacies offered for sale in violation of his orders; sometimes he even sent lictors and guards into dining-rooms to remove illegal dishes, already served, which his watchmen had failed to intercept.

44. Caesar continually undertook great new works for the embellishment of the city, or for the Empire's protection and enlargement. His first projects were a temple of Mars, the biggest in the world, to build which he would have had to fill up and pave the lake where the naval sham-fight had been staged; and an enormous theatre sloping down from the Tarpeian Rock on the Capitoline Hill.

Another task he set himself was the reduction of the Civil Code to manageable proportions, by selecting from the unwieldy mass of statutes only the most essential, and publishing them in a few volumes. Still another was to provide the finest possible public libraries, by commissioning Marcus Varro to collect and classify Greek and Latin books. His engineering schemes included the draining of the Pomptine Marshes and of Lake Fucinus; also a highway running from the Adriatic across the Apennines to the Tiber; and a canal to be cut through the Isthmus of Corinth. In the military field he planned an expulsion of the Dacians from the Black Sea area and Thrace, which they had recently occupied, and then an attack on Parthia by way of Lesser Armenia; but decided not to risk a pitched battle until he had familiarized himself with Parthian tactics.

All these schemes were cancelled by his assassination. Before describing that, I should perhaps give a brief description of his appearance, personal habits, dress, character, and conduct in peace and war.

45. Caesar is said to have been tall, fair, and well-built, with a rather broad face and keen, dark-brown eyes. His health was sound, apart from sudden comas and a tendency to nightmares which troubled him towards the end of his life; but he twice had epileptic fits while on campaign. He was something of a dandy, always keeping his head carefully trimmed and shaved; and has been accused of having certain other hairy parts of his body depilated with tweezers. His baldness was a disfigurement which his enemies harped upon, much to his exasperation; but he used to comb the thin strands of hair forward from his poll, and of all the honours voted him by the Senate and People, none pleased him so much as the privilege of wearing a laurel wreath on all occasions – he constantly took advantage of it.

His dress was, it seems, unusual: he had added wrist-length sleeves with fringes to his purple-striped senatorial tunic, and the belt which he wore over it was never tightly fastened – hence Sulla's warning to the aristocratic party: 'Beware of that boy with the loose clothes!'

46. Caesar's first home was a modest house in the Subura quarter, but later, as Chief Priest, he used the official residence on the Sacred Way. Contemporary literature contains frequent references to his fondness for luxurious living. Having built a country mansion at Nemus from the foundations up, one story goes, he found certain features in it to dislike, so that, although poor at the time and heavily in debt, he tore the whole place down. It is also recorded that he carried tessellated and mosaic pavements with him on his campaigns.

47. Pearls seem to have been the lure that prompted his invasion of Britain; he would sometimes weigh them in the palm of his hand to judge their value, and was also a keen collector of gems, carvings, statues, and Old Masters. So high were the prices he paid for slaves of good appearance and attainments that he became ashamed of his extravagance and would not allow the sums to be entered in his accounts.

48. I find also that, while stationed abroad, he always had dinner served in two separate rooms: one for his officers and Greek friends, the other for Roman citizens and the more important provincials. He paid such strict attention to his domestic economy, however small the detail, that he once put his baker in irons for giving him a different sort of bread from that served to his guests; and executed a favourite freedman for committing adultery with a knight's wife, although no complaint had been lodged by the husband.

49. The only specific charge of unnatural practices ever brought against him was that he had been King Nicomedes' bedfellow – always a dark stain on his reputation and frequently quoted by his enemies. Licinius Calvus published the notorious verses:

> The riches of Bithynia's King
> Who Caesar on his couch abused.

Dolabella called him 'the Queen's rival and inner partner of the royal bed', and Curio the Elder: 'Nicomedes' Bithynian brothel'. Bibulus, Caesar's colleague in the consulship, described him in an edict as 'the Queen of Bithynia ... who once wanted to sleep with a monarch, but now wants to be one'. And Marcus Brutus recorded that, about the same time, one Octavius, a scatterbrained creature who would say the first thing that came into his head, walked into a packed assembly where he saluted Pompey as 'King' and Caesar as 'Queen'. Moreover, Gaius Memmius directly charges Caesar with having joined a group of Nicomedes' debauched young friends at a banquet, where he acted as the royal cup-bearer; and adds that certain Roman merchants, whose names he supplies, were present as guests. Cicero, too, not only wrote in several letters:

Caesar was led by Nicomedes' attendants to the royal bed-chamber, where he lay on a golden couch, dressed in a purple shift ... So this descendant of Venus lost his virginity in Bithynia ...

RESPECTABILITY – AND ALTERNATIVE. *The austere values of the early Roman republic continued to be cherished during the late republican and imperial periods – if, increasingly, by lip service only.*

18 (above). Members of a family on a funerary plaque carved during Caesar's lifetime or shortly thereafter. (Rome, Vatican.)

19 (right). Music and love: this scene on the Grimani altar, although portraying characters of myth, none the less reflects many people's expectations of daily life. First century A.D. *(Venice, Museo Archeologico.)*

but also once interrupted Caesar while he was addressing the House in defence of Nicomedes' daughter Nysa and listing his obligations to Nicomedes himself. 'Enough of that,' Cicero shouted, 'if you please! We all know what he gave you, and what you gave him in return.' Lastly, when Caesar's own soldiers followed his decorated chariot in the Gallic triumph, chanting ribald songs, as they were privileged to do, this was one of them:

> Gaul was brought to shame by Caesar;
>   By King Nicomedes, he.
> Here comes Caesar, wreathed in triumph
>   For his Gallic victory!
> Nicomedes wears no laurels,
>   Though the greatest of the three.

50. His affairs with women are commonly described as numerous and extravagant: among those of noble birth whom he is said to have seduced were Servius Sulpicius's wife Postumia; Aulus Gabinius's wife Lollia; Marcus Crassus's wife Tertulla; and even Pompey's wife Mucia. Be this how it may, both Curio the Elder and Curio the Younger reproached Pompey for having married Caesar's daughter,[18] when it was because of Caesar, whom he had often despairingly called 'Aegisthus',[19] that he divorced Mucia, mother of his three children.

18. Julia.　　19. The lover of Agamemnon's wife Clytaemnestra.

But Marcus Brutus's mother Servilia was the woman whom Caesar loved best, and in his first consulship he bought her a pearl worth 60,000 gold pieces. He gave her many presents during the Civil War, as well as knocking down certain valuable estates to her at a public auction for a song. When surprise was expressed at the low price, Cicero made a neat remark: 'It was even cheaper than you think, because a third (*tertia*) had been discounted.' Servilia, you see, was also suspected at the time of having prostituted her daughter Tertia to Caesar.

51. That he had love-affairs in the provinces, too, is suggested by another of the ribald verses sung during the Gallic triumph:

> Home we bring our bald whoremonger;
> Romans, lock your wives away!
> All the bags of gold you lent him
> Went his Gallic tarts to pay.

52. Among his mistresses were several queens – including Eunoë, wife of Bogudes the Moor whom, according to Marcus Actorius Naso, he loaded with presents; Bogudes is said to have profited equally. The most famous of these queens was Cleopatra of Egypt. He often feasted with her until dawn; and they would have sailed together in her state barge nearly to Ethiopia had his soldiers consented to follow him. He eventually summoned Cleopatra to Rome, and would not let her return to Alexandria without high titles and rich presents. He even allowed her to call the son whom she had borne him by his own name.[20] Some Greek historians say that the boy closely resembled Caesar in features as well as in gait. Mark Antony informed the Senate that Caesar had, in fact, acknowledged Caesarion's paternity, and that other friends of Caesar's, including Gaius Matius and Gaius Oppius, were aware of this. Oppius, however, seems to have felt the need of clearing his friend's reputation; because he published a book to prove that the boy whom Cleopatra had fathered on Caesar was not his at all.

A tribune of the people named Helvius Cinna informed a number of people that, following instructions, he had drawn up a bill for the commons to pass during Caesar's absence from Rome, legitimizing his marriage with any woman, or women, he pleased – 'for the procreation of children'. And to emphasize the bad name Caesar had won alike for unnatural and natural vice, I may here record that the Elder Curio referred

to him in a speech as: 'Every woman's man and every man's woman'.

53. Yet not even his enemies denied that he drank abstemiously. An epigram of Marcus Cato's survives: 'Caesar was the only sober man who ever tried to wreck the Constitution'; and Gaius Oppius relates that he cared so little for good food that when once he attended a dinner party where rancid oil had been served by mistake, and all the other guests refused it, Caesar helped himself more liberally than usual, to show that he did not consider his host either careless or boorish.

54. He was not particularly honest in money matters, either while a provincial governor or while holding office at Rome. Several memoirs record that as Governor in Spain he not only begged his allies for money to settle his debts, but wantonly sacked several Lusitanian towns, though they had accepted his terms and opened their gates to welcome him.

In Gaul he plundered large and small temples of their votive offerings, and more often gave towns over to pillage because their inhabitants were rich than because they had offended him. As a result he collected larger quantities of gold than he could handle, and began selling it for silver, in Italy and the provinces, at 3,000 sestertii to the pound – which was about two-thirds of the official exchange rate.

In the course of his first consulship he stole 3,000 lb of gold from the Capitol, and replaced it with the same weight of gilded bronze. He sold alliances and thrones for cash, making King Ptolemy XII of Egypt give him and Pompey nearly 1,500,000 gold pieces; and later paid his Civil War army, and the expenses of his triumphs and entertainments, by open extortion and sacrilege.

55. Caesar equalled, if he did not surpass, the greatest orators and generals the world had ever known. His prosecution of Dolabella unquestionably placed him in the first rank of advocates; and Cicero, discussing the matter in his *Brutus*, confessed that he knew no more eloquent speaker than Caesar 'whose style is chaste, pellucid, and grand, not to say noble'. Cicero also wrote to Cornelius Nepos:

Very well, then! Do you know any man who, even if he has concentrated on the art of oratory to the exclusion of all else, can speak better than Caesar? Or anyone who makes so many witty remarks? Or whose vocabulary is so varied and yet so exact?

Caesar seems to have modelled his style, at any rate when a beginner, on Caesar Strabo – part of whose

---

20. Caesarion (Ptolemy XV Caesar).

Defence of the Sardinians he borrowed verbatim for use in a trial oration of his own; he was then competing with other advocates for the right to plead a cause. It is said that he pitched his voice high in speaking, and used impassioned gestures which far from displeased his audience.

Several of Caesar's undoubted speeches survive; and he is credited with others that may or may not have been his. Augustus said that the speech 'For Quintus Metellus' could hardly have been published by Caesar himself, and that it appeared to be a version taken down by shorthand writers who could not keep up with his rapid delivery. He was probably right, because on examining several manuscripts of the speech I find that even the title is given not as 'For Metellus' but as 'A Speech Composed for Metellus' – although Caesar purported to deliver it in defence of Metellus and himself against a joint accusation.

Augustus also doubted the authenticity of Caesar's 'Address to my Soldiers in Spain'. It is written in two parts, one speech supposedly delivered before the first battle, the other before the second – though on the latter occasion at least, according to Asinius Pollio, the enemy's attack gave Caesar no time to address his troops at all.

56. He left memoirs of his war in Gaul, and of his civil war against Pompey; but no one knows who wrote those of the Alexandrian, African, and Spanish campaigns. Some say that it was Oppius; others that it was Hirtius, who also finished 'The Gallic War', left incomplete by Caesar, adding a final book. With regard to Caesar's memoirs, Cicero, also in the *Brutus*, observes: 'Caesar wrote admirably; his memoirs are cleanly, directly and gracefully composed, and divested of all rhetorical trappings. And while his sole intention was to supply historians with factual material, the result has been that several fools have been pleased to primp up his narrative for their own glorification; but every writer of sense has given the subject a wide berth.'

Hirtius says downrightly: 'These memoirs are so highly rated by all judicious critics that the opportunity of enlarging and improving on them, which he purports to offer historians, seems in fact withheld from them. And, as his friends, we admire this feat even more than strangers can: they appreciate the faultless grace of his style, we know how rapidly and easily he wrote.'

Asinius Pollio, however, believes that the memoirs show signs of carelessness and inaccuracy. Caesar, he holds, did not always check the truth of the reports that came in, and was either disingenuous or forgetful in describing his own actions. Pollio adds that Caesar must have planned a revision.

Among his literary remains are two books of *An Essay on Analogy*, two more of *Answers to Cato*, and a poem, *The Journey*. He wrote *An Essay on Analogy* while coming back over the Alps after holding assizes in Cisalpine Gaul; *Answers to Cato* in the year that he won the battle of Munda; and *The Journey* during the twenty-four days he spent on the road between Rome and Further Spain.

Many of the letters and despatches sent by him to the Senate also survive, and he seems to have been the first statesman who reduced such documents to book form; previously, Consuls and governor-generals had written right across the page, not in neat columns. Then there are his letters to Cicero; and his private letters to friends, the more confidential passages of which he wrote in cypher: to understand their apparently incomprehensible meaning one must number the letters of the alphabet from 1 to 22, and then replace each of the letters that Caesar has used with the one which occurs three numbers lower – for instance, D stands for A.

It is said that in his boyhood and early youth he also wrote pieces called *In Praise of Hercules* and *The Tragedy of Oedipus* and *Collected Sayings*; but nearly a century later the Emperor Augustus sent Pompeius Macer, his Surveyor of Libraries, a brief, frank letter forbidding him to circulate these minor works.

57. Caesar was a most skilful swordsman and horseman, and showed surprising powers of endurance. He always led his army, more often on foot than in the saddle, went bareheaded in sun and rain alike, and could travel for long distances at incredible speed in a gig, taking very little luggage. If he reached an unfordable river he would either swim or propel himself across it on an inflated skin; and often arrived at his destination before the messengers whom he had sent ahead to announce his approach.

58. It is a disputable point which was the more remarkable when he went to war: his caution or his daring. He never exposed his army to ambushes, but made careful reconnaissances; and refrained from crossing over into Britain until he had collected reliable information about the harbours there, the best course to steer, and the navigational risks. On the other hand, when news reached him that his camp in Germany was being besieged, he disguised himself as a Gaul and

picked his way through the enemy outposts to take command on the spot.

He ferried his troops from Brundusium to Dyrrhachium in the winter season, running the blockade of Pompey's fleet. And one night, when Antony had delayed the supply of reinforcements despite repeated pleas, Caesar muffled his head with a cloak and secretly put to sea in a small boat, alone and incognito; forced the helmsman to steer into the teeth of a gale, and narrowly escaped shipwreck.

59. Religious scruples never deterred him for a moment. At the formal sacrifice before he launched his attack on Scipio and King Juba, the victim escaped; but he marched off at once. He had also slipped and fallen as he disembarked on the coast of Africa, but turned an unfavourable omen into a favourable one by shouting: 'Africa, I have tight hold of you!' Then, to ridicule the prophecy according to which it was the Scipios' fate to be perpetually victorious in Africa, he took about with him a contemptible member of the Cornelian branch of the Scipio family nicknamed 'Salvito' – or 'Greetings! but off with him!' – the 'Off with him!' being a mockery of his way of life.

60. Sometimes he fought after careful tactical planning, sometimes on the spur of the moment – at the end of a march, often; or in miserable weather, when he would be least expected to make a move. Towards the end of his life, however, he took fewer chances; having come to the conclusion that his unbroken run of victories ought to sober him, now that he could not possibly gain more by winning yet another battle than he would lose by a defeat. It was his rule never to let enemy troops rally when he had routed them, and always therefore to assault their camp at once. If the

THE TRADITIONAL ROMAN RELIGION *in Caesar's day was a conglomerate of very ancient rites which aroused the scepticism of many, but which were none the less to endure for several centuries more.*

20 *(above). The* suovetaurilia, *sacrifice of a bull, a sheep, and a pig, was an old Roman rite to purify the fields. The same sacrifice came also to be offered during the quinquennial census and purification of the Roman army and people. Left, the census record is being entered in a book; right, the sacrificial procession approaches the altar. Altar of Domitius Ahenobarbus (Paris, Louvre.)*

21 *(opposite). Sacrificial implements: ladle and jug for libations of wine, knife, axe, and priest's headgear. Frieze from the temple of Vespasian. (Rome, Capitoline Museum.)*

fight were a hard-fought one he used to send the chargers away – his own among the first – as a warning that those who feared to stand their ground need not hope to escape on horseback.

61. This charger of his, an extraordinary animal with feet that looked almost human – each of its hoofs was cloven in five parts, resembling human toes – had been foaled on his private estate. When the soothsayers pronounced that its master would one day rule the world, Caesar carefully reared, and was the first to ride, the beast; nor would it allow anyone else to do so. Eventually he raised a statue to it before the Temple of Mother Venus.

62. If Caesar's troops gave ground he would often rally them in person, catching individual fugitives by the throat and forcing them round to face the enemy again; even if they were panic-stricken – as when one standard-bearer threatened him with the sharp butt of his Eagle and another, whom he tried to detain, ran off leaving the Eagle in his hand.

63. Caesar's reputation for determination is fully borne out by the instances quoted. After Pharsalus, he had sent his legions ahead of him into Asia and was crossing the Hellespont in a small ferry-boat, when Lucius Cassius with ten naval vessels approached. Caesar made no attempt to escape but rowed towards the flagship and demanded Cassius's surrender; Cassius gave it and stepped aboard Caesar's craft.

64. Again, while attacking a bridge at Alexandria, Caesar was forced by a sudden enemy sortie to jump into a row-boat. So many of his men followed him that he dived into the sea and swam 200 yards until he reached the nearest Caesarian ship – holding his left hand above water the whole way to keep certain documents dry; and towing his purple cloak behind him with his teeth, to save this trophy from the Egyptians.

65. He judged his men by their fighting record, not by their morals or social position, treating them all with equal severity – and equal indulgence; since it was only in the presence of the enemy that he insisted on strict discipline. He never gave forewarning of a march or a battle, but kept his troops always on the alert for sudden orders to go wherever he directed. Often he made them turn out when there was no need at all, especially in wet weather or on public holidays. Sometimes he would say: 'Keep a close eye on me!' and then steal away from camp at any hour of the day or night, expecting them to follow. It was certain to be a particularly long march, and hard on stragglers.

66. If rumours about the enemy's strength were causing alarm, his practice was to heighten morale, not by denying or belittling the danger, but on the contrary by further exaggerating it. For instance, when his troops were in a panic at the news of King Juba's approach, he called them together and announced: 'You may take it from me that the King will be here within a few days, at the head of ten infantry legions, thirty thousand cavalry, a hundred thousand lightly armed troops, and three hundred elephants. This being the case, you may as well stop asking questions and making guesses. I have given you the facts, with which I am familiar. Any of you who remain unsatisfied will find themselves aboard a leaky hulk and being carried

SPEECH TO THE ARMY. *Rhetorical ability was considered to be an important qualification for a Roman general, and Caesar possessed it in ample measure.*
22. *Coin of Galba showing the Emperor addressing his men.* (Hirmer.)

across the sea wherever the winds may decide to blow them.'

67. Though turning a blind eye to much of their misbehaviour, and never laying down any fixed scale of penalties, he allowed no deserter or mutineer to escape severe punishment. Sometimes, if a victory had been complete enough, he relieved the troops of all military duties and let them carry on as wildly as they pleased. One of his boasts was: 'My soldiers fight just as well when they are stinking of perfume.' He always addressed them not as 'My soldiers', but as 'Comrades ...', which put them into a better humour; and he equipped them splendidly. The silver and gold inlay of their weapons both improved their appearance on parade and made them more careful not to get disarmed in battle, these being objects of great value. Caesar loved his men dearly; when news came that Titurius's command had been massacred, he swore neither to cut his hair nor to trim his beard until they had been avenged.

68. By these means he won the devotion of his army as well as making it extraordinarily brave. At the outbreak of the Civil War every centurion in every legion volunteered to equip a cavalryman from his savings; and the private soldiers unanimously offered to serve under him without pay or rations, pooling their money so that nobody should go short. Throughout the entire struggle not a single Caesarian deserted, and many of them, when taken prisoners, preferred death to the alternative of serving with the Pompeians. Such was their fortitude in facing starvation and other hardships, both as besiegers and as besieged, that when Pompey was shown at Dyrrhachium the substitute for bread, made of grass, on which they were feeding, he exclaimed: 'I am fighting wild beasts!' Then he ordered the loaf to be hidden at once, not wanting his men to find out how tough and resolute the enemy were, and so lose heart.

Here the Caesarians suffered their sole reverse, but proved their stout-heartedness by begging to be punished for the lapse; whereupon he felt called upon to console rather than upbraid them. In other battles, they beat enormously superior forces. A single company of the Sixth Legion held a redoubt against four Pompeian legions for several hours, though almost every man had been wounded by arrow-shot – 130,000 arrows were afterwards collected on the scene of the engagement. This high level of courage is less surprising when individual examples are considered: for the centurion Cassius Scaeva, blinded in one eye, wounded in thigh and shoulder, and with no less than 120 holes in his shield, continued to defend the approaches to a redoubt. Nor was his by any means an exceptional case. At the naval battle of Massilia, a private soldier named Gaius Acilius grasped the stern of an enemy ship and, when someone lopped off his right hand, nevertheless boarded her and drove the enemy back with the boss of his shield only – a feat rivalling that of the Athenian Cynegirus (brother of the poet Aeschylus), who showed similar courage when maimed in trying to detain a Persian ship after the victory at Marathon.

69. Caesar's men did not mutiny once during the Gallic War, which lasted ten years. In the Civil Wars they were less dependable, but whenever they made insubordinate demands he faced them boldly, and always brought them to heel again – not by appeasement but by sheer exercise of personal authority. At Placentia, although Pompey's armies were as yet undefeated, he disbanded the entire Ninth Legion with

ignominy, later recalling them to the Colours in response to their abject pleas; this with great reluctance and only after executing the ringleaders.

70. At Rome, too, when the Tenth Legion agitated for their discharge and bounty and were terrorizing the city, Caesar defied the advice of his friends and at once confronted the mutineers in person. Again he would have disbanded them, though the African war was still being hotly fought; but by addressing them as 'Citizens' he readily regained their affections. A shout went up: 'We are your soldiers, Caesar, not civilians!' and they clamoured to serve under him in Africa: a demand which he nevertheless disdained to grant. He showed his contempt for the more disaffected soldiers by withholding a third part of the prize-money and land which had been set aside for them.

71. Even as a young man Caesar was well known for the devotion and loyalty he showed his dependants. While praetor in Africa, he protected a nobleman's son named Masintha against the tyranny of Hiempsal, King of Numidia; with such devotion that in the course of the quarrel he caught Juba, the Numidian heir-apparent, by the beard. Masintha, being then declared the King's vassal, was arrested; but Caesar immediately rescued him from the Numidian guards and harboured him in his own quarters for a long while. At the close of this praetorship Caesar sailed for Spain, taking Masintha with him. The lictors carrying their rods of office, and the crowds, who had come to say goodbye, acted as a screen; nobody realized that Masintha was hidden in Caesar's litter.

72. He showed consistent affection to his friends. Gaius Oppius, travelling by his side once through a wild forest, suddenly fell sick; but Caesar insisted on his using the only shelter that offered – a woodcutter's hut, hardly large enough for a single occupant – while he and the rest of his staff slept outside on the bare ground. Having attained supreme power he raised some of his friends, including men of humble birth, to high office and brushed aside criticism by saying: 'If bandits and cut-throats had helped to defend my honour, I should have shown them gratitude in the same way.'

73. Yet, when given the chance, he would always cheerfully come to terms with his bitterest enemies. He supported Gaius Memmius's candidature for the consulship, though they had both spoken most damagingly against each other. When Gaius Calvus, after his cruel lampoons of Caesar, made a move towards reconciliation through mutual friends, Caesar took the initiative

by writing him a friendly letter. Valerius Catullus had also libelled him in his verses about Mamurra,[21] yet Caesar, while admitting that these were a permanent blot on his name, accepted Catullus's apology and invited him to dinner that same afternoon, and never interrupted his friendship with Catullus's father.

74. Caesar was not naturally vindictive; and if he crucified the pirates who had held him to ransom, this was only because he had sworn in their presence to do so; and he first mercifully cut their throats. He could never bring himself to take vengeance on Cornelius Phagita, even though in his early days, while he was sick and a fugitive from Sulla, Cornelius had tracked him down night after night and demanded large sums of hush-money. On discovering that Philemon, his slave-secretary, had been induced to poison him, Caesar ordered a simple execution, without torture. When Publius Clodius was accused of adultery with Caesar's wife Pompeia, in sacrilegious circumstances, and both her mother-in-law Aurelia and her sister-in-law Julia had given the court a detailed and truthful account of the affair, Caesar himself refused to offer any evidence. The Court then asked him why, in that case, he had divorced Pompeia. He replied: 'Because I cannot have members of my household accused or even suspected.'

75. Nobody can deny that during the Civil War, and after, he behaved with wonderful restraint and clemency. Whereas Pompey declared that all who were not actively with the government were against it and would be treated as public enemies, Caesar announced that all who were not actively against him were with him. He allowed every centurion whom he had appointed on Pompey's recommendation to join the Pompeian forces if he pleased. At Ilerda, in Spain, the articles of capitulation were being discussed between Caesar and the Pompeian generals Afranius and Petreius, and the rival armies were fraternizing, when Afranius suddenly decided not to surrender and massacred every Caesarean soldier found in his camp. Yet Caesar could not bring himself to pay Afranius back in the same coin. During the battle of Pharsalus he shouted to his men: 'Spare your fellow-Romans!' and then allowed them to save one enemy soldier apiece, whoever he might be. My researches show that not a single Pompeian was killed at Pharsalus, once the fighting had ended, except Afranius and Faustus and young Lucius Caesar. It is thought that not even these

21. Catullus, *Poems* 29 and 57.

three were killed at his instance, though Afranius and Faustus had taken up arms again after he had spared their lives, and Lucius Caesar had cruelly cut the throats of the dictator's slaves and freedmen, even butchering the wild beasts brought by him to Rome for a public show. Eventually, towards the end of his career, Caesar invited back to Italy all exiles whom he had not yet pardoned, permitting them to hold magistracies and command armies; and went so far as to restore the statues of Sulla and Pompey, which the city crowds had thrown down and smashed. He also preferred to discourage rather than punish any plots against his life, or any slanders on his name. All that he would do when he detected such plots, or became aware of secret nocturnal meetings, was to announce openly that he knew about them. As for slanderers, he contented himself with warning them in public to keep their mouths shut; and good-naturedly took no action either against Aulus Caecina for his most libellous pamphlet or against Pitholaus for his scurrilous verses.

76. Yet other deeds and sayings of Caesar's may be set to the debit account, and justify the conclusion that he deserved assassination. Not only did he accept excessive honours, such as a life-consulship, a life-dictatorship, a perpetual Censorship, the title 'Imperator' put before his name, and the title 'Father of his Country' appended to it, also a statue standing among those of the ancient kings, and a raised couch placed in the orchestra at the Theatre; but took other honours which, as a mere mortal, he should certainly have refused. These included a golden throne in the Senate House, and another on the tribunal; a ceremonial chariot and litter for carrying his statue in the religious procession around the Circus; temples, altars and divine images; a priest of his own cult; a new college of Lupercals to celebrate his divinity; and the renaming of the seventh month as 'July'. Few, in fact, were the honours which he was not pleased to accept or assume.

His third and fourth consulships were merely titular; the dictatorship conferred on him at the same time supplied all the authority he needed. And in both years he substituted two new Consuls for himself during the last quarter, meanwhile letting only tribunes and aediles of the people be elected, and appointing prefects instead of praetors to govern the city during his absence.

One of the Consuls died suddenly on New Year's Eve and, when someone asked to hold office for the remaining few hours, Caesar granted his request. He showed equal scorn of traditional precedent by choosing magistrates several years ahead, decorating ten former praetors with the emblems of consular rank, and admitting to the Senate men of foreign birth, including semi-civilized Gauls, who had been granted Roman citizenship. He placed his own slaves in charge of the Mint and the public revenues, and sent one of his favourites, a freedman's son, to command the three legions stationed at Alexandria.

77. Titus Ampius has recorded some of Caesar's public statements which reveal a similar presumption: that the Republic was nothing – a mere name without form or substance; that Sulla had proved himself a dunce by resigning his dictatorship; and that, now his own word was law, people ought to be more careful how they approached him. Once, when a soothsayer reported that a sacrificial beast had been found to have no heart – an unlucky omen indeed – Caesar told him arrogantly: 'The omens will be more favourable when I wish them to be; meanwhile I am not at all surprised that a beast should lack the organ which inspires our finer feelings.'

78. What made the Romans hate him so bitterly was that when, one day, the entire Senate, armed with an imposing list of honours that they had just voted him, came to where he sat in front of the Temple of Mother Venus, he did not rise to greet them. According to some accounts he would have risen had not Cornelius Balbus prevented him; according to others, he made no such move and grimaced angrily at Gaius Trebatius who suggested this courtesy. The case was aggravated by a memory of Caesar's behaviour during one of his triumphs: he had ridden past the benches reserved for the tribunes of the people, and shouted in fury at a certain Pontius Aquila, who had kept his seat: 'Hey, there, Aquila the tribune! Do you want me to restore the Republic?' For several days after this incident he added to every undertaking he gave: 'With the kind consent of Pontius Aquila.'

79. This open insult to the Senate was emphasized by an even worse example of his arrogance. As he returned to Rome from the Alban Hill, where the Latin Festival had been celebrated, a member of the crowd set a laurel wreath bound with a royal white fillet on the head of his statue. Two tribunes of the people, Epidius Marullus and Caesetius Flavus, ordered the fillet to be removed at once and the offender imprisoned. But Caesar reprimanded and summarily deposed them both: either because the suggestion that he should be crowned King had been so rudely rejected, or else because – this was his own version – they had given him no chance to reject it himself and so earn deserved credit. From that day forward, however, he lay under the odious suspicion of having tried to revive the title of King; though, indeed, when the commons greeted him with 'Long live the King!' he now protested: 'No, I am Caesar, not King'; and though, again, when he was addressing the crowd from the Rostra at the Lupercalian Festival, and Mark Antony, the Consul, made several attempts to crown him, he refused the offer each time and at last sent the crown away for dedication to Capitoline Jupiter. What made matters worse was a persistent rumour that Caesar intended to move the seat of government to Troy or Alexandria, carrying off all the national resources, drafting every available man in Italy for military service, and letting his friends govern the city. At the next meeting of the House (it was further whispered), Lucius Cotta would announce a decision of the Fifteen who had charge of the Sibylline Books, that since these prophetic writings stated clearly: 'Only a king can conquer the Parthians,' the title of King must be conferred on Caesar.

80. Because his enemies shrank from agreeing to this proposal, they pressed on with their plans for his assassination. Several groups, each consisting of two or three malcontents, now united in a general conspiracy. Even the commons had come to disapprove of how things were going, and no longer hid their disgust at Caesar's tyrannical rule but openly demanded champions to protect their ancient liberties. When foreigners were admitted to the Senate someone put up a poster which read: 'Long live our country;[22] but if any newly-appointed senator inquires the way to the Senate House, let nobody direct him there!' And the following popular song was sung everywhere:

> Caesar led the Gauls in triumph,
>   Led them uphill, led them down,
> To the Senate House he took them,
>   Once the glory of our town.
> 'Pull those breeches off,' he shouted,
>   'Change into a purple gown!'

As Quintus Maximus, one of the three-months' Consuls, entered the Theatre, the lictor called out as usual: 'Make way for the Consul!' Cries of protest went up: 'What? For him? He's no Consul!' The deposition of Caesetius and Marullus caused such widespread annoyance that at the next Consular elections the commons

---

22. *Bonum factum* (*sit*), a formula prefixed to edicts.

cast a great many votes in their favour. Someone then wrote on the pedestal of Lucius Brutus's statue: 'If only you were alive now!' and on that of Caesar himself:

> Brutus was elected Consul
> When he sent the kings away;
> Caesar sent the Consuls packing,
> Caesar is our King today.'

More than sixty conspirators banded together against him, led by Gaius Cassius and Marcus and Decimus Brutus. A suggested plan was to wait until the consular elections, when Caesar would take his stand on the wooden bridge along which voters walked to the poll; one group of conspirators would then topple him over, while another waited underneath with daggers drawn. An alternative was to attack him in the Sacred Way or at the entrance to the Theatre. The conspirators wavered between these plans until Caesar called a meeting of the Senate in the Hall of Pompey for the Ides of March; they then decided at once that this would be a convenient time and place.

81. Unmistakable signs forewarned Caesar of his assassination. A few months previously the veterans who had been sent to colonize Capua under the Julian Law were breaking up some ancient tombs in search of stone for their new farm-houses – all the more eagerly when they came across a large hoard of ancient vases. One of these tombs proved to be that of Capys, founder of the city, and there they found a bronze tablet with a Greek inscription to this effect: 'Disturb the bones of Capys, and a man of Trojan stock will be murdered by his kindred, and later avenged at great cost to Italy.' This story should not be dismissed as idle fiction, or a lie, because our authority for it is none other than Cornelius Balbus, a close friend of Caesar's. Soon afterwards news reached Caesar that a herd of horses which he had dedicated to the river Rubicon, after fording it, and allowed to roam untended in the valley, were beginning to show a repugnance for the pasture and shedding bucketfuls of tears. Again, during a sacrifice, the augur Spurinna warned Caesar that the danger threatening him would not come later than the Ides of March; and on the day before the Ides a little bird, called the King Bird, flew into the Hall of Pompey with a sprig of laurel in its beak – pursued by a swarm of different birds from a near-by copse, which tore it to pieces there and then. And on his last night Caesar dreamed that he was soaring above the clouds, and then shaking hands with Jupiter; while his wife

Calpurnia dreamed that the gable ornament, resembling that of a temple, which had been one of the honours voted him by the Senate, collapsed, and there he lay stabbed in her arms! She awoke suddenly and the bedroom door burst open of its own accord.

These warnings, and ill-health, made him hesitate for some time whether to go ahead with his plans, or whether to postpone the meeting. Finally Decimus Brutus persuaded him not to disappoint the Senate, who had been in full session for some time, waiting for him to arrive. It was about ten o'clock when he set off for the House. As he went, someone handed him a note containing details of the plot against his life, but he merely added it to the bundle of petitions in his left hand, which he intended to read later. Several victims were then sacrificed, and despite consistently unfavourable omens, he entered the House, deriding Spurinna as a false prophet. 'The Ides of March have come,' he said. 'Yes, they have come,' replied Spurinna, 'but they have not yet gone.'

23. CAESAR'S DREAM *was not merely a forewarning of death but also an augury of divinization, of joining the gods, as is shown by this relief from the Arch of Trajan at Benevento, where Jupiter god of the sky hands his principal instrument of power, the thunderbolt, to the Emperor.*

82. As soon as Caesar took his seat the conspirators crowded around him as if to pay their respects. Tillius Cimber, who had taken the lead, came up close, pretending to ask a question. Caesar made a gesture of postponement, but Cimber caught hold of his shoulders. 'This is violence!' Caesar cried, and at that moment, as he turned away, one of the Casca brothers with a sweep of his dagger stabbed him just below the throat. Caesar grasped Casca's arm and ran it through with his stylus; he was leaping away when another dagger blow stopped him. Confronted by a ring of drawn daggers, he drew the top of his gown over his face, and at the same time ungirded the lower part, letting it fall to his feet so that he would die with both legs decently

CAEASAR'S WILL. *As* pontifex maximus, *chief priest, Caesar exercised the sacral authority which had formerly belonged to the Roman Kings, and thus supervised the Vestal Virgins, in whose house on the Roman Forum he deposited his will.*
24. *Vesta, the Vestal Virgins and the* pontifex maximus (far right). (Palermo.)

covered. Twenty-three dagger thrusts went home as he stood there. Caesar did not utter a sound after Casca's blow had drawn a groan from him; though some say that when he saw Marcus Brutus about to deliver the second blow, he reproached him in Greek with: 'You, too, my child?'

The entire Senate then dispersed in confusion, and Caesar was left lying dead for some time, until three slave boys carried him home in a litter, with one arm hanging over the side. The physician Antistius conducted the *post mortem* and came to the conclusion that none of the wounds had been mortal except the second one, in the chest. It had been decided to drag the dead man down to the Tiber, confiscate his property, and revoke all his edicts; but fear of Mark Antony, the Consul, and Lepidus, the Master of Horse, kept the assassins from making their plans good.

83. At the request of Lucius Piso, Calpurnia's father, Caesar's will, which he had drafted six months before at his villa near Lavicum, and entrusted to the safekeeping of the Chief Vestal, was unsealed and read in Antony's house. From the time of his first consulship until the outbreak of the Civil War (according to Quintus Tubero) Caesar's principal heir had been his son-in-law Pompey, and he used to read out this part of his will to the assembled troops. In his last will, however, he cancelled the bequest and left three-quarters of his estate, after certain legacies had been deducted,

to Gaius Octavius, afterwards Augustus, and one-eighth each to Lucius Pinarius and Quintus Pedius. These were the three grandsons of his sister. At the close of the will he also adopted Gaius Octavius into the Caesar family, but provided for the possibility of a son being subsequently born to himself and appointed several of the assassins as guardians to the boy. Decimus Brutus even figured among his heirs in the second degree.[23] Caesar left the general public his gardens on the banks of the Tiber for use as a recreation ground, and three gold pieces a man.

84. When the funeral arrangements had been announced, his friends raised a pyre on the Campus Martius near his daughter Julia's tomb, and a gilded

23. Those who would inherit if the heirs in the first degree were prevented by death or unwillingness from accepting the legacy.

CAESAR'S DIVINIZATION

25 (right). *Coin of Augustus showing the comet which was seen after Caesar's death and which was thought to be his soul ascending to the above. Spanish mint, 18–17* B.C., (London, British Museum.)

26 (below). *Funeral procession with musicians and mourners. The bier of the deceased is surmounted by a baldacchino with moon and stars, hinting at his abode in the heavens. First century* A.D. (Aquila, Museo Aquilano.)

shrine on the Rostra resembling that of Mother Venus. In it they set an ivory couch, spread with purple and gold cloth, and from a pillar at its head hung the gown in which he had been murdered. Since a procession of mourners laying funeral gifts would have taken more than a day to file past the pyre, everyone was invited to come there by whatever route he pleased, regardless of precedence. Emotions of pity and indignation for Caesar's murder were aroused at the funeral games by a line from Pacuvius's play *Contest for the Arms of Achilles*:

What, did I save these men that they might murder me?

and by a similar sentiment from Atilius's *Electra*. Mark Antony dispensed with a formal eulogy; instead, he instructed a herald to read, first, the recent decree simultaneously voting Caesar all divine and human honours, and then the oath by which the entire Senate had pledged themselves to watch over his safety. Antony added a very few words of comment. When the ivory funeral couch had been carried down into the Forum by a group of magistrates and ex-magistrates, and a dispute arose as to whether the body should be cremated in the Temple of Capitoline Jupiter or in Pompey's Assembly Hall, two divine forms suddenly appeared, two javelins in their hands and sword at thigh, and set fire to the couch with torches. Immediately the spectators assisted the blaze by heaping on it dry branches and the judges' chairs, and the court benches, with whatever else came to hand. Thereupon the musicians and professional mourners, who had walked in the funeral train wearing the robes that he had himself worn at his four triumphs, tore these in pieces and flung them on the flames – to which veterans who had assisted at his triumphs added the arms they had then borne. Many women in the audience similarly sacrificed their jewellery together with their children's breast-plaques and robes. Public grief was enhanced by crowds of foreigners lamenting in their own fashion, especially Jews, who came flocking to the Forum for several nights in succession.

85. As soon as the funeral was over, the populace, snatching firebrands from the pyre, ran to burn down the houses of Brutus and Cassius, and were repelled with difficulty. Mistaking Helvius Cinna for the Cornelius Cinna who had delivered a bitter speech against Caesar on the previous day, and whom they were out to kill, they murdered him and paraded the streets with his head stuck on the point of a spear. Later they raised a substantial, almost twenty-foot-high column of Numidian marble in the Forum, and inscribed on it: 'To the Father of His Country'. For a long time afterwards they used to offer sacrifices at the foot of this column, make vows there and settle disputes by oaths taken in Caesar's name.

86. Some of his friends suspected that, having no desire to live much longer because of his failing health, he had taken no precautions against the conspiracy, and neglected the warnings of soothsayers and well-wishers. It has also been suggested that he placed such confidence in the Senate's last decree and in their oath of loyalty, that he dispensed even with the armed Spaniards who had hitherto acted as his permanent escort. A contrary view is that as a relief from taking constant precautions, he deliberately exposed himself, just this once, to all the plots against his life which he knew had been formed. Also, he is quoted as having often said: 'It is more important for Rome than for myself that I should survive. I have long been sated with power and glory; but, should anything happen to me, Rome will enjoy no peace. A new Civil War will break out under far worse conditions than the last.'

87. Almost all authorities agree on one thing, that he more or less welcomed the manner of his death. He had once read in Xenophon's *Boyhood of Cyrus* the paragraph about the funeral instructions given by Cyrus on his deathbed, and said how much he loathed the prospect of a lingering end – he wanted a sudden one. And on the day before his murder he had dined at Marcus Lepidus's house, where the topic discussed happened to be 'the best sort of death' – and 'Let it come swiftly and unexpectedly,' cried Caesar.

88. He was fifty-five years old when he died, and his immediate deification, formally decreed, was more than a mere official decree since it reflected public conviction; if only because, on the first day of the Games given by his successor Augustus in honour of this apotheosis, a comet appeared about an hour before sunset and shone for seven days running. This was held to be Caesar's soul, elevated to Heaven; hence the star, now placed above the forehead of his divine image.

The Senate voted that the Assembly Hall where he fell should be walled up; that the Ides of March should be known ever afterwards as 'The Day of Parricide'; and that a meeting of the Senate should never take place on it again.

89. Very few, indeed, of the assassins outlived Caesar for more than three years, or died naturally. All were condemned, and all perished in different ways – some in shipwreck, some in battle, some using the very daggers with which they had murdered Caesar to take their own lives.

II
AUGUSTUS

AFTERWARDS DEIFIED

AUGUSTUS *as* pater patriae, *father of the fatherland.*
28 (above). *Roman coin.* (Hirmer.)

PUBLIC MONUMENTS *in Italy and elsewhere proclaimed that the Roman Empire had at last reached a state of peace.*
27 (opposite). *Arch dedicated to Augustus at Rimini.*

The family of the Octavii, by all accounts, were famous in ancient Velitrae. An 'Octavian Street' runs through the busiest part of the city, and an altar is shown there consecrated by one Octavius, a local commander. Apparently news of an attack by a neighbouring city reached him while he was sacrificing a victim to Mars; snatching the intestines from the fire, he offered them only half-burned, and hurried away to win the battle. The records at Velitrae include a decree that all future offerings to Mars must be made in the same fashion, the carcase of every victim becoming a perquisite of the Octavians.

2. King Tarquinius Priscus admitted the Octavii, among other families, to the Roman Senate, and though Servius Tullius awarded them patrician privileges, they later reverted to plebeian rank until eventually Julius Caesar made them patricians once more. Gaius Rufus was the first Octavius elected to office by the popular vote – he won a quaestorship. His sons Gnaeus and Gaius fathered two very different branches of the family. Gnaeus's descendants held all the highest offices of state in turn; but Gaius's branch, either by accident or choice, remained simple knights until the entry into the Senate of Augustus's father. Augustus's great-grandfather had fought as a colonel under Aemilius Papus[1] in Sicily during the Second Punic War. His grandfather, who enjoyed a comfortable income, was apparently content with a municipal magistracy, and lived to an advanced age. This information is given by others; it is not derived from Augustus's own memoirs, which merely record that he came of a rich old equestrian family, and that his father had been the first Octavius to enter the Senate. Mark Antony wrote scornfully that Augustus's great-grandfather had been only a freedman, a ropemaker from the neighbourhood

1. 205 B.C.

THE ANCESTORS. *Respect for one's ancestors was one of the old Roman virtues, and many Roman homes contained shrines in which ancestral portraits were kept.*
29 (above). *Ancestral busts in small cupboards on a Roman tomb relief.* (Copenhagen, National Museum.)
30 (left). *Man holding busts of his ancestors. Statue of the time of Augustus.* (Rome, Capitoline Museum.)

of Thurii; and his grandfather, a money-changer. This is as much information as I have managed to glean about the paternal ancestors of Augustus.

3. I cannot believe that Gaius Octavius, his father, was also a money-changer who distributed bribes among the voters in the Campus and undertook other electioneering services. He was certainly born rich; from the start of his life a man of wealth and repute, brought up in sufficient affluence to achieve office without having to engage in such practices; and proved a capable administrator. After his praetorship, he became governor of Macedonia, and the Senate commissioned him to pass through Thurii on his way there and disperse a group of outlawed slaves who, having fought under Spartacus and Catiline, were now holding possession of the district. He governed Macedonia courageously and justly, winning a big battle in Thrace, mainly against the Bessians; and letters survive from Cicero reproaching his brother Quintus, then proconsular governor of Asia, for inefficiency, and advising him to make Octavius his model in all diplomatic dealings with allies.

4. Gaius died suddenly on his return to Rome, before he could stand as a candidate for the consulship. He left three children: Octavia the Elder, Octavia the Younger, and Augustus. The mother of Octavia the Elder was Ancharia; the other two were his children by Atia, daughter of Marcus Atius Balbus and Julius Caesar's sister Julia. Balbus's family originated in Aricia, and could boast of many ancestral busts of senators; his mother was also closely related to Pompey the Great. Balbus served first as praetor, and then with a Commission of Twenty appointed under the Julian Law to divide estates in Campania among the commons. Mark Antony likewise tried to belittle Augustus's maternal line by alleging that his great-grandfather Balbus had been born in Africa, and kept first a perfumery and then a bakehouse at Aricia. Cassius of Parma similarly sneers at Augustus as the grandson of a baker and a money-changer, writing in one of his letters: 'Your mother's flour came from a miserable Arician bakery, and the coin-stained hands of a money-changer from Nerulum kneaded it.'

5. Augustus was born just before sunrise on 23 September,[2] while Cicero and Gaius Antonius were Consuls, at Ox-Heads, in the Palatine district; a shrine to him, built soon after his death, marks the spot. The case of a young patrician, Gaius Laetorius by name, figures in the published book of *Senatorial Proceedings*. Pleading his youth and position to escape the maximum punishment for adultery, he further described himself as 'the occupant and, one might even say, guardian of the place first touched at his birth by the God Augustus'. Laetorius begged for pardon in the name of his 'own especial god'. The Senate afterwards consecrated that part of the building by decree.

6. In the country mansion, near Velitrae, which belonged to Augustus's grandfather, a small room, not unlike a butler's pantry, is still shown and described as Augustus's nursery; the local people firmly believe that he was also born there. Religious scruples forbid anyone to enter except for some necessary reason, and after purification. It had long been believed that casual visitors would be overcome by a sudden awful terror; and recently this was proved true when, one night, a new owner of the mansion, either from ignorance or because he wanted to test the truth of the belief, went to sleep in the room. A few hours later he was hurled out of bed by a supernatural agency and found lying half-dead against the door, bedclothes and all.

7. I can prove pretty conclusively that as a child Augustus was called Thurinus ('The Thurian'), perhaps because his ancestors had once lived at Thurii, or because his father had defeated the slaves in that neighbourhood soon after he was born; my evidence is a bronze statuette which I once owned. It shows him as a boy, and a rusty, almost illegible inscription in iron letters gives him this name. I have presented the statuette to the Emperor Hadrian, who has placed it among the Household-gods in his bedroom. Moreover, Augustus was often sneeringly called 'The Thurian' in Antony's correspondence. Augustus answered by confessing himself puzzled: why should his former name be thrown in his face as an insult?

Later he adopted the surname Caesar to comply with the will of his mother's uncle, the Dictator; and then the title Augustus after a motion to that effect had been introduced by Munatius Plancus. Some senators wished him to be called Romulus, as the second founder of the city; but Plancus had his way. He argued that 'Augustus' was both a more original and a more honourable title, since sanctuaries and all places consecrated by the augurs are known as 'august' – the word being either an enlarged form of *auctus*, implying the 'increase' of dignity thus given such places, or a product of the phrase *avium gestus gustusve*, 'the behaviour and feeding of birds', which the augurs observed. Plancus supported his point by a quotation from Ennius's *Annals*:

When glorious Rome had founded been, by augury august.

8. At the age of four Augustus[3] lost his father. At twelve he delivered a funeral oration in honour of his grandmother Julia, Julius Caesar's sister. At sixteen, having now come of age, he was awarded military decorations when Caesar celebrated his African triumph, though he had been too young for overseas service. Caesar then went to fight Pompey's sons in Spain; Augustus followed with a very small escort, along roads held by the enemy, after a shipwreck, too, and in a state of semi-convalescence from a serious illness. This action delighted Caesar, who, moreover, soon formed a high estimate of Augustus's character quite apart from the energetic manner in which he had made the journey.

Having recovered possession of the Spanish provinces, Caesar planned a war against the Dacians and

---

2. 63 B.C.

3. He is generally known as Octavian until 27 B.C., when he was given the title Augustus.

Parthians, and sent Augustus ahead to Apollonia, in Illyria, where he spent his time studying Greek literature. News then came that Caesar had been assassinated, after naming him his heir, and Augustus was tempted, for a while, to put himself under the protection of the troops quartered near by. However, deciding that this would be rash and premature, he returned to Rome and there entered upon his inheritance, despite his mother's doubts and the active opposition of his step-father, Marcius Philippus the ex-Consul. Augustus now levied armies, and governed the Empire: first with Antony and Lepidus as his colleagues; next, for nearly twelve years, with Antony alone; finally by himself for another forty-four years.

9. After this brief outline of Augustus's life, I shall fill in its various phases; but the story will be more readable and understandable if, instead of keeping chronological order, I use subject headings.

He fought five civil wars in all; associated respectively with the names of Mutina, Philippi, Perusia, Sicily, and Actium. Those of Mutina and Actium were against Antony; that of Philippi against Brutus and Cassius; that of Perusia against Antony's brother Lucius; that of Sicily against Sextus Pompeius, son of Pompey the Great.

10. The underlying motive of every campaign was that Augustus felt it his duty, above all, to avenge Caesar and keep his decrees in force. On his return from Apollonia, he decided to surprise Brutus and Cassius by rapid and forceful action ; but they foresaw the danger and escaped, so he had recourse to the law and prosecuted them for murder in their absence. Finding that the officials who should have celebrated Caesar's victory with public Games did not dare to carry out their commission, he undertook the task himself. Because stronger authority was needed to implement his other plans, Augustus announced his candidature for a tribuneship of the people – death had created a vacancy – although he was a patrician but not yet a senator, and thus doubly disqualified from standing. Antony, one of the two Consuls, on whose assistance Augustus had particularly counted, opposed this action and denied him even his ordinary legal rights, except on payment of a heavy bribe. Augustus therefore went over to the senatorial party,[4] well aware that they hated Antony, who was now besieging Decimus Brutus at Mutina and trying to expel him from the province to which he had been appointed by Caesar with the

THE HOUSEHOLD GODS

31 (opposite). *Painting from Pompeii showing, below, the guardian spirits,* genii, *of the master and mistress of the household, in the form of serpents, next to an altar with offerings, and, above, the Lares and the goddess Fortune at an altar.*

32 (above). *Household shrines contained images of the Lares, initially gods of the fields, and later of the house also, and images of the Penates, gods of the house and storeroom. Bronze statuette of a Lar.* (Oxford, Ashmolean Museum.) *(See Ill. 59.)*

4. The *optimates*, or 'best people'.

Senate's approval. On the advice of certain persons, Augustus actually engaged assassins to murder Antony and, fearing retaliation when the plot came to light, spent as much money as he could raise on enlisting a force of veterans to protect himself and the state. The Senate awarded him praetorian rank,[5] gave him the command of this army, and instructed him to join Hirtius and Pansa, the two new Consuls, in lending aid to Decimus Brutus. Augustus brought the campaign to a successful close within three months, after fighting a couple of battles. According to Antony, he ran away from the first of these and did not reappear until the next day, having lost both his charger and his purple cloak. But it is generally agreed that in the second engagement he showed not only skill as a commander but courage as a soldier: when, at a crisis in the fighting, the standard-bearer of his legion was seriously wounded, Augustus himself shouldered the Eagle and carried it for some time.

11. Because Hirtius fell in battle, and Pansa later succumbed to a wound, a rumour went about that Augustus had engineered both deaths with the object of gaining sole control over their victorious armies after Antony was defeated and the state bereaved of its Consuls. Pansa certainly died in such suspicious circumstances that Glyco, his physician, was arrested on a charge of poisoning the wound; and Aquilius Niger goes so far as to assert that in the confusion of battle Augustus despatched Hirtius with his own hand.

12. However, when Augustus heard that Mark Antony had been taken under Lepidus's protection and that the other military commanders, supported by their troops, were coming to terms with these two, he at once deserted the senatorial party. His excuse was that some of them had contemptuously called him 'the boy', while others had not concealed their view that, once publicly honoured, he should be got rid of – to avoid having to pay his veterans and himself what they expected. Augustus showed regret for his former allegiance by imposing a heavier fine on the people of Nursia than they could possibly meet, and then exiling them from their city; they had offended him by erecting a monument to fellow-citizens killed at Mutina, with the inscription: 'Fallen in the cause of freedom!'

13. As member of a triumvirate consisting of Antony, Lepidus, and himself, Augustus defeated Brutus and Cassius at Philippi, though in ill-health at the time. In the first of the two battles fought he was driven out of his camp, and escaped with some difficulty to Antony's command. After the second and decisive one he showed no clemency to his beaten enemies, but sent Brutus's head to Rome for throwing at the feet of Caesar's divine image; and insulted the more distinguished of his prisoners. When one of these humbly asked for the right of decent burial, he got the cold answer: 'That must be settled with the carrion-birds.' And when a father and his son pleaded for their lives, Augustus, it is said, told them to decide which of the two should be spared, by casting lots or playing *morra*.[6] The father sacrificed his life for the son, and was executed; the son then committed suicide; Augustus watched them both die. His conduct so disgusted the remainder of the prisoners, including Marcus Favonius, a well-known imitator of Cato's, that while being led off in chains they courteously saluted Antony as Imperator, but abused Augustus to his face with the most obscene epithets.

The victors divided between them the responsibilities of government. Antony undertook to pacify the eastern provinces if Augustus led the veterans back to Italy and settled them on municipal lands. However, Augustus failed to satisfy either the landowners, who complained that they were being evicted from their estates; or the veterans, who felt entitled to better rewards for their service.

14. At this point Lucius Antonius felt strong enough, as Consul and brother of the powerful Mark Antony, to raise a revolt. Augustus forced him to take refuge in the city of Perusia, which he starved into surrender, but only after being twice exposed to great danger. On the first occasion, before the revolt broke out, he had found a private soldier watching the Games from one of the seats reserved for knights, and ordered his removal by an attendant; when Augustus's enemies then circulated a rumour that the offender had been tortured and executed, an angry crowd of soldiers began to demonstrate at once and Augustus would have lost his life had not the missing soldier suddenly reappeared, safe and unhurt. On the second occasion Augustus was sacrificing close to the walls of Perusia, during the siege, when a party of gladiators made a sortie and nearly cut off his retreat.

15. After the fall of the city Augustus took vengeance on crowds of prisoners and returned the same answer to all who sued for pardon or tried to explain

6. A game in which the contestants thrust out their fingers, the one naming correctly the number thrust out by his opponent being the winner.

their presence among the rebels. It was simply: 'You must die!' According to some historians, he chose 300 prisoners of equestrian or senatorial rank, and offered them on the Ides of March at the altar of the God Julius, as human sacrifices. Augustus fought, it is said, because he wished to offer his secret enemies, and those whom fear rather than affection kept with his party, a chance to declare themselves by joining Lucius Antonius; he would then crush them, confiscate their estates, and thus manage to pay off his veterans.

16. The Sicilian war, one of his first enterprises, lasted for eight years.[7] It was interrupted by two storms that wrecked his fleets – in the summer, too – and obliged him to rebuild them; and by the Pompeians' success in cutting his grain supplies, which forced him to grant a popular demand for an armistice. At last, however, he built an entirely new fleet, with 20,000 freed slaves trained as oarsmen, and formed the Julian harbour at Baiae by letting the sea into the Lucrine and Avernan lakes. Here he exercised his crews all one winter and, when the sailing season opened, defeated Sextus Pompey off the Sicilian coast between Mylae and Naulochus; although on the eve of the battle he fell so fast asleep that his staff had to wake him and ask for the signal to begin hostilities. This must have been the occasion of Mark Antony's taunt: 'He could not face his ships to review them when they were already at their fighting stations; but lay on his back in a stupor and gazed up at the sky, never rising to show that he was alive until his admiral Marcus Agrippa had routed the enemy.'

Augustus has been taken to task for crying out, when he heard that his fleets were sunk: 'I will win this war, even if Neptune does not want me to!' and for removing the god's image from the sacred procession at the next celebration of Games in the Circus. It would be safe to say that the Sicilian was by far his most dangerous campaign. He once landed an army in Sicily and was sailing back to Italy, where the bulk of his forces were stationed, when the Pompeian admirals Demochares and Apollophanes suddenly appeared and he just managed to escape them with a single ship. He was also nearly captured in Calabria: as he walked along the road to Rhegium by way of Epizephyrian Locri, he saw a flotilla of biremes heading for the shore and, not realizing that they were Pompeians, went down to greet them on the beach. Afterwards, while hurriedly escaping by narrow, winding paths, he faced a new

danger. Some years previously he had proscribed the father of Aemilius Paulus, an officer of his staff, one of whose slaves, now seeing a good opportunity to pay off an old score, tried to murder him.

Lepidus, the third member of the triumvirate, whom Augustus had summoned from Africa to his support, thought himself so important as the commander of twenty legions that, when Sextus Pompey had been beaten, he demanded the highest place in the government with terrible threats. Augustus deprived him of his legions and, though successfully pleading for his life, Lepidus spent what was left of it in permanent exile at Circeii.

17. Eventually Augustus broke his friendship with Mark Antony, which had always been a tenuous one and in continuous need of patching; and sought to prove that his rival had failed to conduct himself as befitted a Roman citizen, by ordering the will he had deposited at Rome to be opened and publicly read. It listed among Antony's heirs the children fathered by him on Cleopatra. Nevertheless, when the Senate outlawed Antony, Augustus allowed all his relatives and friends to join him, including Gaius Sosius and Titus Domitius, the Consuls of the year. He also excused Bononia, a city traditionally dependent on the Antonian family, from rallying to his side as the rest of Italy was doing. Presently he defeated Antony in a sea-battle off Actium, where the fighting went on so long that he spent the whole night aboard his flagship.

In winter-quarters on Samos, after this victory, Augustus heard the alarming news of a mutiny at Brundusium among troops whom he had picked from every corps in the Army. They were demanding the bounties due to them and an immediate discharge. He returned to Italy, but ran into two storms: the first between the headlands of the Peloponnese and Aetolia; the second off the Ceraunian Mountains. Some of his galleys went down on both occasions; the rigging of his own vessel carried away and her rudder split. He stayed no more than twenty-seven days at Brundusium, just long enough to pacify the mutineers; then took a roundabout route to Egypt by way of Asia Minor and Syria, besieged Alexandria, where Antony had fled with Cleopatra, and soon reduced it. At the last moment Antony sued for peace, but Augustus forced him to commit suicide – and inspected the corpse. He was so anxious to save Cleopatra as an ornament for his triumph that he actually summoned Psyllian snake-charmers to suck the poison from her self-inflicted wound, supposedly the bite of an asp. Though he allowed the lovers

ANTONY AND CLEOPATRA
33 (above). *Portrait bust of Cleopatra.* (London, British Museum.)
34 (right). *Portrait bust of Mark Antony.* (Kingston Lacy.)

honourable burial in the same tomb, and gave orders that the mausoleum which they had begun to build should be completed, he had the elder of Antony's sons by Fulvia[8] dragged from the image of the God Julius, to which he had fled with vain pleas for mercy, and executed. Augustus also had Caesarion, Julius Caesar's bastard son by Cleopatra, overtaken, and killed him when captured. However, he spared Cleopatra's children by Antony, brought them up no less tenderly than if they had been members of his own family, and gave

them the education which their various positions deserved.

18. About this time he had the sarcophagus containing Alexander the Great's mummy removed from its shrine and, after a long look at its features, showed his veneration by crowning the head with a golden diadem and strewing flowers on the trunk. When asked 'Would you now like to visit the Mausoleum of the Ptolemies?' he replied: 'I came to see a King, not a row of corpses.'

Augustus turned the kingdom of Egypt into a Roman province; and then, to increase its fertility and its yield of grain for the Roman market, set troops to

8. Marcus Antonius the Younger (Antyllus).

EGYPT AND ROME. *From the time of Augustus, the city of Rome became increasingly dependent on the Egyptian grain supply.*

35 (above). *Personification of the river Nile, first century* A.D. *The god is surrounded by symbols of Egypt's fertility: he holds a sheaf of corn and is crowned with corn, while the sixteen babies refer to the annual flooding of the Nile, in which the water usually rose sixteen measures.* (Rome, Vatican.)

clean out the irrigation canals of the Nile Delta which had silted up after many years' neglect. To perpetuate the glory of his victory at Actium, he founded a city close to the scene of the battle and named it Nicopolis – or 'City of Victory' – and made arrangements for the celebration of Games there every five years. He also enlarged an ancient local temple of Apollo, and embellished his camp with trophies taken from Antony's fleet, consecrating the site jointly to Neptune and Mars.

19. Next, he suppressed a series of sporadic riots and revolts; besides certain conspiracies, all of them detected before they became dangerous. The leaders of the conspiracies were, in historical sequence: Lepidus the Younger; Varro Murena, and Fannius Caepio; Marcus Egnatius; Plautius Rufus and Lucius Paulus (the husband of Augustus's grand-daughter), and besides these Lucius Audasius, a feeble old man who had been indicted for forgery; also Asinius Epicadus, a half-breed of partly Parthian origin. Audasius and Epicadus had planned to rescue Augustus's daughter Julia and his grandson Agrippa Postumus from the prison islands where they were confined, and forcibly take them to the legions abroad. But attempts against Augustus's life were made by men from even the lowest walks of life; so I must not forget one Telephus, a slave, whose task it had been to remind a lady of her engagements; he nursed a delusion that he was fated to become emperor, and planned an armed attack on the Senate as well. Then an Illyrian camp-orderly, who had managed to sneak into the Palace without being noticed by the porters, was caught one night near

Nature and the Gods

What is most difficult to understand about the past is what at that time people took for granted. Many aspects of the past look deceptively similar to what we know ourselves until we look more closely and find that we have stumbled upon an entirely different method of looking at life and the universe.

We know of the Romans' love for nature and the countryside from many authors of the republican and imperial periods, and countless Roman artefacts and works of art bear witness to detailed observation of plants and animals which were meticulously portrayed in stone carving or in painting[1]. Such depictions speak of people who, however sophisticated and 'modern' they may have been in many respects, and however long they had lived in cities, retained some part of themselves which was deeply rooted in country life. Nature was full of signs, whether these were the seasonal changes which still punctuate the agricultural year, or whether they were the divine powers which many thoughtful Romans saw at work in these same seasonal changes and in other aspects of nature's rhythms which are different from human rhythms.

The Roman state religion laid down a variety of procedures which were to be followed so that man might correctly interpret those signs and rhythms of nature: for it was thought that exceptional events in human affairs would in some way be preceded and announced by exceptional events in the order of nature. Suetonius narrates numerous occasions when in some manner nature gave an augury of events in the human sphere (Augustus 97; Galba 1).

A Roman, if he were a religious person, experienced a certain tension between the human and the natural orders: for him it could not be the function of religion to relate everything to man, to make man the centre of the universe. Nature, the outside world, retained some primacy. Thus, however much Roman landscape painting might at times crowd in on nature with buildings and ornaments[10], some wildness, something uncontrollable, was left intact in the way in which a Roman viewed his environment. It was this primeval independence which nature retained in Roman religion that ultimately could validate the ancient and obscure rites of the state religion. Many Romans of Suetonius's day considered these rites quaint or even absurd: but there remained a feeling that the rites had or could have a context in nature,

1. Roman garden; painting from the House of Livia ▶

2. Girl dancer; from the temple of Artemis at Sparta

3. Venus of the Sea; painting from Pompeii

4. Ruins of the villa of Tiberius on Capri

5. The childhood of Dionysus; painting from Villa Farnesina

6. Pan and the nymphs; painting from Pompeii

7. Dionysus and Vesuvius; painting from Pompeii

8. The mission of Trioptolemus; Roman silver dish

9. The four Seasons; mosaic from Zliten

however dimly this might be perceived, and that they should therefore be performed.

However, little of this strand in Roman official religion ever entered the realm where it could regularly be reasoned about, ordered or depicted. Instead, in much of their imagery of nature and in their myths, Romans drew on Greek religion and Greek cults[2]. Roman historiography and poetry linked the origins of Rome with Greek stories of the long-distant past, and Roman noble families claimed descent from figures in Greek religion and mythology (Julius 6; Galba 2).

At the same time, nature became populated with anthropomorphic divine figures from the Greek pantheon who were given Latin names and replaced the more impersonal divine powers of ancient Italy and Rome. A wooded corner in the garden of a country seat might remind a weary Roman city dweller of the nymphs and Pan, or Faunus, playing his reed pipes[6]. Dionysus, or Bacchus, the god of ecstasy and wine, was reared by nymphs in the country[5] and could be depicted in a familiar Italian landscape[7], while Aphrodite, or Venus, the sea-born goddess of love, swam over the waves[3].

However, the Romans did not merely receive and repeat Greek myths and sacred tales. In the international framework of the Roman Empire, some of these tales acquired a new, almost universal dimension. The tales acquired this dimension because they were applied to divinities and cult sites far removed from their place of origin, and out of the resulting mingling of Greek, Roman and other elements new forms of religious expression evolved. At the same time, the sheer size of the Empire influenced religious thought and religious speculation. In this way the Greek story from Eleusis near Athens (cf. Augustus 93) of how Triptolemus travelling on a winged chariot had instructed mankind in agriculture could be depicted as a cosmic tableau, framed by personifications of heaven and earth[8].

One of the most universal of Roman images and concepts of nature and the gods was that of the Seasons. Despite its size and its unprecedented human resources, the Roman Empire remained very largely agricultural, and the success or failure of the harvest, the sequence of the seasons, was therefore, for most Romans, a constant preoccupation. In art, the four Seasons were shown as personifications, each with the products of her time of year[9]. The Seasons stood for the abundance of the harvest, for felicity and happiness in this life – and by a transference of meanings which is characteristic of Roman religious thought, they also stood for the felicity and happiness of the departed in the after-life.

◄ 10. Garden landscape with goatherds; painting from Pompeii

EGYPT AND ROME. *Egypt exported not only grain, but also ideas.*

36 (above). *The cult of the Egyptian goddess Isis reached Rome in the first century* B.C. *The altar of Isis from her temple in the Field of Mars: it shows her mystic casket and sacred serpent. The crescent moon was one of her symbols (see Ills. 113 and 149). (Rome, Capitoline Museum.)*

37 (right). *Traditionally, tombs in Roman Italy were built in the form of a house; the tomb of Annia Regilla on the Via Appia is an unusually elaborate example of the second century* A.D. *(See Ill. 131.)*

(opposite). *Gaius Cestius, a contemporary of Augustus, on the other hand, imitated a style of burial current in Egypt in the third millennium* B.C., *and had himself buried in a pyramid on the Via Ostiensis, Rome.*

the imperial bedroom, brandishing a hunting-knife; but since no statement could be extracted from him by torture it is doubtful whether he was really insane or merely pretending to be.

20. Augustus commanded armies in only two foreign wars: against the Dalmatians while he was still in his teens, and against the Cantabrians after defeating Antony. In one of the Dalmatian battles his right knee was bruised by a sling-stone; in another, he had one leg and both arms severely crushed when a bridge collapsed. The remainder of his foreign wars were conducted by his lieutenants; though during some of the Pannonian and German campaigns he either visited the front or kept in close touch with it by moving up to Ravenna, Mediolanum, or Aquileia.

21. Either as commander on the spot, or commander-in-chief, Augustus conquered Cantabria, Aquitania, Pannonia, Dalmatia, and the whole of Illyricum, besides Raetia and the Alpine tribes known as Vindelicians and Salassians. He also checked the raids of the Dacians, inflicting heavy casualties on them – three of their leaders fell in action; drove all the Germans back across the Elbe, except the Suebians and Sigambrians, who surrendered and agreed to settle in Gallic territory near the Rhine; and pacified other tribes who gave trouble.

Yet Augustus never wantonly invaded any country, and felt no temptation to increase the boundaries of the Empire or enhance his military glory; indeed, he made certain barbarian chieftains swear in the Temple of Avenging Mars that they would faithfully keep the peace for which they sued. In some instances he tried to bind them to their oaths by demanding an unusual kind of hostage, namely women; well aware that barbarians do not feel bound to respect treaties secured only by male hostages. But he let them reclaim their hostages as often as they pleased. Even when tribes rebelled frequently or showed particular ill-faith, Augustus's most severe punishment was to sell as slaves the prisoners he took, ordering them to be kept at some distance from their own country and not to be freed until thirty years had elapsed. Such was his reputation for courage and clemency that the very Indians and Scythians – nations of whom we then knew by hearsay alone – voluntarily sent envoys to Rome, pleading for his friendship and that of his people. The Parthians also were ready to grant Augustus's claims on Armenia and, when he demanded the surrender of the Eagles captured from Crassus and Antony,[9] not

only returned them but offered hostages into the bargain; and once, because several rival princes were claiming the Parthian throne, announced that they would elect whichever candidate he chose.

22. The gates of the Temple of Janus Quirinus, which had been closed no more than twice[10] since the foundation of Rome, he closed three times during a far shorter period, as a sign that the Empire was at peace on land and at sea. He enjoyed a triumphal ovation after Philippi, and again after his Sicilian successes – and celebrated three full triumphs, on three successive days, for his victories won in Dalmatia, off Actium, and at Alexandria.

23. He suffered only two heavy and disgraceful defeats, both in Germany, the generals concerned being Lollius and Varus.[11] Lollius's defeat was ignominious rather than of strategic importance; but Varus's nearly wrecked the Empire, since three legions, with their general and all their officers and auxiliary forces, and the general staff, were massacred to a man. When the news reached Rome, Augustus ordered patrols of the city at night to prevent any rising; then prolonged the terms of the provincial governors, so that the allies should have men of experience, whom they trusted, to confirm their allegiance. He also vowed to celebrate Games in honour of Jupiter Best and Greatest as soon as the political situation improved; similar vows had been made during the Cimbrian and Marsian Wars. Indeed, it is said that he took the disaster so deeply to heart that he left his hair and beard untrimmed for months; he would often beat his head on a door, shouting: 'Quinctilius Varus, give me back my legions!' and always kept the anniversary as a day of deep mourning.

24. Augustus introduced many reforms into the Army, besides reviving certain obsolete practices, and exacted the strictest discipline. He grudged even his generals home-leave to visit their wives and granted this only during the winter. When a Roman knight cut off the thumbs of his two young sons to incapacitate them for Army service, Augustus had him and his property publicly auctioned; but, realizing that a group of tax-collectors were bidding for the man, knocked him down to an imperial freedman – with instructions that he should be sent away and allowed a free existence in some country place. He gave the entire Tenth

9. 53, 40, and 36 B.C.

10. In the reign of King Numa and in 235 B.C., after the first Punic War.

11. 15 B.C.; A.D. 9.

Legion an ignominious discharge because of their in-solent behaviour, and when some other legions also demanded their discharge in a similarly riotous man-ner, he disbanded them, withholding the bounty which they would have earned had they continued loyal. If a cohort broke in battle, Augustus ordered the sur-vivors to draw lots, then executed every tenth man, and fed the remainder on barley bread instead of the custo-mary wheat ration. Centurions found absent from their posts were sentenced to death, like other ranks, and any lesser dereliction of duty earned them one of several degrading punishments – such as being made to stand all day long in front of general headquarters, sometimes

PUBLIC MONUMENTS
38 and 39 (above and opposite). *Arches dedicated to Augustus at Aosta and Orange.*

wearing tunics without sword-belts, sometimes carry-ing ten-foot poles, or even sods of turf.

25. When the Civil Wars were over, Augustus no longer addressed the troops as 'Comrades', but as 'Soldiers'; and had his sons and step-sons follow suit.

He thought 'Comrades' too flattering a term: consonant neither with military discipline, nor with peacetime service, nor with the respect due to himself and his family. Apart from the city fire-brigades, and militia companies raised to keep order during food shortages, he enlisted freedmen in the Army only on two occasions. The first was when the veteran colonies on the borders of Illyricum needed protection; the second, when the Roman bank of the Rhine had to be held in force. These soldiers were recruited, as slaves, from the households of well-to-do men and women, and then immediately freed; but he kept them segregated in their original units, not allowing them either to associate with soldiers of free birth or to carry arms of standard pattern.

Most of the decorations with which Augustus rewarded distinguished conduct in the field were valuable silver and gold plaques or collars, rather than the superior distinction of mural crowns.[12] These crowns he awarded as rarely as possible and with due regard to merit; private soldiers sometimes won them. Marcus Agrippa earned the right to fly a blue ensign in recognition of his naval victory off Sicily. The only

12. So called because traditionally earned by the first man who scaled an enemy wall.

fighting men whom Augustus held ineligible for decorations were generals who had already celebrated triumphs, even though they might have fought beside him and shared in his victories; he explained that they themselves had the right to confer such awards at their discretion. The two faults which he condemned most strongly in a military commander were haste and recklessness, and he constantly quoted such Greek proverbs as 'More haste, less speed,' and 'Give me a safe commander, not a rash one,' and the Latin tag: 'Well done is quickly done.' It was a principle of his that no campaign or battle should ever be fought unless the hope of victory was clearly greater than the fear of defeat; and he would compare those who took great risks in the hope of gaining some small advantage to a man who fishes with a golden hook, though aware that nothing he can catch will be valuable enough to justify its loss.

26. Among the public appointments and honours conferred on Augustus before he was officially old enough to receive them were some extraordinary ones and some granted him for life. At the age of nineteen[13] he created himself Consul, marched on Rome as though it were an enemy city, and sent messengers ahead in the name of his army to demand that the appointment should be confirmed. When the Senate hesitated to obey, one Cornelius, a centurion leading his deputation, opened his military cloak, displayed the hilt of his sword, and boldly said: 'If you do not make him Consul, this will!' Nine years later Augustus undertook his second consulship,[14] and his third after an interval of a year. Having held the next nine in sequence, he declined any more for as many as seventeen years; then demanded a twelfth term,[15] and two years later a thirteenth – but only because he wanted to be holding the highest office when his adopted sons, Gaius and Lucius Caesar, successively came of age. He held his sixth, seventh, eighth, ninth, and tenth consulships for a full year each, and the remainder for nine months, or six, or four, or three – except for the second; that was the occasion of his seating himself on the curule chair in front of the Temple of Capitoline Jupiter early on New Year's Day, and resigning his office to a substitute a few hours later. He was absent from Rome at the beginning of his fourth consulship, which found him in Asia; of his fifth, which found him in Samos; and of his eighth and ninth, when he was visiting Tarraco.

27. For ten years Augustus remained a member of

the Triumvirate commissioned to reorganize the government, and though at first opposing his colleagues' plan for a proscription, yet, once this had been decided upon, carried it out more ruthlessly than either of them. They often relented under the pressure of personal influence, or when the intended victims appealed for pity; Augustus alone demanded that no one was to be spared, and even added to the list of proscribed persons the name of his guardian Gaius Toranius, who had been an aedile at the same time as his father Octavius. Julius Saturninus has more to say on this subject: when the proscription was over and Marcus Lepidus, in an address to the House, justified the severe measures that had been taken but encouraged the hope that greater leniency would now be shown, since enough blood had been shed, Augustus spoke in a quite opposite sense. 'I consented to close the list,' he said, 'on condition that I should be allowed a free hand in future.' Later, however, he emphasized his regret for this rigorous attitude by creating Titus Vinius Philopoemen a knight – Philopoemen had, it appears, secretly harboured his patron who was on the list of the proscribed.

Under the Triumvirate, many of Augustus's acts won him the hatred of the people. Once, for instance, while addressing a soldiers' assembly at which a crowd of civilians were also present, he saw a Roman knight named Pinarius transcribing his speech; and had him stabbed there and then as taking too close an interest in the proceedings. Again, a spiteful comment by Tedius Afer, Consul-elect, on some act of Augustus's, provoked him to such frightful threats that Afer committed suicide by jumping from a height. There was also the case of Quintus Gallius the praetor who, while paying Augustus his respects, clutched a set of writing-tablets underneath his robe. Augustus suspected that he had a sword, but dared not have him searched on the spot, for fear of being mistaken; so presently ordered an officer's party to drag him away from the tribunal. Gallius was tortured as if he were a slave; and though he confessed to nothing, Augustus himself tore out his eyes and sentenced him to death. In his own account of the incident, however, Augustus records that Gallius asked for an audience, attacked him unexpectedly, and was removed to prison; that, being then banished from Italy, he disappeared on the way to his place of exile, but whether he was shipwrecked or ambushed by bandits, nobody knew.

The commons awarded Augustus lifelong tribunician power, and on two occasions he chose a colleague to share it with him for a five-year period. The Senate

13. 43 B.C.   14. 33 B.C.   15. 5 B.C.

also voted him the task of supervising public morals and scrutinizing the laws – another lifelong appointment. Thus, although he did not adopt the title of Censor, he was privileged to hold a public census, and did so three times, assisted by a colleague on the first and third occasions, though not the second.

28. Twice Augustus seriously thought of restoring the Republican system: immediately after the fall of Antony, when he remembered that Antony had often accused him of being the one obstacle to such a change; and again when he could not shake off an exhausting illness. He then actually summoned the chief Officers of State, with the rest of the Senate, to his house and gave them a faithful account of the military and financial state of the Empire. On reconsideration, however, he decided that to divide the responsibilities of government among several hands would be to jeopardize not only his own life, but national security; so he did not do so. The results were almost as good as his intentions, which he expressed from time to time and even published in an edict: 'May I be privileged to build firm and lasting foundations for the Government of the State. May I also achieve the reward to which I aspire: that of being known as the author of the best possible Constitution, and of carrying with me, when I die, the hope that these foundations which I have established for the State will abide secure.' And, indeed, he achieved this success, having taken great trouble to prevent his political system from causing any individual distress.

Aware that the city was architecturally unworthy of her position as capital of the Roman Empire, besides being vulnerable to fire and river floods, Augustus so improved her appearance that he could justifiably boast: 'I found Rome built of bricks; I leave her clothed in marble.' He also used as much foresight as could have possibly been provided in guarding against future disasters.

29. Among his very numerous public works three must be singled out for mention: his Forum with the Temple of Avenging Mars; the Palatine Temple of Apollo; and the Temple of Jupiter the Thunderer on the Capitoline Hill. He built his Forum because the two already in existence could not deal with the recent great increase in the number of lawsuits caused by a corresponding increase in population; which was why he hurriedly opened it even before the Temple of Mars had been completed. Public prosecutions and the casting of lots for jury service took place only in this Forum. Augustus had vowed to build the Temple of Mars during the Philippi campaign of vengeance against Julius Caesar's assassins. He therefore decreed that the Senate should meet here whenever declarations of war or claims for triumphs were considered; and that this should be both the starting point for military governors, when escorted to their provinces, and the repository of all triumphal tokens when they returned victorious. The Temple of Apollo was erected in the part of his Palace to which, the soothsayers said, the God had drawn attention by having it struck with lightning. The colonnades running out from it housed Latin and Greek libraries; and in his declining years Augustus frequently held meetings of the Senate in the buildings, or revised jury lists there. A lucky escape on a night march in Cantabria prompted him to build the Temple of Jupiter the Thunderer: a flash of lightning had scorched his litter and killed the slave who was going ahead with a torch.

Some of Augustus's public works were undertaken in the names of relatives: such as the colonnade and basilica of his grandsons Gaius and Lucius; the colonnades of his wife Livia and his sister Octavia; the theatre of his nephew Marcellus. He also often urged leading citizens to embellish the city with new public monuments or to restore and improve ancient ones, according to their means. Many responded: thus the Temple of Hercules and the Muses was raised by Marcius Philippus; that of Diana by Lucius Cornificius; the Hall of Liberty by Asinius Pollio; the Temple of Saturn by Munatius Plancus; a theatre by Cornelius Balbus; an amphitheatre by Statilius Taurus; and a variety of magnificent buildings by Marcus Agrippa.

30. Augustus divided the city into districts and wards; placing the districts under the control of magistrates annually chosen by lot, and the wards under supervisors locally elected. He organized stations of night-watchmen to guard against fires; and, as a precaution against floods, cleared the Tiber channel which had been choked with an accumulation of rubbish and narrowed by projecting houses. Also, he improved the approaches to the city: repaving the Flaminian Way as far as Ariminum, at his own expense, and calling upon men who had won triumphs to spend their prize money on putting the other main roads into good condition.

Furthermore, he restored ruined or burned temples, beautifying these and others with the most lavish gifts: for instance, a single donation to Capitoline Jupiter of 16,000 lb of gold, besides pearls and precious stones to the value of 500,000 gold pieces.

31. Finally, on assuming the office of Chief Priest vacated by the death of Marcus Lepidus – he could not bring himself to divest his former colleague of it,

PUBLIC WORKS IN ROME

40 (above). *The Theatre of Marcellus, built by Augustus in memory of his nephew and son-in-law Marcellus, who had been destined to be his successor, but died in 23* B.C. *The theatre seated over 10,000 people. The top tier indicates the original height of the theatre.*

41 (opposite). *The Pantheon in Rome, inscribed 'Marcus Agrippa three times consul built it'. The present structure is a rebuilding by Hadrian, who added the domed rotunda. Agrippa's original building consisted of the present narthex and a round open enclosure.*

even though he were an exile – Augustus collected all the copies of Greek and Latin prophetic verse then current, the work of either anonymous or unrespected authors, and burned more than two thousand. He kept only the Sibylline Books, and edited even these before depositing them in two gilded cases under the pedestal of Palatine Apollo's image. Since official negligence had allowed the Calendar, reformed by Julius Caesar, to fall into confusion, he put it straight again; and while doing so renamed the month of Sextilis 'August' (although he had been born in September), because it was during Sextilis that he had won his first consulship and his most decisive victories. He increased the priesthood in numbers and dignity, and in privileges, too,

being particularly generous to the College of Vestal Virgins. Moreover, when the death of a Virgin caused a vacancy in this College, and many citizens busily tried to keep their daughters' names off the list of candidates – one of whom would be chosen by lot – Augustus took a solemn oath that if any of his grand-daughters had been of eligible age he would have proposed her.

He also revived certain obsolescent rites and appointments: the augury of the Goddess Safety, the office of Flamen Dialis, the Lupercalian Festival, the Saecular Games, and the Cross-Roads Festival. But at the Lupercalia he forbade any boys to run who had not yet shaved off their first beards; and at the Saecular Games no young people might attend a night perform-

ance unless accompanied by an adult relative. The images of the Cross-Road gods were to be crowned twice a year with wreaths of spring and summer flowers.

Next to the Immortals, Augustus most honoured the memory of those citizens who had raised the Roman people from small beginnings to their present glory; which was why he restored many public buildings erected by men of this calibre, complete with their original dedicatory inscriptions, and raised statues to them, wearing triumphal dress, in the twin colonnades of his Forum. Then he proclaimed: 'This has been done to make my fellow-citizens insist that both I while I live, and my successors, shall not fall below the

standard set by those great men of old.' He also transferred Pompey's statue from the hall in which Julius
Caesar had been assassinated[16] to a marble arch facing
the main entrance of the Theatre.

32. Many of the anti-social practices that endangered public order were a legacy of lawlessness
from the Civil Wars; but some had originated in times
of peace. For example, bandit parties infested the roads
armed with swords, supposedly worn in self-defence,
which they used to overawe travellers – whether free-
born or not – and force them into slave-barracks built
by the landowners.[17] Numerous so-called 'workmen's
guilds', in reality organizations for committing every
sort of crime, had also been formed. Augustus now stationed armed police in bandit-ridden districts, had the
slave-barracks inspected, and dissolved all workmen's
guilds except those that had been established for some
time and were carrying on legitimate business. Since
the records of old debts to the Public Treasury had
become by far the most profitable means of blackmail,
Augustus burned them; also granting title-deeds to the
occupants of city sites wherever the State's claim to
ownership was disputable. When persons had long
been awaiting trial on charges that were not pressed,
and therefore continued to wear mourning in public
– with advantage to nobody, except their gleeful
enemies – Augustus struck the cases off the lists and
forbade any such charge to be renewed unless the
plaintiff agreed to suffer the same penalty, if he lost
the case, as the defendant would have done. To prevent
actions for damages, or business claims, from either not
being heard or being postponed, he increased the legal
term by another thirty days – a period hitherto devoted
to public games in honour of distinguished citizens. He
added a fourth inferior division of jurors to the three
already existing; these so-called 'Ducenarii'[18] judged
cases which involved only small monetary claims. The
minimum age for enrolment in a jury was reduced from

thirty-five to thirty years; but, observing a general
movement to evade jury service, he grudgingly granted
each of the four divisions in turn one year's exemption,
and closed all courts throughout the months of
November and December.

33. Augustus proved assiduous in his administration of justice, often remaining in court until nightfall;
and, if he happened to be unwell, would have his litter
carried up to the tribunal. Sometimes he even judged
cases from his sick-bed in his house. As a judge he was
both conscientious and lenient: once, to save a man
who had obviously committed parricide from being
sewn up in a sack,[19] he is said to have asked the accused:
'I may assume, of course, that you did not kill your
father?'

On another occasion the witnesses to a forged will
were punishable under the Cornelian Law but, besides
the usual two tablets for recording their verdict of
'guilty' or 'not guilty', Augustus handed the jurors a
third, for acquitting any of the accused whose signature
had, in their opinion, either been obtained by false
pretences or attached in error. Every year he referred
to the City Praetor cases in which Roman citizens had
exercised their right of appeal; foreigners' appeals
would be handled by particular ex-Consuls whom he
had appointed to look after the affairs of the province
concerned.

34. The existing laws that Augustus revised, and the
new ones that he enacted, dealt, among other matters,
with extravagance, adultery, unchastity, bribery, and
the encouragement of marriage in the Senatorial and
Equestrian Orders. His marriage law being more rigor-
ously framed than the others, he found himself unable
to make it effective because of an open revolt against
several of its clauses. He was therefore obliged to withdraw or amend certain penalties exacted for a failure
to marry; to increase the rewards he offered for large
families; and to allow a widow, or widower, three years'
grace before having to marry again. Even this did not
satisfy the knights, who demonstrated against the law
at a public entertainment, demanding its repeal;
whereupon Augustus sent for the children whom his
grand-daughter Agrippina had borne to Germanicus,
and publicly displayed them, some sitting on his own
knee, the rest on their father's – and made it quite clear
by his affectionate looks and gestures that it would not
be at all a bad thing if the knights imitated that young

16. See Julius Caesar 81.

17. See Tiberius 8.

18. Men whose property amounted to 200,000 sestertii (2,000 gold
pieces).

42. OCTAVIA *was married to Mark Antony for reasons
of state and was divorced by him in 32 B.C. She none the
less cared for his children by his first wife Fulvia and by
Cleopatra. (Paris, Louvre.)*

19. Parricides were sewn up in a sack with a dog, a cock, a snake,
and a monkey, and cast into a river or the sea.

M·CORNELIO·M·F·PAL·STATIO·L·FECER

CHILDREN

43 (opposite). *Mater Natuta, a very ancient Roman deity, protected children, especially during puberty. Her festival was celebrated on 11 June by married women.* (Florence, Museo Archeologico.)

44 (above). *Scenes from a child's life: being nursed, and fondled by the father, practising adult pursuits, and going to school. The child died at eight. Sarcophagus.* (Paris, Louvre.)

man's example. When he then discovered that bachelors were getting betrothed to little girls, which meant postponing the responsibilities of fatherhood, and that married men were frequently changing their wives, he dealt with these evasions of the law by shortening the permissible period between betrothal and marriage, and by limiting the number of lawful divorces.

35. The Senatorial Order now numbered more than 1,000 persons, some of whom were popularly known as the 'Orcus Men',[20] having secured admission after Caesar's death through influence or bribery. The sight of this sad and ill-assorted rabble decided Augustus to restore the Order to its former size and repute by two new acts of enrolment. First, each member was allowed to nominate one other; then Augustus and Agrippa together reviewed the list and announced their own

20. After Orcus (Pluto), the god of the underworld.

choice. When Augustus presided on this second occasion he is said to have worn a sword and a steel corselet beneath his tunic, with ten burly senatorial friends crowding around him. According to Cremutius Cordus, the senators were not even then permitted to approach Augustus's chair, except singly and after the folds of their robes had been carefully searched. Though shaming some of them into resignation, he did not deny them the right to wear senatorial dress, or to watch the Games from the orchestra seats, or to attend the Order's public banquets. He then encouraged those selected for service to a more conscientious (and less inconvenient) discharge of their duties, by ruling that each member should offer incense and wine at the altar of whatever temple had been selected for a meeting; that such meetings should not be held more than twice a month – at the beginning and in the middle – and that, during September and October, no member need attend apart from the few whose names were drawn by lot to provide a quorum for the passing of decrees. He also arranged that a Council of the Senate should be created and its members chosen by lot every six months, their duty being to study the drafts of bills which would later be laid before the House as a whole. During debates of critical importance Augustus shelved the custom of calling on members in order of seniority, and instead singled out speakers arbitrarily; this was intended to make all present take an alert interest in proceedings and feel responsible for constructive thought, instead of merely rising to remark: 'I agree with the last speakers.'

36. Among Augustus's other innovations were: a

ban on the publication of *Proceedings of the Senate*;[21] a statutory interval between the conclusion of city magistracies and their holders' departure to appointments abroad; a fixed mule-and-tent allowance to provincial governors, replacing the system by which they contracted for these necessities and charged them to the Public Treasury; the transference of the Treasury from the control of city quaestors to that of ex-praetors or praetors; and the ruling that the Board of Ten, instead of the ex-quaestors, should convoke the so-called Centumviral Court.

37. To give more men some experience of governmental duties he created new offices dealing with the upkeep of public buildings, roads and aqueducts; the clearing of the Tiber channel; and the distribution of grain to the people – also a prefecture of the city, a Board of Three for choosing new senators, and another for inspecting the troops of knights, whenever this was needed. He also revived the long obsolete custom of appointing Censors; increased the number of praetors; and requested not one colleague but two whenever he held a consulship. The Senate, however, refused this last plea: everyone shouting that it was sufficient detraction from his supreme dignity to acknowledge even a single colleague.

38. Augustus showed equal generosity in recognizing military talent, by letting full triumphs be voted to more than thirty of his generals, and triumphant regalia to an even larger number.

Senators' sons were now encouraged to familiarize themselves with the administration; they might wear purple-striped gowns immediately upon coming of age and attend meetings of the House. When their military careers began, they were not merely given colonelcies in regular legions, but the command of cavalry squadrons; and Augustus usually appointed two to the command of each squadron, thus ensuring that none of them lacked experience in this arm of the service.

He frequently inspected the troops of knights, and revived the long-forgotten custom of making them ride in procession; yet he withdrew from accusers their right of challenging knights to dismount while the parade was in progress; and those who were so old or infirm that they would look ridiculous, if they took part, might now send their riderless mounts to the starting point and report to Augustus on foot. Later, all knights over thirty-five years of age who did not

wish to retain their chargers were excused the embarrassment of publicly surrendering them.

39. With the assistance of ten senators, Augustus cross-examined every knight on his personal affairs. Some, whose lives proved to have been scandalous, were punished; others were degraded; but in most cases he was content to reprimand culprits with greater or less severity. The luckiest were those whom he obliged merely to take the tablets handed them, and read his censure in silence where they stood. Knights who had borrowed money at a low rate of interest, in order to invest it at a higher, earned Augustus's particular displeasure.

40. If insufficient candidates of the required senatorial rank presented themselves for election as tribunes of the people, Augustus nominated knights to fill the vacancies; but allowed them, when their term of office had expired, either to remain members of the Equestrian Order or to become senators, whichever they preferred. Since many knights had lost so much money during the Civil Wars that for fear of penalization under the law regarding theatres they refrained from taking their seats in the fourteen rows reserved for the Order, he announced that they were not liable to punishment under the law governing theatres – which did not apply to anyone who had once been a knight, or who was a knight's son.

Augustus revised the roll of citizens, ward by ward; and tried to obviate the frequent interruptions of their trades or businesses which the public grain-distribution entailed, by handing out tickets, three times a year, valid for a four months' supply; but was implored to resume the former custom of monthly distributions, and consented. He also revived the traditional election privileges and attempted to suppress bribery by the imposition of various penalties; besides distributing on Election Day a bounty of ten gold pieces from the Privy Purse to every member both of the Fabian tribe – the Octavian family were Fabians – and of the Scaptian tribe, which included the Julians. His object was to protect the candidates against demands for further emoluments.

Augustus thought it most important not to let the native Roman stock be tainted with foreign or servile blood, and was therefore very unwilling to create new Roman citizens, or to permit the manumission of more than a limited number of slaves. Once, when Tiberius requested that a Greek dependant of his should be granted the citizenship, Augustus wrote back that he could not assent unless the man put in a personal appearance and convinced him that he was worthy of the honour. When Livia made the same request for a Gaul from a tributary province, Augustus turned it down, saying that he would do no more than exempt the fellow from tribute – 'I would far rather forfeit whatever he may owe the Privy Purse than cheapen the value of the Roman citizenship.' Not only did he make it extremely difficult for slaves to be freed, and still more difficult for them to attain full independence, by strictly regulating the number, condition, and status of freedmen; but he ruled that no slave who had ever been in irons or subjected to torture could become a citizen, even after the most honourable form of manumission.

Augustus set himself to revive the ancient Roman dress, and once, on seeing a group of men in dark cloaks among the crowd, quoted Virgil indignantly:

Behold them, conquerors of the world, all clad in Roman togas!

and instructed the aediles that no one should ever again be admitted to the Forum, or its environs, unless he wore a toga and no cloak.

41. His generosity to all classes was displayed on many occasions. For instance, when he brought the treasures of the Ptolemies to Rome at his Alexandrian triumph, so much cash passed into private hands that the interest rate on loans dropped sharply, while real estate values soared. Later, he made it a rule that whenever estates were confiscated and the funds realized by their sale exceeded his requirements, he would grant interest-free loans for fixed periods to anyone who could offer security for twice the amount. The property qualification for senators was now increased from 8,000 to 12,000 gold pieces, and if any member of the Order found that the value of his estate fell short of this, Augustus would make up the deficit from the Privy Purse. His awards of largesse to the people were frequent, but differed in size: sometimes it was four gold pieces a head, sometimes three, sometimes two and a half; and even little boys benefited, though hitherto eleven years had been the minimum age for a recipient. In times of food shortage he often sold grain to every man on the citizens' list at a very cheap rate; occasionally he supplied it free; and doubled the number of free money-coupons.

42. However, to show that he did all this not to win popularity but to improve public welfare, he once sharply reminded the people, when they complained of the scarcity and high price of wine, that: 'Marcus Agrippa, my son-in-law, has made adequate provision for thirsty citizens by building several aqueducts.' Again, he replied to a demand for largesse which he had, in fact, promised: 'I always keep my word.' But when they demanded largesse for which no such promise had been given, he issued a proclamation in which he called them a pack of shameless rascals, and added that though he had intended to make them a money present, he would now tighten his purse-strings. Augustus showed equal dignity and strength of character on another occasion when, after announcing a distribution of largesse, he found that the list of citizens had been swelled by a considerable number of recently freed slaves. He gave out that those to whom he had promised nothing were entitled to nothing, and that he refused to increase the total sum; thus the original beneficiaries must be content with less. In one period of exceptional scarcity he found it impossible to cope with the public distress except by expelling every useless mouth from the city, such as the slaves in the slave-market, all members of gladiatorial schools, all foreign residents with the exception of physicians and teachers, and a number of household-slaves. He writes that when at last the grain supply improved: 'I had a good mind to discontinue permanently the supply of grain to the city, reliance on which had discouraged Italian agriculture; but refrained because some politician would be bound one day to revive the dole as a means of ingratiating himself with the people.' Nevertheless, in his handling of the food problem he now began to consider the interests of farmers and grain merchants as much as the needs of city dwellers.

43. None of Augustus's predecessors had ever provided so many, so different, or such splendid public shows. He records the presentation of four Games in his own name and twenty-three in the names of other city magistrates who were either absent or could not afford the expense. Sometimes plays were shown in all the various city districts, and on several stages, the actors speaking the appropriate local language; and gladiators fought not only in the Forum or the Amphitheatre, but in the Circus and Enclosure as well; or the show might, on the contrary, be limited to a wild-beast hunt. He also held athletic competitions in the Campus Martius, for which he put up tiers of wooden seats; and dug an artificial lake beside the Tiber, where the present Caesarian Grove stands, for a mock sea-battle. On these occasions he posted guards in different parts of the city to prevent ruffians from turning the emptiness of the streets to their own advantage. Chariot-races

THE GRAIN SUPPLY. *In a primitive economy, where transport is difficult and often irregular, it is a primary task of government to ensure an adequate supply of food in cities. The matter is regularly alluded to on the Roman coinage.*
45 (left). *Ears of corn on a coin of Augustus from Ephesus, 27–20 B.C. (London, British Museum.)*
46 (right). *Annona, personification of the annual harvest, with Ceres, goddess of the corn, on a Roman coin of Nero. (London, British Museum.)*

and foot-races took place in the Circus, and among those who hunted the wild beasts were several volunteers of distinguished family. Augustus also ordered frequent performances of the Troy Game[22] by two troops, of older and younger boys; it was an admirable tradition, he held, that the scions of noble houses should make their public début in this way. When Nonius Asprenas fell from his horse at one performance and was crippled, Augustus comforted him with a golden torque and the hereditary surname of 'Tor-

22. See Julius Caesar 39.

quatus'. Soon afterwards, however, he discontinued the Troy Game, because Asinius Pollio the orator attacked it bitterly in the House; his grandson, Aeserninus, having broken a leg too.

Even Roman knights sometimes took part in stage plays and gladiatorial shows until a Senatorial decree put an end to the practice. After this, no person of good family appeared in any show, with the exception of a young man named Lycius; he was a dwarf, less than two feet tall and weighing only 17 lb, but had a tremendous voice. At one of the Games, Augustus allowed the people a sight of the first group of Parthian hostages ever sent to Rome by leading them down the middle of the arena and seating them two rows behind himself. And whenever anything strange or remarkable was brought to the city, he used to exhibit it in some convenient place on days when no public shows were being given: for instance, a rhinoceros in the Enclosure; a tiger on the stage of the Theatre; and a serpent nearly ninety feet long in front of the Comitium.

Once Augustus happened to be ill on the day that he had vowed to hold Games in the Circus, and was obliged to lead the sacred procession lying in a litter; and when he opened the Games celebrating the dedication of Marcellus's Theatre, and sat down in his chair of state, it gave way and sent him sprawling on his back. A panic started in the Theatre during a public performance in honour of Gaius and Lucius; the audience feared that the walls might collapse. Augustus, finding that he could do nothing else to pacify or reassure them, left his own box and sat in what seemed to be the most threatened part of the auditorium.

44. He issued special regulations to prevent the disorderly and haphazard system by which spectators secured seats for these shows; having been outraged by the insult to a senator who, on entering the crowded theatre at Puteoli, was not offered a seat by a single member of the audience. The consequent Senatorial decree provided that at every public performance, wherever held, the front row of stalls must be reserved for senators. At Rome, Augustus would not admit the envoys of independent or allied kingdoms to seats in the Orchestra, on learning that some were mere freedmen. Other rules of his included the separation of soldiers from civilians; the assignment of special seats to married commoners, to boys not yet come of age, and, close by, to their tutors; and a ban on the wearing of dark cloaks, except in the back rows. Also, whereas men and women had hitherto always sat together, Augustus confined women to the back rows even at gladiatorial shows: the only ones exempt from this rule being the Vestal Virgins, for whom separate accommodation was provided, facing the praetor's tribunal. No women at all were allowed to witness the athletic contests; indeed, when the audience clamoured at the Games for a special boxing match to celebrate his appointment as Chief Priest, Augustus postponed this until early the next morning, and issued a proclamation to the effect that it was the Chief Priest's desire that women should not attend the Theatre before ten o'clock.

45. He had a habit of watching the Games from the upper rooms of houses overlooking the Circus, which belonged to his friends or freedmen; but occasionally he used the imperial box, and even took his wife and children there with him. Sometimes he did not appear until the show had been running for several hours, or even for a day or more; but always excused his absences and appointed a substitute president. Once in his seat, however, he watched the proceedings intently; either to avoid the bad reputation earned by Julius Caesar for reading letters or petitions, and answering them, during such performances, or just to enjoy the fun, as he frankly admitted doing. This enjoyment led him to offer special prizes at Games provided by others, or give the victors valuable presents from the Privy Purse;

and he never failed to reward, according to their merits, the competitors in any Greek theatrical contests that he attended. His chief delight was to watch boxing, particularly when the fighters were Italians – and not merely professional bouts, in which he often used to pit Italians against Greeks, but slogging matches between untrained roughs in narrow city alleys.

To be brief: Augustus honoured all sorts of professional entertainers by his friendly interest in them; maintained, and even increased, the privileges enjoyed by athletes; banned gladiatorial contests if the defeated fighter were forbidden to plead for mercy; and amended an ancient law empowering magistrates to punish stage-players wherever and whenever they pleased – so that they were now competent to deal only with misdemeanours committed at games or theatrical performances. Nevertheless, he insisted on a meticulous observance of regulations during wrestling matches and gladiatorial contests; and was exceedingly strict in checking the licentious behaviour of stage-players. When he heard that Stephanio, a Roman actor, went about attended by a page-boy who was really a married woman with her hair cropped, he had him flogged through all the three theatres – those of Pompey, Balbus, and Marcellus – and then exiled. Acting on a praetor's complaint, he had a comedian named Hylas publicly scourged in the hall of his own residence; and expelled Pylades not only from Rome, but from Italy too, because when a spectator started to hiss, he called the attention of the whole audience to him with an obscene movement of his middle finger.

46. After thus improving and reorganizing Rome, Augustus increased the population of Italy by personally founding twenty-eight veteran colonies. He also supplied country towns with municipal buildings and revenues; and even gave them, to some degree at least, privileges and honours equalling those enjoyed by the City of Rome. This was done by granting the members of each local senate the right to vote for candidates in the City Elections; their ballots were to be placed in sealed containers and counted at Rome on polling day. To maintain the number of knights and encourage an increase in the population, he allowed any township to nominate men capable of taking up such senior Army posts as were reserved for the Equestrian Order; and, to encourage the birth-rate of the Roman commons, offered a bounty of ten gold pieces for every legitimate son or daughter whom a citizen could produce, on his tours of the city wards.

47. THE ALTAR OF PEACE, ARA PACIS, *was in-augurated on 4 July 13* B.C., *to celebrate the return of Augustus from the provinces of the Empire to Rome. A carved frieze surrounding the altar shows the procession which on that day went to the altar's site in the Field of Mars to offer sacrifice. Augustus, and behind him Tiberius, are on the far left, followed by four priests with spiked hats. Agrippa, centre, is preceded by a man carrying an axe; behind him is his wife Julia, daughter of Augustus, and between the two their son Lucius Caesar.*

Antonia, daughter of Mark Antony (see Ill. 34) and Octavia (see Ill. 42), holds her little son by the hand. She and her husband are talking to each other, while in the background Octavia, her finger on her lips, bids them be silent. The little boy with the laurel wreath is Gnaeus Domitius Ahenobarbus – his son was to be the Emperor Nero. This procession portrays Augustus and members of his family as he wished them to appear and be: wearing the traditional Roman dress, living good and useful lives, with their children to succeed them. (Rome.)

47. Augustus kept for himself all the more vigorous provinces – those that could not be safely administered by an annual governor; the remainder went to proconsuls chosen by lot. Yet, as occasion arose, he would change the status of provinces from imperial to senatorial, or contrariwise, and paid frequent visits to either sort. Finding that certain city-states which had treaties of alliance with Rome were ruining themselves through political irresponsibility, he took away their independence; but also granted subsidies to others crippled by public debts, rebuilt some cities which had been devastated by earthquakes, and even awarded Latin rights or full citizenship to states that could show a record of faithful service in the Roman cause. So far as I know, Augustus inspected every province of the Empire, except Sardinia and North Africa, and would have toured these, too, after his defeat of Sextus Pompey in Sicily, had not a sequence of gales prevented him from sailing; later, he had no particular reason, nor any opportunity, for visiting either province.

48. He nearly always restored the kingdoms which he had conquered to their defeated dynasties, or combined them with others, and followed a policy of linking together his royal allies by mutual ties of friendship or intermarriage, which he was never slow to propose. Nor did he treat them otherwise than as integral parts of the Empire, showing them all consideration and finding guardians for those who were not yet old enough to rule, until they came of age – and for those who suffered from mental illness, until they recovered. He also brought up many of their children with his own, and gave them the same education.

49. His military dispositions were as follows. The legions and their auxiliaries were distributed among the various provinces; one fleet being stationed at Misenum, and another at Ravenna, to command respectively the Western and Eastern Mediterranean. The rest of his armed forces served partly as city police, partly as his own bodyguards; for after Antony's defeat he had disbanded a company of men from Calagurris, and a company of Germans after the Varus disaster – both of which had served in his personal bodyguard. However, he never kept more than three cohorts on duty at Rome, and even these had no permanent camp; the remainder he stationed in nearby towns, changing them regularly from summer to winter quarters. Augustus also standardized the pay and allowances of the entire Army – at the same time fixing the period of service and the bounty due on its completion – according to military rank; this would discourage them from revolting, when back in civil life, on the excuse that they were either too old or had insufficient capital to earn an honest living. In order to have sufficient funds always in hand for the upkeep of his military establishment and for pensioning off

veterans, he formed an Army Treasury maintained by additional taxation. At the beginning of his reign he kept in close and immediate touch with provincial affairs by relays of runners strung out at short intervals along the highways; later, he organized a chariot service, based on posting stations – which has proved the more satisfactory arrangement, because post-boys can be cross-examined on the situation as well as delivering written messages.

50. The first seal Augustus used for safe-conducts, dispatches, and private letters was a sphinx; next came a head of Alexander the Great; lastly, his own head, cut by Dioscurides, the seal which his successors continued to employ. He not only dated every letter, but entered the exact hour of the day or night when it was composed.

51. There are numerous positive proofs of Augustus's clemency and considerate behaviour. Without supplying a full list of the political enemies whom he pardoned and allowed to hold high government office, it will be enough to record that a fine was the sole punishment he awarded Junius Novatus, a plebeian, for circulating a most damaging libel on him under the name of Agrippa Postumus; and that Cassius Patavinus, another plebeian, who openly boasted at a large banquet that he would enjoy assassinating him and had the courage, too, escaped with a mild form of exile. Then again hearing, at an inquiry into the case of Aemilius Aelianus from Corduba, that the most serious of the many charges brought against him was one of 'vilifying Caesar', Augustus pretended to lose his temper and told the counsel for the prosecution: 'I wish you could prove that charge! I'll show Aelianus that I have a nasty tongue, too, and vilify him even worse!' He then dropped the whole inquiry and never resumed it. When Tiberius mentioned the matter in a letter, with more violent expostulations against Aelianus, Augustus replied: 'My dear Tiberius, you must not give way to youthful emotion, or take it to heart if anyone speaks ill of me; let us be satisfied if we can make people stop short at unkind words.'

52. Although the voting of temples to popular proconsuls was a commonplace, he would not accept any such honour, even in the provinces, unless his name were coupled with that of Rome. He even more vigorously opposed the dedication of a temple to himself at home, and went so far as to melt down the silver statues previously erected, and to spend the silver coined from them on golden tripods for Palatine Apollo. When the people would have forced a dictatorship

ITALY AND AENEAS ON THE ALTAR OF PEACE

48. *Personification of Italy, or the Earth, surrounded by symbols of abundance and happiness.* (Rome.)

49. *Near the end of his long wanderings from Troy to Italy (see Ill. 4), Aeneas dreamt that he would find a sow with thirty young on the site of what was to be Alba Longa, the mother city of Rome. Aeneas is shown with his son Ascanius making ready to sacrifice the sow; in the background is an Etruscan-style temple.* (Rome.)

on him he fell on his knee and, throwing back his gown to expose his naked breast, implored their silence.

53. He always felt horrified and insulted when called 'My Lord'. Once, while he was watching a comedy, one of the players spoke the line:

O just and generous Lord!

whereupon the entire audience rose to their feet and applauded, as if the phrase referred to Augustus. A look and a gesture soon quelled this unsuitable flattery, and the next day he issued an edict of stern reprimand. After this he would not let even his adopted children, or grandchildren, use the obsequious word (though it might be only in joke), either when talking to him or about him. Augustus did his best to avoid leaving or entering any city in broad daylight, because that would have obliged the authorities to give him a formal welcome or send-off. During his consulships, he usually went on foot through the streets of Rome, and on other occasions in a closed litter. His morning audiences were open to commoners as well as knights and senators, and he behaved very sociably to all who came with requests – once a petitioner showed such nervousness that Augustus laughed and said: 'Anyone would think you were offering a penny to an elephant!' On days when the Senate was in session and the members had therefore refrained from paying their customary call at his home, he would enter the House and greet each of them in turn by name, unprompted; and after the conclusion of business said goodbye in the same fashion, not requiring them to rise. He exchanged social calls with many noblemen, and always attended their birthday celebrations, until he grew elderly and was jostled by a crowd at a betrothal party. When a senator named Cerrinius Gallus, whom Augustus knew only slightly, went suddenly blind and decided to starve himself to death, he paid him a visit and spoke so consolingly that Gallus changed his mind.

54. Augustus's speeches in the House would often be interrupted by such remarks as 'I don't understand you!' or 'I'd dispute your point if I got the chance.' And it happened more than once that, exasperated by recriminations which lowered the tone of the debates, he left the House in angry haste, and was followed by shouts of: 'You ought to let senators say exactly what they think about matters of public importance!' When every senator was required to nominate one other for enrolment in the reformed Order, Antistius Labeo chose Marcus Lepidus, an old enemy of Augustus's, then living in exile. Augustus asked: 'Surely there are others more deserving of this honour?' Labeo answered: 'A man is entitled to his own opinion.' Yet Augustus never punished anyone for showing independence of mind on such occasions, or even for behaving insolently.

55. He remained unmoved by the lampoons on him, which were distributed about the House, but took trouble to prove their pointlessness; and instead of trying to discover their authors, merely moved that henceforth it should be a criminal offence to publish any defamatory libel, either in prose or verse, signed with another's name.

56. Though replying in a public proclamation to various ugly and damaging jokes current at his expense, he vetoed a law that would have suppressed free speech in wills. Whenever assisting at the City Elections he used to take the candidates with him on a tour of the wards and canvass for them in the traditional manner. He would also cast a vote himself, in his own tribe, to show that he remained a man of the people. If called upon to give evidence in court he answered questions patiently and did not even mind being contradicted. Augustus's new Forum is so narrow because he could not bring himself to evict the owners of the houses which would have been demolished had his original plan been carried out. He never nominated his adopted sons for offices of state without adding: 'If they deserve this honour.' Once, while they were still boys, and the entire theatre audience stood up to cheer them, he expressed his annoyance in no uncertain terms. Although anxious that his friends should take a prominent share in the administration, he expected them to be bound by the same laws as their fellow-citizens and equally liable to public prosecution. When Cassius Severus had brought a charge of poisoning against Augustus's close friend Nonius Asprenas, Augustus

VICTORY AND CLEMENCY. *In many places, Roman conquest brought with it diverse forms of suppression and extortion. Roman propaganda, however, presented the situation in a different and more dignified idiom.*
50. *Augustus, enthroned and holding a globe, receives a figure of Victory with a palm branch.*
51. *Augustus, enthroned, receives the submission of a barbarian enemy and spares him. Cup from Boscoreale.* (Paris, Collection Rothschild.)

asked the Senate what they wished him to do. 'I find myself in a quandary,' he said, 'because to speak in Nonius's defence might be construed as an attempt to shield a criminal, whereas my silence would suggest that I was treacherously prejudicing a friend's chance of acquittal.' Since the whole House consented to his presence in court, he sat quietly for several hours on the benches of the advocates and witnesses, but abstained even from testifying to Nonius's character. He did, however, appear for some of his own dependants, among them a former staff-officer named Scutarius, who had been accused of slander. Yet he intervened successfully in only once case, and then by a personal appeal to the plaintiff in the presence of the judges; this was Castricius, to whom he was indebted for the disclosure of Murena's conspiracy.

57. The degree of affection that Augustus won by such behaviour can easily be gauged. The grateful senatorial decrees may, of course, be discounted as to a certain extent inspired by a sense of obligation. But the Equestrian Order voluntarily and unanimously decided to celebrate his birthday, spreading the festivities over two days; and once a year men of all classes would visit the Curtian Lake, into which they threw coins for his well-being in fulfilment of a vow. They would also climb to the Capitol on New Year's Day with money presents, even if he happened to be out of town. With the sum that thus accrued Augustus bought valuable images of the gods, which he set up in each of the city wards: among them the Apollo of Sandal Street, and Jupiter of the Tragedians.

When his house on the Palatine Hill burned down, a fund for its rebuilding was started by the veterans, the guilds[23] and the tribes; to which people of every sort made further individual contributions according to their means. Augustus, to show his gratitude for the gift, took a token coin from each heap, but no more than a single silver piece. His homecomings after tours of the Empire were always acclaimed with respectful good wishes and songs of joy as well; and it became a custom to cancel all punishments on the day he set foot in Rome.

58. In a universal movement to confer on Augustus the title 'Father of his Country', the first approach was made by the commons, who sent a deputation to him at Antium; when he declined this honour a huge crowd met him outside the Theatre with laurel wreaths, and repeated the request. Finally, the Senate followed suit

23. Probably the guilds of the scribes and other minor officials.

but, instead of issuing a decree or acclaiming him with shouts, chose Valerius Messala to speak for them all when Augustus entered the House. Messala's words were:

'Caesar Augustus, I am instructed to wish you and your family good fortune and divine blessings; which amounts to wishing that our entire State will be fortunate and our country prosperous. The Senate agree with the People of Rome in saluting you as Father of your Country.'

With tears in his eyes, Augustus answered – again I quote his exact words: 'Fathers of the Senate, I have at last achieved my highest ambition. What more can I ask of the immortal gods than that they may permit me to enjoy your approval until my dying day?'

59. Augustus's private physician, Antonius Musa, who had pulled him through a serious illness, was honoured with a statue, bought by public subscription and set up beside Aesculapius's. The will of more than one householder directed that his heirs should take sacrificial victims to the Capitol and carry a placard before them as they went, inscribed with an expression of their gratitude for Augustus's having been allowed to outlive the testator. Some Italian cities voted that their official year should commence on the anniversary of his first visit to them; and a number of provinces not only erected temples and altars to him, but arranged for most of their cities to hold games in his honour at five-yearly intervals.

60. Each of the allied kings who enjoyed Augustus's friendship founded a city called 'Caesarea' in his own dominions; and all clubbed together to provide funds for completing the Temple of Olympian Zeus at Athens, which had been begun centuries before, and dedicating it to his genius. These kings would often leave home, dressed in the togas of their honorary Roman citizenship, without any emblems of royalty whatsoever, and visit Augustus at Rome, or even while he was visiting the provinces; they would attend his morning audiences with the simple devotion of family dependants.

ROMAN MEDICINE
52. *Aesculapius, God of Medicine and Healing, and his daughter Salus (Health). Serpents were sacred to Aesculapius. Roman votive relief.* (Paris, Louvre.)
53. *Roman surgical instruments.* (Bingen, Museum.)

61. This completes my account of Augustus's civil and military career, and of how he governed the Empire, in all parts of the world, in peace and war. Now follows a description of his private life, his character, and his domestic fortunes, from his youth until the last day of his life.

At the age of twenty, while Consul for the first time, Augustus lost his mother; and at the age of fifty-four, his sister Octavia. He had been a devoted son and brother while they lived, and conferred the highest posthumous honours on them at their deaths.

62. As a young man he was betrothed to the daughter of Publius Servilius Isauricus, but on his reconciliation with Mark Antony after their first disagreement, the troops insisted that they should become closely allied by marriage; so, although Antony's step-daughter Claudia – borne by his wife Fulvia to Publius Clodius – was only just of marriageable age, Augustus married her; however, he quarrelled with Fulvia and divorced Claudia before the union had been consummated. Soon afterwards he married Scribonia, both of whose previous husbands had been ex-consuls, and by one of whom she had a child. Augustus divorced her, too, 'because,' as he wrote, 'I could not bear the way she nagged at me' – and immediately took Livia

AUGUSTUS AND LIVIA

54 (left). *Portrait of Livia.* (Copenhagen, Ny Carlsberg.)

55 (right). *Portrait of Augustus as a young man.* (Rome. Capitoline Museum.)

Drusilla away from her husband, Tiberius Nero, though she was pregnant at the time. Livia remained the one woman whom he truly loved until his death.

63. Scribonia bore him a daughter, Julia; but to his great disappointment the marriage with Livia proved childless, apart from a premature birth. But Julia's first husband was Marcellus, his sister Octavia's son, then hardly more than a child; and, when he died, Augustus persuaded Octavia to let her become Marcus Agrippa's wife – though Agrippa was now married to one of Marcellus's two sisters, and had fathered children on her. At Agrippa's death, Augustus cast about for a new son-in-law, even if he were only a knight, eventually choosing Tiberius, his step-son; this meant, however, that Tiberius must divorce his wife, who had already given

him an heir. Julia was betrothed first to Antony's son Antonius[24] and then to Cotiso, King of the Getae, whose daughter Augustus himself proposed to marry in exchange; or so Antony writes.

64. Julia bore Agrippa three sons – Gaius, Lucius, and Agrippa Postumus; and two daughters – Julia the Younger, and Agrippina the Elder. Augustus married this Julia to Lucius Paulus whose father, of the same name, was Censor; and Agrippina to Germanicus – grandson of his sister.[25] He then adopted Gaius and Lucius, and brought them up at the Palace, after buying them from Agrippa by a token sale. He trained his new sons in the business of government while they were still young, sending them as commanders-in-chief to the provinces when only Consuls-elect. The education of his daughter and grand-daughters included even spinning and weaving; they were forbidden to say or do anything, either publicly or in private, that could not decently figure in the imperial day-book. He took severe measures to prevent them forming friendships without his consent, and once wrote to Lucius Vinicius, a young man of good family and conduct: 'You were very ill-mannered to visit my daughter at Baiae.' Augustus gave Gaius and Lucius reading, swimming and other simple lessons, for the most part acting as their tutor himself; and was at pains to make them model their handwriting on his own. Whenever they dined in his company he had them sit at his feet on the so-called lowest couch; and, while accompanying him on his travels, they rode either ahead of his carriage, or one on each side of it.

65. His satisfaction with the success of this family and its training was, however, suddenly dashed by Fortune. He came to the conclusion that the Elder and the Younger Julia had both been indulging in every sort of vice; and banished them. When Gaius then died in Lycia, and Lucius eighteen months later at Massilia, Augustus publicly adopted his remaining grandchild Agrippa Postumus and, at the same time, his step-son Tiberius; a special bill to legalize this act was passed in the Forum.[26] Yet he soon disinherited Postumus, whose behaviour had lately been vulgar and brutal, and packed him off to Surrentum.

When members of his family died Augustus bore his loss with far more resignation than when they disgraced themselves. The deaths of Gaius and Lucius did

not break his spirit; but after discovering his daughter Julia's adulteries, he refused to see visitors for some time. He wrote a letter about her case to the Senate, staying at home while a quaestor read it to them. He even considered her execution; at any rate, hearing that one Phoebe, a freedwoman in Julia's confidence, had hanged herself, he cried: 'I should have preferred to be Phoebe's father!' Julia was forbidden to drink wine or enjoy any other luxury during her exile; and denied all male company, whether free or slave, except by Augustus's special permission and after he had been given full particulars of the applicant's age, height, complexion, and of any distinguishing marks on his body – such as moles or scars. He kept Julia for five years on a prison island before moving her to the mainland, where she received somewhat milder treatment. Yet nothing would persuade him to forgive his daughter; and when the Roman people interceded several times on her behalf, earnestly pleading for her recall, he stormed at a popular assembly: 'If you ever bring up this matter again, may the gods curse you with daughters and wives like mine!' While in exile Julia the Younger gave birth to a child, which Augustus refused to allow to be acknowledged or reared. Because Agrippa Postumus's conduct, so far from improving, grew daily more irresponsible, he was transferred to an island, and held there under military surveillance. Augustus then asked the Senate to pass a decree making Postumus's banishment permanent; but whenever his name, or that of either Julia, came up in conversation he would sigh deeply, and sometimes quote a line from the *Iliad*:

Ah, never to have married, and childless to have died!

referring to them as 'my three boils' or 'my three running sores'.

66. Though slow in making friends, once Augustus took to a man, he showed great constancy and not only rewarded him as his qualities deserved, but even condoned his minor shortcomings. Indeed, it would be hard to recall an instance when one of Augustus's friends fell from favour; apart from Salvidienus Rufus and Cornelius Gallus, two nobodies whom he promoted, respectively, to a consulship and the governorship of Egypt. Rufus, for taking part in a plot, was handed over to a Senatorial Court and sentenced to death; Gallus, for showing ingratitude and an envious nature, was at first merely denied access to Augustus's house, or the privilege of living in any imperial province; but charges were later brought against him, and

24. Marcus Antonius the Younger (Antyllus).
25. Octavia.
26. i.e., a *lex curiata*, passed by the *comitia curiata*.

he, too, died by order of the Senate. Augustus commended the loyal House for feeling as strongly as they did on his behalf, but complained with tears of the unfortunate position in which he was placed: the only man in Rome who could not punish his friends merely by an expression of disgust for them – the matter must always be taken further. However, Augustus's other friends all continued rich and powerful so long as they lived, despite occasional coolnesses; each ranking among the leaders of his Order. It will be enough to mention in this context his annoyance at Marcus Agrippa's show of impatience and at Maecenas's inability to hold his tongue. Agrippa had felt that Augustus was not behaving as warmly towards him as usual, and that Marcellus was being preferred to him; he resigned all his offices and went off to Mytilene; Maecenas was guilty of confiding a state secret to his wife Terentia – namely that Murena's conspiracy had been disclosed.

Augustus expected the affection that he showed his friends to be warmly reciprocated even in the hour of death. For, although nobody could call him a legacy-hunter – indeed, he could never bear to benefit under the will of a man personally unknown to him – yet he was almost morbid in his careful weighing of a friend's death-bed tributes. His disappointment if they economized in their bequests to him, or failed to make at least some highly complimentary mention of his name, was only too apparent; nor could he repress his satisfaction if they remembered him with loving gratitude. But whenever any testator, of whatever Order, left him either legacies or shares in promised inheritances, Augustus at once resigned his rights in favour of the man's grown-up sons or daughters, if he had any; and, in the case of minors, kept the money until the boys came of age or the girls married, whereupon he handed it over, increased by the accumulated interest.

67. Augustus behaved strictly but graciously and kindly towards his dependants and slaves, and honoured some of his freedmen, such as Licinus, Celadus, and others, with his close intimacy. A slave named Cosmus, who had complained of him in the vilest terms, was punished merely by being put in irons. Once, when Augustus and his steward Diomedes were out walking together and a wild boar suddenly charged at them, Diomedes took fright and dodged behind his master. Augustus later made a joke of the incident, though he had been in considerable danger, preferring to call Diomedes a coward than anything worse – after all, his action had not been premeditated.

Yet, when one Polus, a favourite freedman, was convicted of adultery with Roman matrons, Augustus ordered him to commit suicide; and sentenced Thallus, an imperial secretary, to have his legs broken for divulging the contents of a letter – his fee had been twenty-five gold pieces. And because Gaius Caesar's tutor and attendants used their master's sickness and subsequent death as an excuse for arrogant, greedy behaviour in his province, Augustus had them flung into a river with weights tied around their necks.

68. As a young man Augustus was accused of various improprieties. For instance, Sextus Pompey jeered at his effeminacy; Mark Antony alleged that Julius Caesar made him submit to unnatural relations as the price of adoption; Antony's brother Lucius added that, after sacrificing his virtue to Caesar, Augustus had sold his favours to Aulus Hirtius in Spain, for 3,000 gold pieces, and that he used to soften the hair on his legs by singeing them with red-hot walnut shells. One day at the Theatre an actor came on the stage representing a eunuch priest of Cybele, the Mother of the Gods; and, as he played his timbrel, another actor exclaimed:

Look, how this invert's finger beats the drum!

Since the Latin phrase could also mean: 'Look how this invert's finger *sways the world*!' the audience took the line for a hint at Augustus and broke into enthusiastic applause.

69. Not even his friends could deny that he often committed adultery, though of course they said, in justification, that he did so for reasons of state, not simple passion – he wanted to discover what his enemies were at by getting intimate with their wives or daughters. Mark Antony accused him not only of indecent haste in marrying Livia, but of hauling an ex-consul's wife from her husband's dining-room into the bedroom – before his eyes, too! He brought the woman back, says Antony, blushing to the ears and with her hair in disorder. Antony also writes that Scribonia was divorced for having said a little too much when a rival got her claws into Augustus; and that his friends used to behave like Toranius, the slave-dealer, in arranging his pleasures for him – they would strip mothers of families, or grown girls, of their clothes and inspect them as though they were up for sale. A racy letter of Antony's survives, written before he and Augustus had quarrelled privately or publicly:

What has come over you? Do you object to my sleeping with Cleopatra? But we are married; and it is not even as though this were anything new – the affair started nine years ago. And what about you? Are you faithful to Livia Drusilla? My congratulations if, when this letter arrives, you have not been in bed with Tertullia, or Terentilla, or Rufilla, or Salvia Titisenia – or all of them. Does it really matter so much where, or with whom, you perform the sexual act?

70. Then there was Augustus's private banquet, known as 'The Feast of the Divine Twelve', which caused a public scandal. The guests came dressed as gods or goddesses, Augustus himself representing Apollo; and our authority for this is not only a spiteful letter of Antony's, which names all the twelve, but the following well-known anonymous lampoon:

> Those rogues engaged the services
>   Of a stage manager;
> So Mallia found six goddesses
>   And six gods facing her!
>
> Apollo's part was lewdly played
>   By impious Caesar; he
> Made merry at a table laid
>   For gross debauchery.
>
> Such scandalous proceedings shocked
>   The Olympians. One by one
> They quit and Jove, his thunders mocked,
>   Vacates the golden throne.

What made the scandal even worse was that the banquet took place at a time of food shortage; and on the next day people were shouting: 'The Gods have gobbled all the grain!' or 'Caesar is Apollo, true – but he's Apollo of the Torments' – this being the god's aspect in one city district. Some found Augustus a good deal too fond of expensive furniture, Corinthian bronzes, and the gaming table. While the proscriptions were in progress someone had scrawled on the base of his statue:

> I do not take my father's line;
>   His trade was silver coin, but mine
>   Corinthian vases –

the belief being that he enlarged the proscription lists with names of men who owned vases of this sort.

During the Sicilian War another rhyme was current:

> He took a beating twice at sea,
>   And threw two fleets away.
> So now to achieve one victory
>   He tosses dice all day.

71. Augustus easily disproved the accusation (or slander, if you like) of prostituting his body to men, by the decent normality of his sex-life, then and later;

and that of having over-luxurious tastes by his conduct at the capture of Alexandria, where the only loot he took from the Palace of the Ptolemies was a single agate cup – he melted down all the golden dinner services. However, the charge of being a womanizer stuck, and as an elderly man he is said to have still harboured a passion for deflowering girls – who were collected for him from every quarter, even by his wife! Augustus did not mind being called a gambler; he diced openly, in his old age too, simply because he enjoyed the game – not only in December, when the licence of the Saturnalia justified it, but on other holidays, as well, and actually on working days. That this is quite true a letter in his own handwriting proves:

My dear Tiberius,

... we had the same company for dinner, except that Vinicius and the elder Silius were also invited; and we gambled like old men all through the meal, both yesterday and today. Anyone who threw the Dog or a six put a silver piece in the pool for each of the dice; and anyone who threw Venus scooped the lot.[27]

And another letter runs:

My dear Tiberius,

We spent the Quinquatria[28] very pleasantly, keeping the gaming table warm by playing all day long. Your brother Drusus made fearful complaints about his luck, yet in the long run was not much out of pocket. He went down heavily at first, but we were surprised to see him slowly recouping most of his losses. I lost two hundred gold pieces; however, that was because, as usual, I behaved with excessive sportsmanship. If I had dunned every player who had forfeited his stakes to me, or not handed over my legitimate winnings when dunned myself, I should have been at least five hundred to the good. Well, that is how I like it: my generosity will gain me immortal glory, you may be sure!

And to his daughter Julia he wrote:

Enclosed please find two and a half gold pieces in silver coin: which is the sum I give each of my dinner guests in case they feel like dicing or playing 'odd and even' at table.

72. Augustus's other personal habits are generally agreed to have been unexceptionable. His first house, once the property of Calvus the orator, stood close to the Roman Forum at the top of the Ringmakers' Stairs; thence he moved to what had been Hortensius's house on the Palatine Hill. His new palace was remarkable for

27. 'The Dog' was two aces; and 'Venus' was when each of the dice showed a different number.
28. The five-day festival of Minerva.

neither size nor elegance; the courts being supported by squat columns of peperino stone, and the living-rooms innocent of marble or elaborately tessellated floors. There he slept in the same bedroom all the year round for over forty years; although the winter climate of Rome did not suit his health. Whenever he wanted to be alone and free of interruptions, he could retreat to a study at the top of the house, which he called 'Syra-cuse' or 'my little workshop'. He would hide himself away either here or else in a suburban villa owned by one of his freedmen; but, if he fell ill, always took refuge in Maecenas's mansion. He spent his holidays at seaside resorts, or on some island off the Campanian coast, or in country towns near Rome, such as Lanuvium, or Praeneste or Tibur – where he often ad-ministered justice in the colonnades of Hercules's Temple. Such was his dislike of all large pretentious country houses that he went so far as to demolish one built by his grand-daughter Julia on too lavish a scale. His own were modest enough and less remarkable for their statuary and pictures than for their landscape gardening and the rarities on display: for example, at Capreae he had collected the huge skeletons of extinct sea and land monsters popularly known as 'Giants' Bones', and the weapons of ancient heroes.

73. How simply Augustus's palace was furnished may be deduced by examining the couches and tables still preserved, many of which would hardly be con-sidered fit for a private citizen. He is said to have always slept on a low bed, with a very ordinary coverlet. On all but special occasions he wore clothes woven and sewn for him by either Livia, Octavia, Julia, or one of his grand-daughters. His gowns were neither tight nor full, and the purple stripe on them was neither narrow nor broad; but his shoes had rather thick soles to make him look taller. And he always kept a change of better shoes and clothes at hand; he might be unexpectedly called upon to appear in an official capacity.

74. He gave frequent dinner parties, very formal ones, too; paying strict attention to social precedence and personal character. Valerius Messala writes that the sole occasion on which Augustus ever invited a freedman to dine was when he honoured Menas for delivering Sextus Pompey's fleet into his power; and even then Menas was first enrolled on the list of free-born citizens. However, Augustus himself records that he once invited an ex-member of his bodyguard, the freedman whose villa he used as a retreat. At such din-ner parties he would sometimes arrive late and leave early, letting his guests start and finish without him.

The meal usually consisted of three courses, though in expansive moods Augustus might serve as many as six. There was no great extravagance, and a most cheerful atmosphere, because of his talent for making shy guests, who either kept silent or muttered to their neighbours, join in the general conversation. He also enlivened the meal with performances by musicians, actors, or even men who gave turns at the Circus – but more often by professional story-tellers.

75. Augustus spared no expense when celebrating national holidays and behaved very light-heartedly on occasion. At the Saturnalia, for instance, or whenever else the fancy took him, he whimsically varied the value of his gifts. They might consist of rich clothing and gold or silver plate; or every sort of coin, including specimens from the days of the early monarchy, and foreign pieces; or merely lengths of goat-hair cloth, or sponges, or pokers, or tongs – all ticketed with mislead-ing and riddling descriptions of the objects concerned.

At some dinner parties he would also auction tickets for prizes of most unequal value, and paintings with their faces turned to the wall, for which every guest present was expected to bid blindly, taking his chance like the rest: he might either pick up most satisfactory bargains, or throw away his money.

76. In this character sketch I need not omit his eat-ing habits. He was frugal and, as a rule, preferred the food of the common people, especially the coarser sort of bread, small fishes, fresh hand-pressed cheese, and green figs of the second crop; and would not wait for dinner, if he felt hungry, but ate anywhere. The follow-ing are verbatim quotations from his letters:

I had a snack of bread and dates while out for my drive today ...

and:

On the way back in my litter from the Regia, I munched an ounce of bread and a few hard-skinned grapes.

and again:

My dear Tiberius,

Not even a Jew fasts so scrupulously on his sabbaths[29] as I have done today. Not until dusk had fallen did I touch a thing; and that was at the baths, before I had my oil rub, when I swallowed two mouthfuls of bread.

This failure to observe regular mealtimes often resulted in his dining alone, either before or after his

29. Augustus is confusing the sabbaths with the annual Day of Atonement.

guests, and touching nothing while the meal was in progress.

77. Augustus was also a habitually abstemious drinker. During the siege of Mutina, according to Cornelius Nepos, he never took more than three drinks of wine-and-water at dinner. In later life his limit was a pint; if he ever exceeded this he would deliberately vomit. Raetian was his favourite, but he seldom touched wine between meals; instead, he would moisten his throat with a morsel of bread dunked in cold water; or a slice of cucumber or the heart of a young lettuce; or a sour apple either fresh or dried.

78. After lunch he used to rest for a while without removing clothes or shoes; one hand shading his eyes, his feet uncovered. When dinner was over he would retire to a couch in his study, where he worked late until all the outstanding business of the day had been cleared off; or most of it. Then he went to bed and slept seven hours at the outside, with three or four breaks of wakefulness. If he found it hard to fall asleep again on such occasions, as frequently happened, he sent for readers or story-tellers; and on dropping off would not wake until the sun was up. He could not bear lying sleepless in the dark with no one by his side; and if he had to officiate at some official or religious ceremony that involved early rising – which he also loathed – would spend the previous night at a friend's house as near the appointed place as possible. Even so, he often needed more sleep than he got, and would doze off during his litter journeys through the city if anything delayed his progress and the bearers set the litter down.

79. Augustus was remarkably handsome and of very graceful gait even as an old man; but negligent of his personal appearance. He cared so little about his hair that, to save time, he would have two or three barbers working hurriedly on it together, and meanwhile read or write something, whether they were giving him a haircut or a shave. He always wore so serene an expression, whether talking or in repose, that a Gallic chief once confessed to his compatriots: 'When granted an audience with the Emperor during his passage across the Alps I would have carried out my plan of hurling him over a cliff had not the sight of that tranquil face softened my heart; so I desisted.'

Augustus's eyes were clear and bright, and he liked to believe that they shone with a sort of divine radiance: it gave him profound pleasure if anyone at whom he glanced keenly dropped his head as though dazzled by looking into the sun. In old age, however, his left eye had only partial vision. His teeth were small, few, and decayed; his hair, yellowish and rather curly; his eyebrows met above the nose; he had ears of moderate size, a nose projecting a little at the top and then bending slightly inward, and a complexion intermediate between dark and fair. Julius Marathus, Augustus's freedman and recorder, makes his height 5 feet 7 inches; but this is an exaggeration, although, with body and limbs so beautifully proportioned, one did not realize how small a man he was, unless someone tall stood close to him.

80. His body is said to have been marred by blemishes of various sorts – a constellation of seven birthmarks on his chest and stomach, exactly corresponding in form, order, and number with the Great Bear; and a number of hard, dry patches suggesting ringworm, caused by an itching of his skin and a too frequent and vigorous use of the scraper at the Baths. He had a weakness in his left hip, thigh, and leg, which occasionally gave him the suspicion of a limp; but this was improved by the sand-and-reed treatment. Sometimes the forefinger of his right hand would be so numbed and shrunken by cold that it hardly served to guide a pen, even when strengthened with a horn finger-stall. He also suffered from bladder pains which, however, ceased to trouble him once he had passed gravel in his urine.

81. Augustus survived several grave and dangerous illnesses at different periods. The worst was after his Cantabrian conquest, when abscesses on the liver reduced him to such despair that he consented to try a remedy which ran counter to all medical practice: because hot fomentations afforded him no relief, his physician Antonius Musa successfully prescribed cold ones. He was also subject to certain seasonal disorders which recurred every year: in early spring a tightness of the diaphragm; and when the sirocco blew, catarrh. These so weakened his constitution that either hot or cold weather caused him great distress.

82. In winter he wore no fewer than four tunics and a heavy woollen gown above his undershirt; and below that a woollen chest protector; also underpants and woollen gaiters. In summer he slept with the bedroom door open, or in the courtyard beside a fountain, having someone to fan him; and could not bear the rays even of the winter sun, but always wore a broad-brimmed hat when he walked in the open air, even at home. He preferred to travel by litter, at night, and his bearers kept so leisurely a pace that they were two days in arriving at Praeneste or Tibur; yet, whenever it was possible

to reach his destination by sea, he did so. Indeed, he pampered his health, especially by not bathing too often, and being usually content with an oil rub – or with a sweat-bath beside a fire, after which he took a douche of water either warmed or allowed to stand in the sun until it had lost its chill. When hot brine or warm Albulan water[30] was prescribed for his rheumatism he did no more than sit on a wooden bath-seat – calling it by the Spanish name *dureta* – and alternately dip his hands and feet into the bath.

83. As soon as the Civil Wars were over Augustus discontinued his riding and fencing exercises on the Campus Martius and used, instead, to play catch with two companions, or hand-ball with several. But soon he was content to go riding, or take walks, muffled in a cloak or blanket, that ended with a sprint and some jumping. Sometimes he went fishing as a relaxation; sometimes he played at dice, marbles, or nuts in the company of little boys, and was always on the lookout for ones with pretty faces and cheerful chatter, especially Syrians and Moors – he loathed people who were dwarfish or in any way deformed, regarding them as freaks of nature and bringers of bad luck.

84. Even in his boyhood Augustus had studied rhetoric with great eagerness and industry, and during the Mutina campaign, busy though he was, is said to have read, written, and declaimed daily. From that time onwards he carefully drafted every address intended for delivery to the Senate, the popular Assembly, or

30. From the sulphur springs flowing into the River Anio.

THE EMPEROR AND THE CITIZEN

56 (opposite). *The cuirassed statue of Augustus from Primaporta shows on the breastplate the return of the Roman Eagles which had been captured by the Parthians to Tiberius, who received them as Augustus's delegate. The scene is surrounded by personifications of earth and sky which hint at claims to universal dominion. The gesture of the outstretched right arm is that of the general addressing his troops.* (Rome, Vatican.)

57 (left). *Statue of Augustus from the Via Labiaca: the Emperor is here portrayed in his role as a citizen and chief priest; when making a sacrifice, the toga was drawn over the wearer's head.* (Rome, Terme Museum.)

the troops; though gifted with quite a talent for extempore speech. What is more, he avoided the embarrassment of forgetting his words, or the drudgery of memorizing them, by always reading from a manuscript. All important statements made to individuals, and even to his wife Livia, were first committed to notebooks and then repeated aloud; he was haunted by a fear of saying either too much or too little if he spoke off-hand. His articulation of words, constantly practised under an elocution teacher, was pleasant and rather unusual; but sometimes, when his voice proved inadequate for addressing a large crowd, he called a herald.

85. Augustus wrote numerous prose works on a variety of subjects, some of which he read aloud to a group of his closer friends as though in a lecture-hall: the *Reply to Brutus's Eulogy of Cato*, for instance. In this case, however, he tired just before the end – being then already an old man – and handed the last roll to Tiberius, who finished it for him. Among his other works were *An Encouragement to the Study of Philosophy* and thirteen books of *My Autobiography*, which took the story only up to the time of the Cantabrian War. He made occasional attempts at verse composition; including *Sicily*, a short poem in hexameters, and an equally short collection of *Epigrams*, most of them composed at the Baths. Both these books survive; but growing dissatisfied with the style of his tragedy, *Ajax*, which he had begun in great excitement, he destroyed it. When friends asked: 'Well, what has Ajax been doing lately?' he answered: 'Ajax has fallen on my sponge.'

86. He cultivated a simple and easy oratorical style, avoiding purple passages, artfully contrived prose-rhythms, and 'the stink of far-fetched phrases', as he called it; his main object being to say what he meant as plainly as possible. An anxiety not to let his audience or his readers lose their way in his sentences explains why he put such prepositions as *to* or *in* before the names of cities,[31] and why he often repeated the same conjunction several times where a single appearance would have been less awkward, if more confusing. He expressed contempt for both innovators and archaizers, as equally mischievous, and would attack them with great violence: especially his dear friend Maecenas, whose 'myrrh-distilling ringlets' he parodied mercilessly. Even Tiberius, who had a habit of introducing obsolete and pedantic phrases into his

speeches, did not escape Augustus's ridicule, and Antony was for him a madman who wrote 'as though he wanted to be wondered at rather than understood'. He made fun of Antony's bad taste and inconsistent literary style: 'Your use of antique diction borrowed by Sallust from Cato's *Origins* suggests that you are in two minds about imitating Annius Cimber or Veranius Flaccus. Or are you trying to acclimatize in Latin the nonsensicalities of those garrulous Asiatic orators?' And to a letter praising the intelligence of his grand-daughter Agrippina, he adds: 'But please take great care to avoid affectation in writing or talking.'

87. Augustus's everyday language must have contained many whimsical expressions of his own coinage, to judge from letters in his own handwriting. Thus, he often wrote 'they will pay on the Greek Kalends'; which meant 'never' – because the reckoning by Kalends is a purely Roman convention. Another of his favourite remarks was: 'Let us be satisfied with *this* Cato!' – meaning that one should make the most of contemporary circumstances, however poorly they might compare with the past. He also had a favourite metaphor for swift and sudden actions: 'Quicker than boiled asparagus.' Here is a list of unusual synonyms which constantly appear in Augustus's letters:

baceolus (dolt) for: *stultus* (fool)
pulleiaceus (wooden-headed) for: *cerritus* (crazy)
vapide se habere (feel flat) for: *male se habere* (feel bad)
betizare (be a beetroot) for: *languere* (be languid) –
on the analogy of the colloquial form *lachanizare*.

Among his grammatical peculiarities occur the forms *simus* for *sumus* (we are), and *domos* for *domuos* (of home), to which he always clung as a sign that they were his considered choice. I have noticed one particular habit of his: rather than break a long word at the end of a line and carry forward to the next whatever letters were left over, he would write these underneath the first part of the word and draw a loop to connect them with it.

88. Instead of paying a strict regard to orthography, as formulated by the grammarians, he inclined towards phonetic spelling. Of course, most writers make such slips as transposing or omitting whole syllables, as well as single letters; so I should not have mentioned that Augustus often did the same but for my surprise on finding, in more than one book of memoirs, the story that he once retired a governor of consular rank for being ill-educated enough to write *ixi* for *ipsi* (the same men). When Augustus wrote in cypher he simply sub-

---

31. It was correct to omit them.

stituted the next letter of the alphabet for the one required, except that he wrote AA for X.

89. He had ambitions to be as proficient in Greek as in Latin, and did very well at it. His tutor was Apollodorus of Pergamum, who accompanied him to Apollonia, though a very old man, and taught him elocution. Afterwards Augustus spent some time with Areus the philosopher, and his sons Dionysius and Nicanor, who broadened his general education; but never learned to speak Greek with real fluency, and never ventured on any Greek literary composition. Indeed, if he ever had occasion to use the language he would write down whatever it might be in Latin and get someone to make a translation. Yet nobody could describe him as ignorant of Greek poetry, because he greatly enjoyed the Old Comedy, and often put plays of that period on the stage. His chief interest in the literature of both languages was the discovery of moral precepts, with suitable anecdotes attached, capable of public or private application; and he would transcribe passages of this sort for the attention of his generals or provincial governors, whenever he thought it necessary. He even read whole volumes aloud to the Senate, and issued proclamations commending them to the people – such as Quintus Metellus's *On the Need for Larger Families*, and Rutilius's *On the Height of Buildings* – just to prove that he had been anticipated in his recommendations by far earlier thinkers.

Augustus gave all possible encouragement to intellectuals: he would politely and patiently attend readings not only of their poems and historical works, but of their speeches and dialogues; yet objected to being made the theme of any work unless the author were known as a serious and reputable writer, and often warned the praetors not to let his name be vulgarized by its constant occurrence in prize orations.

90. As for Augustus's attitude to religion: he is recorded to have been scared of thunder and lightning, against which he always carried a piece of seal-skin as an amulet, and to have taken refuge in an underground vault whenever a heavy storm threatened – because, as I have already mentioned, he had once narrowly escaped being struck on a night march which frightened him badly.

91. Warnings conveyed in dreams, either his own or those dreamed by others, were not lost on him: for example, before the battle of Philippi, when so ill that he decided not to leave his tent, he changed his mind on account of a friend's dream – most fortunately, too,

as it proved. For the camp was captured and a party of the enemy, breaking into the tent, plunged their swords through and through his bed under the impression that he was still in it, tearing the bed-clothes to ribbons. Every spring he had a series of ugly dreams, but none of the horrid visions seen in them came true; whereas what he occasionally dreamed at other seasons tended to be reliable. One day, after he had paid frequent visits to the Temple of Jupiter the Thunderer, founded by himself on the Capitoline Hill, Capitoline Jupiter approached him in a dream with a complaint that the newcomer was stealing his worshippers. He replied: 'I put the Thunderer so close to your Temple because I had decided to give you a janitor.' When Augustus awoke, he hung a set of bells from the gable of the new building to make it look like a front door. Because of another dream he used to sit in a public place once a year holding out his hand for the people to give him coppers, as though he were a beggar.

92. Augustus had absolute faith in certain premonitory signs: considering it bad luck to thrust his right foot into the left shoe as he got out of bed, but good luck to start a long journey or voyage during a drizzle of rain, which would ensure success and a speedy return. Prodigies made a particularly strong impression on him. Once, when a palm tree pushed its way between the paving stones in front of his house he had it transplanted to the inner court beside his family gods, and lavished care on it. When he visited Capreae, the drooping branches of a moribund old oak suddenly regained their vigour, which so delighted him that he arranged to buy the island from the city of Neapolis in exchange for Aenaria. He also had a superstition against starting a journey on the day after a market-day, or undertaking any important task on the Nones of a month – although, in this case, as he explained to Tiberius in a letter, it was merely the unlucky *non*-sound of the word that affected him.

93. Augustus showed great respect towards all ancient and long-established foreign rites, but despised the rest. Once, for example, after becoming an adept in the Eleusinian Mysteries at Athens, he judged a case at Rome in which the privileges of the priests of the Attic Ceres[32] were questioned. Since certain religious secrets had to be quoted in the evidence, he cleared the court, dismissed his legal advisers and settled the dispute *in camera*. On the other hand, during his journey through Egypt he would not go out of his way, however slightly, to honour the divine Apis bull; and

32. Demeter.

praised his grandson Gaius for not offering prayers when he visited Jerusalem.

94. At this point it might be well to list the omens, occurring before, on, and after the day of Augustus's birth, from which his future greatness and lasting good fortune could clearly be prognosticated.

In ancient days part of the city wall of Velitrae had been struck by lightning and the soothsayers prophesied that a native of the place would one day rule the world. Confidence in this prediction led the citizens to declare immediate war against Rome, and to keep on fighting until they were nearly wiped out; only centuries later did the world-ruler appear in the person of Augustus.

According to Julius Marathus, a public portent warned the Roman people some months before Augustus's birth that Nature was making ready to provide them with a king; and this caused the Senate such consternation that they issued a decree which forbade the rearing of any male child for a whole year. However, a group of senators whose wives were expectant prevented the decree from being filed at the Treasury and thus becoming law – for each of them hoped that the prophesied king would be his own son.

Then there is a story which I found in a book called *Theologumena*, by Asclepiades of Mendes. Augustus's mother, Atia, with certain married women friends, once attended a solemn midnight service at the Temple of Apollo, where she had her litter set down, and presently fell asleep as the others also did. Suddenly a serpent glided up, entered her, and then glided away again. On awakening, she purified herself, as if after intimacy with her husband. An irremovable coloured mark in the shape of a serpent, which then appeared on her body, made her ashamed to visit the public baths any more; and the birth of Augustus nine months later suggested a divine paternity. Atia dreamed that her intestines were carried up to Heaven and overhung all lands and seas; and Octavius, that the sun rose from between her thighs.

Augustus's birth coincided with the Senate's famous debate on the Catilinarian conspiracy, and when Octavius arrived late because of Atia's confinement, Publius Nigidius Figulus the astrologer, hearing at what hour the child had been delivered, cried out: 'The ruler of the world is now born.' Everyone believes this story.

Octavius, during a subsequent expedition through the wilder parts of Thrace, reached a grove sacred to Father Liber,[33] where he consulted the priests about his son's destiny. After performing certain barbaric rites, they gave him the same response as Figulus; for the wine they had poured over the altar caused a pillar of flame to shoot up far above the roof of the shrine into the sky – a sign never before granted except to Alexander the Great when he sacrificed at that very altar. That night Octavius had another dream: his son appeared in superhuman majesty, armed with the thunderbolt, sceptre, and regal ornaments of Jupiter Best and Greatest, crowned with a solar diadem, and riding in a belaurelled chariot drawn by twelve dazzlingly white horses.

Gaius Drusus records that, one evening, the infant Augustus was placed by the nurse in his cradle on the ground-floor, but had vanished by daybreak; at last a search party found him lying on the top of a lofty tower, his face turned towards the rising sun. Once, when he was just learning to talk at his grandfather's country seat, the frogs broke into a loud chorus of croaking: he told them to stop, and it is locally claimed that no frog has croaked there since. On a later occasion, as he sat lunching in a copse beside the Appian Way, close to the fourth milestone, an eagle, to his great surprise, swooped at him, snatched a crust from his hand, carried it aloft – and then, to his even greater surprise, glided gently down again and restored what it had stolen.

Quintus Catulus, after rededicating the Capitol,[34] dreamed two dreams on successive nights. First, Jupiter Best and Greatest beckoned to one of several noblemen's sons who were playing near his altar, and slipped an image of the Goddess Rome into the fold of his gown. Then Catulus dreamed that he saw the same boy sitting in the lap of Capitoline Jupiter; he tried to have him removed, but the God countermanded the order because the boy was being reared as the saviour of Rome. Next day, Catulus met Augustus, looked at him with startled eyes – they had never met before – and pronounced him the identical boy of his dreams. Another version of Catulus's first dream is that a crowd of noblemen's children were begging Jupiter for a guardian; the God then pointed to one of them, saying: 'Whatever you need, ask him!', lightly touched the boy's mouth with his fingers and laid them on his own lips.

On a New Year's Day, Cicero escorted Julius Caesar, as Consul, to the Capitol and happened to tell his friends what he had dreamed the night before: a boy

33. Dionysus (Bacchus).   34. See Julius Caesar 15.

of noble features, let down from Heaven by a golden chain, stood at the Temple door, and was handed a whip by Capitoline Jupiter. At that moment, Cicero's eye caught Augustus, whom his grand-uncle Caesar had brought to the ceremony but whom few of those present knew by sight. He cried: 'There goes the very boy!'

When Augustus celebrated his coming of age, the seams of the senatorial gown which Caesar had allowed him to wear split and it fell at his feet. Some of the bystanders interpreted the accident as a sign that the Senatorial Order itself would some day be brought to his feet.

As Julius Caesar was felling a wood near Munda in Spain to clear a site for his camp, he noticed a palm-tree and ordered it to be spared, as a presage of victory. The tree then suddenly put out a new shoot which, a few days later, had grown so tall as to overshadow it. What was more, a flock of doves began to nest in the fronds, although doves notoriously dislike hard, spiny foliage. This prodigy was the immediate reason, they say, for Caesar's desire that his grand-nephew, and no one else, should succeed him.

At Apollonia, Augustus and Agrippa together visited the house of Theogenes the astrologer, and climbed upstairs to his observatory; they both wished to consult him about their future careers. Agrippa went first and was prophesied such almost incredibly good fortune that Augustus expected a far less encouraging response, and felt ashamed to disclose the time of his birth. Yet when at last, after a deal of hesitation, he grudgingly supplied the information for which both were pressing him, Theogenes rose and flung himself at his feet; and this gave Augustus so implicit a faith in the destiny awaiting him that he even ventured to publish his horoscope, and struck a silver coin stamped with Capricorn, the sign under which he had been born.

95. When he returned to Rome from Apollonia at news of Caesar's assassination, the sky was clear of clouds, but a rainbow-like halo formed around the sun; and suddenly lightning struck the tomb of Caesar's daughter Julia. Then, when he first took the auspices as Consul, twelve vultures appeared, as they had appeared to Romulus; and the livers of all the sacrificial victims were seen to be doubled inwards at the bottom – an omen which, experts in soothsaying agreed, presaged a wonderful future for him.

96. Augustus even foreknew the successful conclusion of his wars. At Bononia, where the army of the Triumvirs Augustus, Antony, and Lepidus was stationed, an eagle perched on Augustus's tent and defended itself vigorously against the converging attack of two ravens, bringing both of them down. This augury was noted and understood by the troops as portending a rupture between their three leaders, which later took place. On Augustus's way to Philippi, a Thessalian stopped him to report having been assured of victory by Caesar's ghost, whom he met on a lonely road. Sacrificing one day before the walls of Perusia, Augustus had failed to secure a satisfactory omen, and sent for more victims; at this point the enemy made a sudden sortie from the beleaguered city, and carried off the entire sacrificial apparatus. The soothsayers unanimously reassured him that whatever disasters had been threatened by the omens would fall upon the present possessors of the entrails, and this proved to be true.

On the eve of the naval battle off Sicily, Augustus was walking along the shore when a fish leaped from the sea and fell at his feet. Before Actium, he was about to board his ship and give the signal for hostilities to begin, when he met a peasant driving an ass, and asked his name. The peasant replied: 'I am Eutychus ("Prosper") and my ass is called Nicon ("Victory").' To commemorate the victory Augustus set up bronze statues of Eutychus and his ass on the camp site, which he made into a sacred enclosure.

97. Next, we come to Augustus's death and subsequent deification, both of which were predicted by evident signs. While he was closing a *lustrum*, or five-year period, with a purificatory ceremony in the crowded Campus Martius, an eagle circled around him several times, then flew to the near-by temple and perched above the first 'A' of Agrippa's name. As soon as Augustus noticed this he ordered Tiberius, who was acting as his colleague in the Censorship, to read out the usual vows for the next five-year period; because, though having composed and recorded them on a tablet, he would not make himself responsible for vows payable after his death. At about the same time lightning melted the initial letter of his name on the inscription below one of his statues. This was interpreted to mean that he would live only another hundred days, since the remainder of the word, namely AESAR, is the Etruscan for 'god' – C being the Roman numeral 100.

Again, when sending Tiberius off to Illyricum and planning to accompany him as far as Beneventum, Augustus got held up by a long list of cases, and cried: 'I will stay here no longer, whoever tries to detain me!'

58. ACTIUM, *where Augustus won his decisive naval victory over Antony, was a site hallowed by a temple of Apollo, god of prophecy, which, according to Roman legend, had been founded by Trojans. In years to follow, Apollo was therefore invoked as the special protector of the Augustan order. Roman altar of the first century* A.D., *showing the Goddess Roma and Apollo with his griffin and cithara, in front of a tripod, symbol of prophecy.* (Tunis, Musée du Bardo.)

These words were subsequently recalled as prophetic. He started off for Beneventum by road but, on reaching Astura, met with a favourable breeze and decided to take ship that evening – although night-voyages were against his usual habits – and so caught a chill, the first symptom of which was diarrhoea.

98. After coasting past Campania, with its islands, he spent the next four days in his villa on Capreae, where he rested and amused himself. As he had sailed through the Gulf of Puteoli, the passengers and crew of a recently arrived Alexandrian ship had put on white robes

and garlands, burned incense, and wished him the greatest of good fortune – because, they said, they owed their lives to him and their liberty to sail the seas: in a word, their entire freedom and prosperity. This incident gratified Augustus so deeply that he gave each member of his staff forty gold pieces, making them promise under oath to spend them only on Alexandrian trade goods. What was more, he made the last two or three days of his stay on Capreae the occasion for distributing, among other little presents, Roman togas and Greek cloaks to the islanders; insisting that the Romans should talk Greek and dress like Greeks, and that the Greeks should do the opposite. He sat for a long time watching the gymnastic training of the many local *ephebi*[35] (Capreae being a very conservative settlement). Afterwards he invited these young men to a banquet at which he presided, and not merely allowed but expected them to play jokes, and freely scramble for the tokens which he threw, entitling the holders to fruit, sweetmeats, and the like. In fact, he indulged in every form of fun.

Augustus called the residential centre of Capreae 'the Land of Do-nothings', because some of his staff, now settled on the island, were growing so lazy; and referred to his friend Masgaba, who had died there in the previous year, as 'Ktistes', meaning 'the Founder'. When he noticed from his dining-room window that a crowd of torchbearers were attending Masgaba's tomb, he improvised this Greek line:

I see the Founder's tomb ablaze with fire . . .

then asked Thrasyllus, Tiberius's astrologer, who was reclining opposite him and did not understand the reference: 'What poet wrote that?' Thrasyllus hesitated, and Augustus capped his own line, reciting:

With torches, look, they honour Masgaba!

and again asked: 'Who wrote that?' Thrasyllus, unable to divine the authorship, mumbled: 'Both lines are very good, whoever the poet was.' Augustus burst out laughing and made a joke of it.

He next crossed over to Neapolis, although his stomach was weak from an intermittent recurrence of the same trouble, and watched an athletic competition which was held in his honour every five years. Finally, he started off with Tiberius and said goodbye to him at Beneventum. Feeling worse on the homeward jour-

ney, he took to his bed at Nola, and sent messengers to recall Tiberius – now headed for Illyricum. At his arrival Augustus had a long talk with him in private, after which he attended to no further important business.

99. On the day that he died, Augustus frequently inquired whether rumours of his illness were causing any popular disturbance. He called for a mirror, and had his hair combed and his lower jaw, which had fallen from weakness, propped up. Presently he summoned a group of friends and asked: 'Have I played my part in the farce of life creditably enough?' adding the theatrical tag:

If I have pleased you, kindly signify
Appreciation with a warm goodbye.

Then he dismissed them, but when fresh visitors arrived from Rome, wanted to hear the latest news of the daughter of Drusus the Younger[36] who was ill. Finally, he kissed his wife with: 'Goodbye, Livia: never forget our marriage!' and died almost at once. He must have longed for such an easy exit, for whenever he had heard of anyone having passed away quickly and painlessly, he used to pray: 'May Heaven grant the same *euthanasia* to me and mine!' The only sign that his wits were wandering, just before he died, was his sudden cry of terror: 'Forty young men are carrying me off!' But even this may be read as a prophecy rather than a delusion, because forty Praetorians were to form the guard of honour that conveyed him to his lying-in-state.

100. Augustus died in the same room as his father Octavius. That was 19 August A.D. 14, at about 3 p.m., the Consuls of the year being Sextus Pompeius and Sextus Appuleius. In thirty-five days' time he would have attained the age of seventy-six. Senators from the neighbouring municipalities and veteran colonies bore the body, in stages, all the way from Nola to Bovillae – but at night, owing to the hot weather, laying it during the daytime in the town hall or principal temple of every halting place. From Bovillae, a party of Roman knights carried it to the vestibule of his house at Rome.

The senators vied with one another in proposing posthumous honours for Augustus. Among the motions introduced were the following: that his funeral procession should pass through the Triumphal Gate preceded by the image of Victory from the Senate House, and that boys and girls of the nobility should

35. Youths who had reached their nineteenth year but were not yet old enough to become full citizens.

36. Julia Livilla.

59. BEGINNINGS OF THE IMPERIAL CULT. *Although Augustus prohibited cults addressed to him personally, his reign did see the beginnings of the imperial cult. Thus, when Augustus reorganized the districts of Rome, each district was given a shrine for the cult of its Lares (see Ills. 31 and 32), which became known as the Lares of the Emperor, whose Genius, guardian spirit, was worshipped along with them. The altar here shown was dedicated 'to the Lares of Augustus' by the presidents of the district, who are represented sacrificing on one of its sides. A flute-player, in the background, accompanies the ritual, while two attendants hold the sacrificial animals, a pig for the Lares, and a bull for the Genius of the Emperor. Another side of the altar displays the statue of a Lar holding a branch of laurel.* (Rome, Conservatori.)

sing his dirge; that on the day of his cremation iron rings should be worn instead of gold ones; that his ashes should be gathered by priests of the leading Colleges; that the name of the month 'August' should be transferred to September, because Augustus had been born in September but had died in the month now called August; and that the whole period between his birth and death should be officially entered in the Calendar as 'the Augustan Age'.

Though it was decided not to pay him excessive honours, he was given two funeral eulogies – by Tiberius from the forecourt of Julius Caesar's Temple, and by Tiberius's son Drusus from the Old Rostra – after which a party of senators shouldered the body and took it to a pyre on the Campus Martius, where it was burned; and an ex-praetor actually swore that he had seen Augustus's spirit soaring up to Heaven through the flames. Leading knights, barefoot, and wearing unbelted tunics, then collected his ashes and placed them in the family Mausoleum. He had built this himself, during his sixth consulship, between the Flaminian Way and the Tiber; at the same time converting the neighbourhood into a public park.

101. Augustus's will, composed on 3 April of the previous year, while Lucius Plancus and Gaius Silius were Consuls, occupied two note-books, written partly in his own hand, partly in those of his freedmen Polybius and Hilarion. The Vestal Virgins to whose safe-keeping he had entrusted these documents now produced them, as well as three rolls, also sealed by him. All were opened and read in the House. It proved that he had appointed Tiberius and Livia heirs to the bulk of his estate, directing that Tiberius should take two-thirds and adopt the name 'Augustus', while Livia

60. DIVINIZATION
Coin of Tiberius: the coin depicts a scene which occurred in Rome on several occasions; a carriage with the statue of the deceased Emperor, in this case Augustus, is drawn by four elephants. In the ancient world, elephants were associated with light, victory and eternity. The legend reads, 'The Senate and People of Rome to the divinized Augustus'. (London, British Museum.)

took the remaining third and adopted the name 'Augusta'. The heirs in the second degree were to be Tiberius's son Drusus, entitled to one-third of the reversion; and Germanicus, with his three sons, jointly entitled to the remainder. Many of Augustus's relatives and friends figured among the heirs in the third degree. He also left a bequest of 400,000 gold pieces to the Roman commons in general; 35,000 to the two tribes with which he had family connections; ten to every Praetorian guardsman; five to every member of the city cohorts; three to every legionary soldier. These legacies were to be paid on the nail, because he had always kept enough cash for the purpose. There were other minor bequests, some as large as 200 gold pieces, which were not to be settled until a year after his death because:

... my heirs will not receive more than 1,500,000 gold pieces; for, although my friends have bequeathed me some 14,000,000 in the last twenty years, nearly the whole of this sum, besides what came to me from my father, from my adoptive father, and from others, has been used for the benefit of the State.

He had given orders that 'should anything happen' to his daughter Julia, or his grand-daughter of the same name, their bodies must be excluded from the Mausoleum. One of the three sealed rolls contained directions for his own funeral; another, a record of his reign, which he wished to have engraved on bronze and posted at the entrance to the Mausoleum; the third, a statement of how many serving troops were stationed in different parts of the Empire, what money reserves were held by the Public Treasury and the Privy Purse, and what revenues were due for collection. He also supplied the names of freedmen and slave-secretaries who could furnish details, under all these heads, on demand.

61. THE MAUSOLEUM OF AUGUSTUS IN ROME

III
TIBERIUS

The patrician branch of the Claudian House – there was a plebeian branch, too, of equal influence and distinction – came to Rome, which had then been only recently founded, from the Sabine town of Regilli, bringing with them a large train of dependants. They did so at the invitation of Titus Tatius, who was either Romulus's co-king or (according to a more widely held version of the story) reigned at a later period and shared the government of the city with Atta Claudius, the head of the Claudians, about six years after the expul-

62 (above). TIBERIUS.
Coin of his reign. (London, British Museum.)

TIBERIUS AND THE CLAUDIANS
63 (opposite). *Portrait head of Tiberius.* (Munich, Antikensammlung.)
64 (right). *Claudia Quinta, ancestress of Tiberius, pulls the boat of Cybele, the Great Mother (see Ill. 148) up the Tiber with her girdle. The event occurred in 204* B.C. *Altar of the Great Mother.* (Rome, Capitoline Museum.)

sion of the Kings. The Claudians were enrolled among the patrician houses, and also publicly decreed an estate beyond the Anio for their dependants to farm, and a family burial ground at the foot of the Capitoline Hill. In course of time they amassed twenty-eight consulships, five dictatorships, seven censorships, six triumphs, and two ovations. Many different forenames and surnames were used by members of the House, but they unanimously decided to ban the forename Lucius, because one Lucius Claudius had been convicted as a highwayman and another as a murderer; and added the surname Nero, which is Sabine for 'strong and energetic'.

2. History records many distinguished services and equally grave injuries done to the state by Claudians. Let me quote only a few instances. Appius Claudius the Blind advised the Senate that an alliance with King Pyrrhus[1] would not be in the national interest. Claudius Caudex was the first to take a fleet across the Straits of Messina, and expelled the Carthaginians from Sicily.[2] Tiberius Nero intercepted Hasdrubal as he arrived in Italy from Spain with powerful reinforcements for his brother Hannibal, and defeated him before a junction could be effected.[3]

On the debit side of the ledger must be set Claudius Regillianus's attempt, while one of the ten commissioners for codifying the laws, to enslave and seduce a free-born girl – a wicked act which made the commons desert Rome in a body, for the second time, leaving the patricians to their own devices. Then there was Claudius Russus, who set up a crowned image of himself at the town called Appius's Forum, and attempted to conquer Italy with the help of his armed dependants. And Claudius Pulcher who, as Consul, took the auspices before a naval battle off Sicily and, finding that the sacred chickens had refused their feed, cried: 'If they will not eat, let them drink!' He threw them into the sea, fought the battle in defiance of their warning, and lost it.[4] When the Senate then ordered Claudius to appoint a dictator, he seemed to be making a joke of the critical military situation when he chose one Glycias, his dispatch-rider.

An equal disparity may be found between the records of the Claudian women. There was a Claudia who, when the ship which was bringing the sacred image of the Idaean Mother-goddess to Rome grounded on a Tiber mud-bank, publicly prayed that she might be allowed to refloat it, in proof of her perfect chastity; and did so.[5] Against her achievement may be set that of Claudius Pulcher's sister. She was riding through the crowded streets in a carriage, and making such slow progress that she shouted: 'If only my brother were alive to lose another fleet! That would thin out the population a little!' She was consequently tried for treason in the People's Court, as had happened to no woman before her.[6] All these Claudians were aristocrats and pillars of the patrician party, with the sole exception of Publius Clodius, who found he could best expel Cicero from Rome by becoming the adoptive son of a plebeian – as it happened, a man younger than himself.[7] Moreover, they were so rude and violent in their attitude towards the commons that, not even when tried on a capital charge, would any of them condescend to wear suppliant dress or sue for mercy; and some, in their constant quarrels with the tribunes of the people, actually dared to strike them, though their persons were officially sacrosanct. Once, when a Claudian was about to celebrate a triumph without first obtaining the commons' consent, his sister, a Vestal Virgin, mounted the decorated chariot and rode with him all the way to the Capitol, thus making it sacrilege for the tribunes of the people to halt the procession.[8]

3. Tiberius was doubly a Claudian: his father having been descended from the original Tiberius Nero, and his mother from Appius Pulcher, both of them sons of Appius the Blind. His maternal grandfather had, however, been adopted into the Livian family. The Livians were originally plebeians, but had also achieved great distinction: winning eight consulships, two censorships, three triumphs, and the titles of Dictator and Master of the Horse. Among the best-known members of this House were Livius Salinator, and the two Drusi. Livius Salinator had been convicted of malpractices while Consul, and fined; yet was re-elected by the commons to a second term and even appointed Censor – whereupon he set a mark of ignominy against the names of every tribe, to register his disapproval of their fickleness.[9] The first Drusus gained this honourable surname by killing an enemy chieftain called Drausus in single combat, and it became hereditary.[10] He is also said to have brought back from Gaul, where he was a governor of praetorian rank, the gold which his ancestors had paid to the Senonians in ransom for captured Rome;[11] this contradicts the tradition that the treasure had already been redeemed by the dictator

1. 280 B.C.   2. 264 B.C.   3. 207 B.C.   4. 249 B.C.

5. 204 B.C.   6. 246 B.C.   7. 60 B.C.; see Julius Caesar 20.
8. 143 B.C.   9. 204 B.C.   10. 283 B.C.   11. 390 B.C.

Camillus. His great-great-grandson, known as 'The Senate's Patron' because of his stalwart opposition to the reforms of the Gracchi brothers, left a son who was treacherously murdered by the opposing party while carrying on the same policy in similar circumstances and with equal resolution.

4. Tiberius's father Nero, a quaestor, commanded Julius Caesar's fleet during the Alexandrian War and was largely responsible for his eventual victory. Caesar showed his appreciation by making Nero a priest, in substitution of Publius Scipio, and sent him to plant colonies in Gaul, including those of Narbo and Arelate. Yet at Caesar's death when, to prevent further rioting, all the other senators voted for an amnesty, Nero moved that rewards should be conferred on the assassins. Later he was elected praetor; but towards the end of his term two of the triumvirs, Antony and Lepidus, quarrelled among themselves; so he retained the emblems of office longer than was his legal right and followed Antony's brother Lucius, then Consul, to Perusia. When Perusia fell, only Nero of all Roman magistrates in the city scorned to capitulate. He stood loyally by his convictions, and escaped to Praeneste, thence to Neapolis, and after a vain attempt at enlisting a force of slaves with a promise of arms and freedom, took refuge in Sicily. There Sextus Pompeius was slow to grant him an audience and denied him the use of the fasces.[12] Taking offence, Nero crossed over to Greece where he joined Mark Antony. On the conclusion of peace he presently returned in Antony's train to Rome; and with him came his wife Livia Drusilla, who had borne him one son and was pregnant of another. Yet when Augustus wanted to marry Livia, Nero surrendered her to him, and died soon afterwards. The elder son was named Tiberius Nero; the younger, Drusus.

5. Some believe that Tiberius was born at Fundi, but their only evidence is that his maternal grandmother originated there, and that a statue of Fortune has since been set up in the town by decree. The bulk of trustworthy opinion makes him born on the Palatine Hill in the course of the civil war which was to be decided at Philippi; the date being given as 16 November, and the Consuls as Marcus Aemilius Lepidus and Lucius Munatius Plancus – the latter for his second term. Both date and birthplace are, indeed, recorded in the Calendar and the official gazette; yet some writers still insist that he was born in the previous year,

12. Emblems of office.

during the consulship of Hirtius and Pansa, or in the following year, during that of Servilius Isauricus and Mark Antony's brother Lucius.

6. His childhood and youth were beset with hardships and difficulties, because Nero and Livia took him wherever they went in their flight from Augustus. At Neapolis, as they secretly slipped down to the port, he nearly betrayed them twice by crying, when their companions tried to assist them in their peril by snatching little Tiberius first from his nurse's breast, and then from Livia's arms. He was next hurried all over Sicily and Greece, where his parents entrusted him to the public care of the Spartans, who happened to be clients of the Claudii. But while Livia was escaping with him from Sparta by night he almost lost his life when she ran into a sudden forest fire which scorched her hair and part of her robe. The presents which were given him in Sicily by Sextus Pompeius's sister Pompeia, a cloak, a brooch, and some gold plaques, are still preserved and exhibited at Baiae. On their return to Rome, a senator named Marcus Gallius made a will adopting Tiberius; he accepted the inheritance, but soon dropped the name of Gallius, the testator having been one of Augustus's political opponents.

At the age of nine Tiberius mounted on the Rostra to deliver his father's funeral eulogy, and four or five years later took part in Augustus's triumph after Actium, mounted on the left trace-horse of his decorated chariot, while Marcellus, Octavia's son, rode the right. He also presided at the City Festival and led the detachment of elder boys in the Troy Game at the Circus.

7. The principal events between Tiberius's coming of age and his accession to the throne may be summarized as follows. He staged a gladiatorial contest in memory of his father Nero, and another in memory of his grandfather Drusus. The first took place in the Forum, the second in the amphitheatre; and he persuaded some retired gladiators to appear with the rest, by paying them 1,000 gold pieces each. There were theatrical performances, too, but Tiberius did not attend them. Livia and Augustus financed these lavish entertainments.

Tiberius married Vipsania Agrippina, daughter of Augustus's admiral Marcus Agrippa and granddaughter of Caecilius Atticus, the Roman knight to whom Cicero addressed many of his letters. It proved a happy marriage; but when Vipsania had already borne him a son, Drusus, whose paternity he acknowledged, and found herself pregnant again, he was

Towns

Apart from warfare, the foundation of new towns, or the re-foundation of existing ones, was the principal means of spreading the Roman way of life in the conquered provinces of the Empire.

Many Roman statesmen and generals, and even some Emperors, as well as authors, among them Suetonius, were born and grew up in such provincial towns, and the Romans had little doubt that civilized life could not take place without towns.

Towns represented both the most positive, and the most negative, even destructive elements of Roman culture.

In any town of importance, theatrical performances of various types were a regular occurrence; they ranged from the production of classical Greek and Roman tragedies and comedies[5] to less serious but more popular dramatic displays such as those mentioned by Suetonius (Nero 12, for example). Chariot-racing[6] was another popular diversion, and it became almost a political institution in the city of Rome: for it became customary that on the occasion of races at which the Emperor was present, the people would voice their various expectations and discontents in the hope that a remedy would be found – as often it was, seeing that by this means an angry crowd could, at least for the time being, be placated. Chariot-racing and gladiatorial displays, while being valued as entertainment, also had the function of bringing the inhabitants of a town together, seated according to their rank: senators, priests, knights, soldiers and the remainder of the people were accommodated in the auditorium in seats which denoted their station within the social order.

In an autocratic state where communications were often poor, public displays therefore had very considerable symbolic significance: they mirrored the order of society, and thereby validated it and made it convincing, be it in Rome or in any provincial town. The attention which Augustus was prepared to pay to these displays (Augustus 45) thus expressed something beyond an interest in the performance in itself or courtesy to the other spectators: with the fine sensitivity to the political and social aura of his day for which he was noted, Augustus, by attending the games, accepted and laid claim to his own pre-eminent position.

In later centuries, public displays were not without reason one of the features of the Roman order which were singled out for criticism by Christians – by people, that is, who, even if not explicitly, disagreed in principle with many fundamental aspects of Roman social and political organization. This disagreement was voiced about the weakest link in the complex structure that was the Roman Empire, that is, the

1. Tall buildings in a town; painting from a villa at Boscoreale ▶

2. Architectural perspectives;
paintings in Nero's Golden House

3. Town and country;
paintings from a villa at Boscoreale

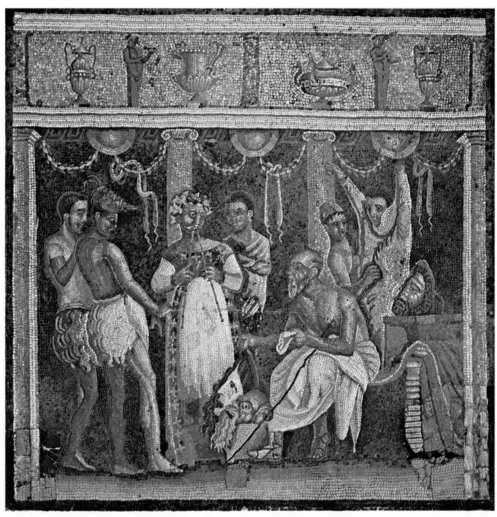

5. Playwright and actors; mosaic from Pompeii

6. A chariot race; mosaic found in Barcelona

7. The harbour of a Roman town; painting from Stabiae

8. The Roman Forum; the three surviving columns of the Temple of Castor and Pollux above the steps of the Basilica Julia

9. A street in Pompeii

10. The Roman theatre at Leptis Magna, North Africa

Empire's failure to contain violence. For violence did not happen only in warfare. It happened in the struggles for the imperial office which Suetonius describes, and it happened, in ritualized form, in the regular contests of the public games, gladiatorial shows, naval battles, and wild-beast hunts (Julius 39; Augustus 43; Gaius 18 etc.), which at times exploded into rioting. This was the destructive element in Roman city life and Roman culture, and was an ineradicable part of that culture.

The public shows and games of Roman towns played out certain aspects of the Roman order in a concentrated and intensified version: at the same time, the daily life of the street could be equally intense, and much more diverse. The shows stood for Rome, and for a universal empire: the life of the streets showed up the limitations of Roman grandiosity and universality. Daily pursuits continued, with a generous admixture of regional variation and of the seedy side of life, in both of which, as Suetonius narrates, even Emperors were participants (Nero 26; Otho 2).

During the first century A.D., *the population of Rome steadily rose: the newcomers were traders, slaves, individuals in search of their fortune, or in search of the food rations which were distributed to the people of the capital free of charge. This accumulation of population in Rome and other cities gave rise to new styles of urban architecture, which are often regarded as characteristic of the Roman Empire: spaciously planned public meeting places[8], squares, theatres[10], arcaded walks, as well as street after street of crowded apartment buildings for those who could not pay for more private forms of housing.*

While average living conditions in cities could be comfortable, they were often crowded and far from ideal; the running of cities and such amenities as they did have was made possible by Roman engineering on the one hand, and Roman government on the other.

Buildings, in the Roman world as now, created life-styles, but they also created artistic vision. Innumerable architectural perspectives from the very simple[2] to the very elaborate[3], which were painted on the walls of Roman houses and palaces, bear witness to the Roman preoccupation with architectural form in terms of its function to provide habitation for human beings on the one hand and to channel perception of man-made space on the other.

But Roman towns were not just buildings, whether buildings as objects of utility or as mediating artistic vision. They were at the same time the products of life-styles and occupations which were initiated by Roman conquest and were perpetuated during the century and a half of peace in the Mediterranean world which Roman defence of the frontiers was able to achieve[7]. As the Roman slogan had it, 'to vanquish the proud', the enemies of the Roman Empire, made it possible to 'spare those who had been conquered', the inhabitants of the Empire.

Towns were the products of Roman peace, the pax Romana, *the creation and internal workings of which Suetonius describes.*

required to divorce her and hurriedly marry Augustus's daughter Julia. Tiberius took this very ill. He loved Vipsania and strongly disapproved of Julia, realizing, like everyone else, that she had felt an adulterous passion for him while still married to his father-in-law Agrippa. Tiberius continued to regret the divorce so heartily that when, one day, he accidentally caught sight of Vipsania and followed her with tears in his eyes and intense unhappiness written on his face, precautions were taken against his ever seeing her again.

At first he lived on good terms with Julia and dutifully reciprocated her love; but gradually conceived such a loathing for her that, after their child had died in infancy at Aquileia, he broke off marital relations. On the death in Germany of his brother Drusus, Tiberius brought the body back to Rome, walking in front of the coffin all the way.

8. Tiberius's civil career began with his defence, against various charges, of King Archelaus,[13] also the people of Tralles and the Thessalians, at a court presided over by Augustus. Next, he appeared before the Senate as advocate of the people of Laodicea, Thyatira, and Chios who had appealed for relief, because of losses incurred in an earthquake. When Fannius Caepio plotted against Augustus with Varro Murena, Tiberius acted as public prosecutor and secured their condemnation on a charge of high treason. Meanwhile he had undertaken two special commissions: to reorganize the defective grain supply and to inquire into the state of slave-barracks throughout Italy – the owners having made a bad name for themselves by confining lawful travellers in them, and by harbouring men who would rather pass as slaves than be drafted for military service.

9. His first campaign was fought against the Cantabrians, as a colonel; next, he took an army to the east, where he restored King Tigranes of Armenia, personally crowning him on his own official dais; then he proceeded to recover the standards, captured by the Parthians from Marcus Crassus at Carrhae. For a year or so after this Tiberius governed Gallia Comata, where barbarian raids and feuds between the chieftains had caused considerable unrest. After that he fought consecutively in the Alps, Pannonia, and Germany. The first of these campaigns brought about the subjugation of the Raetians and Vindelicians; the second that of the Breuci and Dalmatians; and in the third he took some 40,000 German prisoners, whom he brought

13. Of Cappadocia.

across the Rhine and settled in new homes on the Gallic bank. Tiberius's exploits were rewarded with an ovation, followed by a regular triumph; and it seems that what was then a novel honour had previously been conferred on him, namely triumphal regalia. He became in turn quaestor, praetor, and Consul, almost without an interval, and always before he was old enough to qualify officially as a candidate. A few years later he held another consulship, and was given the tribunician power for a five-year period.

10. Yet, though in the prime of life, in excellent health, and at the height of his career, Tiberius suddenly decided to go into retirement, and withdraw as completely as possible from state affairs. His motive may have been an inveterate dislike of Julia, whom he dared not charge with adultery or divorce on any other grounds; or it may have been a decision not to bore his fellow-countrymen by remaining too long in the public eye – perhaps he even hoped to increase his reputation by a prolonged absence from Rome, so that if the need of his services were ever felt he would be recalled. Another view is that since Augustus's grandchildren Gaius and Lucius, now also his adopted sons, had recently come of age, Tiberius voluntarily resigned his established position as second man in the Empire and left the political field open for them. This was, in fact, the reason which he afterwards gave, and their father Agrippa had done much the same when Augustus's nephew Marcellus began his official career – retiring to the island of Mytilene so as not to overshadow Marcellus by his great reputation, or be mistaken for a rival. At the time, however, Tiberius applied for leave of absence merely on the ground that he was weary of office and needed a rest; nor would he consider either Livia's express pleas for him to stay, or Augustus's open complaints in the Senate that this was an act of desertion. On the contrary, he defeated their vigorous efforts to blunt his resolution, by a four days' hunger-

ROME AT WAR. *The triumphal monument of Trajan at Adamklissi records the course of Roman warfare and its effects.*
65 (top left). *Two Dacian women, one with a baby.*
66 (top right). *Roman horseman in chain mail.*
67 (bottom left). *Roman soldier with short sword fighting a Dacian; a wounded Dacian sits on the ground.*
68 (bottom right). *Dacian prisoners.*

strike. In the end he sailed off: and leaving Julia and Drusus, his son by Vipsania, behind at Rome, hurried down to Ostia without saying a word to any of the friends who came to say goodbye, and kissing only very few of them before he went aboard his ship.

11. As Tiberius coasted past Campania, news reached him that Augustus was ill; so he cast anchor for a while. But when tongues began to wag, accusing him of standing by in the hope of seizing the throne, he at once made the best of his way to Rhodes, though the wind was almost dead against him. He had cherished pleasant memories of that beautiful and healthy island since touching there, during his return voyage from Armenia, many years before; and contented himself with a modest town house and a nearby country villa which was not on a grand scale either. Here he behaved most unassumingly: after dismissing his lictors and runners he would often stroll about the gymnasium where he greeted and chatted with simple Greeks almost as if they were his equals.

It happened once that, in arranging the next day's programme, he had expressed a wish to visit the local sick. His staff misunderstood him. Orders went out that all the patients in town should be carried to a public colonnade and there arranged in separate groups according to their ailments. Tiberius was shocked; for a while he stood at a loss, but at last went to see the poor fellows, apologizing even to the humblest and least important for the inconvenience he had caused them.

In Rhodes he exercised his tribunician power on a single recorded occasion only. It was his custom to attend the schools and halls where professors of philosophy lectured, and listen to the ensuing discussions. Once, when two sophists had started a violent argument, an impudent member of the audience dared abuse him for joining in and appearing to support one sophist at the expense of the other. Tiberius slowly retired to his house, from which he all at once reappeared with a group of lictors; then, instructing a herald to summon the scurrilous wretch before his tribunal, presently ordered him off to gaol.

Soon afterwards, Tiberius learned that Julia had been banished for immoral and adulterous behaviour, and that his name had been used by Augustus on the bill of divorce sent her. The news delighted him, but he felt obliged to send a stream of letters urging a reconciliation between Augustus and her; and though well aware that Julia deserved all she got, allowed her to keep whatever presents she had at any time received

from him. When the term of his tribunician power expired he asked Augustus's leave to return and visit his family, whom he greatly missed; and confessed at last that he had settled in Rhodes only because he wished to avoid the suspicion of rivalry with Gaius and Lucius. Now that both were fully grown and the acknowledged heirs to the throne, he explained, his reasons for keeping away from Rome were no longer valid. Augustus, however, turned down the plea, telling him to abandon all hope of visiting his family, whom he had been so eager to desert.

12. Thus Tiberius remained, most unwillingly, in Rhodes; and could hardly persuade Livia to wheedle him the title of ambassador from Augustus, as an official cloak for his disfavour.

His days were now clouded with danger and fear. Although he lived a quiet private life in the country, wishing to avoid contact with all important men who landed, unwelcome attentions continued to be paid him; because no general or magistrate sailing along the southern coast of Asia Minor ever failed to break his journey at Rhodes. Besides, he had even greater reasons for anxiety. When Tiberius had visited Samos to greet his step-son Gaius Caesar, Governor of the East, the slanders spread by Marcus Lollius, Gaius's guardian, ensured him a chilly welcome. Again, some centurions of Tiberius's creation, who had returned to camp from leave, were said to have circulated mysterious messages to a number of persons, apparently incitements to treason. When Augustus informed Tiberius of this suspicion, he answered with reiterated demands that some responsible person, of whatever rank, should be detailed to visit Rhodes and there keep unceasing watch on what he did and said.

13. Tiberius discontinued his usual exercise on horseback and on foot in the parade ground; wore a Greek cloak and slippers instead of Roman dress; and for two years, or longer, grew daily more despised and shunned – until the people of Nemausus were encouraged to overturn his statues and busts. One day, at a private dinner party attended by Gaius Caesar, Tiberius's name cropped up, and a guest rose to say that if Gaius gave the order he would sail straight to Rhodes and 'fetch back the Exile's head' – for he had come to be known simply as 'the Exile'. This incident brought home to Tiberius that his situation was not only worrying but perilous, and he pleaded most urgently for a recall to Rome; Livia supported him with equal warmth, and Augustus at last gave way. But this was partly due to a fortunate chance: Augustus had

left the final decision on Tiberius's case to Gaius, who happened at the time to be on rather bad terms with Lollius, and therefore did as Augustus wished, though stipulating that Tiberius should take no part, and renounce all interest, in politics.

14. So Tiberius returned to Rome after an absence of more than seven years, with the same unshaken belief in a glorious future that certain presages and prophecies had fixed in his mind since early childhood. Just before his birth, for instance, Livia had tried various means of foretelling whether her child would be male or female; one was to take an egg from underneath a broody hen and warm it alternately in her own hands and in those of her women – and she successfully hatched a cock-chick which already had a fine comb. Also, while Tiberius was a mere infant, Scribonius the astrologer prophesied for him an illustrious career and a crownless kingship – though, of course, nobody in those days knew that the Caesars would soon become kings in all but name. Again, when he first commanded an army,[14] and was marching through Macedonia into Syria, the altars consecrated by the victorious Caesarians at Philippi, twenty-two years previously, were suddenly crowned with spontaneous fires. Later, on his way to Illyricum, he stopped near Patavium to visit Geryon's oracle; there he drew a lot which advised him to throw golden dice into the fountain of Aponus, if he wished his inquiries to be answered. He did so, and made the highest possible cast; one can still see the same dice shining through the water. Finally, a few days before the letter arrived recalling him from Rhodes, an eagle – a bird never previously seen in the island – perched upon the roof of his house; and on the very eve of this welcome news the tunic into which he was changing seemed to be ablaze. When the ship hove in sight Tiberius happened to be strolling along the cliffs with Thrasyllus the learned astrologer, whom he had made a member of his household. Now, Tiberius was losing faith in Thrasyllus's powers of divination, and regretted having rashly confided secrets to him; for, despite his rosy predictions, everything seemed to be going wrong. Thrasyllus was, indeed, in immediate danger of being pushed over the cliff when he pointed out to sea and announced that the distant ship brought good news; a lucky stroke which persuaded Tiberius of his trustworthiness.

15. On his return to Rome Tiberius introduced his son Drusus to public life, but immediately afterwards

moved from the house of the Pompeys in the 'Keels' to another residence in the Gardens of Maecenas on the Esquiline Hill where he lived in strict retirement merely looking after his private affairs and undertaking no official duties. Before three years had passed, however, Gaius and Lucius Caesar were both dead; Augustus then adopted Tiberius as a son, along with Agrippa Postumus, their only surviving brother; and Tiberius was himself obliged to adopt his nephew Germanicus. He thereupon ceased to act as the head of the Claudian family, surrendering all the privileges which this position entailed; and, because now theoretically in pupillage to his adoptive father Augustus, made no more gifts, freed no more slaves, and did not even accept any inheritances and legacies, apart from entering them as an addition to his personal property.[15] Yet Augustus did everything possible to advance Tiberius's reputation, especially after having to disown Agrippa Postumus; for by this time it had become pretty clear who the next Emperor must be.

16. Tiberius was given another three years of tribunician power, with the task of pacifying Germany; and the Parthian envoys who visited Augustus at Rome, with messages from their King, were instructed to present themselves before Tiberius, too, in Germany. There followed the Illyrian revolt, which he was sent to suppress, and which proved to be the most bitterly fought of all foreign wars since Rome had defeated Carthage. Tiberius conducted it for three years at the head of fifteen legions and a correspondingly large force of auxiliaries. Supplies were always short, and conditions arduous; but, though often called back to Rome, he never allowed the powerful and adjacent enemy forces to assume the offensive. Tiberius was well paid for his stubbornness, by finally reducing the whole of Illyricum – a stretch of country enclosed by Italy, Noricum, the Danube, Thrace, Macedonia, and the Adriatic Sea – to complete submission.

17. This feat appeared in a still more glorious light when Quinctilius Varus fell in Germany with his three legions: but for the timely conquest of Illyricum, most people realized, the victorious Germans would have made common cause with the Pannonians. Tiberius was therefore voted a triumph and many other distinctions. Proposals were made for decreeing him the

15. i.e., treating them as *peculium*, the savings of a son under his father's control (or of a slave), which technically belonged to his father (or master).

surname Pannonicus, or 'the Unconquered', or 'the Devoted'; but Augustus vetoed all these in turn, promising on each occasion that Tiberius would be satisfied with what he intended to bequeath him. Tiberius himself postponed his triumph because of the public mourning for Varus; but entered Rome dressed in a senatorial gown and wreathed with laurel. A tribunal had been built in the Enclosure; on it were four chairs of state, behind which the Senate stood, ranged in a semicircle. Tiberius mounted the steps and took his seat at Augustus's side, the two outer chairs being occupied by the Consuls. From this place of honour he greeted the populace, and was then escorted around the appropriate temples.

18. In the following year Tiberius visited Germany and, finding that the disaster there had been due to Varus's rashness and neglect of precautions against surprise, refrained from taking any strategic decisions without the assent of his military council. This was a notable departure from habit; hitherto he had always had complete confidence in his own independent judgement, but was now relying on a large body of advisers. He also took more elaborate precautions than usual. At every crossing of the Rhine he strictly limited the amount of permissible baggage, and would not signal the advance unless he had first inspected every transport wagon, to make sure that none carried anything but what was permitted and necessary. Once across the river, he made it his practice to eat on the bare turf, slept in the open as often as not, and always committed his Daily and Emergency Orders to writing. Moreover, any officer who was in doubt about any matter was required to consult him personally at any hour of the day or night.

19. Tiberius imposed the severest discipline on his men: reviving obsolete methods of punishment or branding them with ignominy for misbehaviour. He even degraded a legionary commander because he had sent a few soldiers across the river as escort for one of his freedmen who was hunting there. Although leaving so little to fortune and chance, Tiberius would enter a battle with far greater confidence if, on the previous

69. A ROMAN DEFEAT
Cenotaph of Marcus Caelius from Bologna, one of the fallen in the 'war of Varus' (quoting the inscription). It was erected by the dead man's brother. (Bonn, Rheinisches Landesmuseum.)

night, the lamp by which he was working went out all of a sudden, without human agency; he used to say that he and his fighting ancestors had always found this a reliable omen of good luck. At the conclusion of his campaign an assassin of the tribe of the Bructeri gained admittance to headquarters, disguised as an attendant, but betrayed himself by nervousness and confessed under torture.

20. Two years after going to Germany Tiberius returned and celebrated the postponed Illyrian triumph; and with him went those generals whom he had recommended for triumphal regalia. He dismounted and knelt at the feet of his adoptive father before proceeding up the Capitoline Hill to the Temple of Jupiter. Tiberius showed gratitude to the Pannonian leader Bato, who had chivalrously allowed the Roman army to escape when trapped in a gorge, by giving him rich presents and a home at Ravenna. Then he provided a thousand-table public banquet, and gave three gold pieces to every male guest. The money fetched by the sale of his spoils went to restore the Temple of Concord and that of the Heavenly Twins; both buildings being rededicated in his own name and that of his dead brother Drusus.

21. Soon afterwards the Consuls introduced a measure which gave Tiberius joint control of the provinces with Augustus, and the task of assisting him to carry out the next five-year census. When the usual purificatory sacrifices had been completed he set off for Illyricum; but was immediately recalled by Augustus, whom he found in the throes of his last illness. They spent a whole day together in confidential talk. I am well aware of the story that, when Tiberius finally took his departure, Augustus's attendants overheard him saying: 'Poor Rome, doomed to be masticated by those slow-moving jaws!' I am also aware that, according to some writers, he so frankly disliked Tiberius's dour manner as to interrupt his own careless chatter whenever he entered; and that, when begged by Livia to adopt her son, he is suspected of having agreed the more readily because he selfishly foresaw that, with a successor like Tiberius, his death would be increasingly regretted as the years went by. Yet how could so prudent and far-sighted an Emperor have acted as blindly as this in a matter of such importance? My belief is that Augustus weighed Tiberius's good qualities against the bad, and decided that the good tipped the scale; he had, after all, publicly sworn that his adoption of Tiberius was in the national interest, and had often referred to him as an outstanding general and

THE TRIUMPH OF TIBERIUS. *The triumph was the highest honour which a Roman general could receive.*
70 (above). *Tiberius in his triumphal chariot. Silver cup from Boscoreale.* (Paris, Collection Rothschild.)
71 (left). *Triumphal arch of Orange of the Tiberian period, displaying captured arms.*

the only one capable of defending Rome against her enemies. In support of my contention let me quote the following passages from Augustus's correspondence:

... Goodbye, my very dear Tiberius, and the best of luck go with you in your battles on my behalf – and the Muses! Goodbye, dearest and bravest of men and the most conscientious general alive! If anything goes wrong with you, I shall never smile again!

*

... Your summer campaigns, dear Tiberius, deserve my heartiest praise; I am sure that no other man alive could have conducted them more capably than yourself in the face of so many difficulties and the war-weariness of the troops. All those who served with you agree with me that Ennius's well-known line about Quintus Fabius Cunctator should be amended in your favour, *Alone he saved us by his watchful eye.*[16]

*

... If any business comes up that demands unusually careful thought, or that annoys me, I swear by the God of Truth that I miss my dear Tiberius more than I can say. And the Homeric tag runs in my head:

If he came with me, such his wisdom is,
We should escape the fury of the fire.

*

... When people tell me, or I read, that constant campaigning is wearing you out, damnation take me if I don't get goose-flesh in sympathy! I beg you to take things easy, because if you were to fall ill the news would kill your mother and me, and the whole country would be endangered by doubts about its leadership.

*

... My state of health is of little importance compared with yours. I pray that the Gods will always keep you safe and sound for us, if they have not taken an utter aversion to Rome.

22. Tiberius revealed Augustus's death only after getting rid of young Agrippa Postumus, whom the colonel appointed to guard him in the prison island had received a written order to execute. So much is known, but some doubt remains whether this order was left by Augustus to be acted on when he died; or whether Livia wrote it in his name; or whether, if so, Tiberius knew anything of the matter. At all events, when the colonel arrived to report that he had done his duty, Tiberius disowned the order and threatened to make him answerable for this unauthorized execution. Tiberius was, it seems, trying merely to avoid immediate unpopularity; for he shelved the inquiry and allowed the incident to be forgotten.

23. With Agrippa out of the way, Tiberius used his tribunician power to convene the Senate and break the news of Augustus's death. After reading a few words of a prepared speech, he suddenly groaned aloud and, protesting that grief had robbed him of his voice and that he wished his life would also be taken, handed the scroll to his son Drusus the Younger, who finished the task. Augustus's will was then brought in, and a freedman read it aloud; all senators present who had witnessed the document being first called upon to acknowledge their seals – witnesses of lower rank

would presently do the same outside the House. The preamble to the will ran as follows: 'Since fate has cruelly carried off my sons Gaius and Lucius, Tiberius shall inherit two-thirds of my property ...' This wording strengthened the suspicion that Augustus had nominated Tiberius as his successor only for want of any better choice.

24. Tiberius did not hesitate to exercise imperial power immediately by calling on the Praetorians to provide him with a bodyguard; which was to be Emperor in fact and in appearance. Yet a long time elapsed before he assumed the position of Emperor. When his friends urged him to accept it he went through the farce of scolding them for the suggestion, saying that they did not realize what a monstrous beast the monarchy was; and kept the Senate guessing by his carefully evasive answers and hesitations, even when they threw themselves at his feet imploring him to change his mind. This made some of them lose patience, and in the confusion a voice was heard shouting: 'Oh, let him either take it or leave it!' And another senator openly taunted him with: 'Some people are slow to do what they promise; you are slow to promise what you have already done.' Finally, with a great show of reluctance, and complaints that they were forcing him to become a miserable and overworked slave, Tiberius accepted the title of Emperor; but hinted that he might later resign it. His actual words were: 'Until I grow so old that you may be good enough to grant me a respite.'

25. His hesitation was caused by fear of the dangers that threatened him from many quarters, and often led him to declare that he was holding a wolf by the ears. One Clemens, a slave of Agrippa Postumus, had recruited a fairly large force to avenge his dead master; Lucius Scribonius Libo, a nobleman, was secretly planning a revolt; and mutinies now broke out in Illyricum and Germany. Both bodies of mutineers demanded very large concessions – particularly that they should be paid at the same rate as the Praetorian guardsmen. The army in Germany also refused to acknowledge an Emperor whom they had not chosen themselves, and did all they could to make their commander, Germanicus, accept the supreme office despite his flat refusal. A fear that they might succeed was the main reason for Tiberius's plea to the Senate: 'Pray assign me any part in the government you please; but remember that no single man can bear the whole burden of Empire – I need a colleague, or perhaps several colleagues.' He then gave out that he was

16. *Vigilando*, by being watchful; the word in the original was *cunctando*, by delaying.

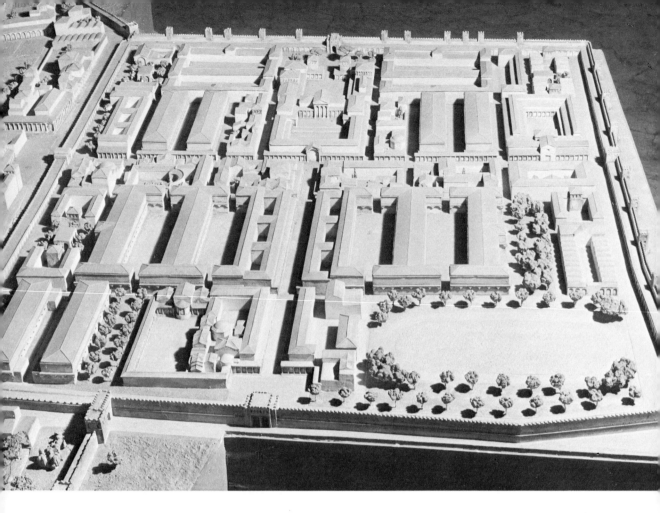

THE PRAETORIAN GUARD. *The presence of the Praetorian Guard in the centre of Rome made the military foundations of imperial government an ever present and not always welcome reality to the citizens.*
72. Model of the camp of the Praetorian Guards in Rome. Outer wall of the camp of the Praetorian Guards, which was integrated into the town walls of Rome in the late third century.

dangerously ill, so that Germanicus would wait with more patience for an early succession, or at least a share in the sovereignty. However, both mutinies were suppressed; Tiberius tricked Clemens into surrender; and in the following year he finally brought Libo in front of a Senatorial Court – though hitherto he had merely kept on his guard, not feeling powerful enough to take active measures against him. Thus, when Libo took part in a sacrifice among the priests, Tiberius, who was with him, had substituted a leaden knife for the sharp

double-bladed steel one which Libo would use; and later refused his plea for a private audience unless Drusus the Younger was present, and even then pretended to need the support of Libo's arm as they walked up and down together, and clung tightly to it.

26. These immediate anxieties past, Tiberius at first behaved with great discretion, and almost as modestly as if he had never held public office. Of the many high honours voted him, he accepted none but a few unimportant ones, and could hardly be persuaded to let his birthday, which fell on the day of the Plebeian Games, be honoured by the addition of a two-horse chariot to the state procession in the Circus. He vetoed all bills for the dedication of temples and priests to his divinity, and reserved the right to sanction even the setting up of his statues and bust – which might not be placed among the images of the gods, but lodged in temples merely as adornments. Proposals that all citizens should swear to approve his past and future actions, and that the months of September and October

should be renamed respectively 'Tiberius' and 'Livius' (after his mother) met with his veto. He also declined to set the title 'Imperator' before his name, or 'Father of His Country' after; or to let the Civic Crown – which had been voted to Augustus for preserving the lives of his fellow-citizens – be fixed above his own palace door; and even refrained from using the title 'Augustus', though his by right of inheritance, in any letters except those addressed to foreign monarchs and princes.[17] On becoming Emperor, he held no more than three consulships[18]: one for a few days, the next for three months, and the third – during his absence in Capreae – from New Year until 15 May.

27. Such was his hatred of flatterers that he refused to let senators approach his litter, whether in greeting or on business; and one day, when an ex-Consul came to apologize for some fault and tried to embrace his knees in suppliant fashion, Tiberius retreated so

17. This is not correct.   18. A.D. 18, 21 and 31.

A ROMAN PROVINCE: THE WAR MACHINE
73 (left). *Two German captives on a column base from the Roman legionary camp at Mainz.* (Mainz, Mittelrheinisches Landesmuseum.)
74 (right). *Roman cavalryman riding over a fallen enemy. This was a widely spread iconography, which spells out the impersonality of warfare. Tombstone of a Roman soldier.* (Mainz, Mittelrheinisches Landesmuseum.)

A ROMAN PROVINCE: DAILY LIFE. *The tastes of Italy were to some extent reflected in the Roman provinces, but indigenous lifestyles outlasted Roman conquest.*

75 (opposite). *The master of an estate dressed in indigenous clothes returns from the hunt and receives the payments of his tenants. The pilasters and capitals which frame the reliefs imitate Italian designs. (Trier, Landesmuseum.)*

76 (top left). *The ship-owner Blussus and his wife Menimane with their son. Their names and attire are Celtic, but the inscription is in Latin. Tombstone, c. A.D. 50. (Mainz, Mittelrheinisches Landesmuseum.)*

77 (top right). *The Three Mothers, Celtic goddesses of fertility, holding fruits on their laps are honoured with a votive relief bearing a Latin inscription. The donors, a married couple and their son, are shown in the background. (Bonn, Rheinisches Landesmuseum.)*

78 (right). *Potter's invoice using a mixture of Celtic and Roman letters. (Rodez, Musée Fénaille.)*

hurriedly that he tumbled over backwards. And if any-one, either in conversation or a speech, spoke of him in too fulsome terms, Tiberius would interrupt and sternly correct the phrase. Once, when addressed as 'My Lord and Master', he gave warning that no such insult must ever again be thrown at him. Another man referred to 'your sacred occupations', and a third said that he had 'approached the Senate by his authority'; Tiberius made them change these words to 'your laborious occupations' and 'his advice'.

28. He was, moreover, quite unperturbed by abuse, slander, or lampoons on himself and his family, and would often say that liberty to speak and think as one pleases is the test of a free country. When the Senate asked that those who had offended in this way should be brought to book, he replied: 'We cannot spare the time to undertake any such new enterprise. Open that window, and you will let in such a rush of denunciations as to waste your whole working day; everyone will take this opportunity of airing some private feud.' A remarkably modest statement of his is recorded in the *Proceedings of the Senate*: 'If So-and-so challenges me, I shall lay before you a careful account of what I have said and done; if that does not satisfy him, I shall reciprocate his dislike of me.'

29. All this was the more noteworthy, because Tiberius showed an almost excessive courtesy when addressing individual senators, and the House as a body. Once, on the floor of the House, he found himself disagreeing with Quintus Haterius, and said: 'You will, I hope, forgive me if I trespass on my rights as a senator by speaking rather more plainly than I should.' Then he turned to the House with: 'Let me repeat, gentlemen, that a right-minded and true-hearted statesman who has had as much sovereign power placed in his hands as you have placed in mine, should regard himself as the servant of the Senate; and often of the people as a whole; and sometimes of private citizens, too. I do not regret this view, because I have always found you to be generous, just, and indulgent masters.'

30. He even made a pretence at restoring popular liberties by seeing that the Senate and magistrates enjoyed their former dignities; and by referring all public and private business, however important or un-important, to the House, asking for advice in every mat-ter that concerned the national revenue, the allocation of monopolies, and the construction or repair of public buildings. He actually consulted them about the draft-ing or disbanding of troops, the stationing of legions and auxiliaries, the extension of military commands, the choice of generals to conduct particular campaigns, and how to answer letters from foreign potentates. When the commander of a cavalry squadron was accused of robbery with violence, Tiberius compelled him to plead his case before the Senate. He always entered the House unattended, except for one day when he was sick and carried in on a litter; and even then he dismissed his bearers immediately.

31. If decrees were passed in defiance of his wishes, he abstained from complaint: for example, when he had insisted that city magistrates should stay at home and transact their official business, but the Senate allowed a praetor-elect to travel overseas, with the privileges of an ambassador. And on expressing the opinion that a road could rightfully be made at Trebia with a legacy bequeathed the city towards the building of a new theatre, he was overruled and the testator's intentions were respected. Once it happened that the Senate put a motion to the vote; Tiberius went into the minority lobby and not a soul followed him.

He left a great deal of public business to the magi-strates and the ordinary processes of law; and the Con-suls grew so important again that an African delegation came before them, complaining that they could make no headway with Caesar, to whom they had been sent. Nor was this at all remarkable; everyone knew that he even stood up when the Consuls appeared, and made way on meeting them in the streets.

32. Some governors of consular rank earned a rebuff by addressing their dispatches to Tiberius rather than the Senate and asking him to approve awards of mili-tary honours as though they were not entitled to give these at their own discretion. He also congratulated a praetor who, when he assumed office, revived the ancient custom of publicly eulogizing his own ances-tors; and he attended the funerals of important citizens, to the extent of witnessing their cremation. Tiberius never presumed on his position by riding rough-shod over men of lesser rank. He summoned to Rome the Rhodian magistrates who had sent him a public report without adding the usual complimentary formula, yet did not reprimand them when they appeared; merely instructing them to repair the omis-sion, and sending them home again. During his stay at Rhodes a professor of literature named Diogenes used to lecture every Sabbath – and, when Tiberius wanted to hear him some other day of the week, sent a slave out to say: 'Come back on the seventh day!' Diogenes now turned up at Rome and waited at the Palace door to pay Tiberius his respects; Tiberius's

only revenge was a mild message: 'Come back in the seventh year.' He answered some governors who had written to recommend an increase in the burden of provincial taxation, with: 'A good shepherd shears his flock; he does not flay them.'

33. Very gradually Tiberius showed that he was the real ruler of the Empire, and though at first his policy was not always consistent, he nevertheless took considerable pains to be helpful and to further the national interest. At first, too, he intervened in matters of state only when abuses had to be checked; revoking certain orders published by the Senate, and sometimes offering to sit on the tribunal beside the magistrates, or at one end of the dais, in an advisory capacity. And if it came to his ears that influence was being used to acquit a criminal in some court or other, he would suddenly appear and address the jury either from the floor or from the tribunal; asking them to remember the sanctity of the Law and their oath to uphold it, and the serious nature of the crime on which their verdict was required. He also undertook to arrest any decline in public morality due to negligence or licence.

34. Tiberius cut down the expenses of public entertainments by lowering the pay of actors and setting a limit to the number of gladiatorial combats on any given festival. Once he protested violently against an absurd rise in the cost of Corinthian bronze statues, and of high-quality fish – three mullets had been offered for sale at 100 gold pieces each! His proposal was that a ceiling should be imposed on the prices of household furniture, and that market values should be annually regulated by the Senate. At the same time the aediles were to restrict the amount of food offered for sale in cook-shops and eating-houses; even banning pastry. And to set an example in his campaign against waste he often served, at formal dinner parties, half-eaten dishes left over from the day before – or only one side of a wild boar – which, he said, contained everything that the other side did.

He issued an edict against promiscuous kissing and the giving of good-luck gifts at New Year. On the receipt of such a gift he had formerly always returned one four times as valuable, and presented it personally; but he discontinued this practice when he found the whole of January becoming spoilt by a stream of gift-givers who had been denied an audience on New Year's Day.

35. An ancient Roman custom revived by Tiberius was the punishment of married women guilty of improprieties, by the decision of a family council; so long

as a public prosecutor had not intervened. When one Roman knight had sworn that he would never divorce his wife whatever she did, but found her in bed with his son, Tiberius absolved him from his oath. Married women of good family but bad reputation were beginning to ply openly as prostitutes, and to escape punishment for their adulteries by renouncing the privileges of their class; and wastrels of both the Senatorial and Equestrian Orders purposely got themselves reduced in rank so as to evade the law forbidding their appearance on the stage or in the arena. All such offenders were now exiled, which discouraged any similar sheltering behind the letter of the law. Tiberius degraded a senator on hearing that he had left Rome just before the first of July,[19] in order to secure a house at a cheaper rental later on, when there would be less demand. He cancelled the quaestorship of another man who had married a woman the day before he cast lots for a province, but divorced her the next day.[20]

36. He abolished foreign cults at Rome, particularly the Egyptian and Jewish, forcing all citizens who had embraced these superstitious faiths to burn their religious vestments and other accessories. Jews of military age were removed to unhealthy regions, on the pretext of drafting them into the army; the others of the same race or of similar beliefs were expelled from the city and threatened with slavery if they defied the order. Tiberius also banished all astrologers except such as asked for his forgiveness and undertook to make no more predictions.

37. Tiberius safeguarded the country against banditry and brigandage by decreasing the distance between military posts; and at Rome provided the Praetorian Guards, who had hitherto been billeted in scattered lodging houses, with a regular camp. He also discountenanced city riots, and if any broke out, crushed them without mercy. The theatregoers had formed factions in support of rival actors, and once when their quarrels ended in bloodshed, Tiberius exiled not only the faction leaders but the actors who had been the occasion of the riot; nor would he ever give way to popular entreaties by recalling them. Trouble occurred in Pollentia, a Ligurian town at the northern foot of the Apennines, where the townsfolk would not let the corpse of a leading centurion be removed from the market-place until his heirs had agreed to meet their importunate demands for a free gladiatorial show.

19. The date for renting and letting houses and rooms.
20. Meaning uncertain.

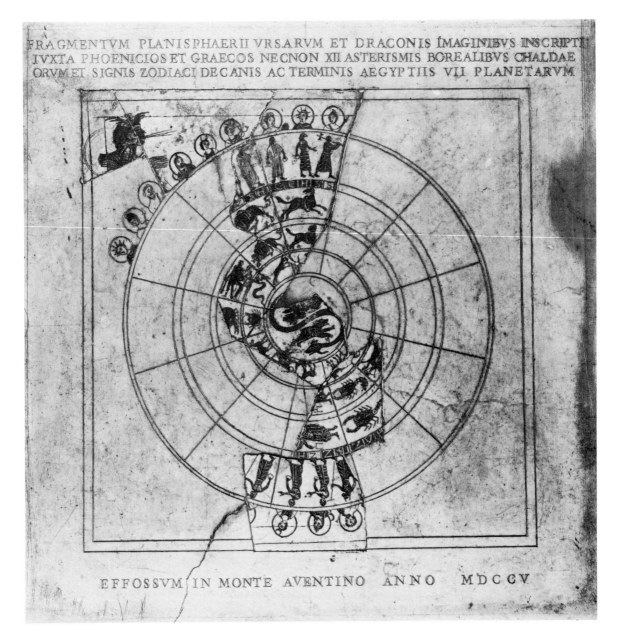

helped to crystallize and articulate whatever opposition already existed.

79 (above). *The tablet of Bianchini, from Rome, an astrological dicing board. In the centre is the constellation Draco with the Great and Little Bears. The band surrounding these shows twelve animals, one for each hour of the day; next is the zodiac, shown twice. In the next*

band, each of the twelve signs of the zodiac is subdivided into three sections, decans: a divinity rules each of the decans, as shown in this band. Round the edge are the faces of the seven planetary gods, repeated several times. (Paris, Louvre.)

80 (above). *The vault of heaven with the zodiac, held up by Egyptian divinities. In the centre is the Great Bear,* represented as the foreleg of a bull; it is held by a hippopotamus goddess. The outer circle shows the decans. Relief from the temple of Hathor, goddess of the sky, which was built in the reign of Tiberius. (Paris, Louvre.)

Tiberius detached one cohort from Rome, and another from the kingdom of Cottius, to converge on Pollentia, after disguising their destination. They had orders to enter the town simultaneously by opposite gates, suddenly display their weapons, blow trumpets, and consign most of the inhabitants and magistrates to life-imprisonment.

He also abolished the traditional right of sanctuary throughout the Empire; and punished the people of Cyzicus for their outrageous treatment of certain Roman citizens, by withdrawing the freedom conferred on them as a reward for services in the Mithridatic War. After his accession to the throne, he undertook no campaigns, but delegated the task of dealing with enemy outbreaks to his generals, sanctioning aggressive action only if it seemed unavoidable. He disciplined foreign kings suspected of ill-will towards Rome by threats and reprimands rather than punitive expeditions; and decoyed some of them with glowing promises to Rome – where they were detained at his pleasure. Among them were Maroboduus the German, Rhascuporis the Thracian, and Archelaus of Cappadocia – whose kingdom he reduced to provincial status.

38. In the first two years of his reign Tiberius did not once set foot outside the gates of Rome; and even after that the farthest town he visited was Antium, where he occasionally spent a few days. Yet he announced from time to time that he would make a tour of the provinces and inspect the troops there; and almost every year made preparations for a journey by chartering transport and requesting the Roman municipalities and colonies to have supplies of food and drink ready when he approached. At last he even allowed people to make vows for his safe return from the promised tour, which earned him the humorous nickname of 'Callipedes' – the original Callipedes having been a comic actor, famous for his realistic imitation of a long-distance runner, in which he never moved from the same spot.

39. After the loss of his son Drusus the Younger at Rome, and his adopted son Germanicus in Syria, Tiberius retired to Campania – from which almost everyone swore he would not return, but would soon die there. This prediction was not far out, because Rome had, in fact, seen the last of him, and he narrowly escaped death a few days later. He was dining at a country house called 'The Cavern',[21] near Tarracina,

21. Spelunca.

when some huge rocks fell from the roof of the natural cave which served as a banqueting hall and gave the house its name, killing several guests and attendants close to him.

40. His pretext for the progress through Campania was that he must dedicate a temple to Capitoline Jupiter at Capua, and a temple to Augustus at Nola. But, these tasks done, he crossed over to the isle of Capreae, which fascinated him by having only one small landing-beach – the remainder of its coast consisted of sheer cliffs surrounded by deep water. However, a catastrophe at Fidenae recalled him to the mainland almost at once in response to the pressing entreaties of its people: the amphitheatre had collapsed during a gladiatorial show, and more than 20,000 people lay dead in the ruins. Tiberius now gave audiences to everyone who demanded them, and was the readier to make amends because he had given orders on leaving the city some days previously that he must not be disturbed throughout his journey.

41. On his return to Capreae he let all affairs of state slide: neither filling vacancies that occurred in the Equestrian Order, nor making new appointments to senior military posts, or the governorships of any province. Spain and Syria were left without their governors of consular rank for several years. He allowed the Parthians to overrun Armenia; the Dacians and Sarmatians to ravage Moesia; and the Germans to invade Gaul – a negligence as dangerous to the Empire as it was dishonourable.

42. But having found seclusion at last, and no longer feeling himself under public scrutiny, he rapidly succumbed to all the vicious passions which he had for a long time tried, not very successfully, to disguise. I shall give a faithful account of these from the start. Even as a young officer he was such a hard drinker that his name, Tiberius Claudius Nero, was displaced by the nickname 'Biberius Caldius Mero' – meaning: 'Drinker of hot wine with no water added'. When already Emperor and busily engaged on the reform of public morals, he spent two whole days and the intervening night in an orgy of food and drink with Pomponius Flaccus and Lucius Piso – at the conclusion of which he made Flaccus Governor of Syria and Piso City Prefect: actually eulogizing them in their commissions as 'good fellows at all hours of the day or night'. Being invited to dinner by Cestius Gallus, a lecherous old spendthrift whom Augustus had ignominiously removed from the Senate and whom he had himself reprimanded only a few days previously,

LOVE AND LUCK. *Romans often viewed personal contentment with a lover and wellbeing in general, especially in relation to nature, as related to each other.*
81 (above). *A pair of lovers on a moulded bowl of the first century* A.D. (Arezzo, Museo della Confraternità dei Laici.)
82 (right). *Priapus, god of gardens and orchards, painted for good luck on the vestibule wall of the House of the Vettii at Pompeii.*

Tiberius accepted on condition that the dinner should follow Gallus's usual routine; and that the waitresses should be naked. At another banquet a very obscure candidate for the quaestorship drained a huge two-handled tankard of wine at Tiberius's challenge, whereupon he was preferred to rival candidates from the noblest families. Tiberius also paid Asellius Sabinus 2,000 gold pieces, to show his appreciation of a dialogue in which a mushroom, a fig-picker, an oyster, and a thrush took part in a competition; and established a new office, Comptroller of Pleasures, first held by a knight named Titus Caesonius Priscus.

43. On retiring to Capreae he made himself a private sporting-house, where sexual extravagances were practised for his secret pleasure. Bevies of girls and young men, whom he had collected from all over the Empire as adepts in unnatural practices, and known as *spintriae*, would copulate before him in groups of three, to excite his waning passions. A number of small rooms were furnished with the most indecent pictures and statuary obtainable, also certain erotic manuals from Elephantis in Egypt; the inmates of the establishment would know from these exactly what was expected of them. He furthermore devised little nooks of lechery in the woods and glades of the island, and had boys and girls dressed up as Pans and nymphs prostituting themselves in front of caverns or grottoes; so that the island was now openly and generally called 'Caprineum'.[22]

44. Some aspects of his criminal obscenity are

22. A play on the word *caper* (goat).

almost too vile to discuss, much less believe. Imagine training little boys, whom he called his 'minnows', to chase him while he went swimming and get between his legs to lick and nibble him. Or letting babies not yet weaned from their mother's breast suck at his breast or groin – such a filthy old man he had become! Then there was a painting by Parrhasius, which had been bequeathed him on condition that, if he did not like the subject, he could have 10,000 gold pieces instead. Tiberius not only preferred to keep the picture but hung it in his bedroom. It showed Atalanta performing fellatio with Meleager.

The story goes that once, while sacrificing, he took an erotic fancy to the acolyte who carried the incense casket, and could hardly wait for the ceremony to end before hurrying him and his brother, the sacred trumpeter, out of the temple and indecently assaulting them both. When they jointly protested at this disgusting behaviour he had their legs broken.

45. What nasty tricks he used to play on women, even those of high rank, is clearly seen in the case of Mallonia whom he summoned to his bed. She showed such an invincible repugnance to complying with his lusts that he set informers on her track and during her very trial continued to shout: 'Are you sorry?' Finally she left the court and went home; there she stabbed herself to death after a violent tirade against 'that filthy-mouthed, hairy, stinking old man'. So a joke at his expense, slipped into the next Atellan farce, won a loud laugh and went the rounds at once:

> The old goat goes
> For the does
> With his tongue.

46. Tiberius was close-fisted to the point of miserliness, never paying his staff a salary when on a foreign mission, but merely providing their keep. On the sole occasion that he behaved liberally to these friends of his, Augustus bore the expense. Tiberius then arranged them in three categories according to their rank; the first were given 6,000 gold pieces, the second 4,000 and the third, whom he described not as 'his friends' but as 'his Greeks', 2,000.

47. No magnificent public works marked his reign: his only two undertakings, the erection of Augustus's Temple and the restoration of Pompey's Theatre, still remained uncompleted at the end of all those years. He hardly ever attended public shows given by others, because he gave none himself and did not want to be asked for any – especially after the crowd forced him, on one of his rare visits to the theatre, to buy the free-dom of a comic actor named Actius. Though relieving the financial distress of a few senators at his accession, he avoided having to repeat this generous act by announcing that, in future, imperial assistance would be restricted to such persons as could prove to the satisfaction of the Senate that they were not responsible for their financial embarrassment. Shame and pride then prevented many impoverished senators from making an application; among these Hortalus, grandson of the orator Quintus Hortensius, whose income was very moderate indeed but whom Augustus's impassioned pleas had encouraged to beget four children.

48. Tiberius showed large-scale generosity no more than twice. On the first occasion he offered a public loan of a million gold pieces, free of interest, for three years, because a decree which he had persuaded the Senate to pass – ordering all money-lenders to invest two-thirds of their capital in agricultural land, provided that their debtors at once disbursed in cash two-thirds of what they owed – failed to relieve the acute economic crisis. On the second occasion,[23] he paid for the rebuilding of certain blocks of houses on the Caelian Hill which had been destroyed in a fire. This, too, was an emergency measure during bad times; yet he made such a parade of his open-handedness as to rename the whole hill 'The Augustan'. After doubling the legacies bequeathed by Augustus to the army, Tiberius never gave them anything beyond their pay; except for the ten gold pieces a head which the Praetorian Guard won for not joining Sejanus's revolt, and sums awarded the legions in Syria for their refusal to set consecrated statues of Sejanus among their standards. He granted few veterans their discharge, reckoning that, if they died while still with the Colours, he would be spared the expense of the customary discharge bounty. The only free money grant any province got from him was when an earthquake destroyed some cities in Asia Minor.

49. As the years went by, this stinginess turned to rapacity. It is notorious that he forced the wealthy Gnaeus Lentulus Augur to name him as his sole heir and then to commit suicide, by playing on his nervous apprehensions; and that he gratified Quirinius,[24] a rich and childless ex-Consul, by executing the highly aristocratic Aemilia Lepida – she was Quirinius's divorced wife and he accused her of an attempt to poison him twenty years previously! Tiberius also confiscated the property of leading Spanish, Gallic, Syrian, and Greek provincials on trivial and absurd

---

23. A.D. 27.   24. The 'Cyrenius' of *Luke* II.2.

charges, such as keeping part of their wealth in ready cash.[25] He made many states and individuals forfeit their ancient immunities and mineral rights, and the privilege of collecting taxes. As for Vonones, King of Parthia, whom his subjects had dethroned but who, under the impression that he was confiding himself to Roman protection, escaped to Antioch with a huge treasure, Tiberius treacherously robbed and killed him.

50. Tiberius's first hostile action against his own family was when his brother Drusus the Elder wrote to him privately suggesting that they should jointly persuade Augustus to restore the Republican constitution; Tiberius produced the letter. Then he turned against the rest. After coming to power he showed so little loyalty or kindness for his exiled wife Julia that he did not have the decency to confirm her father's decree which merely confined her to a town, but restricted her to a single house where visitors were forbidden. He even deprived her of the annual allowance hitherto paid her by Augustus, on the pretext that no mention of this had appeared in his will and that consequently, under common law, she was no longer entitled to draw it. Tiberius then complained that his mother Livia vexed him by wanting to be co-ruler of the Empire; which was why he avoided frequent meetings or long private talks with her. Although he did occasionally need and follow Livia's advice, he disliked people to think of him as giving it serious consideration. A Senatorial decree adding 'Son of Livia' as well as 'Son of Augustus' to his honorific titles so deeply offended him that he vetoed proposals to confer 'Parent of the Country' or any similarly high-sounding title on her. What is more, he often warned Livia to remember that she was a woman and must not interfere in affairs of state. He became especially insistent on this point when a fire broke out near the Temple of Vesta and news reached him that Livia was directing the populace and soldiery in person, as though Augustus were still alive, and urging them to redouble their efforts.

51. Afterwards Tiberius quarrelled openly with his mother. The story goes that she repeatedly urged him to enrol in the jurors' list the name of a man who had been granted citizenship. Tiberius agreed to do so on one condition – that the entry should be marked 'forced upon the Emperor by his mother'. Livia lost her temper and produced from a strong-box some of Augustus's old letters to her commenting on Tiberius's

sour and stubborn character. Annoyance with her for hoarding these documents so long, and then spitefully confronting him with them, is said to have been his main reason for retirement to Capreae. At all events he visited her exactly once in the last three years of her life, and only for an hour or two at that; and when she presently fell sick, made no effort to repeat the visit. Livia then died, and he spoke of attending her funeral, but did not come. After several days her corpse grew so corrupt and noisome that he sent to have it buried; but vetoed her deification on the pretext that she had herself forbidden this. He also annulled her will, and began taking his revenge on all her friends and confidants – even those whom, as she died, she had appointed to take charge of her funeral rites – and went so far as to condemn one of them, a knight, to the treadmill.

52. Tiberius had no paternal feelings either for his son Drusus the Younger, whose vicious and dissolute habits offended him, or for his adopted son Germanicus. When Drusus died Tiberius was not greatly concerned, and went back to his usual business almost as soon as the funeral ended, cutting short the period of official mourning; in fact, when a Trojan delegation arrived with condolences somewhat belatedly, Tiberius grinned, having apparently got over his loss, and replied: 'May I condole with you, in return, on the death of your eminent fellow-citizen Hector?' Also, he described Germanicus's glorious victories as wholly ineffective, and far more than the country could afford; so little affection did he feel for him! He actually sent the Senate a letter of complaint when Germanicus hurried to Alexandria and there relieved a sudden disastrous famine, without consulting him. It is even believed that he arranged for Gnaeus Piso, the Governor of Syria, to poison Germanicus; and that Piso, when tried on this charge, would have produced his instructions had they not been taken from him when he confronted Tiberius with them, whereupon he was executed. As a result of these events, 'Give us back Germanicus!' was written on the walls throughout Rome and shouted all night. Tiberius later strengthened popular suspicion by his cruel treatment of Germanicus's wife Agrippina and her children.

53. When Agrippina said more than was wise in her complaints about her husband's death, Tiberius took her by the hand, quoting the Greek line:

And if you are not queen, my dear, have I then done you wrong?

and this was the last conversation that he ever condescended to have with her. Indeed, since she seemed

---

25. i.e., for revolutionary purposes.

scared of tasting an apple which he handed her at dinner, the invitation to his table was never repeated;
he said that she had charged him with attempted
poisoning. Yet the whole scene had been carefully
stage-managed: he would offer the apple as a test of
her feelings for him, and she would suspect that it
carried certain death, and refuse it. At last he falsely
accused her of planning to take sanctuary beside the
image of her grandfather Augustus, or with the army
abroad; and exiled her to the prison island of Pandataria. In punishment for her violent protests he ordered
a centurion to give her a good flogging; in the course
of which she lost an eye. Then she decided to starve
herself to death and, though he had her jaws prized
open for forcible feeding, succeeded. So he wickedly
slandered her memory, persuading the Senate to decree her birthday a day of ill-omen, and boasting of his
clemency in not having her strangled and thrown out
on the Stairs of Mourning. He even allowed a bill to
be passed congratulating him on this pious attitude
and voting a golden commemorative gift to Capitoline
Jupiter.

54. By Germanicus, Tiberius had three grandsons,[26] Nero, Drusus and Gaius, and another
(Tiberius) by Drusus the Younger. He recommended
Nero and Drusus, the eldest of Germanicus's sons, to
the Senate; and celebrated their coming-of-age ceremonies by giving largesse to the populace. But when
he found that, at the New Year celebrations, prayers
for their safety were being added to his own, he asked
the Senate to decide whether this was a proper procedure; suggesting that such honours should be conferred only on men who had served their country long
and meritoriously. After this he made no secret of his
dislike for the young pair and arranged that all sorts
of false charges should be brought against them; then
cleverly contrived that whenever they expressed their
natural indignation at his schemes a witness would
always be standing by. This gave him grounds for writing the Senate so harsh a complaint that both were declared public enemies and starved to death – Nero on
the island of Pontia, Drusus in a Palace cellar. It is
believed that Nero was forced to commit suicide when
an executioner, announcing that he had come with the
Senate's warrant, displayed the noose for hanging him
and the hooks for dragging his corpse to the Tiber. As
for Drusus, his hunger was such that he tried to eat
the flock from his mattress; and their bodies were

26. By adoption of Germanicus. Gaius was known as Caligula.

chopped in so many pieces that great difficulty was later
found in collecting them for burial.

55. Tiberius had asked the Senate to choose him a
Council to advise him on public affairs, consisting of
twenty men – in addition to certain old friends and intimates – only two or three of whom died natural deaths.
All the rest he killed, one way or another; including
Aelius Sejanus, who dragged many others to ruin with
him. Tiberius felt no affection for Sejanus, but had
given him plenary powers as being efficient and cunning enough to do what was required of him – namely,
to make away with Germanicus's children and ensure
that Tiberius's true grandson and namesake should
become the next Emperor.

56. He acted no less cruelly towards the Greeklings
who were his associates and whose company gave him
special pleasure. One day he asked a man named Xeno,
who had been discoursing in a rather affected style:
'What nasty dialect may that be?' 'It is Doric,' replied
Xeno. Tiberius mistook this for a taunting reference
to his own exile in Rhodes, where Doric is spoken; and
banished Xeno to the Aegean island of Cinaria. At the
dinner table he used to pose questions arising from his
daily study. Seleucus, a professor of literature, had
been finding out from the imperial servants what books
he was reading, and came prepared with all the right
answers; hearing of this, Tiberius dismissed him from
the company, and later forced him to commit suicide.

57. Some signs of Tiberius's savage and dour
character could be distinguished even in his boyhood.
Theodorus the Gadarene, who taught him rhetoric,
seems to have been the first to do so, since, on having
occasion to reprove Tiberius, he would call him 'mud,
kneaded with blood!' But after he became Emperor,
while he was still gaining popular favour by a pretence
of moderation, there could be no doubt that Theodorus had been right. Once, as a funeral procession was
passing, a humorist hailed the corpse and asked him
to tell Augustus's ghost that his bequests to the commons had not yet been duly paid. Tiberius ordered the
man to be arrested and brought before him. 'I will give
you your due at once,' he said, and ordered his execution with: 'Why not go to my father yourself and tell
him the truth about those legacies?' Soon afterwards
a Roman knight named Pompeius appeared in the
Senate to lodge a strong protest against some action
of Tiberius. Tiberius threatened imprisonment,
shouting: 'You're Pompeius, aren't you? I'll make a
Pompeian of you unless you hold your tongue!' – a

disagreeable pun on the name of Pompey the Great and the fate of his party in times gone by.

58. About this time a praetor asked Tiberius whether, in his opinion, courts should be convened to try cases of treason. Tiberius replied that the law must be enforced; and enforce it he did, most savagely, too. One man was accused of decapitating an image of Augustus with a view to substituting another head; his case was tried before the Senate and, finding a conflict of evidence, Tiberius had the witnesses examined under torture. The offender was convicted, which provided a precedent for far-fetched accusations: people could now be executed for beating a slave, or changing their own clothes, close to an image of Augustus, or for carrying a ring or coin, bearing Augustus's head, into a lavatory or a brothel; or for criticizing anything Augustus had ever said or done. The climax came when a man died merely for letting an honour be voted him by his native town council on the same day that honours had once been voted to Augustus.

59. Tiberius did so many other wicked deeds under the pretext of reforming public morals – but in reality to gratify his lust for seeing people suffer – that many satires were written against the evils of the day, incidentally expressing gloomy fears about the future; such as the following:

> You cruel monster! I'll be damned, I will,
> If even your own mother loves you still.
>
> *
>
> You are no knight – Caesar's adopted son
> May own no cash to qualify as one;
> And banishment in Rhodes cancelled your right
> To be a citizen – far less a knight.
>
> *
>
> Saturn's golden age has passed,
> Saturn's age could never last;
> Now while Caesar holds the stage
> This must be an iron age.
>
> *
>
> He is not thirsty for neat wine
> As he was thirsty then,
> But warms him up a tastier cup –
> The blood of murdered men.
>
> *
>
> Here is a Sulla, men of Rome, surnamed
> Sulla the Fortunate – to your misfortune;
> Here is a Marius come back at last
> To capture Rome; here is an Antony
> Uncivilly provoking civil strife,

> His hands thrice dyed in costly Roman blood.
> Confess: 'Rome is no more!' All who return
> To reign, from banishment, reign bloodily.

At first Tiberius dismissed these verses as the work of bilious malcontents who were impatient with his reforms and did not really mean what they said. He would remark: 'Let them hate me, so long as they respect me!' But, as time went on, his conduct justified every line they had written.

60. A few days after he came to Capreae a fisherman suddenly intruded on his solitude by presenting him with an enormous mullet, which he had lugged up the trackless cliffs at the rear of the island. Tiberius was so scared that he ordered his guards to rub the fisherman's face with the mullet. The scales skinned it raw, and the poor fellow shouted in his agony: 'Thank Heaven, I did not bring Caesar that huge crab I also caught!' Tiberius sent for the crab and had it used in the same way.

A guardsman once stole a peacock from the imperial aviary and was sentenced to death. On another occasion, during a country jaunt, the bearers of Tiberius's litter were held up by a bramble thicket; he had the senior centurion of the Praetorian Guard, whose task it was to choose the right path, stretched on the ground and flogged until he nearly died.

61. Soon Tiberius broke out in every sort of cruelty and never lacked for victims: these were, first, his mother's friends and even acquaintances; then those of his grandsons and daughter-in-law; finally, those of Sejanus. With Sejanus out of the way his savageries increased; which proved that Sejanus had not, as some thought, been inciting him to commit them, but merely providing the opportunities that he demanded. Nevertheless, in Tiberius's brief and sketchy autobiography we find him daring to assert that Sejanus had been killed because he had found him persecuting Nero and Drusus, the sons of Germanicus; the fact being that he had himself put Nero to death when Sejanus was already an object of suspicion, and Drusus after he had fallen from power. A detailed list of Tiberius's barbarities would take a long time to compile; I shall content myself with a few samples. Not a day, however holy, passed without an execution; he even desecrated New Year's Day. Many of his men victims were accused and punished with their children – some actually by their children – and the relatives forbidden to go into mourning. Special awards were voted to the informers who had denounced them and, in certain circum-

stances, to the witnesses too. An informer's word was always believed. Every crime became a capital one, even the utterance of a few careless words. A poet found himself accused of slander – he had written a tragedy which presented King Agamemnon in a bad light – and a historian had made the mistake of describing Caesar's assassins, Brutus and Cassius, as 'the last of the Romans'. Both these authors were executed without delay, and their works – though once publicly read before Augustus, and accorded general praise – were called in and destroyed. Tiberius denied those who escaped with a prison sentence not only the solace of reading books, but the privilege of talking to their fellow-prisoners. Some of the accused, on being warned to appear in court, felt sure that the verdict would be 'guilty' and, to avoid the trouble and humiliation of a trial, stayed at home and severed an artery; yet Tiberius's men bandaged their wounds and hurried them, half-dead, to prison. Others obeyed their summons and then drank poison in full view of the Senate. The bodies of all executed persons were flung on the Stairs of Mourning, and dragged to the Tiber with hooks – as many as twenty a day, including women and children. Tradition forbade the strangling of virgins; so, when little girls had been condemned to die in this way, the executioner began by violating them. Tiberius used to punish with life those who wished to die. He regarded death as a comparatively light affliction, and on hearing that a man named Carnulus had forestalled his execution by suicide, exclaimed: 'Carnulus has got away!' Once, during a gaol inspection, a prisoner begged to be put out of his misery; Tiberius replied: 'No; we are not yet friends again.' An ex-consul has recorded in his memoirs that he attended a banquet at which Tiberius was suddenly asked loudly by a dwarf, standing among a group of jesters near the table: 'What of Paconius? Why is he still alive after being charged with treason?' Tiberius told him to hold his saucy tongue; but a few days later requested the Senate to make a quick decision about Paconius's execution.

62. On eventually discovering that his own son, Drusus the Younger, had after all died, not as a result of his debauched habits, but from poison administered by his wife Livilla in partnership with Sejanus, Tiberius grew enraged and redoubled his cruelties until nobody was safe from torture and death. He spent whole days investigating the Drusus affair, which obsessed him to such a degree that when a man whose guest he had been at Rhodes arrived in response to his own friendly invitation, he mistook him for an impor-

tant witness in the case and had him put to the torture at once. When the truth came out he actually executed the man to avoid publicizing the scandal.

In Capreae they still show the place at the cliff top where Tiberius used to watch his victims being thrown into the sea after prolonged and exquisite tortures. A party of marines were stationed below, and when the bodies came hurtling down they whacked at them with oars and boat-hooks, to make sure that they were completely dead. An ingenious torture of Tiberius's devising was to trick men into drinking huge draughts of wine, and then suddenly to knot a cord tightly around their genitals, which not only cut into the flesh but prevented them from urinating. Even more people would have died, it is thought, had Thrasyllus the astrologer not persuaded him, deliberately it is said, to postpone his designs by an assurance that he still had many years of life in hand. These victims would have included his remaining grandsons, Gaius whom he suspected, and Tiberius Gemellus whom he hated as having been born from adultery. The story is credible, because he sometimes used to express envy of Priam for having outlived his entire family.

63. Much evidence is extant, not only of the hatred that Tiberius earned but of the state of terror in which he himself lived, and the insults heaped upon him. He forbade anyone to consult soothsayers, except openly and with witnesses present; and even attempted to suppress all oracles in the neighbourhood of Rome – but desisted for fear of the miraculous power shown by the sacred Lots, which he brought to Rome in a sealed chest from the Temple of Fortune at Praeneste. They vanished and did not become visible again until returned to the same temple.

THE GODDESS FORTUNA OF PRAENESTE *foretold the future by lots. The dictator Sulla built her a magnificent temple at Praeneste, of which extensive remains survive.*
83. *The temple of Fortuna at Praeneste was a round building which was approached via a series of terraces and staircases. The plan of these can be distinguished from the surviving remains. The present building above the upper terrace follows the outline of the Roman semicircular colonnade which gave access to the temple behind.*
84. *Beneath this colonnade lies a semicircular space ringed by steps where ritual dances were probably performed.*

Tiberius had assigned provinces to certain ex-Consuls whom he distrusted; but, not daring to relax his surveillance, detained them in Rome for several years until their successors had been appointed. Meanwhile, they relayed his frequent instructions to their lieutenants and agents in the provinces which they officially governed, yet were unable to visit.

64. After exiling Agrippina and her two sons he always moved them from one place of confinement to another in closed litters, with their wrists and ankles fettered and a military escort to prevent all persons met on the road from even stopping to watch the litter go by, let alone glance inside.

65. Becoming aware that Sejanus's birthday was being publicly celebrated, and that golden statues had been raised to him everywhere, as a preliminary step to his usurpation of the throne, Tiberius found some difficulty in getting rid of him and did so at last by subterfuge rather than by the exercise of imperial authority. First of all, to detach Sejanus from his own immediate entourage, while pretending to honour him, Tiberius appointed him his colleague in a fifth consulship,[27] which he assumed solely for this purpose ten years after the fourth; but did not visit Rome for his inauguration. Next, he made Sejanus believe that he would soon marry into the imperial family and be awarded tribunician power; and then, taking him off his guard, sent a shamefully abject message to the Senate begging, among other things, to be fetched into their presence under military escort by one of the two Consuls[28] – he complained that he was a lonely old man. But he had taken precautions against the revolt which he feared might yet break out, by ordering that his grandson Drusus (the son of Germanicus), who was still alive, should be released if necessary from his prison at Rome and appointed commander-in-chief. He thought, indeed, of taking refuge at the headquarters of some provincial army and had a naval flotilla standing by to carry him off the island; where he waited on a cliff top for the distant bonfire signals (announcing all possible eventualities), which he had ordered to be sent in case his couriers might be delayed. Even when Sejanus's conspiracy had been suffocated Tiberius did not show the least sign of increased confidence, but remained in the so-called Villa of Jupiter for the next nine months.

27. A.D.31.
28. i.e., the 'suffect' Consuls appointed to succeed Tiberius and Sejanus for the latter part of the year.

66. His uneasiness of mind was aggravated by a perpetual stream of reproaches from all sides; every one of his condemned victims either cursed him to his face or arranged for a defamatory notice to be posted in the theatre seats occupied by senators. His attitude to these reproaches varied markedly: sometimes shame made him want nobody to hear about the incident, sometimes he laughed and deliberately publicized it. He even had a scathing letter from Artabanus, King of Parthia, in which he was accused of murdering his immediate family, with other persons, and of slothful and dissolute living; and recommended to satisfy the intense and pardonable longings of his people, who loathed him, by committing suicide at the earliest possible moment.

67. At last, growing thoroughly disgusted with himself, he as good as confessed his misery. A letter to the Senate began in this strain. 'My lords, if I know what to tell you, or how to tell it, or what to leave altogether untold for the present, may all the gods and goddesses in Heaven bring me to an even worse damnation than I now daily suffer!' According to one body of opinion he had foreseen that he would, in time, yield to his vices and earn universal hatred or dislike; which made him, when he became Emperor, refuse, point-blank, the title 'Father of His Country' offered by the Senate, and also forbid them to swear an oath approving in advance and retrospect of whatever he said or did – for fear that his shame would be intensified when he turned out to be unworthy of such honours. This conclusion may, in fact, be deduced from his formal reply to the two proposals:

So long as my wits do not fail me, you can count on the consistency of my behaviour; but I should not like you to set the precedent of binding yourselves to approve a man's every action; for what if something happened to alter that man's character?

And again:

If you ever feel any doubts about my character or my sincere regard for you – but may I die before that happens! – the title 'Father of His Country' will not recompense me for the loss of your regard, and you will be ashamed either of having given me the title without sufficient deliberation, or of having shown inconsistency by changing your opinion of me.

68. Tiberius was strongly and heavily built, and above average height. His shoulders and chest were broad, and his body perfectly proportioned from top to toe. His left hand was more agile than the right, and so strong that he could poke a finger through a sound,

newly-plucked apple or into the skull of a boy or young man. He had a handsome, fresh-complexioned face, though subject to occasional rashes of pimples. The letting his back hair grow down over the nape seems to have been a family habit of the Claudii. Tiberius's eyes were remarkably large and possessed the unusual power of seeing at night and in the dark, when he first opened them after sleep; but this phenomenon disappeared after a minute or two. His gait was a stiff stride, with the neck poked forward, and if ever he broke his usual stern silence to address those walking with him, he spoke with great deliberation and eloquent movements of the fingers. Augustus disliked these mannerisms and put them down to pride, but frequently assured both the Senate and the commons that they were natural and not intentional defects. Tiberius enjoyed excellent health almost to the end of his reign, although after the age of thirty he never called in a doctor or asked one to send him medicine.

69. He lacked any deep regard for the gods or other religious feelings, his belief in astrology having persuaded him that the world was wholly ruled by fate. Yet thunder had a most frightening effect on Tiberius: whenever the sky wore an ugly look he would put on a laurel wreath which, he supposed, would make him lightning-proof.

70. Tiberius was deeply devoted to Greek and Latin literature. In Latin oratory, he was a follower of Messala Corvinus, whom he had listened to in his youth, when Messala was already an old man. But he ruined his style with so many affectations and pedantries that his extempore speeches were considered far better than the prepared ones. He also wrote an *Elegy on the Death of Lucius Caesar* and Greek verses in the manner of his favourites Euphorion, Rhianus, and Parthenius, whose busts he placed in the public libraries among those of the classics – thus prompting several scholars to publish rival commentaries on these poets and dedicate them to him. However, he had a particular bent for mythology and carried his researches in it to such a ridiculous point that he would test professors of Greek literature – whose society, as I have already mentioned, he cultivated above all others – by asking them questions like: 'Who was Hecuba's mother?' – 'What name did Achilles assume when he was among the girls?'[29] – 'What song did the Sirens sing?' Furthermore, on

ODYSSEUS *listens to the singing and playing of the Sirens. He has had himself tied to the mast of his ship, lest he, like others, be enchanted by the Sirens' song, go to and be devoured by them.*
85. *Etruscan cinerary urn.* (Volterra, Museo Guarnacci.)

29. i.e., when he was disguised as a girl at the court of King Lycomedes.

his first entrance into the Senate after the death of Augustus he showed equal respect for the gods and for his adoptive father's memory by reviving the example set long ago by King Minos of Crete when informed of his son Androgeus's murder: he used wine and incense in his sacrifice, but dispensed with the customary flutists.

71. Tiberius spoke Greek fluently, but there were occasions when he stuck to Latin, especially at Senate meetings: indeed, he once apologized to the House for the foreign word 'monopoly', explaining that he could find no native equivalent. And he objected to the Greek word 'emblems' – meaning metal ornaments riveted on wine cups – when it appeared in a decree: if a one-word Latin equivalent could not be found, he said, a periphrasis of several words must serve. At another time he gave orders that a soldier who had been asked, in Greek, to give evidence on oath, must answer either in Latin or not at all.

72. During the entire period of Tiberius's retirement from Rome he only twice attempted to return. On the first occasion he sailed up the Tiber in a trireme as far as the park near the artificial lake, having posted troops along both banks to order away anyone who came from the city to meet him; but, after a distant view of the city walls, sailed back, it is not known why. On the second occasion he rode up the Appian Way as far as the seventh milestone, but then retreated because of a frightening portent. This was the death of a pet snake which he used to feed with his own hands. When about to do so as usual he found it half eaten by a swarm of ants; and a soothsayer warned him: 'Beware the power of the mob.' He hurried back to Campania, fell ill at Astura, yet felt strong enough to continue with his journey. At Circeii he disguised his ill-health by attending the garrison Games, and even threw down javelins at a wild boar let loose in the arena. He twisted the muscles of his side by this effort, and then aggravated his condition by sitting in a draught while overheated. Nevertheless, he resolutely went on to Misenum without any change in daily routine, continuing to engage in banquets and other diversions – partly because he now never practised self-denial, partly because he wanted nobody to realize how ill he was. Indeed, when the physician Charicles, on leaving the dining table, kissed his hand in farewell, Tiberius suspected a covert attempt to feel his pulse and begged Charicles to sit down again. Then he kept the party going until very late, and when it ended, followed his nightly habit of standing in the middle of the banqueting hall, with a lictor beside him, for a personal good-night to each of the departing guests.

73. Meanwhile he read in the *Proceedings of the Senate* a paragraph to the effect that some persons whom he had sent for trial merely as 'named by an informer' had been discharged without a hearing. 'This is contempt!' he shouted furiously, and decided to return at all costs to Capreae, the only place where he felt safe to take vigorous action. But bad weather and increasing sickness delayed his voyage; and he died soon afterwards in a country house which had once belonged to Lucullus. He was then seventy-seven years old and had reigned for nearly twenty-three years. It was 16 March, and the Consuls of the year were Gnaeus Acerronius Proculus and Gaius Pontius Nigrinus.

Some believe that he had been given a slow, wasting poison by Gaius; others that, when convalescent after fever, he demanded food but was refused it. According to one account, he fainted and on regaining consciousness asked for the seal-ring which had meanwhile been removed from his left hand. Seneca writes that Tiberius, realizing how near his end was, removed the ring himself, as if to give it to someone; but then clung to it a while before replacing it on his finger; that he afterwards lay quiet for some little time with the fist clenched, until summoning his servants; and that, when no one answered, he got out of bed, collapsed, and died.

74. On his last birthday Tiberius dreamed that the enormous, beautiful statue of Apollo of Temenos, which he had brought from Syracuse to erect in the library of the new temple,[30] came in to announce: 'Tiberius will never dedicate me!' A few days before his death the Capreae lighthouse was wrecked by an earthquake. At Misenum the dead embers of the fire which had been put into a brazier to warm his dining room suddenly blazed up again, early in the evening, and continued to glow until late that night.

75. The first news of his death caused such joy at Rome that people ran about yelling: 'To the Tiber with Tiberius!' and others offered prayers to Mother Earth and the Infernal Gods to give him no home below except among the damned. There were also loud threats to drag his body off with a hook and fling it on the Stairs of Mourning; for popular resentment against his savage behaviour was now increased by a fresh outrage. It so happened that the Senate had

30. The temple of the deified Augustus.

decreed a ten days' stay of execution in the case of all persons sentenced to death, and Tiberius died the very day on which the period of grace expired for some of them. They threw themselves on the mercy of the public but, since Gaius was still away, there was no one who could be approached with an appeal; and the gaolers, afraid of acting illegally, carried out the sentence of strangling them and throwing their bodies on the Stairs of Mourning. Thus the hatred of Tiberius grew hotter than ever – his cruelty, it was said, continued even after his death – and when the funeral procession left Misenum, the cry went up: 'Take him to the amphitheatre at Atella! Give him only a half-burning.'[31] However, the soldiers carried the corpse on to Rome, where it was cremated with due ceremony.

76. Two years before his death Tiberius had drawn a will in his own handwriting; an identical copy was also found in the handwriting of a freedman. Both these documents had been signed and sealed by witnesses of the very lowest class. In them, Gaius son of Germanicus and Tiberius Gemellus son of Drusus the Younger were named as Tiberius's co-heirs; and if either should die, the survivor was to be the sole heir. Tiberius left legacies to several other persons, including the Vestals; with a bounty for every serving soldier in the army and every member of the Roman commons. Separate bequests to the city wardmasters were added.

31. Meaning uncertain.

THE SPIRITS OF THE DEAD. *The dead were believed to live on in some form of existence which reflected life on earth. They were thought to be beings who in some way participated in the divine, and offerings were accordingly made to them, both collectively and individually.*
86. *Funerary altar inscribed 'To the divine departed spirits (the same term is translated as 'Infernal Gods' in the text) of Petronia Sabina'.* (Rome, Terme Museum.)

IV
GAIUS (CALIGULA)

Germanicus, the father of Gaius Caesar, the son of Drusus and Antonia the Younger, was adopted by Tiberius, his paternal uncle. After serving as quaestor five years, before the legal age, he became Consul, without holding the usual intermediate offices, and at Augustus's death the Senate appointed him to command the forces in Germany. Though the legions there were unanimously opposed to Tiberius's succession and would have acclaimed Germanicus Emperor, he showed a remarkable example of filial respect and determination by diverting their attention from this project; he took the offensive in Germany, and won a triumph. As Consul-elect for the second time he was hurried off to restore order in the East, before being able to take office. There he defeated the King of Armenia, and reduced Cappadocia to provincial status, but succumbed to a protracted illness at Antioch, being thirty-three years old when he died. Because of the dark stains which covered his body, and the foam on his lips, poison was suspected; significantly, also, they found the heart intact among his bones after cremation – a heart steeped in poison is supposedly proof against fire.

2. According to the general verdict, Tiberius craftily arranged Germanicus's death with Gnaeus Piso as his intermediary and agent. Piso had been appointed to govern Syria and there, deciding that he must make an enemy either of Germanicus or of Tiberius, took every opportunity to provoke Germanicus, even when on his sickbed, by the meanest acts and speeches; behaviour for which the Senate condemned him to death on his return to Rome, after he had narrowly escaped a popular lynching.

87. GAIUS CALIGULA
Coin from Rome. (Hirmer.)

3. Germanicus is everywhere described as having been of outstanding physical and moral excellence. He was handsome, courageous, a past-master of Greek and Latin oratory and letters, conspicuously kind-hearted, and gifted with the powerful desire and capacity for winning respect and inspiring affection. Only his legs were somewhat undeveloped, but he strengthened them by assiduous exercise on horseback after meals. He often fought and killed an enemy in hand-to-hand combat; and did not cease to plead causes in the Law Courts even when he had gained a triumph. Some of his Greek comedies are extant, besides other literary works. At home or abroad he always behaved modestly, would dispense with lictors when visiting any free or allied town, and offered sacrifices at whatever tombs of famous men he came across. On deciding to bury under one mound all the scattered remains of Varus's fallen legionaries, he led the search party himself and took the initiative in the collection. Towards his detractors Germanicus showed such tolerance and leniency, regardless of their identity or motives, that he would not even break with Piso (who was cancelling his orders and plaguing his subordinates) until he found that spells and potions were being used against him. And then he did no more than renounce his friendship by uttering the traditional formula, and leave testamentary instructions for his family to take vengeance on Piso if anything should happen to himself.

4. Such virtuous conduct brought Germanicus rich rewards. He was so deeply respected and loved by all his kindred that Augustus – I need hardly mention his other relatives – wondered for a long time whether to make him his successor, but at last ordered Tiberius to adopt him. Germanicus, many writers record, had won such intense popular devotion that he was in danger of being mobbed to death whenever he arrived at Rome or took his leave again. Indeed, when he came

PROPAGANDA FOR THE IMPERIAL FAMILY *was intended to convince the people of Rome that they had a stable – and respectable – government.*
88 (above and right). *Commemorative coin for Agrippina, mother of Gaius Caligula.* (Hirmer.)

back from Germany after suppressing the native uprising, all the cohorts of the Praetorian Guard marched out in welcome, despite orders that only two were to do so; and the entire people of Rome – all ages and ranks and both sexes – flocked as far as the twentieth milestone to meet him.

5. But the most spectacular proof of the devotion in which Germanicus had been held appeared on the day of his death and immediately afterwards. On the day when he died the populace stoned temples and upset altars; people threw their Household-gods into the street, and refused to acknowledge their newly-born children. Even the barbarians who were fighting us, or one another, are said to have made immediate peace as though a domestic tragedy had afflicted the whole world; some princes shaving their own beards, and their wives' heads, in token of profound grief. The King of Kings himself cancelled his hunting parties

and banquets with his grandees, which is a sign of public mourning in Parthia.

6. While Rome was still stunned and distressed by the first news of his illness, and waiting for further bulletins, a rumour that he had recovered suddenly went the rounds one evening after dark, and sent people rushing to the Capitol with torches and sacrificial victims. So eager were they to register their vows that the Temple gates were almost torn down. Tiberius was awakened by the joyful chant:

> All is well again at Rome,
> All is well again at home,
> Here's an end to all our pain:
> Germanicus is well again!

When the news of his death finally broke, neither edicts nor official expressions of sympathy could console the populace; mourning continued throughout the festal days of December. The renown of the dead man and the bitterness of his loss were accentuated by the horrors which followed; for everyone believed, and with good reason, that moral respect for Germanicus had alone kept Tiberius from displaying the cruelty of his wicked heart – which was soon to burst forth.

7. Germanicus married Agrippina the Elder, daughter of Marcus Agrippa and Julia, who bore him nine children. Two died in infancy, and a third, an extremely likeable boy, during early childhood. Livia dedicated a statue of him, dressed as a cupid, to Capito-

line Venus; Augustus kept a replica in his bedroom and used to kiss it fondly whenever he entered. The other children – three girls, Agrippina the Younger, Drusilla, and Livilla, born in successive years; and three boys, Nero, Drusus, and Gaius Caesar – survived their father; but Tiberius later brought charges against Nero and Drusus, whom he persuaded the Senate to execute as public enemies.

8. Gaius Caesar was born on 31 August A.D. 12, during the consulship shared by his father with Gaius Fonteius Capito. His birthplace is disputed. According to Gnaeus Lentulus Gaetulicus, he was born at Tibur; but, according to Pliny the Elder, near Treveri, in the village of Ambitarvium, just above the junction of the Moselle and the Rhine. Pliny supports his view by mentioning certain local altars inscribed 'IN HONOUR OF AGRIPPINA'S PUERPERIUM' (i.e. child-bearing), also a verse, which went the rounds at Gaius's accession and suggests that he was born in the winter quarters of the legions:

> Born in a barracks,
>   Reared in the arts of war:
> A noble nativity
>   For a Roman Emperor!

The *Gazette*, however, gives his birthplace as Antium; and my researches convince me that this is correct. Pliny shows that Gaetulicus tried to flatter the proud young monarch by pretending that he came from Tibur, a city sacred to Hercules; and that he lied with greater confidence because Germanicus did have a son named Gaius Caesar born there, whose lovable character as a boy, and premature death, I have already mentioned. Nevertheless, Pliny is himself mistaken in his chronology since historians of Augustus's reign agree that Germanicus's first visit to Gaul took place after he had been Consul, by which time Gaius was already born. Moreover, the inscription on the altar does not prove Pliny's point, since Agrippina bore Germanicus two daughters in Gaul, and any confinement is a *puerperium*, regardless of the child's sex – girls were formerly called *puerae* as often as *puellae*, and boys *puelli* as often as *pueri*. Finally, there is a letter which Augustus wrote a few months before he died, to his grand-daughter Agrippina the Elder; the Gaius mentioned in it must have been the future Emperor because no other child of that name was alive at the time. It reads: 'Yesterday I made arrangements for Talarius and Asillius to bring your son Gaius to you on the eighteenth of May, if the gods will. I am also sending with him one of my slaves, a doctor who, as I have told Germanicus in a letter, need not be returned to me if he proves of use to you. Goodbye, my dear Agrippina! Keep well on the way back to your Germanicus.' Clearly, Gaius could not have been born in a country to which he was first taken from Rome at the age of nearly two! This letter also weakens my confidence in that piece of verse. So we are, I think, reduced to accepting the only other authority, namely the *Gazette*, especially since Gaius preferred Antium to any other city, and treated it as his native place; he even planned, they say, to transfer the seat of imperial government there, when he wearied of Rome.

9. He won his surname Caligula ('Bootikin') from an army joke, because he grew up among the troops and wore the miniature uniform of a private soldier. An undeniable proof of the hold on their affections which this early experience of camp-life gave him is that when they rioted at the news of Augustus's death and were ready for any madness, the mere sight of little Gaius unquestionably calmed them down. As soon as they realized that he was being removed to a neighbouring city to protect him from their violence, they were overcome by contrition; some of them seized and stopped his carriage, pleading to be spared this disgrace.

10. Gaius also accompanied Germanicus to Syria. On his return he lived with his mother and next, after she had been exiled, with his great-grandmother Livia,[1] whose funeral oration he delivered from the Rostra though he had not yet come of age. He then lived with his grandmother Antonia until Tiberius summoned him to Capreae, at the age of eighteen. He assumed his manly gown and shaved his first beard as soon as he arrived there; but this was a most informal occasion, compared with his brothers' coming-of-age celebrations. The courtiers tried every trick to lure or force him into making complaints against Tiberius; always, however, without success. He not only failed to show any interest in the murder of his relatives, but affected an amazing indifference to his own ill-treatment, behaving so obsequiously to his adoptive grandfather, and to the entire household, that someone said of him, very neatly: 'Never was there a better slave, or a worse master!'

11. Yet even in those days he could not control his natural brutality and viciousness. He loved watching

---

1. Livia's correct designation was Julia Augusta (after the death of Augustus).

tortures and executions; and, disguised in wig and
robe, abandoned himself nightly to the pleasures of
gluttonous and adulterous living. Tiberius was ready
enough to indulge a passion which Gaius had for
theatrical dancing and singing, on the ground that it
might have a civilizing influence on him. With characteristic shrewdness, the old Emperor had exactly
gauged the young man's vicious inclinations, and
would often remark that Gaius's advent portended
his own death and the ruin of everyone else. 'I am nurs-
ing a viper for the Roman people,' he once said, 'and
a Phaëthon for the whole world.'[2]

12. Gaius presently married Junia Claudilla,
daughter of the distinguished Marcus Silanus; after

2. In mythology, Phaëthon fell from his fiery sun-chariot and
scorched the earth.

which he was first appointed Augur, in place of his
brother Drusus, and then promoted to the Priesthood,
in compliment to his dutiful behaviour and exemplary
life. This encouraged him in the hope of becoming
Tiberius's successor, because Sejanus's downfall had
reduced the Court to a shadow of its former self – and
when Junia died in childbirth, he seduced Ennia
Naevia, wife of Macro, the Guards Commander; not
only swearing to marry her if he became Emperor, but
putting the oath in writing. Having through her
wormed his way into Macro's favour, he poisoned
Tiberius, as some assert, issuing orders for the imperial
ring to be removed while he was still breathing; and
then, suspecting that he was trying not to let it go, he
had him smothered with a pillow – or even throttled
Tiberius with his own hands, and when a freedman
cried out in protest at this wicked deed, crucified him
at once. All this may be true; some writers report that
Gaius later confessed at least to intended parricide. He
would often boast, that is to say, of having carried a
dagger into Tiberius's bedroom with the dutiful
intention of avenging his mother and brothers; but,
according to his own account, found Tiberius asleep
and, restrained by feelings of pity, threw down the
dagger and went out. Tiberius, he said, was perfectly
aware of what had happened, yet never dared question
him, or take any action in the matter.

13. Gaius's accession seemed to the Roman people
– one might almost say, to the whole world – like a
dream come true. The memory of Germanicus and
compassion for a family that had been practically wiped

out by successive murders, made most provincials and soldiers, many of whom had known him as a child, and the entire population of Rome as well, show extravagant joy that he was now Emperor. When he escorted Tiberius's corpse from Misenum to Rome he was, of course, dressed in mourning, but a dense crowd greeted him uproariously with altars, sacrifices, torches, and such endearments as 'star', 'chicken', 'baby', and 'pet'.

14. On his arrival in the city the Senate (and a crowd of people who had forced their way into the House) immediately and unanimously conferred absolute power upon him. They set aside Tiberius's will – which made his other grandson, then still a child, joint-heir with Gaius – and so splendid were the celebrations that 160,000 victims were publicly sacrificed during the next three months, or perhaps even a shorter period.

A few days later Gaius visited the prison islands off Campania, and vows were uttered for his safe return – at that time no opportunity of demonstrating a general concern for his welfare was ever disregarded. When he fell ill, anxious crowds besieged the Palace all night. Some swore that they would fight as gladiators if the gods allowed him to recover; others even carried placards volunteering to die instead of him. To the great love in which he was held by his own people, foreigners added their own tribute of devotion. Artabanus, King of the Parthians, who always expressed outspoken hatred and contempt for Tiberius, made unsolicited overtures of friendship to Gaius, attended a conference with the Governor of Syria and, before

returning across the river Euphrates, paid homage to the Roman Eagles and standards, and to the statues of the Caesars.

15. Gaius strengthened his popularity by every possible means. He delivered a funeral speech in honour of Tiberius to a vast crowd, weeping profusely all the while; and gave him a magnificent burial. But as soon as this was over he sailed for Pandataria and the Pontian Islands to fetch back the remains of his mother and his brother Nero; and during rough weather, too, in proof of devotion. He approached the ashes with the utmost reverence and transferred them to the urns with his own hands. Equally dramatic was his gesture of raising a standard on the stern of the bireme which brought the urns to Ostia, and thence up the Tiber to Rome. He had arranged that the most distinguished knights available should carry them to the Mausoleum in two biers, at about noon, when the streets were at their busiest; also appointing an annual day of funeral sacrifices, in addition to Circus Games, in honour of his mother, at which her image would be paraded in a covered carriage. He honoured his father's memory by renaming the month of September 'Germanicus'; and sponsored a Senatorial decree which awarded his grandmother Antonia, at a blow, all the honours won by Livia Augusta in her entire lifetime. As fellow-Consul he chose his uncle Claudius, who had hitherto been a mere knight; and adopted young Tiberius Gemellus when he came of age, giving him the official title of 'Prince of the Youth'.

Gaius caused the names of his sisters to be included

in all oaths, in the following terms: '... I will not value
my life or that of my children less highly than I do the
safety of the Emperor Gaius and his sisters!' – and in
the consular motions, as follows: 'Good fortune attend
the Emperor Gaius and his sisters!'

An equally popular step was his recall of all exiles,
and dismissal of all criminal charges whatsoever that
had been pending since earlier times. The batches of
written evidence in his mother's and brothers' cases
were brought to the Forum at his orders, and burned,
to set at rest the minds of such witnesses and informers
as had testified against them; but first he swore before
Heaven that he had neither read nor touched a single
document. He also refused to examine a report supposedly concerning his own safety, on the ground that
nobody could have any reason to hate him, and that
he gave no hearing to informers.

16. Gaius drove from the city the perverts known
as *spintriae*, and could with difficulty be restrained
from drowning the lot. He gave permission for the
works of Titus Labienus, Cremutius Cordus, and Cassius Severus, which had been banned by order of the
Senate, to be routed out and republished – stating it
to be entirely in his interest that posterity should be

*SYMBOLS OF EMPIRE. The Romans had an elaborate
language of symbols with religious overtones to convey the
majesty and universality of the Empire. Some of these
symbols were depicted on military standards, which themselves were objects of cult.*
91 (above). *Winged Victories stand on either side of a
shield adorned with the imperial laurel wreath and the
eagle, bird of Jupiter, which holds a thunderbolt in its
claws. Relief of the first century* A.D. *(Rome, Capitoline
Museum.)*
92 (opposite). *Roman soldiers carrying standards. Relief
from the monument of Trajan at Adamklissi.*

in full possession of all historical facts; also, he revived
Augustus's practice, discontinued by Tiberius, of
publishing an imperial budget; invested the magistrates with full authority, not requiring them to apply
for his confirmation of sentences; and strictly and scrupulously scanned the list of knights but, though
publicly dismounting any who had behaved in a wicked
or scandalous manner, merely omitted the names of

those guilty of lesser misbehaviour from the list which he read out. Gaius's creation of a fifth judicial division aided jurors to keep abreast of their work; his reviving of the electoral system was designed to restore popular control over the magistracy. He honoured faithfully and uncritically every one of the bequests in Tiberius's will, though this had been set aside by the Senate, and in that of his maternal great-grandmother Livia, which Tiberius had suppressed; abolished the Italian half-per-cent auction tax; and paid compensation to a great many people whose houses had been damaged by fire. Any king whom he restored to the throne was awarded the arrears of taxes and revenue that had accumulated since his deposition – Antiochus of Commagene, for example, got a refund of a million gold pieces from the Public Treasury. To show his interest in every kind of noble action he awarded 8,000 gold pieces to a freedwoman who, though put to extreme torture, had not revealed her patron's guilt. These acts won him many official honours, among them a golden shield, carried once a year to the Capitol by the priestly colleges marching in procession, and followed by the Senate, while children of noble birth chanted an anthem in priase of his virtues. By a senatorial decree the festival of Parilia[3] was transferred to the day of his accession, as though Rome had now been born again.

17. Gaius held four consulships: the earliest for two months, from 1 July; the next for the whole month of January; the third for the first thirteen days of January; and the fourth for the first seven. Only the last two were in sequence.[4] He assumed his third consulship without a colleague. Some historians describe this as a high-handed breach of precedent; but unfairly, because he was then quartered at Lugdunum, where the news that his fellow Consul-elect had died in Rome, just before the New Year, had not reached him in time. He twice presented every member of the commons with three gold pieces; and twice invited all the senators and knights, with their wives and children, to an extravagant banquet. At the first of these banquets he gave every man a toga and every woman a red or purple scarf. He also added to the gaiety of Rome by extending the customary four days of the Saturnalia with a fifth, known as 'Youth Day'.

18. Gaius held several gladiatorial contests, some in Statilius Taurus's amphitheatre, and others in the En-

closure; diversifying them with prize-fights between the best boxers of Africa and Campania, and occasionally allowing magistrates or friends to preside at these instead of doing so himself. Again, he staged a great number of different theatrical shows of various kinds and in various buildings – sometimes at night, with the whole city illuminated – and would scatter vouchers among the audience entitling them to all sorts of gifts, over and above the basket of food which was everyone's due. At one banquet, noticing with what extraordinary gusto a knight seated opposite dug into the food, he sent him his own heaped plate as well; and rewarded a senator, who had been similarly enjoying himself, with a praetorship, though it was not yet his turn to hold this office. Many all-day Games were celebrated in the Circus and, between races, Gaius introduced panther-baiting and the Trojan war dance. For certain special Games, when all the charioteers were men of senatorial rank, he had the Circus decorated in red and green. Once, while he was inspecting the Circus equipment, from the Gelotian House which overlooks it, a group of people standing in the near-by balconies called out: 'What about a day's racing, Caesar?' So, on the spur of the moment, he gave immediate orders for Games to be held.

19. One of his spectacles was on such a fantastic scale that nothing like it had ever been seen before. He collected all available merchant ships and anchored them in two lines, close together, the whole way from Baiae to the mole at Puteoli, a distance of more than three and a half Roman miles. Then he had earth heaped on their planks, and made a kind of Appian Way along which he trotted back and forth for two consecutive days. On the first day he wore oak-leaf crown, sword, buckler, and cloth-of-gold cloak, and rode a gaily caparisoned charger. On the second, he appeared in charioteer's costume driving a team of two famous horses, with a boy named Dareus, one of his Parthian hostages, displayed in the car beside him; behind came the entire Praetorian Guard, and a group of his friends mounted in Gallic chariots. Gaius is, of course, generally supposed to have built the bridge as an improvement on Xerxes's famous feat of bridging the much narrower Hellespont. Others believe that he planned this huge engineering feat to terrify the Germans and Britons, on whom he had his eye. But my grandfather used to tell me as a boy that, according to some courtiers in Gaius's confidence, the reason for the bridge was this: when Tiberius could not decide whom to appoint as his successor, and inclined towards his

---

3. Commemorating the birth of Rome.
4. An error. He was Consul in the years A.D. 37, 39, 40 and 41.

natural grandson,[5] Thrasyllus the astrologer had told him: 'As for Gaius, he has no more chance of becoming Emperor than of riding a horse dryshod across the Gulf of Baiae.'

20. Gaius gave several shows abroad – Athenian Games at Syracuse in Sicily, and miscellaneous Games at Lugdunum in Gaul, where he also held a competition in Greek and Latin oratory. The loser, it appears, had to present the winners with prizes and make speeches praising them; while those who failed miserably were forced to erase their entries with either sponges or their own tongues – unless they preferred to be thrashed and flung into the neighbouring river.

21. He completed certain projects half finished by Tiberius: namely the Temple of Augustus and Pompey's Theatre; and began the construction of an aqueduct in the Tibur district, and of an amphitheatre near the Enclosure. (His successor Claudius finished the aqueduct; but work on the amphitheatre was abandoned.) Gaius rebuilt the ruinous ancient walls and temples of Syracuse, and among his other projects were the restoration of Polycrates's palace at Samos, the completion of Didymaean Apollo's temple at Ephesus, and the building of a city high up in the Alps. But he was most deeply interested in cutting a canal through the Isthmus[6] in Greece, and sent a leading-centurion there to survey the site.

22. So much for the Emperor; the rest of this history must deal with the Monster.

He adopted a variety of titles: such as 'Pious', 'Son of the Camp', 'Father of the Army', 'Best and Greatest of Caesars'. But when once, at the dinner table, some foreign kings who had come to pay homage were arguing which of them was the most nobly descended, Caligula interrupted their discussion by declaiming Homer's line:

Nay, let there be one master, and one king!

And he nearly assumed a royal diadem then and there, turning the semblance of a principate into an autocracy. However, after his courtiers reminded him that he already outranked any prince or king, he insisted on being treated as a god – sending for the most revered or artistically famous statues of the Greek deities (including that of Jupiter at Olympia), and having their heads replaced by his own.

Next, Gaius extended the Palace as far as the Forum; converted the shrine of Castor and Pollux into its vesti-

bule; and would often stand beside these Divine Brethren to be worshipped by all visitants, some of whom addressed him as 'Jupiter Latiaris'. He established a shrine to himself as God, with priests, the costliest possible victims, and a life-sized golden image, which was dressed every day in clothes identical with those that he happened to be wearing. All the richest citizens tried to gain priesthoods here, either by influence or bribery. Flamingos, peacocks, black grouse, guinea-hens, and pheasants were offered as sacrifices, each on a particular day of the month. When the moon shone full and bright he always invited the Moon-goddess to sexual intercourse in his bed; and during the day would indulge in whispered conversations with Capitoline Jupiter, pressing his ear to the god's mouth, and sometimes raising his voice in anger. Once he was overheard threatening the god: 'If you do not raise me up to Heaven I will cast you down to Hell.' Finally he announced that Jupiter had persuaded him to share his home; and therefore connected the Palace with the Capitol by throwing a bridge across the Temple of the God Augustus; after which he began building a new house inside the precincts of the Capitol itself, in order to live even nearer.

23. Because of Agrippa's humble origin Gaius loathed being described as his grandson, and would fly into a rage if anyone mentioned him, in speech or song, as an ancestor of the Caesars. He nursed a fantasy that his mother had been born of an incestuous union between Augustus and his daughter Julia; and not content with thus discrediting Augustus's name, cancelled the annual commemorations of Agrippa's victories at Actium and off Sicily, declaring that they had proved the disastrous ruin of the Roman people. He called his great-grandmother Livia a 'Ulysses in petticoats', and in a letter to the Senate dared describe her as of low birth – 'her maternal grandfather Aufidius Lurco having been a mere local senator at Fundi' – although the public records showed Lurco to have held high office at Rome. When his grandmother Antonia asked him to grant her a private audience he insisted on taking Macro, the Guards Commander, as his escort. Unkind treatment of this sort hurried her to the grave though, according to some, he accelerated the process with poison and, when she died, showed so little respect that he sat in his dining room and watched the funeral pyre burn. One day he sent a colonel to kill young Tiberius Gemellus without warning; on the pretext that Tiberius had insulted him by taking an antidote against poison – his breath smelled of it. Then he forced his

5. Tiberius Gemellus.   6. The Isthmus of Corinth.

father-in-law, Marcus Silanus, to cut his own throat with a razor, the charge being that he had not followed the imperial ship when it put to sea in a storm, but had stayed on shore to seize power at Rome if anything happened to himself. The truth was that Silanus, a notoriously bad sailor, could not face the voyage; and Tiberius's breath smelled of medicine taken for a persistent cough which was getting worse. Gaius preserved his uncle Claudius merely as a butt for practical jokes.

24. It was his habit to commit incest with each of his three sisters and, at large banquets, when his wife reclined above him, placed them all in turn below him. They say that he ravished his sister Drusilla before he came of age: their grandmother Antonia, at whose house they were both staying, caught them in bed together. Later, he took Drusilla from her husband, the former Consul Lucius Cassius Longinus, openly treating her as his lawfully married wife; and when he fell dangerously ill left Drusilla all his property, and the Empire too. At her death he made it a capital offence to laugh, to bathe, or to dine with one's parents, wives, or children while the period of public mourning lasted; and was so crazed with grief that he suddenly rushed from Rome by night, drove through Campania, took ship to Syracuse, and returned just as impetuously without having shaved or cut his hair in the meantime. Afterwards, whenever he had to take an important oath, he swore by Drusilla's divinity, even at a public assembly or an army parade. He showed no such extreme love or respect for the two surviving sisters, and often, indeed, let his boy friends sleep with them; and at Aemilius Lepidus's trial, felt no compunction about denouncing them as adulteresses who were party to plots against him – openly producing letters in their handwriting (acquired by trickery and seduction) and dedicating to Mars the Avenger the three swords with which, the accompanying placard alleged, they had meant to kill him.

25. It would be hard to say whether the way he got married, the way he dissolved his marriages, or the way he behaved as a husband was the most disgraceful. He attended the wedding ceremony of Gaius Piso and Livia Orestilla, but had the bride carried off to his own home. After a few days, however, he divorced her and two years later banished her, suspecting that she had returned to Piso in the interval. According to one account he told Piso, who was reclining opposite him at the wedding feast: 'Hands off my wife!' and abducted her from the table at once; and announced

the next day that he had taken a wife in the style of Romulus and Augustus.[7] Then he suddenly sent for Lollia Paulina, wife of Gaius Memmius, a Governor of consular rank, from his province, because somebody had remarked that her grandmother was once a famous beauty; but soon discarded her, forbidding her ever again to sleep with another man. Caesonia was neither young nor beautiful, and had three daughters by a former husband, besides being recklessly extravagant and utterly promiscuous; yet he loved her with a passionate faithfulness and often, when reviewing the troops, used to take her out riding in helmet, cloak and shield. For his friends he even paraded her naked; but would not allow her the dignified title of 'wife' until she had borne him a child, whereupon he announced the marriage and the birth simultaneously. He named the child Julia Drusilla; and carried her around the temples of all the goddesses in turn before finally entrusting her to the lap of Minerva, whom he called upon to supervise his daughter's growth and education. What finally convinced him of his own paternity was her violent temper; while still an infant she would try to scratch her little playmates' faces and eyes.

26. It would be trivial and pointless to record how Gaius treated such relatives and friends as his cousin King Ptolemy of Mauretania (the son of King Juba and grandson of Antony by his daughter Cleopatra Selene), or Macro the Guards Commander, with his wife Ennia, by whose help he had become Emperor. Their very nearness and services to him earned them cruel deaths.

Nor was he any more respectful or considerate in his dealings with the Senate, but made some of the highest officials run for miles beside his chariot, dressed in their togas; or wait in short linen tunics at the head or foot of his dining couch. Often he would send for men whom he had secretly killed, as though they were still alive, and remark off-handedly a few days later that they must have committed suicide. When two Consuls forgot to announce his birthday, he dismissed them and left the country for three days without officers of state. One of his quaestors was charged with conspiracy; Gaius had him stripped and spread on the ground, to give the soldiers who flogged him a firmer foothold.

He behaved just as arrogantly and violently towards the other orders of society. A crowd bursting into the Circus about midnight to secure free seats angered him so much that he had them driven away with clubs; more than a score of knights, as many married women,

7. See Augustus 69.

and numerous others were crushed to death in the ensuing panic. Gaius liked to stir up trouble in the Theatre by scattering gift vouchers before the seats were occupied, thus tempting commoners to invade the rows reserved for knights. During gladiatorial shows he would have the canopies removed at the hottest time of the day and forbid anyone to leave; or take away the usual equipment, and pit feeble old fighters against decrepit wild animals; or stage comic duels between respectable householders who happened to be physically disabled in some way or other. More than once he closed down the granaries and let the people go hungry.

27. The following instances will illustrate his bloodthirstiness. Having collected wild animals for one of his shows, he found butcher's meat too expensive and decided to feed them with criminals instead. He paid no attention to the charge-sheets, but simply stood in the middle of a colonnade, glanced at the prisoners lined up before him, and gave the order: 'Kill every man between that bald head and the other one over there!' Someone had sworn to fight in the arena if Gaius recovered from his illness; Gaius forced him to fulfil this oath, and watched his swordplay closely, not letting him go until he had won the match and begged abjectly to be released. Another fellow had pledged himself, on the same occasion, to commit suicide; Gaius, finding that he was still alive, ordered him to be dressed in wreaths and fillets, and driven through Rome by the imperial slaves – who kept harping on his pledge and finally flung him over the embankment into the river. Many men of decent family were branded at his command, and sent down the mines, or put to work on the roads, or thrown to the wild beasts. Others were confined in narrow cages, where they had to crouch on all fours like animals; or were sawn in half – and not necessarily for major offences, but merely for criticizing his shows, or failing to swear by his Genius.

Gaius made parents attend their sons' executions, and when one father excused himself on the ground of ill-health, provided a litter for him. Having invited another father to dinner just after the son's execution, he overflowed with good-fellowship in an attempt to make him laugh and joke. He watched the manager of his gladiatorial and wild-beast shows being flogged with chains for several days running, and had him killed only when the smell of suppurating brains became insupportable. A writer of Atellan farces was burned alive in the amphitheatre, because of a line which had an amusing *double-entendre*. One knight, on the point of being thrown to the wild beasts, shouted that he was innocent; Gaius brought him back, removed his tongue, and then ordered the sentence to be carried out.

28. Once he asked a returned exile how he had been spending his time. To flatter him the man answered: 'I prayed continuously to the gods for Tiberius's death, and your accession; and my prayer was granted.' Gaius therefore concluded that the new batch of exiles must be praying for his own death; so he sent agents from island to island and had them all killed. Being anxious that one particular senator should be torn in pieces he persuaded some of his colleagues to challenge him as a public enemy when he entered the House, stab him with their pens, and then hand him over for lynching to the rest of the Senate; and was not satisfied until the victim's limbs, organs, and guts had been dragged through the streets and heaped up at his feet.

29. Gaius's savage crimes were made worse by his brutal language. He claimed that no personal trait made him feel prouder than his 'inflexibility' – by which he must have meant 'brazen impudence'. As though mere deafness to his grandmother Antonia's good advice were not enough, he told her: 'Bear in mind that I can treat anyone exactly as I please!' Suspecting that young Tiberius Gemellus had taken drugs as prophylactics to the poison he intended to administer, he scoffed: 'Can there really be an antidote against Caesar?' And, on banishing his sisters, he remarked: 'I have swords as well as islands.' One ex-praetor, taking a cure at Anticyra, made frequent requests for an extension of his sick leave; Gaius had him put to death, suggesting that if hellebore had been of so little benefit over so long a period, he must need to be bled. When signing the execution list he used to say: 'I am clearing my accounts.' And one day, after sentencing a number of Gauls and Greeks to die in the same batch, he boasted of having 'subdued Gallo-Graecia'.

30. The method of execution he preferred was to inflict numerous small wounds, and his familiar order: 'Make him feel that he is dying!' soon became proverbial. Once, when the wrong man had been killed owing to a confusion of names, he announced that the victim had equally deserved death; and often quoted Accius's line:

Let them hate me, so long as they fear me.

He would indiscriminately abuse the Senate as having

been friends of Sejanus, or informers against his mother and brothers (at this point producing the papers which he was supposed to have burned!); and exclaim that Tiberius's cruelty had been quite justified since, with so many accusers, he was bound to believe their charges. The Knights earned his constant displeasure for spending their time, or so he complained, at the play or the Games. On one occasion the people cheered the team he opposed; he cried angrily: 'I wish all you Romans had only one neck!' When a shout arose in the amphitheatre for Tetrinius the bandit to come out and fight, he said that all those who called for him were Tetriniuses too. A group of net-and-trident gladiators, dressed in tunics, put up a very poor show against the five men-at-arms[8] with whom they were matched; but when he sentenced them to death, one of them seized a trident and killed each of the victorious team in turn. Gaius then publicly expressed his horror at what he called 'this most bloody murder', and his disgust with those who had been able to stomach the sight.

31. He went about complaining how bad the times were, and particularly that there had been no public disasters like the Varus massacre under Augustus, or the collapse of the amphitheatre at Fidenae under Tiberius. The prosperity of his own reign, he said, would lead to its being wholly forgotten, and he often prayed for a great military catastrophe, or for some famine, plague, fire, or earthquake.

32. Everything that he said and did was marked with equal cruelty, even during his hours of rest and amusement and banqueting. He frequently had trials by torture held in his presence while he was eating or otherwise enjoying himself; and kept an expert headsman in readiness to decapitate the prisoners brought in from gaol. When the bridge across the sea at Puteoli was being blessed, he invited a number of spectators from the shore to inspect it; then abruptly tipped them into the water. Some clung to the ships' rudders, but he had them dislodged with boat-hooks and oars, and left to drown. At a public dinner in the city he sent to his executioners a slave who had stolen a strip of silver from a couch; they were to lop off the man's hands, tie them around his neck so that they hung on his breast, and take him for a tour of the tables, displaying a placard in explanation of his punishment. On another occasion a gladiator[9] from the school against whom he was fencing with a wooden sword fell down deliberately; whereupon Gaius drew a real dagger,

8. *Secutores.*   9. *Murmillo.*

HOMER AND VIRGIL. *Homer's* Iliad *tells the story of the Trojan war and his* Odyssey *is about the wanderings of Odysseus (see Ill. 85), one of the Greek heroes who fought at Troy. The hero of Vergil's* Aeneid *is the Trojan Aeneas; the poem relates how his followers reached Italy and settled there (see Ill. 49). Most educated Romans knew large parts of these three poems by heart.*

93 (above). *Homer* (bottom left) *is crowned by the World and Time, while History offers incense to him on an altar. Above are Apollo, the Muses and Zeus. Second century* B.C. *(London, British Museum.)*

94 (opposite). *Virgil between two Muses; the scroll in his left hand is open at the verse near the beginning of the* Aeneid *in which the poet addresses his Muse. Roman mosaic. (Tunis, Musée du Bardo.)*

stabbed him to death, and ran about waving the palm-branch of victory. Once, while presiding appropriately robed at the sacrificial altar, he swung his mallet, as

if at the victim, but instead felled the assistant priest.[10]
At one particularly extravagant banquet he burst into
sudden peals of laughter. The Consuls, who were reclining next to him, politely asked whether they might
share the joke. 'What do you think?' he answered. 'It

10. Gaius was dressed as the *popa*, whose job it was to knock the
victim out. The assistant priest was the *cultrarius* who had the duty
of cutting its throat.

occurred to me that I have only to give one nod and
both your throats will be cut on the spot!'

33. As an example of his sense of humour, he played
a prank on Apelles, the tragic actor, by standing beside
a statue of Jupiter and asking: 'Which of us two is the
greater?' When Apelles hesitated momentarily, Gaius
had him flogged, commenting on the musical quality
of his groans for mercy. He never kissed the neck of
his wife or mistress without saying: 'And this beautiful

throat will be cut whenever I please.' Sometimes he even threatened to torture Caesonia as a means of discovering why he was so devoted to her.

34. In his insolent pride and destructiveness he made malicious attacks on men of almost every epoch. Needing more room in the Capitol courtyard, Augustus had once shifted the statues of certain celebrities to the Campus Martius; these Gaius dashed to the ground and shattered so completely, inscriptions and all, that they could not possibly be restored. After this no statue or bust of any living person anywhere could be set up without his permission. He toyed with the idea of suppressing Homer's poems – for he might surely claim Plato's privilege of banishing Homer from his republic? As for Virgil and Livy, he came very near to having their works and busts removed from the libraries, claiming that Virgil had no talent and little learning; and that Livy was a wordy and inaccurate historian. It seems, also, that he proposed to abolish the legal profession; at any rate, he often swore by Hercules that no lawyer could give advice contrary to his will.

35. He deprived the noblest men at Rome of their ancient family emblems – Torquatus lost his golden collar, Cincinnatus his lock of hair, and Gnaeus Pompeius the surname 'Great' belonging to his ancient house. He invited King Ptolemy to visit Rome, welcomed him with appropriate honours, and then suddenly ordered his execution – as mentioned above – because at Ptolemy's entrance into the amphitheatre during a gladiatorial show the fine purple cloak which

DRINKING AND DRUNKENNESS

95 (below). *Tavern scene in Pompeii: two men embrace while a woman brings a drink; she says, 'Who ordered? Take it. Come, Oceanus, drink up.'* (Naples, Museum.)
96 (opposite). *The hero Hercules lies on the ground drunk. Cherubs play with his club and quiver, while Omphale queen of Lydia and her attendants watch with an air of surprise. The story was something of a cautionary tale of the ancient world.* (Naples, Museum.)

he wore had attracted universal admiration. Any good-looking man with a fine head of hair whom Gaius ran across – he himself was bald – had the back of his scalp brutally shaved. One Aesius Proculus, a leading-centurion's son, was so well-built and handsome that people nicknamed him 'Giant Cupid'. Without warning, Gaius ordered Aesius to be dragged from his seat in the amphitheatre into the arena, and matched first with a Thracian net-fighter, then with a man-at-arms. Though Aesius won both combats, he was thereupon dressed in rags, led fettered through the streets to be jeered at by women, and finally executed; the truth being that however low anyone's fortune or condition might be, Gaius always found some cause for envy. Thus he sent a stronger man than the then Sacred King of Lake Nemorensis to challenge him, after many years of office.[11] A chariot-fighter called Porius drew such tremendous applause for freeing his slave in celebration of a victory at the Games that Gaius indignantly rushed from the amphitheatre. In so doing he tripped over the fringe of his robe and pitched down the steps, at the bottom of which he complained that the people who ruled the world seemed to take greater notice of a gladiator's trifling gesture than of all their deified emperors, or even the one still among them.

36. He had not the slightest regard for chastity, either his own or others', and was accused of homosexual relations, both active and passive, with Marcus Lepidus, also Mnester the comedian,[12] and various foreign hostages; moreover, a young man of consular family, Valerius Catullus, revealed publicly that he had buggered the Emperor, and quite worn himself out in the process. Besides incest with his sisters, and a notorious passion for the prostitute Pyrallis, he made advances to almost every woman of rank in Rome; after inviting a selection of them to dinner with their husbands he would slowly and carefully examine each in turn while they passed his couch, as a purchaser might assess the value of a slave, and even stretch out his hand and lift up the chin of any woman who kept her eyes modestly cast down. Then, whenever he felt so inclined, he would send for whoever pleased him best, and leave the banquet in her company. A little later he would return, showing obvious signs of what he had been about, and openly discuss his bed-fellow in detail, dwelling on her good and bad physical points and commenting on her sexual performance. To some of these unfortunates he issued, and publicly registered, divorces in the name of their absent husbands.

37. No parallel can be found for Gaius's far-fetched extravagances. He invented new kinds of baths, and the most unnatural dishes and drinks – bathing in hot and cold perfumed bath-oils, drinking valuable pearls dissolved in vinegar, and providing his guests with golden bread and golden meat; and would remark that a man must be either frugal or Caesar. For several days in succession he scattered largesse from the roof of the Julian Basilica; and built Liburnian galleys, with ten banks of oars, jewelled sterns, multi-coloured sails, and with huge baths, colonnades and banqueting halls aboard – not to mention vines and fruit-trees of different varieties. In these vessels he used to take early-morning cruises along the Campanian coast, reclining on his couch and listening to songs and choruses. Villas and country-houses were run up for him regardless of expense – in fact, Gaius seemed interested only in doing the apparently impossible – which led him to construct moles in deep, rough water far out to sea, drive tunnels through exceptionally hard rocks, raise flat ground to the height of mountains, and reduce mountains to the level of plains; and all at immense speed, because he punished delay with death. But why give details? Suffice it to record that, in less than a year, he squandered Tiberius's entire fortune of 27 million gold pieces, and an enormous amount of other treasure besides.

38. When impoverished and in need of funds, he concentrated on wickedly ingenious methods of raising funds by false accusations, auctions, and taxes. He ruled that no man could lawfully enjoy Roman citizenship acquired by any ancestor more remote than his father; and when confronted with certificates of citizenship issued by Julius Caesar or Augustus, rejected them as antiquated and obsolete. He also disallowed all property returns to which, for whatever reason, later additions had been appended. If a leading-centurion had bequeathed nothing either to Tiberius or himself since the beginning of the former's reign, he would rescind the will on the ground of ingratitude; and voided those of all other persons who were said to have intended making him their heir when they died, but had not done so. This caused widespread alarm, and even people who did not know him personally would tell their friends or children that they had left him everything; but if they continued to live after the declaration he considered himself tricked, and sent several of them

11. The priest of Diana at Nemu was by tradition a fugitive slave who had killed his predecessor.

12. *Pantominus* (see Key to Terms).

presents of poisoned sweets. Gaius conducted these cases in person, first announcing the sum he meant to raise, and not stopping until he had raised it. The slightest delay nettled him, and he once passed a single sentence on a batch of more than forty men charged with various offences, and then boasted to Caesonia, when she woke from her nap, that he had done very good business since she dozed off.

He would auction whatever properties were left over from a show; driving up the bidding to such heights that many of those present, forced to buy at fantastic prices, found themselves ruined and committed suicide by opening their veins. A famous occasion was when Aponius Saturninus fell asleep on a bench, and Gaius warned the auctioneer to keep an eye on the senator of praetorian rank who kept nodding his head at him. Before the bidding ended Aponius had unwittingly bought thirteen gladiators for a total of 90,000 gold pieces.

39. While in Gaul Gaius did so well by selling the furniture, jewellery, slaves, and even the freedmen of his condemned sisters at immense prices that he decided to do the same with the furnishings of the Old Palace. So he sent to Rome, where his agents commandeered public conveyances, and even draught animals from the bakeries, to fetch the stuff north; which led to a bread shortage in the city, and to the loss of many lawsuits, because litigants who lived at a distance were unable to appear in court and meet their bail. He then used all kinds of procurers' tricks for disposing of the furniture: scolding the bidders for their avarice, or for their shamelessness in being richer than he was, and pretending grief at this surrender of imperial property to commoners. Discovering that one wealthy provincial had paid the men who issued the Emperor's invitations 2,000 gold pieces to be smuggled into a banquet, he was delighted that the privilege of dining with him should be valued so highly and, when next day the same man turned up at the auction, made him pay 2,000 gold pieces for some trifling object – but also sent him a personal invitation to dinner.

40. The tax-collectors were ordered to raise new and unprecedented levies, and found this so profitable that he detailed his Guards colonels and centurions to collect the money instead. No class of goods or individuals now avoided duty of some kind. He imposed a fixed tax on all foodstuffs sold in any quarter of the city, and a charge of $2\frac{1}{2}$ per cent on the money involved in every lawsuit and legal transaction whatsoever; and devised special penalties for anyone who compounded or abandoned a case. Porters had to hand over an eighth part of their day's earnings and prostitutes their standard fee for a single sexual act – even if they had quitted their profession and were respectably married; pimps and ex-pimps also became liable to this public tax, and even marriage was not exempt.

41. These new regulations having been announced by word of mouth only, many people failed to observe them, through ignorance. At last he acceded to the urgent popular demand, by posting the regulations up, but in an awkwardly cramped spot and written so small that no one could take a copy. He never missed a chance of securing loot: setting aside a suite of Palace rooms, he decorated them worthily, opened a brothel, stocked it with married women and free-born boys, and then sent his pages around the squares and public halls, inviting all men, of whatever age, to come and enjoy themselves. Those who appeared were lent money at interest, and clerks openly wrote down their names under the heading 'Contributors to the Imperial Revenue'.

Gaius did not even disdain to make profits from gambling, and when he played at dice he would always cheat and lie. Once he interrupted a game by giving up his seat to the man behind him and going out into the courtyard. A couple of rich knights passed; Gaius immediately had them arrested and confiscated their property; then resumed the game in high spirits, boasting that his luck had never been better.

42. His daughter's birth gave him an excuse for further complaints of poverty. 'In addition to the burden of sovereignty,' he said, 'I must now shoulder that of fatherhood' – and promptly took up a collection for her education and dowry. He also announced that New Year gifts would be welcomed on 1 January; and then sat in the Palace porch, grabbing the handfuls and lapfuls of coin which a mixed crowd of all classes pressed on him. At last he developed a passion for the feel of money and, spilling heaps of gold pieces on an open space, would walk over them barefoot, or else lie down and wallow.

43. Gaius had only a single taste of warfare, and even that was unpremeditated. At Mevania, where he went to visit the river Clitumnus and its sacred grove, someone reminded him that he needed Batavian recruits for his bodyguard; which suggested the idea of a German expedition. He wasted no time in summoning regular legions and auxiliaries from all directions, levied troops everywhere with the utmost strictness, and collected military supplies of all kinds on an

Living and the Family

The family was the basic unit of living in Roman times. The fundamental events of a lifetime, birth, marriage, death, were centred around it, and very few people would opt out of this network of human relations and styles of living. The family made its demands, which were sanctioned by long tradition, but it also gave its support.

These facts were reflected in Roman imperial politics: whenever possible, the imperial succession was arranged on a family basis, whenever possible the closest suitable relative to the deceased Emperor would succeed. In this respect, imperial politics overrode one of the most firmly held principles of the Roman Republic, namely that ideally candidates to public office should be freely elected by the people. Therefore, while in public life the transition from Republic to Empire brought with it profound ideological and political changes, not so much changed in the patterns in which individuals arranged their daily private life.

Romantic and idealizing love was not often thought to be a necessary qualification for marriage. Poets of the late Republic and early Empire often idealized the women whom they loved, but the portraits which emerge from their poems, while they may have contributed to later renderings of feminine beauty by artists[1 and 8], are very different from the canon of feminine virtues which are spelt out on many funerary inscriptions of married women of the period. As regards the latter, the ideals which were to be aspired to by them – to be the wife of one man, to care for children, to weave – fitted less into the context of metropolitan Rome, a capital city of great sophistication, than into the Rome of earlier centuries, a town which was only beginning to emerge from its agricultural roots.

With the new choices and the freedom which the affluence and the political and social instability of the late Republic brought with them, not all women found the old ways acceptable. One such was Julia, the daughter of Augustus, who was exiled by her father for having a love affair and for her involvement with the fashionable intelligentsia of Rome (cf. Augustus 101), among them the poet Ovid, whose work The Art of Love *displeased Augustus. We catch a haunting glimpse of this world in a painting of the period which depicts a marriage: after performing the marriage ceremonies, a sad-faced bride sits on a couch next to her husband, who – seemingly in vain – tries to reassure her.*

The transition of marriage achieved, however, family life took its course, with its tale of births[7] and deaths. Perspectives could become very inward-looking in such a context: fortune-telling[9] and the interpretation of dreams occupied many people, and the resulting predictions could reach far beyond the immediate family circle (for example Caesar

1. Woman playing the cithara; painting from a villa at Boscoreale ▶

2. Mosaic floor, signed by the artist Hephaistion

3. Courtyard of the house of the Brothers, Pompeii

4. Portrait of a couple; painting from Pompeii   5 (*overleaf*). Reconstructed Roman room from a villa at Boscoreale

6 (*opposite*). The Portland Vase

7. Washing a baby; relief from Perge

8. Portrait of a Roman lady

81). Here, as in the patterns of family living, ancient patterns lived on from generation to generation: a poet might in a playful mood describe the matrons of early imperial Rome participating in an old-fashioned festival of Mars: the reality was not so playful when year after year women would seek out the same venerable shrine with their inmost hopes and desires.

The late Republic and early Empire brought with them new fashions, new tastes, new activities, which changed the lives of the women of Rome. But ultimately the lives of men, in the circles which Suetonius describes, changed far more deeply than the lives of women. For when the Republic collapsed, these men lost the expectation of an independent political career for which they had been brought up: the hope of being a statesman in one's own right was replaced by the hope of steady advancement in the imperial service, granted by the Emperor or his delegates, as a reward for loyal service.

At the same time, Rome became culturally and materially more sophisticated, and, as some observers of the time maintained, more decadent. The sophistication is borne out by a wide range of refined products which were at the disposal of the affluent. In the Roman Empire, many objects of daily use were mass-produced for the customers of every day. Thus, floor after floor in a Roman house might be covered in mosaics, but these were a world apart from a mosaic laid by an artist who would sign his name to it, mosaic such as Cicero imagined when he said that a good orator chooses his words as carefully as a mosaicist chooses his tesserae[2]. Objects for more personal use could be equally carefully chosen, both in material and in craftsmanship[6].

Many of the objects which Roman men and women used every day or had around them, as well as Roman architectural decoration, reflect these people's love for and attachment to nature. Whether it was fruits on a twig, light reflected in a glass of water or images of bliss in the world of nature which were derived from Greek and Roman myth, artists untiringly depicted such scenes for their patrons. And the patrons in their turn lived, when they could, in houses where a courtyard enclosed a small garden[3], a microcosm of the world of nature which lived in their awareness of what lay beyond houses and towns.

◀ 9. Fortune-teller; mosaic from Pompeii

unprecedented scale. Then he marched off so rapidly and hurriedly that the Guards cohorts could not keep up with him except by breaking tradition: they had to tie their standards on the pack-mules. Yet, later, he became so lazy and self-indulgent that he travelled in a litter borne by eight bearers; and, whenever he approached a town, made the inhabitants sweep the roads and lay the dust with sprinklers.

44. After reaching his headquarters, Gaius showed how keen and severe a commander-in-chief he intended to be by ignominiously dismissing any general who was late in bringing along from various places the auxiliaries he required. Then, when he reviewed the legions, he discharged many veteran leading-centurions on grounds of age and incapacity, though some had only a few more days of their service to run; and, calling the remainder a pack of greedy fellows, scaled down their retirement bonus to sixty gold pieces each.

All that he accomplished in this expedition was to receive the surrender of Adminius, son of the British King Cunobelinus,[13] who had been banished by his father and come over to the Romans with a few followers. Gaius, nevertheless, wrote an extravagant dispatch to Rome as if the whole island had surrendered to him, and ordered the couriers not to dismount from their post-chaise on reaching the outskirts of the city but make straight for the Forum and the Senate House, and take his letter to the Temple of Mars the Avenger for personal delivery to the Consuls, in the presence of the entire Senate.

45. Since the chance of military action appeared very remote, he presently sent a few of his German bodyguard across the Rhine, with orders to hide themselves. After lunch scouts hurried in to tell him excitedly that the enemy were upon him. He at once galloped out, at the head of his friends and part of the Guards cavalry, to halt in the nearest thicket, where they chopped branches from the trees and dressed them like trophies; then, riding back by torchlight, he taunted as timorous cowards all who had failed to follow him, and awarded his fellow-heroes a novel fashion in crowns – he called it 'The Ranger's Crown' – ornamented with sun, moon, and stars. On another day he took some hostages from an elementary school and secretly ordered them on ahead of him. Later, he left his dinner in a hurry and took his cavalry in pursuit of them, as though they had been fugitives. He was no less melodramatic about this foray: when he returned

13. Shakespeare's Cymbeline.

to the hall after catching the hostages and bringing them back in irons, and his officers reported that the army was marshalled, he made them recline at table, still in their corselets, and quoted Virgil's famous advice: 'Be steadfast, comrades, and preserve yourselves for happier occasions!' He also severely reprimanded the absent Senate and People for enjoying banquets and festivities, and for hanging about the theatres or their luxurious country-houses while the Emperor was exposed to all the hazards of war.

46. In the end, he drew up his army in battle array facing the Channel and moved the arrow-casting machines and other artillery into position as though he intended to bring the campaign to a close. No one had the least notion what was in his mind when, suddenly, he gave the order: 'Gather sea-shells!' He referred to the shells as 'plunder from the ocean, due to the Capitol and to the Palace', and made the troops fill their helmets and tunic-laps with them; commemorating this victory by the erection of a tall lighthouse, not unlike the one at Pharos, in which fires were to be kept going all night as a guide to ships. Then he promised every soldier a bounty of four gold pieces, and told them: 'Go happy, go rich!' as though he had been excessively generous.

47. He now concentrated his attention on his forthcoming triumph. To supplement the few prisoners and the deserters who had come over from the barbarians, he picked the tallest Gauls of the province – 'those worthy of a triumph' – and some of their chiefs as well. These had not only to grow their hair and dye it red, but also to learn German and adopt German names. The triremes used in the Channel were carted to Rome overland most of the way; and he sent a letter ahead instructing his agents to prepare a triumph more lavish than any hitherto known, but at the least possible expense; and added that everyone's property was at their disposal.

48. Before leaving Gaul he planned, in an access of unspeakable cruelty, to massacre the legionaries who long ago, at news of Augustus's death, had mutinously besieged the headquarters of his father Germanicus, who was their commander; he had been there himself as a little child. His friends barely restrained him from carrying this plan out, and he could not be dissuaded from ordering the execution of every tenth man; for which purpose they had to parade without arms, not even wearing their swords, and surrounded by armed horsemen. But when he noticed that a number of legionaries, scenting trouble, were slipping away to

fetch their weapons, he hurriedly fled from the gathering and headed straight for Rome. There, to distract attention from his inglorious exploits, he openly and vengefully threatened the Senate who, he said, had cheated him of a well-earned triumph – though in point of fact he had expressly stated, a few days before, that they must do nothing to honour him, on pain of death.

49. So, when the distinguished senatorial delegates met him with an official plea for his immediate return, he shouted: 'I am coming, and this' – tapping the hilt of his sword – 'is coming too!' He was returning only to those who would really welcome him; namely, the knights and the people; so far as the senators were concerned he would never again consider himself their fellow-citizen, or their Emperor, and forbade any more of them to meet him. Having cancelled, or at least postponed, his triumph he entered the city on his birthday, and received an ovation. Within four months he was dead.

But meanwhile he had dared commit fearful crimes, and contemplated even worse ones: such as murdering the most distinguished of the senators and knights, and then moving the seat of government first to Antium, and afterwards to Alexandria. So that none may doubt this, let me record that two books were found among his papers entitled *The Dagger* and *The Sword*, each of them containing the names and addresses of men whom he had planned to kill. A huge chest filled with a variety of poisons also came to light. It is said that when Claudius later threw this into the sea, quantities of dead fish, cast up by the tide, littered the neighbouring beaches.

50. Physical characteristics of Gaius:

Height: tall.
Complexion: pallid.
Body: hairy and badly built.
Neck: thin.
Legs: spindling.
Eyes and temples: hollow.
Forehead: broad and forbidding.
Scalp: almost hairless, especially on the top.

Because of his baldness and hairiness he announced that it was a capital offence for anyone either to look down on him as he passed or to mention goats in any context. He worked hard to make his naturally forbidding and uncouth face even more repulsive, by practising fearful and horrifying grimaces in front of a mirror. Gaius was, in fact, sick both physically and mentally. In his boyhood, he suffered from epilepsy; and

although in his youth he was not lacking in endurance, there were times when he could hardly walk, stand, think, or hold up his head, owing to sudden faintness. He was well aware that he had mental trouble, and sometimes proposed taking a leave of absence from Rome to clear his brain; Caesonia is reputed to have given him an aphrodisiac which drove him mad. Insomnia was his worst torment. Three hours a night of fitful sleep were all that he ever got, and even then terrifying visions would haunt him – once, for instance, he dreamed that he had a conversation with an apparition of the sea. He tired of lying awake the greater part of the night, and would alternately sit up in bed and wander through the long colonnades, calling out from time to time for daylight and longing for it to come.

51. I am convinced that this brain-sickness accounted for his two contradictory vices – over-confidence and extreme timorousness. Here was a man who despised the gods, yet shut his eyes and buried his head beneath the bedclothes at the most distant sound of thunder; and if the storm came closer, would jump out of bed and crawl underneath. In his travels through Sicily he poked fun at the miraculous stories associated with local shrines, yet on reaching Messana suddenly fled in the middle of the night, terrified by the smoke and noise which came from the crater of Etna. Despite his fearful threats against the barbarians, he showed so little courage after he had crossed the Rhine and gone riding in a chariot through a defile, that when someone happened to remark: 'What a panic there would be if the enemy unexpectedly appeared!' he immediately leaped on a horse and galloped back to the bridges. These were crowded with camp servants and baggage, but he had himself passed from hand to hand over the men's heads, in his impatience at any delay. Soon afterwards, hearing of an uprising in Germany, he decided to escape by sea. He fitted out a fleet for this purpose, finding comfort only in the thought that, should the enemy be victorious and occupy the Alpine summits as the Cimbrians had done, or Rome as the Senonian Gauls had done, he would at least be able to hold his overseas provinces. This was probably what later gave Gaius's assassins the idea of quieting his turbulent soldiers with the story that rumours of a defeat had scared him into sudden suicide.

52. Gaius paid no attention to traditional or current fashions in his dress; ignoring male conventions and even the human decencies. Often he made public appearances in a cloak covered with embroidery and encrusted with precious stones, a long-sleeved tunic

and bracelets; or in silk (which men were forbidden by law to wear) or even in a woman's robe; and came shod sometimes with slippers, sometimes with buskins, sometimes with military boots, sometimes with women's shoes. Often he affected a golden beard and carried a thunderbolt, trident, or serpent-twined staff in his hand. He even dressed up as Venus and, even before his expedition, wore the uniform of a triumphant general, including sometimes the breastplate which he had stolen from Alexander the Great's tomb at Alexandria.

53. Though no man of letters, Gaius took pains to study rhetoric, and showed remarkable eloquence and quickness of mind, especially when prosecuting. Anger incited him to a flood of words and thoughts, he moved about excitedly while speaking, and his voice carried a great distance. At the start of every speech he would warn the audience that he proposed to 'draw the sword which he had forged in his midnight study'; yet so despised all polished and elegant style that he discounted Seneca, then at the height of his fame, as a 'mere text-book orator', or 'sand without lime'. He often published confutations of speakers who had successfully pleaded a cause; or composed speeches for both the prosecution and the defence of important men who were on trial by the Senate – the verdict depending entirely on the caprice of his pen – and would invite the knights by proclamation to attend and listen.

54. Gaius practised many other various arts as well, most enthusiastically, too. He made appearances as a Thracian gladiator, as a singer, as a dancer, fought with real weapons, and drove chariots in many circuses in a number of places. Indeed, he was so proud of his voice and his dancing that he could not resist the temptation of supporting the tragic actors at public performances; and would repeat their gestures by way of praise or criticism. On the very day of his death he seems to have ordered an all-night festival, intending to take advantage of the free-and-easy atmosphere for making his stage debut. He often danced at night, and once, at about midnight, summoned three senators of consular rank to the Palace; arriving half-dead with fear, they were conducted to a stage upon which, amid a tremendous racket of flutes and clogs, Gaius suddenly burst, dressed in cloak and ankle-length tunic, performed a song and dance, and disappeared again. Yet, with all these gifts, he could not swim a stroke!

55. On those whom he loved he bestowed an almost insane passion. He would shower kisses on Mnester the comedian, even in the theatre; and if anyone made the slightest noise during a performance, Gaius had the offender dragged from his seat and beat him with his own hands. To a knight who created some disturbance while Mnester was on the stage, he sent instructions by a centurion to go at once to Ostia and convey a sealed message to King Ptolemy in Mauretania. The message read: 'Do nothing at all, either good or bad, to the bearer.'

He chose Thracian gladiators to officer his German bodyguard. He reduced the defensive armour of the men-at-arms; and when a gladiator of this sort, called Columbus, won a fight but was lightly wounded, Gaius had him treated with a virulent poison which he afterwards called 'Columbinum' – at any rate that was how he described it in his catalogue of poisons. He supported the Leek-Green faction with such ardour that he would often dine and spend the night in their stables and, on one occasion, gave the driver Eutychus presents worth 20,000 gold pieces. To prevent Incitatus, his favourite horse, from being disturbed he always picketed the neighbourhood with troops on the day before the races, ordering them to enforce absolute silence. Incitatus owned a marble stable, an ivory stall, purple blankets, and a jewelled collar; also a house, a team of slaves, and furniture – to provide suitable entertainment for guests whom Gaius invited in its name. It is said that he even planned to award Incitatus a consulship.

56. Such frantic and reckless behaviour roused murderous thoughts in certain minds. One or two plots for his assassination were discovered; others were still awaiting a favourable opportunity, when two men put their heads together and succeeded in killing him, thanks to the co-operation of his most powerful freedmen and the Guards' commanders. These commanders had been accused of being implicated in a previous plot and, although innocent, realized that Gaius hated and feared them. Once, in fact, he had subjected

VENUS AND PRIAPUS
97. *Marble statue of Venus and Priapus from Pompeii. It was found in what may have been a brothel. Venus was the goddess of love, known for her adulterous love affairs, and Priapus was a god of fertility, the subject of obscene stories and allusions.* (Naples, Museum.)

them to public shame and suspicion, taking them aside and announcing, as he waved a sword, that he would gladly kill himself if they thought him deserving of death. After this he accused them again and again, each to the other, and tried to make bad blood between them. At last they decided to kill him about noon at the conclusion of the Palatine Games, the principal part being claimed by Cassius Chaerea. Gaius had persistently teased Cassius, who was no longer young, for his supposed effeminacy. Whenever he demanded the watchword, Gaius used to give him 'Priapus', or 'Venus'; and if he came to acknowledge a favour, always stuck out his middle finger for him to kiss, and waggled it obscenely.

57. Many omens of Gaius's approaching murder were reported. While the statue of Olympian Jupiter was being dismantled before removal to Rome at his command, it burst into such a roar of laughter that the scaffolding collapsed and the workmen took to their heels; and a man named Cassius appeared immediately afterwards saying that he had been ordered, in a dream, to sacrifice a bull to Jupiter. The Capitol at Capua was struck by lightning on the Ides of March, which some interpreted as portending another imperial death; because of the famous murder that had taken place on that day. At Rome, the Palace doorkeeper's lodge was likewise struck; and this seemed to mean that the owner of the Palace stood in danger of attack by his own guards. On asking Sulla the soothsayer for his horoscope, Gaius learned that he must expect to die very soon. The Oracle of Fortune at Antium likewise warned him: 'Beware of Cassius!' whereupon, forgetting Chaerea's family name, he ordered the murder of Cassius Longinus, Governor of Asia at the time. On the night before his assassination he dreamed that he was standing beside Jupiter's heavenly throne, when the God kicked him with a toe of his right foot and sent him tumbling down to earth. Some other events that occurred on the morning of his death were also read as portents. For instance, blood splashed him as he was sacrificing a flamingo; Mnester danced the same tragedy of Cinyras that had been performed by the actor Neoptolemus during the Games at which King Philip of Macedonia was assassinated; and in a farce[14] called *Laureolus*, at the close of which the leading character, a highwayman, had to die while escaping and vomit blood, the understudies were so anxious to dis-

play their proficiency at dying that they flooded the stage with blood. A nocturnal performance by Egyptians and Ethiopians was also in rehearsal: a play staged in the Underworld.

58. On 24 January then, just past midday, Gaius, seated in the Theatre, could not make up his mind whether to adjourn for lunch; he still felt a little queasy after too heavy a banquet on the previous night. However, his friends persuaded him to come out with them, along a covered walk; and there he found some boys of noble family who had been summoned from Asia, rehearsing the Trojan war-dance. He stopped to watch and encourage them, and would have taken them back to the Theatre and held the performance at once, had their principal not complained of a cold. Two different versions of what followed are current. Some say that Chaerea came up behind Gaius as he stood talking to the boys and, with a cry of 'Take this!' gave him a deep sword-wound in the neck, whereupon Cornelius Sabinus, the other colonel, stabbed him in the breast. The other version makes Sabinus tell certain centurions implicated in the plot to clear away the crowd and then ask Gaius for the day's watchword. He is said to have replied: 'Jupiter', whereupon Chaerea, from his rear, yelled: 'So be it!' – and split his jawbone as he turned his head. Gaius lay writhing on the ground. 'I am still alive!' he shouted; but word went round: 'Strike again!' and he succumbed to thirty further wounds, including sword-thrusts through the genitals. His bearers rushed to help him, using their litter-poles; and soon his German bodyguard appeared, killing several of the assassins and a few innocent senators into the bargain.

59. He died at the age of twenty-nine after ruling for three years, ten months and eight days. His body was moved secretly to the Lamian Gardens, half-cremated on a hastily-built pyre, and then buried beneath a shallow covering of sods. Later, when his sisters returned from exile they exhumed, cremated, and entombed it. But all the city knew that the Gardens had been haunted until then by his ghost, and that something horrible appeared every night at the scene of the murder until at last the building burned down. Caesonia was murdered by a centurion at the same time, and their daughter's brains were dashed out against a wall.

60. The condition of the times could be judged by the sequel: at first no one would believe that he had really been assassinated, and suspected that the story was invented and circulated by himself to discover

---

14. Mime. The understudies came on afterwards and imitated the actions of the star.

what people thought of him. The conspirators had no particular candidate for Emperor in mind, and the senators were so unanimously bent on restoring the Republic that the Consuls summoned the first assembly not to the House, because it was named the Julian Building, but to the Capitol. Some wanted all memory of the Caesars obliterated, and their temples destroyed.

People commented on the fact that every Caesar named 'Gaius' had died by the sword, beginning with Gaius Julius Caesar Strabo, murdered in Cinna's day.[15]

15. No: Gaius, Julius Caesar's father, had died without violence; and so had Augustus's grandson, Gaius Caesar.

V

CLAUDIUS

AFTERWARDS DEIFIED

When, three months after her marriage to Augustus, Livia gave birth to Decimus (later Nero) Drusus[1] – the father of the future Emperor Claudius – people naturally suspected that he was the product of adultery with his stepfather. This provoked the following epigram:

> How fortunate those parents are for whom
> Their child is only three months in the womb!

Drusus commanded an army against the Raetians, and subsequently against the Germans, while holding the successive ranks of quaestor and praetor. He was the first Roman general to navigate the North Sea; and also excavated the Drusus Canals, as they still call them.[2] After defeating the local tribes in a series of battles, Drusus drove them far back into the wild interior and did not cease his dispute until checked by an apparition: a barbarous woman of phenomenal size who warned him in Latin to venture no farther.

1. Drusus the Elder.   2. Connecting the Rhine with the Yssel.

These campaigns earned Drusus an ovation, with triumphal regalia; and he became Consul directly the praetorship ended. On resuming the war he died at his summer headquarters,[3] thenceforth known as 'The Accursed Camp'. His body was carried to Rome by relays of leading citizens from the various citizen municipalities and veterans' colonies which lay along the route. There a waiting deputation of magistrates' clerks took it to a pyre on the Campus Martius. The army put up a monument in his honour, round which the soldiers were to make a ceremonial run each year on a stated day, when the communities of Gaul would pay their respects with prayers and sacrifices. The Senate voted Drusus many honours, among them a marble

3. 9 B.C.

THE EMPEROR AS JUPITER. *The greatest honour which a Roman republican leader could achieve was the triumph (see Ill. 70). During the celebration he was clothed like the statue of Jupiter on the Capitol, for he represented the god who had brought victory to Roman arms. After the end of the republic, this honour was bestowed only on the Emperor, who at the same time came to be viewed as Jupiter's counterpart on earth.*
98 (opposite). *Claudius as Jupiter. The eagle, bird of Jupiter, stands next to him.* (Olympia, Museum.)

CLAUDIUS
99. *Coin from Rome.* (London, British Museum.)

arch on the Appian Way decorated with trophies, and the surname Germanicus to be held by himself and his descendants.

Drusus was, they say, no less eager for personal glory than devoted to republicanism. Not content with gaining victories over the enemy, he had a long-standing ambition to win 'The Noblest Spoils';[4] and used to chase German chieftains across the battlefield at great risk to his life. He also openly announced that, as soon as he came to power, he would restore the old form of government.

This must be why some writers allege that Augustus suspected him of being a revolutionary, recalled him from his province and, when he did not come back at once, had him poisoned. I think it right not to suppress this view, though it seems to me most improbable; in point of fact, Augustus felt so deep a love for Drusus while he lived that, as he admitted to the Senate on one occasion, he considered him no less his heir than were his sons;[5] and his funeral speech to the people not only eulogized Drusus but included a prayer that the gods would make these young Caesars closely resemble him, and grant them as honourable a death. Nor did he think it enough to have an adulatory inscription carved on Drusus's tomb, in verses of his own composition: he also wrote his biography in prose.

Antonia the Younger bore Drusus several children,

100. THE NOBLEST SPOILS *were the armour of the leader of the enemy, captured by a Roman general in single combat. They are shown on this relief of the first century* B.C. (?) *with two trophies.* (Rome, Capitoline Museum.)

three of whom survived him: Germanicus, Livilla, and Claudius.

2. Claudius was born at Lugdunum, in the consulship of Iullus Antonius and Fabius Africanus, on 1 August 10 B.C., the very day when the first altar was dedicated there to Augustus the God; and he was given the name Tiberius Claudius Drusus. Subsequently he assumed the surname Germanicus after his brother had been admitted into the Julian House as Tiberius's adopted son. He lost his father while he was still a baby. Nearly the whole of his childhood and youth was so troubled by various diseases that he grew dull-witted and had little physical strength; and on reaching the age at which he should have won a magistracy or chosen a private career, was considered by his family incapable of doing either.

Even adult status did not free him from the supervision of a tutor, about whom he later wrote: 'The man was a barbarian, an ex-transport officer who had been assigned the task of punishing me savagely whatever I might do.' Claudius's weak health also accounted for his being muffled in a cloak – an unprecedented sight

4. The armour of an enemy leader, taken from him in hand-to-hand combat by a Roman general.

5. i.e., Gaius and Lucius, his grandsons whom he adopted.

– while presiding at the Gladiatorial Games given by Germanicus and himself to honour their father's memory; and, at his coming of age, he was taken up to the Capitol in a litter, about midnight, without the customary solemn procession.

3. Though he applied himself seriously to literature while still a child, and published several samples of his proficiency in its various departments, this did not advance him to public office or inspire the family with brighter hopes for his future.

Claudius's mother, Antonia, often called him 'a monster: a man whom Nature had not finished but had merely begun'; and, if she ever accused anyone of stupidity, would exclaim: 'He is a bigger fool even than my son Claudius!' Livia, his grandmother, never failed to treat him with the deepest scorn, and seldom addressed him personally; her reproofs came in the form of brief, bitter letters or oral messages. When his sister Livilla heard someone predict that he would one day succeed to the throne, she prayed openly and aloud that the Roman people might be spared so cruel and undeserved a misfortune. Finally, to show what opinions, favourable and otherwise, his great-uncle, Augustus, held of him, I quote the following extracts from the imperial correspondence:

4. My dear Livia,
As you suggested, I have now discussed with Tiberius what we should do about your grandson Claudius at the coming Games of Mars. We both agreed that a decision ought to be taken once and for all. The question is whether he has – shall I say? – full command of all his senses. If so, I can see nothing against sending him through the same degrees of office as his brother; but should he be deemed physically and mentally deficient, the public (which always likes to scoff and mock at such things) must not be given a chance of laughing at him and us. I fear that we shall find ourselves in constant trouble if the question of his fitness to officiate in this or that capacity keeps cropping up. We should therefore decide in advance whether he can or cannot be trusted with offices of state.

As regards the immediate question in your last letter, I have no objection to his taking charge of the priests' banquet at the Festival of Mars, if he lets his relative, the son of Silvanus, stand by to see that he does not make a fool of himself. But I am against his watching the Games in the Circus from the imperial box, where the eyes of the whole audience would be on him. I am also against his being made his brother's assistant during the Latin Festival on the Alban Mount, merely to avoid the embarrassment of appointing him City Prefect at Rome for the occasion; because if capable of the former appointment, he is also capable of the latter.

In short, my dear Livia, I am anxious that a decision should

be reached on this matter once and for all, to save us from further alternations of hope and despair. You are at liberty to show this part of my letter to our kinswoman Antonia for her perusal . . .

Augustus wrote to Livia on another occasion:

. . . While you are away, I shall certainly invite young Tiberius Claudius to dine every day; rather than leave him to the exclusive company of Athenodorus and Sulpicius. If only he would show greater concentration and behave with less capriciousness in his choice of someone to imitate in his movements, deportment and gait. I am sorry for the poor fellow, because in serious matters, when not wool-gathering, he shows a very decent character.

And again:

My dear Livia,
I'll be damned if your grandson Tiberius Claudius hasn't given me a very pleasant surprise! How on earth anyone who talks so confusedly can nevertheless speak in public with such clearness, saying all that needs to be said, I simply do not understand.

However, it is clear what decision Augustus eventually took; because he gave Claudius no honours except a seat in the College of Augurs, and listed him in his will among heirs to the sixth part of his estate – relatives so distant as to be practically strangers – and in the third degree. The only legacy Claudius got was a mere 1,000 gold pieces.

5. When his paternal uncle Tiberius succeeded Augustus, Claudius asked to be given some office of state. Tiberius sent him the consular regalia. Claudius then pressed for the duties of the office as well. Tiberius's reply ran: 'The forty gold pieces I sent you were meant to be squandered on toys during the Saturnalia and Sigillaria.'[6] After that Claudius renounced all hopes of a political career, spending an obscure and idle life between his suburban mansion and a villa in Campania. Since his intimates included men of the lowest class, Claudius's reputation for stupidity was further enhanced by stories of his drunkenness and love of gambling. Yet, despite this behaviour, many men of distinction continued to visit him, and he never lost the people's respect.

6. The Knights twice chose Claudius as head of a deputation to the Consuls: the first time was when they requested the privilege of carrying Augustus's body back to Rome on their shoulders; the second, when

6. An extension of the Saturnalia in December, when gifts of little statuettes (*sigilla*) were made.

Sejanus's conspiracy had been suppressed and they were offering felicitations. At Claudius's appearance in the theatre or amphitheatre, the entire Equestrian Order would rise and take off their cloaks as a mark of honour. The Senate, for their part, voted that he should be made an extraordinary member of the Augustan priesthood, who were as a rule chosen by lot; and when one day his mansion burned down they decreed that it should be rebuilt at public expense, and that he should have the honour of addressing the House among men of consular rank. Tiberius, however, vetoed this second decree on the ground that Claudius's ill-health prevented him from participating in

THE CONSULSHIP *was the highest magistracy, or civilian political office, of the Roman republic. Two Consuls were elected every year by the people. When a Consul appeared in public, he was accompanied by ten lictors, each of whom carried a bundle of rods tied round an axe – a token of the Consul's executive power. During the Empire, Consuls were, in effect, nominated by the Emperor, and they had little political power. But they continued fulfilling the ceremonial duties of their office: principally, they presided at the official games.*

101 (left). *Two lictors. Roman bronze, second century* A.D. (Berlin West, Staatliche Museen.)

102 (below). *Magistrate presiding at chariot races; his wife stands next to him. Funerary relief.* (Rome, Lateran.)

debates; and undertook that the cost of rebuilding the mansion would be defrayed out of his own pocket. Claudius was listed again only with heirs of the third degree – this time to a third part of the estate – in Tiberius's will; but he did secure a legacy of some 25,000 gold pieces and a commendation (in a list of Tiberius's relatives) to the armies, the Senate, and the People of Rome.

THE GAMES, *public displays consisting of gladiatorial combats, wild-beast hunts, chariot races, even mock naval battles, were a fundamental part of public life in any major Roman city (see Ill. 14), especially in Rome itself.*
103 (top). *Gladiators and trumpeters. Roman relief of the imperial period.* (Munich, Antikensammlung.)
104 (centre). *Chariot race, painting from Pompeii.* (Naples, Museum.)
105 (bottom). *Warships.* (Pompeii, House of the Vettii.)

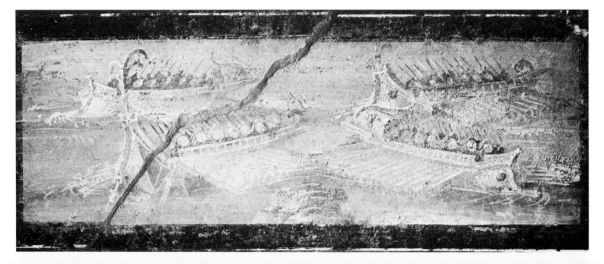

7. As soon as Claudius's nephew Gaius became Emperor and tried every means of gaining popularity, Claudius entered on his belated public career as Gaius's colleague in a two-months' consulship; and when he first entered the Forum with the consular rods, an eagle swooped down and perched on his shoulder. He also drew lots for a second consulship, and won one that would fall due four years later. Claudius often presided as Gaius's substitute at the Games, where the audience greeted him with: 'Long live the Emperor's Uncle!' and 'Long live Germanicus's Brother!'

8. Nevertheless, these honours did not protect him from frequent insults. If ever he arrived a little late in the dining hall, there was nothing for it but to tour the tables in search of a vacant couch; and when he took his usual after-dinner nap the company would pelt him with olives and date stones. Some jokers exercised their wit by putting slippers on his hands as he lay snoring, and then gave him a sudden blow of a whip or cane to wake him, so that he rubbed his face with them.

9. At times he found himself in real danger. He was nearly deposed from his first consulship for having taken so long to set up statues of Gaius's brothers Nero and Drusus; and later had a variety of vexatious accusations brought against him, not only by strangers but by his own servants. When the Senate sent him, with other envoys, to congratulate Gaius, in Germany, on the detection of a conspiracy headed by Lepidus and Gaetulicus,[7] the Emperor felt so furiously annoyed that his uncle, of all people, had been entrusted with this mission – as if to a child in need of a guardian – that according to one account, Claudius was thrown into the Rhine fully dressed, just as he had come. Afterwards, by way of humiliation, Gaius gave orders that he should be the last man of consular rank called upon to speak in any debate. The Senate even found that a will witnessed by him was a forgery; and as a climax, he had to pay a fee of 80,000 gold pieces for entering Gaius's new priesthood. This sum he borrowed from the Treasury; but could not meet the obligation, and his property was formally advertised for sale in accordance with the law.

10. Having spent the better part of his life in circumstances like these, Claudius became Emperor, at the age of fifty, by an extraordinary accident. When the assassins of Gaius shut everyone out, pretending that he wished to be alone, Claudius went off with the rest and retired to a room called the Hermaeum; but

presently heard about the murder and slipped away in alarm to a near-by balcony, where he hid trembling behind the door curtains. A Guardsman, wandering vaguely through the Palace, noticed a pair of feet beneath the curtain, pulled their owner out for identification and recognized him. Claudius dropped on the floor and clasped the soldier's knees, but found himself acclaimed Emperor. The man took him to his fellow-soldiers who were angry, confused, and at a loss what to do; however, they placed him in a litter and, because his own bearers had run off, took turns at carrying him to the Praetorian Camp. Claudius was filled with terror and despair; in his passage through the streets everyone cast him pitying glances as if he were an innocent man being hurried to execution. Once safely inside the rampart of the camp, Claudius spent the night among the sentries, confident now that no immediate danger threatened, but feeling little hope for the future since the Consuls, with the approval of the Senate and the aid of city cohorts, had seized the Forum and Capitol, and were determined to maintain public liberty.[7]

When the tribunes of the people summoned him to visit the House and there advise on the situation, Claudius replied that he was being forcibly detained and could not come. The Senate, however, was dilatory in putting its plans into effect because of the tiresome recriminations of those who held opposing opinions. Meanwhile, crowds surrounded the building and demanded a monarchy, expressly calling for Claudius; so he allowed the Guards to acclaim him Emperor and to swear allegiance. He also promised every man 150 gold pieces, which made him the first of the Caesars to purchase the loyalty of his troops.

11. No sooner had Claudius's power been established than he gave priority to the task of obliterating all records of those two days when there had been talk of changing the form of government. He ordered a general amnesty and forgetfulness for what had been done and said during that period, and observed it himself, apart from executing a few of the colonels and centurions who had conspired against Gaius – to make an example of them and because they had, he knew, planned his own murder as well. Next, to show his family devotion, he always used 'By Augustus!' as the most sacred and frequent of his oaths; made the Senate decree his grandmother Livia divine honours, as well as an elephant-drawn carriage for her image, to match

7. i.e., restore the Republic.

that of Augustus, during ritual processions around the Circus; and instituted public sacrifices to the shades of his parents and annual Circus Games on his father's birthday, during which the image of his mother – now posthumously given the title of 'Augusta', which she had refused while alive – was paraded in a carriage. He also never missed a chance of keeping green the fame of his brother Germanicus; he entered a Greek comedy written by him for a theatrical contest at Neapolis, and awarded it first prize in accordance with the decision of the judges. Nor did he fail to honour Antony; in one proclamation he begged the people 'to celebrate my father Drusus's birthday all the more heartily because it happens likewise to have been that of my maternal grandfather Antony'. Moreover, he completed the marble arch in honour of Tiberius near Pompey's Theatre voted some years before by the Senate, but neglected by Gaius; and while annulling all Gaius's edicts, would not allow the day of his assassination to be proclaimed a public festival, although it marked the beginning of his own reign.

12. Claudius did not presume to accept excessive honours, even refusing the forename 'Imperator'; and let the betrothal of his daughter, and the birthday of his grandson, be celebrated quietly, with private ceremonies only. He recalled no exile from banishment without senatorial permission, and when wishing to bring the Guards' Commander and some colonels into the House, or to have the judicial decisions of his provincial agents ratified, would ask the Senate for these privileges as a favour; and approached the Consuls for leave to hold fairs on his private estates. Often he sat among the advisory board during trials in magistrates' courts; and at public games would rise with the audience and show his delight by clapping and shouting. When the tribunes of the people appeared before his judge's chair, he apologized to them because, owing to lack of space, they had to stand so that he could hear them. This sort of behaviour endeared him to the people so soon that when a rumour went around of his having been ambushed and assassinated on a journey to Ostia, everyone was aghast and began accusing the troops of treachery and the senators of murder. The magistrates had to bring two or three witnesses forward on the Rostra, followed by several more, to assure the city that he was safe and on the way home.

13. Nevertheless, various attempts were made on his life: by dissident individuals, by a group of conspirators, and by a civil war. First, a member of the public with a dagger was arrested about midnight near Claudius's bedroom. Two knights were found waiting to kill him – one with a sword-cane, as he left the Theatre; the other with a hunting-knife, as he sacrificed in the Temple of Mars. Then Asinius Gallus and Statilius Corvinus, grandsons respectively of the orators Pollio and Messala, brought some of Claudius's own freedmen and slaves into a plot for his deposition. Lastly, Furius Camillus Scribonianus, Governor of Dalmatia, started a civil war; but because of a superstitious terror which caused his rebellious legions to repent, it was smothered in less than five days. For, on being ordered to march off and rally around their new Emperor, they found that some divine intervention prevented them from dressing the Eagles with garlands and perfumes, and that the standards resisted all attempts to pull them out of the ground.

14. Claudius held four more consulships: the first two in successive years, the others at four-yearly intervals. The fourth lasted for six months, the remainder only for two; and he took over the third from a Consul who had just died – a thing which no other emperor had ever done before. During these terms of office and, indeed, at all times, Claudius was a most conscientious judge: sitting in court even on his own birthday and those of his family, sometimes actually on ancient popular holidays or days of ill-omen. Instead of always observing the letter of the law, he let himself be guided by his sense of equity, and when he thought the punishments prescribed were either too lenient or too severe, changed them accordingly. Thus, should plaintiffs have lost their cases in a lower court by demanding more damages than the law sanctioned, he allowed a re-trial. But if anyone were found guilty of some really shocking crime, Claudius exceeded the legal penalty and condemned him to the wild beasts.

15. However, his behaviour in hearing and deciding cases varied unpredictably: sometimes he was wise and prudent, sometimes thoughtless and hasty, sometimes downright foolish and apparently out of his senses. One man had presented himself for jury-service without disclosing that he was exempt, because of the number of his children; Claudius, revising the roster, expunged his name, remarking that he showed an unwholesome liking for the jury-box. A juror, challenged in court on the ground that he had a case of his own pending, replied: 'The objection is irrelevant; I am not called upon to plead before Caesar.' Claudius intervened, instructing the juryman to bring his case up at once, since the way he handled it would show how far he might be trusted while judging the other.

A woman once refused to admit that she was the mother of a young man produced in court, and a conflict of evidence arose; but the truth came out when Claudius ordered her to marry the man. He had a tendency to decide against whichever party in a suit happened to be absent, without troubling to ask whether or not this might have been unavoidable. After a man was found guilty of forgery, the crowd shouted: 'He ought to have his hands cut off!' Claudius immediately sent for an executioner, with block and cleaver, to act on this suggestion.

Again, during a wrangle between counsel as to whether a man accused of wrongfully posing as a Roman citizen should wear a Roman toga or a Greek mantle in court, Claudius demonstrated his fair-mindedness by making him wear a mantle when accused and a toga when defended. Before one case opened, it is said, he wrote out the following verdict, which he subsequently delivered: 'I decide in favour of the party which has told the truth.' Such behaviour so greatly discredited Claudius that he came into open and widespread contempt – so much so that when a lawyer kept apologizing for the non-appearance of a provincial witness whom Claudius had summoned, but would not explain it, repeated questioning at last elicited the answer: 'He is dead; I trust the excuse is legitimate.' Another lawyer thanked Claudius for letting him defend a client, and added: 'Though this is, of course, established practice.' Old people I know have told me that litigants imposed so rudely on his good nature that they would not only call him back after he had closed the court, but would catch at the hem of his toga, and even at his foot, in their efforts to detain him. Though all this may sound incredible, I must also record that one little Greek lawyer lost his temper with Claudius during a hearing and burst out: 'And as for you, you're a stupid old idiot!'

It is a matter of common knowledge that when a Roman knight was being falsely accused of unnatural offences against women – the charge had been framed by private enemies who would stop at nothing – and saw that Claudius was admitting the evidence of common prostitutes, he hurled a stylus and set of wax tablets in his face, shouting: 'A curse on your stupid, cruel ways!' Claudius's cheek was badly gashed.

16. The office of Censor had been allowed to lapse since the days of Plancus and Paulus, sixty years previously,[8] but Claudius assumed it; and here he proved

as inconsistent in his general principles as in his particular decisions. He kept the name of a young criminal on a list of knights which he was reviewing, and set no black mark against it; simply because the father denied that he had any complaints to make himself. 'This young man has a Censor of his own,' was Claudius's judgement. Another knight, though a notorious seducer of girls and married women, escaped with a caution: 'Restrain your passions, or at least go more carefully in future. Why should it be any business of mine who your mistress may be?' Once a man's friend persuaded Claudius to remove the black mark which stood against his name. 'But I want the erasure to show,' he insisted. Then there was the Greek nobleman struck from the roster of jurymen and actually deprived of his rights as a Roman citizen, because he did not know Latin. Moreover, Claudius would not let anyone employ a lawyer, when asked to give an account of his life, but made him speak for himself as best he could. Many knights were also struck from the list, much to their surprise, on the novel charge of going abroad without consulting the Emperor and obtaining leave of absence; since one of them had been acting as adviser to a king in his province, Claudius brought up the case of Rabirius Postumus who, in former times, had followed King Ptolemy to Alexandria in the hope of recovering a loan, and was tried for treason when he came back.

His attempts to remove still other names failed, the information collected by his agents proving so inaccurate. He found to his great shame that most of those charged with being bachelors or childless, or too poor to sustain their rank, were in fact married, or fathers of families, or quite comfortably off; and one knight, accused of having attempted suicide with a dagger, tore off his clothes and cried: 'Then show me the scar!' Among Claudius's memorable acts as Censor was the purchase of a beautiful silver chariot, offered for sale in the Sigillarian Street; he then had it hacked to pieces before his eyes! Two of the twenty edicts which he once published on a single day were: 'This year's vintage is unusually abundant, so everyone must pitch his wine-jars well,' and: 'Yew-juice is sovereign against snake-bite.'

17. Claudius's sole campaign was of no great importance. The Senate had already voted him triumphal regalia, but he thought it beneath his dignity to accept these, and decided that Britain was the country where a real triumph could be most readily earned. Its conquest had not been attempted since Julius Caesar's

8. 22 B.C.

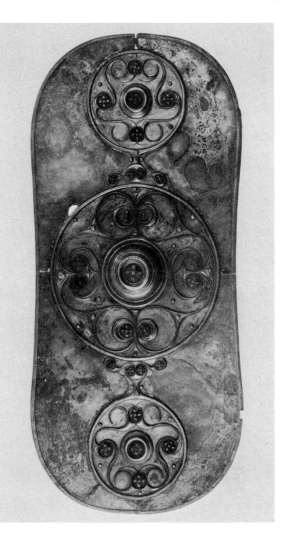

BRITAIN *at the time of the Roman conquest consisted of a series of independent Celtic kingdoms, whose culture and art forms were distinct from those of Rome. Celtic art is characterized by its flowing and at the same time intricate abstract designs.*

106 (above). *Celtic bronze vessel from Aylesford, Kent.* (London, British Museum.)

107 (right). *Celtic shield from Battersea.* (London, British Museum.)

day; and the Britons were now threatening vengeance because of a Roman refusal to return certain deserters. Sailing from Ostia, Claudius was twice nearly wrecked off the Ligurian coast, and again near the Stoechades Islands, but made port safely at Massilia. In consequence he marched north through Gaul until reaching Gesoriacum; crossed the Channel from there; and was back in Rome six months later. He had fought no battles and suffered no casualties, but reduced a large part of the island to submission. His triumph was a very splendid one, and among those whom he invited to witness it were his provincial governors, and certain exiles as well. The emblems of his victory included the naval crown,[9] representing the crossing and conquest, so to speak, of the Ocean, which he set on the Palace gable beside the civic crown.[10] His wife, Messalina, followed the chariot in a covered carriage, and behind her marched the generals who had won triumphal regalia in Britain. All wore purple-bordered togas except Marcus Crassus Frugi; having earned this same honour on a previous occasion, he now came dressed in a palm-embroidered tunic and rode a caparisoned charger.

9. Decorated with the beaks of ships.
10. Of oak-leaves; awarded for the saving of Roman citizens' lives.

BRITAIN: ROMAN CONQUEST AND SETTLEMENT. *Roman military architecture followed the same basic patterns throughout the Empire, regardless of indigenous architectural forms. It thus typifies the unifying effect of Roman government in the Mediterranean world and beyond. A Roman camp consisted of a rectangular enclosure surrounded by a wall and one or more ditches; inside, two streets intersecting at right angles gave access to the camp's various buildings.*

108 (opposite, top). *The Celtic fortification of Maiden Castle in Dorset was constructed on different principles: it is an earthwork which follows the natural contours of the land. Maiden Castle was conquered by Vespasian, the future Emperor.*

109 (opposite, below). *Housesteads, on Hadrian's Wall, was built almost a century later, in a different part of Britain, but follows the same basic design.*

110 (above). *The outlines of the Roman town of Silchester are still visible on this aerial photograph. The course of the town walls is marked by a circuit of trees, and in the foreground the main streets show up in a slightly lighter colour.*

18. Claudius always interested himself in the proper upkeep of the city and the regular arrival of grain supplies. When an obstinate fire ravaged the Aemilian quarter, he lodged at the Election hut on the Campus Martius for two nights running; and, because a force of Guards and another of Palace servants proved insufficient to cope with the blaze, made the magistrates summon the commons from every city district and then sat, with bags of coin piled before him, recruiting fire-fighters; whom he paid, on the nail, whatever seemed a suitable fee for their services.

Once, after a series of droughts had caused a scarcity of grain, a mob stopped Claudius in the Forum and pelted him so hard with curses and stale crusts that he had difficulty in regaining the Palace by a side-door; as a result he took all possible steps to import grain, even during the winter months – insuring merchants against the loss of their ships in stormy weather (which guaranteed them a good return on their ventures), and offering a large bounty for every new grain-transport built, proportionate to its tonnage.

19. The shipowner, if he happened to be a Roman

SEAFARING *in the ancient world could be a dangerous occupation, for which men prayed for supernatural aid.* III. *Altars dedicated to Tranquillity and to the Winds.* (Rome, Capitoline Museum.)

citizen, was exempted from the Papian-Poppaean Law;[11] if only a possessor of Latin rights, acquired full Roman citizenship; if a woman, enjoyed the privileges granted to mothers of four children. These regulations have never since been modified.

20. Claudius's public works, though not numerous, were important. They included, in particular, an aqueduct begun by Gaius; the draining of the Fucine Lake and the building of the harbour at Ostia – though he knew that Augustus had turned down the Marsians'

11. Which increased sanctions against celibacy.

frequent requests for emptying the Lake, and that Julius Caesar, while often on the point of excavating the harbour at Ostia, had always abandoned the project as impractical. Claudius also brought the cool and abundant springs called the Caerulean and the Curtian, or Albudignan, as well as the New Anio, into Rome; the water ran along a stone aqueduct, with lofty arches, now known by his name, and was then distributed into a number of ornamental reservoirs. He undertook the Fucine drainage scheme as much for profit as for glory: a group of businessmen had offered to shoulder the expense if he awarded them the reclaimed land. The outlet took eleven years to dig, although 30,000 men were kept continuously at work; it was three miles long, and his engineers had to level part of a hill and tunnel through the remainder. At Ostia, Claudius constructed a new port by throwing out curved breakwaters on either side of the harbour and built a deep-water mole by its entrance. For the base of this mole he used the

ship in which Caligula had transported a great obelisk from Heliopolis; it was first sunk, then secured with piles, and finally crowned with a very tall lighthouse – like the Pharos at Alexandria – that guided ships into the harbour at night by the beams of a lamp.

21. Claudius often distributed largesse to the people, and gave numerous magnificent public shows; not only the traditional ones in the customary places, but others, including novelties and ancient revivals, where nobody had ever seen them staged before.

Pompey's Theatre was damaged by fire, and when Claudius held Games at its rededication he first sacrificed in the temples above the auditorium, and then walked down the aisle between packed and silent tiers, to inaugurate the Games from a raised seat in the orchestra.

He also celebrated Saecular Games, on the excuse that Augustus had staged them before they were really due; though his own *History* mentions how much

SHIPPING. *Most overseas imports into Rome, especially grain, passed through the port of Ostia near Rome; construction of a new harbour there was begun by Claudius and completed by Nero.*

112. *The harbour of Ostia with two seagoing ships; the one on the left has the Roman wolf and twins on its sails (see Ill. 5), and behind it can be seen the lighthouse of Ostia. In the front, off centre, is a statue of Neptune, god of the sea, and to the right is the sign to avert the evil eye. Roman relief.* (Rome, Museo Torlonia.)

trouble Augustus took to reckon the intervals separating their occurrences in the past, and to recommence the series, after the tradition had long been broken, when the correct year came round once more. Therefore, when the Herald invited the people, in the ancient formula, to 'attend games which nobody present has ever seen or will ever see again', a shout of laughter arose. Not only had many persons present witnessed Saecular Games, but some actors were even billed to take part in them for the second time. Claudius often gave chariot races in the Vatican Circus, too, sometimes introducing wild-beast shows between every five events.

The barred-off chariot compartments at the starting-post in the Great Circus had been built of volcanic tufa and wood. Claudius substituted marble for the tufa, provided goals of gilded metal, and also reserved seats for the senators, who had hitherto sat among the common people. Besides the chariot races he staged the so-called Troy Game; a panther hunt by a squadron of Guards cavalry under their colonels and the Commander in person; and a show in which Thessalian horsemen drove wild bulls across the arena, tired them out, leaped on them, seized hold of their horns and then threw them to the ground.

Among the many Gladiatorial Games presented by him in various places, was an annual one in the Guards Camp, without wild beasts or fancy equipment, to celebrate his accession; another of the usual kind in the Enclosure; and a third, also in the Enclosure, but not part of the regular programme. This last show ran for a few days only and he himself called it 'The Picnic', because the first time he invited the people, by his heralds, 'to take pot-luck, as it were'.

Claudius never behaved less formally than at these Picnics – exposing his left hand in plebeian fashion when he distributed prizes, instead of keeping it decently covered by his toga, and counting the number of gold pieces on his fingers – 'One, two, three . . .' he would shout. He urged the audience to enjoy themselves, addressing them all indiscriminately as 'My lords', and cracking stupid and far-fetched jokes. Once, on hearing the cry: 'Bring on The Dove!'[12] he yelled back: 'Certainly, but he'll take a bit of catching!' Yet when four brothers pleaded for the discharge of their father, a chariot-fighter, Claudius presented him with the customary wooden sword amid resounding cheers, and then circulated a note: 'You now see the great advantage of having a large family; it can win favour and protection even for a gladiator.' He also staged, on the Campus Martius, the realistic storm and sack of a town, with a tableau of the British king's surrender, at which he presided in his purple campaigning cloak.

12. The nickname of a famous gladiator.

Before allowing the water to escape from the Fucine Lake, he arranged to have a sham seafight on it; but when the gladiators shouted: 'Hail, Caesar, we salute you, we who are about to die!' he answered: 'Or not, as the case may be.' They unanimously took him up on this and refused to fight, insisting that his words amounted to a pardon. Claudius grew so angry that he was on the point of sending troops to massacre them all, or burning them in their ships; however, he changed his mind, jumped from his throne and, hobbling ridiculously down to the lakeside, threatened and coaxed the gladiators into battle. Twelve Rhodian triremes then engaged twelve Sicilian ones; the signal for the fight being given by a mechanical silver Triton, which emerged from the Lake bottom and blew a conch.

22. In matters of religious ritual, civil and military customs, and the social status of all classes at home and abroad, Claudius not only revived obsolescent traditions but invented new ones. He never admitted a priest into a college without first taking a personal oath that he thought him worthy of the honour; and required the praetor to call an assembly whenever an earthquake shock was registered at Rome, and proclaim a public holiday. If a bird of evil omen perched on the Capitol, Claudius would go to the Rostra in his capacity as Chief Priest, order artisans and slaves to withdraw, and then read out the customary formula of supplication which the populace repeated after him.

23. Until this reign there had been two terms in the Law Courts, the summer and the winter; Claudius made them continuous. Another of his changes was to institute permanent courts, both at Rome and under the governors of the provinces, for judging fiduciary cases, instead of entrusting them to the annually appointed Roman magistrates. He cancelled Tiberius's supplement to the Papian-Poppaean Law which implied that men over sixty years of age could not beget children; and sponsored a law authorizing the Consuls, contrary to the customary procedure, to choose guardians for orphans; and passed another law, ruling that no person who had been exiled from a province might enter the city or even Italy.

A new form of punishment which forbade some persons to go more than three miles outside Rome was likewise introduced by Claudius. Whenever about to deal with any business of peculiar importance in the House, he would take his seat either between the two Consuls or else on the bench kept for tribunes of the people. Hitherto, when Romans wished to travel

113. THE MELTING POT. *From the first century* B.C., *Rome became an increasingly international city, where people, customs and religions from all parts of the then known world converged. This diversity is illustrated by a bronze statuette of the goddess Fortune: she holds the rudder and horn of plenty which are her own attributes; but on her head she wears the headdress of Isis with the crescent moon of the moon goddess added to it (see Ill. 36). She also has the wings of the goddess Victory, round her right arm coils the serpent of Salus (Health; see Ill. 52), and she wears the deerskin of Dionysus, god of wine.* (Berlin West, Staatliche Museen.)

abroad, the Senate had considered their applications; Claudius reserved the right to deal with these himself.

24. He awarded consular regalia even to his provincial agents of the second class; and if any of them declined this promotion, would not allow them to remain knights. At the beginning of his reign Claudius undertook to create no new senator unless he could prove that his ancestors had been Roman citizens for five generations; presently, however, he awarded this rank to the son of a freedman on the sole condition that he should get himself adopted by a knight. Then, to forestall criticism, he gave out that Appius the Blind, who had founded the Claudian House and been appointed Censor, used to allow freedmen's sons into the Senate; yet this was to misread the word 'freedmen' which, in those days, meant the free-born sons of ex-slaves, not the ex-slaves themselves.

Claudius relieved the quaestors of their obligation to keep the roads paved, expecting them to stage gladiatorial shows instead; next, he withdrew those on duty at Ostia and in Gaul and gave them back their custodianship of the Public Treasury in the Temple of Saturn, which had previously, as now once more, been held by praetors or ex-praetors.

When he awarded triumphal regalia to Lucius Junius Silanus (the prospective husband of his daughter[13]) and to numerous elder men at Rome, all on the slightest of excuses, the legions circulated a joint petition begging that he would issue the same honour to every provincial governor of consular rank on his appointment – otherwise he would try to win it in the field by provoking hostilities. He granted Aulus Plautius an ovation, going out to meet him when he entered the city and courteously giving him the wall on his way up to the Capitol and down again. Moreover, Gabinius Secundus was permitted to adopt the surname 'Cauchius' for his victory over the Cauchi, a German tribe.

25. Claudius made new regulations for the military careers of knights: after commanding an infantry cohort, they were promoted to a cavalry squadron, and then rose to a full colonelcy. He also introduced a so-called 'supernumerary' army service for performance in name only, though it counted as effective; and persuaded the House to issue a decree, forbidding soldiers to pay complimentary calls on senators. Any freedman who tried to pass himself off as a knight found his property confiscated; and if one proved ungrateful to his

13. Octavia.

former master and caused him annoyance, back he went to slavery – Claudius told the lawyers engaged in such cases that a patron should not be placed in the disgraceful position of having to sue his own freedman.

Finding that a number of sick or worn-out slaves had been marooned by their owners on the Island of Aesculapius in the Tiber, to avoid the trouble of giving them proper medical attention, Claudius freed them all and ruled that none who got well again should return to the control of his former owner; furthermore, that any owner who made away with a sick slave, rather than abandon him, should be charged with murder. One of his edicts banned travel through any Italian town except on foot, in a sedan-chair, or in a litter. He also stationed cohorts as fire brigades at Puteoli and Ostia.

It now became illegal for foreigners to adopt the names of Roman families, and any who usurped the rights of Roman citizens were executed in the Esquiline Field. Tiberius had converted the provinces of Greece and Macedonia into a private domain of his own; Claudius gave them back to the Senate. He deprived the Lycians of national independence to punish their love of savage vendettas; but restored the Rhodians' independence to express his pleasure at their recantation of their faults. In granting the Trojans, as founders of the Roman race, perpetual exemption from tribute, he supported his act by reading aloud an ancient letter written in Greek to King Seleucus, from the Senate and People of Rome, with a promise of loyal friendship on condition that Seleucus should 'keep their Trojan kinsfolk free from all imposts'. Because the Jews at Rome caused continuous disturbances at the instigation of Chrestus,[14] he expelled them from the city. When the German envoys first visited the Theatre, they took their seats among the common people, but, noticing the Parthian and Armenian envoys seated with the Senators in the Orchestra, went to join them – were they not just as brave and nobly born? Claudius admired their simple confidence and let them remain there. Augustus had been content to prohibit any Roman citizen in Gaul from taking part in the savage and terrible Druidic cult; Claudius abolished it altogether. On the other hand, he attempted to transfer the Eleusinian Mysteries from Attica to Rome; and had the ruined Temple of Venus on Mount Eryx in Sicily restored at the expense of the Public Treasury. When-

ever he concluded a treaty with foreign rulers, he sacrificed a sow in the Forum, using the ancient formula of the Fetial priests. Yet all these acts, and others like them – indeed, one might say, everything that Claudius did throughout his reign – were dictated by his wives and freedmen: he practically always obeyed their whims rather than his own judgement.

26. Claudius was twice betrothed while still a boy: to Augustus's great-grand-daughter Aemilia Lepida, and to Livia Medullina, surnamed Camilla, of the family of the ancient dictator Camillus. However, when Aemilia Lepida's parents offended Augustus her engagement was broken off; and Livia Medullina died of some illness on what should have been her wedding day. His first wife, Plautia Urgulanilla, whose father had won a triumph, he divorced for scandalous misbehaviour and the suspicion of murder; his next, Aelia Paetina, daughter of an ex-consul, he also divorced, for slight offences. Then he married Valeria Messalina, daughter of his cousin Messala Barbatus. But it turned out that she was not only guilty of other disgraceful crimes, but had gone so far as to commit bigamy with Gaius Silius, and even sign a formal marriage contract before witnesses; so Claudius executed her and told the assembled Praetorian Guard that, having been unfortunate in his wives, he was resolved to live a celibate life in future – they could kill him if he did not keep his word!

Almost at once, however, he planned either to marry Lollia Paulina, Gaius's widow, or to re-marry his divorced wife Aelia Paetina; but it was Agrippina, daughter of his brother Germanicus, who hooked him. She had a niece's privilege of kissing and caressing Claudius, and exercised it with a noticeable effect on his passions: when the House next met, he persuaded a group of senators to propose that a union between him and her should be compulsorily arranged, in the public interest; and that other uncles should likewise be free to marry their nieces, though this had hitherto counted as incest. The wedding took place with scarcely a single day's delay, but no other uncle cared to follow Claudius's example, except one freedman, and one leading-centurion whose marriage he and Agrippina both attended.

27. He had children by three of his wives. Urgulanilla bore him Drusus and Claudia; Paetina had a daughter Antonia; and Messalina presented him with Octavia and a son, first named Germanicus and then Britannicus. He lost Drusus just before he came of age, choked by a pear which he had playfully thrown up

14. i.e., apparently Christ (who had been crucified in the reign of Tiberius).

and caught in his open mouth; since he had been betrothed, only a few days previously, to Sejanus's daughter, the rumour that Sejanus murdered him becomes still less plausible. Claudia's real father was Claudius's freedman Boter. Claudius disavowed paternity and, though she was born nearly five months after the divorce, had her laid naked outside Urgulanilla's house-door. Antonia was twice married: first to Gnaeus Pompeius and then to Faustus Sulla, both young noblemen of the highest birth. Octavia was betrothed to Lucius Silanus before marrying Claudius's step-son, Nero; and Britannicus was born on the twenty-second day of his father's reign, while he was also Consul for the second time. Claudius would often pick little Britannicus up and show him to the troops, or to the audience at the Games, either seated in his lap or held at arms' length. His cry: 'Good luck to you, my boy!' was loudly echoed on all sides. Of his three sons-in-law, Claudius adopted only Nero; Pompeius and Sulla were put to death.

28. Among Claudius's favourite freedmen were Posides the eunuch, to whom he actually awarded, at his British triumph, the decoration of the headless spear, along with soldiers who had fought in the field. For Felix he had an equally high regard, giving him command of infantry cohorts and cavalry squadrons, and the Governorship of Judaea; this Felix married three queens. Then there was Harpocras, who earned the privileges of riding through Rome in a litter and staging public entertainments as though he were a knight. Claudius had an even higher regard for Polybius, his literary mentor, who often walked between the two Consuls. But his firmest devotion was reserved for Narcissus, his secretary, and Pallas, his treasurer, whom he encouraged the Senate to honour with large gifts of money and the insignia of quaestors and praetors as well. They were able to acquire such riches, by illegitimate means, that when one day Claudius complained how little cash was left in the imperial treasury, someone answered neatly that he would have heaps of pocket money if only his two freedmen took him into partnership.

29. As I mention above, Claudius fell so deeply under the influence of these freedmen and wives that he seemed to be their servant rather than their emperor; and distributed honours, army commands, indulgences or punishments according to their wishes, however capricious, seldom even aware of what he was about. I need not dwell on matters of lesser importance: how he revoked grants, cancelled edicts, bra-

zenly amended the texts of letters-patent he had issued, or even openly substituted new versions for the old. Suffice it to record that he executed his father-in-law Appius Silanus; Julia, daughter of Tiberius's son Drusus; and Julia, daughter of his own brother Germanicus – all on unsupported charges and without the right to plead in self-defence. Gnaeus Pompeius, who had married his daughter Antonia, was stabbed to death while in bed with a favourite boy-friend; and Lucius Silanus, whom Claudius had betrothed to his daughter Octavia, lost his praetorship and, four days later, had orders to commit suicide; this was the very New Year's Day on which Claudius married Agrippina. He executed thirty-five senators and 300 Roman knights, with so little apparent concern that once, when a centurion reported that So-and-so the ex-Consul was now duly dispatched, and Claudius denied having given any such command, his freedmen satisfied him that the soldiers had done right not to wait for instructions before taking vengeance on an enemy of the Emperor. It is impossible, however, to believe that they tricked Claudius into signing the marriage contract between Messalina and her lover Silius by an assurance that the marriage was a mere fiction: a transference of portended dangers threatening 'Messalina's husband' from himself to someone else.

30. Claudius had a certain majesty and dignity of presence, which showed to best advantage when he happened to be standing or seated and especially when he was in repose. This was because, though tall, well-built, with a handsome face, a fine head of white hair and a firm neck, he stumbled as he walked owing to the weakness of his knees; and because, both in his lighter moments and at serious business, he had several disagreeable traits. These included an uncontrolled laugh, a horrible habit, under the stress of anger, of slobbering at the mouth and running at the nose, a stammer, and a persistent nervous tic of the head, which was apparent at all times but especially when he exerted himself to the slightest extent.

31. His health was wretched until he succeeded to the throne, when it suddenly became excellent, except for violent stomach-aches which often, he said, made him think of suicide.

32. He gave many splendid banquets, usually in large halls, and at times invited no fewer than 600 guests. One banquet was held close to the debouchment of the Fucine Lake on the day it was emptied; but the water came rushing out in a deluge and almost drowned him. His sons and daughters, like

those of other distinguished figures, were always expected to dine with him, sitting in old-fashioned style at the ends of the couches on which their parents reclined. Once, when a guest was believed to have pocketed a golden bowl, Claudius invited him again the next evening, this time setting a small earthenware basin in front of him. Some say that he planned an edict to legitimize the breaking of wind at table, either silently or noisily – after hearing about a man who was so modest that he endangered his health by an attempt to restrain himself.

33. No matter what time it was or where Claudius happened to be, he always felt ready for food or drink. One day, while he was judging a case in Augustus's Forum, the delicious smell of cooking assailed his nostrils; it was being prepared for the priestly college of the Salii in the adjacent Temple of Mars. He descended from the tribunal, closed the court, and went up to the place where the priests were, taking his place beside them. It was seldom that Claudius left a dining-hall except gorged and sodden; he would then go to bed and sleep supine with his mouth wide open – thus allowing a feather to be put down his throat, which would bring up the superfluous food and drink as vomit.

He slept in short snatches, being usually awake before midnight; but he would sometimes nod off during the daytime in court, and then the lawyers had difficulty in rousing him, however loud they shouted. His feelings for women were extremely passionate, but boys and men left him cold. So fervent was his devotion to dice that he published a book on the subject, and used to play, while out driving, on a special board fitted to his carriage which kept the game from upsetting.

34. His cruelty and bloodthirstiness appeared equally in great and small matters. For instance, if evidence had to be extracted under torture, or parricide punished, he allowed the law to take its course without delay and in his own presence. Once, when an old-fashioned execution had been ordered at Tibur and the criminals had been tied to their stakes, no executioner could be found to carry it out; but Claudius summoned one from Rome and was so set on witnessing the procedure that he waited until dusk for the man's arrival. At gladiatorial shows, whether or not they were staged by himself, he ruled that all combatants who fell accidentally should have their throats cut – above all net-fighters, so that he could gaze on their death agony. When a pair of gladiators mortally wounded each other he sent for their swords and had pocket-knives made

from them for his personal use. Claudius so greatly enjoyed wild-beast shows and the fencing matches during the luncheon interval that, after he had spent the whole morning in the amphitheatre from daybreak until noon, he would dismiss the audience, keep his seat, and not only watch the regular combats but extemporize others between the stage carpenters, and similar members of the theatre staff, as a punishment for the failure of any mechanical device to work as it should. He even forced one of his pages to enter the arena just as he was, and fight in his toga.

35. Claudius was so timid and suspicious that, though making a show of simplicity in the early days of his reign, as I mentioned above, he never attended a banquet unless with an escort of javelin-bearing Guards, and waited upon by soldiers performing the duties of servants. Before entering a sick-room he always had it carefully gone over: pillows and mattresses were prodded, and bedclothes shaken out. Later, he even required all visitors to be searched when they came to pay him a morning call, and excused no one the most thorough examination. Indeed, it was not until the end of his reign that he reluctantly gave up the practice of having women, boys, and girls pawed about during these examinations, and of removing the stylus-case from every caller's attendant or secretary. Camillus the rebel felt sure that Claudius could be frightened into abdication and retirement merely by an impudent, threatening and insulting letter, without the need of declaring war; and Claudius did in fact summon his leading advisers and ask them whether he should comply with Camillus's demands.

36. Baseless rumours of conspiracies caused Claudius such alarm that he attempted to abdicate. After the arrest of the man who, as I mentioned, was caught with a dagger while the Emperor was sacrificing, he sent out heralds to call an immediate meeting of the Senate, at which he protested loudly and tearfully that no place was safe for him any longer; and failed to appear in public during the next few days. Nor did Messalina's wounding and insulting behaviour destroy the extravagant love he bore her, so much as terror that she planned to seat her lover Silius on the throne; and when the crisis occurred he fled in ignominious terror to the Guards' Camp, asking again and again as he went: 'Am I still Emperor?'

37. At the slightest hint of danger he would take instant precaution and vengeance against his supposed enemy, however insignificant, once he began to feel at all uneasy. On one occasion a morning caller, one of

two parties to a legal case, took Claudius aside and told him: 'In my dreams last night you were murdered.' Then a little later on, pretending to recognize his assailant, he pointed out his own opponent in the lawsuit, as he was handing in his petition. Claudius had the petitioner arrested as if caught in the act, and hurried away to execution. Appius Silanus is said to have been the victim of a similar ruse; for when Messalina and Narcissus decided to get rid of him they agreed that Narcissus should run in alarm to Claudius's bedroom just before dawn and pretend that he had dreamed of a violent attack on the Emperor by Appius. Messalina would then awake and exclaim with pretended astonishment: 'Why, I too have dreamed the same dream for the last few nights.' They would have already sent Appius a summons to visit Claudius, so that when someone else announced that he was forcing his way into the imperial quarters, Claudius would take this as positive proof that the dreams were true, accuse Appius of attempted murder and sentence him to death. The plan worked; and the next day Claudius blandly told the Senate what had happened, thanking the freedman[15] for exercising such vigilance even while asleep.

38. In one edict he confessed to the faults of anger and resentment; but sought to excuse them, and drew a distinction between them, undertaking that his anger would never last long, nor his resentment be unjustified. Then there was his bitter letter reprimanding the citizens of Ostia because they had sent no ships to meet him when he entered the Tiber, which made him feel reduced to the rank of a commoner; yet he as suddenly forgave them and sent what amounted to an apology for the warmth of his remarks.

If pestered in public by applicants at unsuitable times, Claudius used to push them away with his own hands. Among the innocent people whom he banished without a hearing were a quaestor's clerk who had once treated him too violently in a court case before his accession; and a senator of praetorian rank who, while aedile, had fined Claudius's tenants for illegally selling cooked food and then whipped his bailiff because he protested. The same resentment made Claudius deprive the aediles of their control over the cook-shops.

Instead of keeping quiet about his stupidity, Claudius explained, in a number of short speeches, that it had been a mere mask assumed for the benefit of Gaius, and that he owed both life and throne to it. Nobody, however, believed him, and soon a book was

published entitled *Fools' Rise to Power*; the thesis being that no one would act the fool unless he were a fool already.

39. Among other things, Claudius's scatter-brainedness and shortsightedness – or to use the Greek terms, his *meteoria* and *ablepsia* – were marvelled at. After executing Messalina, he went in to dinner, and presently asked: 'Why is she not here?' On several occasions he sent for men to give him advice or throw dice with him; and, when they did not appear, followed this up with a reproachful message calling them lazy sleepers – quite unaware that he had just sentenced them to death.

While planning his illegitimate marriage with Agrippina, he constantly made references to her in speeches: such as 'my daughter and foster-child, born and bred in my lap, so to speak'. And shortly before adopting his step-son Nero – as though this were not wrong enough, when he already possessed a grown-up son – gave out with pride more than once that nobody had ever yet been adopted into the Claudian family.

40. Often, in fact, Claudius showed such absent-mindedness in speech and action that it might have been thought that he neither knew nor cared to whom, or in whose hearing, or when or where, he was speaking. He intervened in a senatorial debate on the subject of butchers and wine-sellers with the sudden question: 'But I ask you, my lords, how can anyone live without an occasional snack?' Then he rambled off into a speech about the abundance of city taverns in his youth and how he often used to go the round of them himself.

One of his reasons for supporting the candidature of a would-be quaestor was: 'His father brought me a cool drink of water, long ago, when I was sick and very thirsty.' Of a witness who had been presented before the House, he said: 'Though in fact my mother's freedwoman and personal maid, she always treated me as her patron; I stress this point because even now certain members of my household staff refuse to do so.'

Once, when the men of Ostia made a public petition to him, he lost his temper and shouted from the tribunal that he owed them no consideration, and that surely he was free, if anyone was! Every day, and almost at every hour and minute of the day, he would let fall such remarks as: 'What? Do you take me for a Telegenius?'[16] and: 'Very well, curse me if you like, but keep your hands off!' with other more inept ones,

15. Narcissus.

16. Unknown; evidently some mythical or historical figure famous for his stupidity.

such as would have come ill even from a private citizen,
let alone an Emperor who, far from lacking eloquence
and education, had devoted his whole life to liberal
studies.

41. While still a boy Claudius had started work on
a Roman history, encouraged by Livy, and assisted by
Sulpicius Flavus. But when he gave his first public
reading to a packed audience he found it difficult to
finish because he constantly threw cold water upon his
own performance. As he started to read, a very fat man
came in, sat down, and broke several benches, which
excited considerable merriment. Even when silence
had been restored Claudius could not help recalling the
sight and going off into peals of laughter.

As Emperor he continued work on this history, from
which a professional gave frequent readings. It opened
with the murder of Julius Caesar, then skipped a few
years and started again at the close of the Civil Wars;
because he realized, from his mother's and grandmother's admonitions, that he would not be allowed
to publish a free and unvarnished report on the intervening period. Of the first part two volumes survive;
of the second, forty-one.

Moreover, he wrote eight volumes of an autobiography which are liable to criticism for their lack of
taste rather than any lack of style; as well as *A Defence
of Cicero against the Aspersions of Asinius Gallus* – quite
a learned work. Claudius also added three new letters
of his own invention to the Latin alphabet – maintain-
ing that they were most necessary. He had written a
book on the subject before his accession, and afterwards met with no obstacle in getting the letters officially adopted. They may still be found in a number of
books, in the *Official Gazette*, and in inscriptions on
public buildings.

42. Claudius also studied Greek with great application, and took every opportunity of professing his love
for this language, which he declared to be the finest
of all. Once, when a barbarian addressed him both in
Greek and in Latin, he replied: 'Since you come armed
with both our languages ...' Also, while eulogizing
Greece to the Senate, he called it a province which had
endeared itself to him by a devotion to the same literary
studies as he pursued himself; and often answered
Greek envoys with a carefully composed oration in
their own tongue. Claudius often used to quote lines
of Homer from the tribunal and, after punishing a personal enemy or conspirator, made a habit of giving the
following hexameter line as a watchword to the Colonel
of the Guard:

Let him be first to attack, but be sure that you counter him
boldly.

To conclude, he even wrote books in Greek: twenty
volumes of Etruscan history, and eight of Carthaginian. The city of Alexandria acknowledged these
works by adding a new wing to the Museum called
'The Claudian' in his honour; and having the Etruscan
history read aloud, in the manner of public recitations,
from beginning to end once a year by relays of readers
in the old wing; and the Carthaginian history, likewise,
in the new.

43. In his last years Claudius made it pretty plain
that he repented of having married Agrippina and
adopted Nero. For example, when his freedmen congratulated him on having found a certain woman guilty
of adultery, he remarked that he himself seemed fated
to marry wives who 'were unchaste but remained un-
chastened'; and presently, meeting Britannicus,
embraced him with deep affection. 'Grow up quickly,

THE ETRUSCANS, *who ruled Rome during the period of the Kings (up to 510* B.C., *according to the traditional chronology), were in turn gradually absorbed by the Romans and ceased having an independent political organization. But much of their religion and culture lived on in a Roman context.*

114 (left). *The arch was an essential component of Roman architectural design and Roman engineering; in Italy, its use was pioneered by the Etruscans. Arched city gate of Etruscan Volterra with barrel vault inside, c. 300 B.C.*
115 (above). *Terracotta model of a temple: like some Roman temples which were constructed in the Etruscan style, it is surrounded by columns which are engaged in the wall (see Ill. 15), rather than having a free-standing colonnade like Greek temples. First century* B.C. *(Rome, Villa Giulia.)*

my boy,' he said, 'and I will then explain what my policy has been.' With that he quoted in Greek from the tale of Telephus and Achilles:

The hand that wounded you shall also heal,

and declared his intention of letting Britannicus come of age because, although immature, he was tall enough to wear the toga of manhood; adding 'which will at last provide Rome with a true-born Caesar'.

44. Soon afterwards he composed his will and made all the magistrates put their seals to it as witnesses; but Agrippina, being now accused of many crimes by informers as well as her own conscience, prevented him from going any further.

Most people think that Claudius was poisoned; but when, and by whom, is disputed. Some say that the eunuch Halotus, his official taster, administered the

drug while he was dining with the priests in the Citadel; others, that Agrippina did so herself at a family banquet, poisoning a dish of mushrooms, his favourite food. An equal discrepancy exists between the accounts of what happened next. According to many, he lost his power of speech, suffered frightful pain all night long, and died shortly before dawn. A variant version is that he fell into a coma but vomited up the entire contents of his overloaded stomach and was then poisoned a second time, either by a gruel – the excuse being that he needed food to revive him – or by means of an enema, the excuse being that his bowels required relief and must be emptied too.

45. Claudius's death was not revealed until all arrangements had been completed to secure Nero's succession. As a result, people made vows for his safety as though he still lived, and a troop of actors were summoned, under the pretence that he had asked to be diverted by their antics. He died on 13 October A.D. 54, during the consulship of Asinius Marcellus and Acilius Aviola, in his sixty-fourth year, and the fourteenth of his reign. He was given a princely funeral and officially deified, an honour which Nero later neglected and then cancelled; but which Vespasian restored.

46. The main omens of Claudius's death included the rise of a long-haired star, known as a comet, lightning that struck his father's tomb, and an unusual mortality among magistrates of all ranks. There is also evidence that he foresaw his end and made no secret of it: while choosing the Consuls he provided for no appointment after the month in which he died; and on his last visit to the House offered an earnest plea for harmony between his children,[17] begging the Senate to guide both of them with great care through the years of their youth. During a final appearance on the tribunal he said more than once that he had reached the close of his career; though everyone present cried: 'The Gods forbid!'

17. Britannicus and Nero.

THE ETRUSCANS. *Until the end of antiquity, the Etruscans were known for their skill in divination. One of the methods was divination from the entrails, especially the liver, of animals. This form of divination was also practised in Rome.*

116 (opposite). *Winged demon inspecting a liver; a sacrificial knife lies in front of him and the image is surrounded by a Dionysiac wine-scroll. Etruscan mirror, fourth century* B.C. *(Rome, Vatican.)*

117 (below). *Etruscan bronze model of a liver inscribed with information for the use of diviners. (Piacenza.)*

VI
NERO

Two branches of the Domitian family distinguished themselves – the Calvini and the Ahenobarbi. The Ahenobarbi were named after their founder, Lucius Domitius; the tradition being that once, on his return to Rome from the country, he met a pair of twins looking more like gods than men, who told him to give the Senate and the people the news of a victory, of which nothing had hitherto been heard.[1] In proof of their divinity the twins stroked his cheeks and thereby turned his beard from black to the colour of bronze – a physical peculiarity which became dominant among his descendants. Having gained seven consulships, a triumph, and two censorships, and been raised to patrician rank, they all continued to use the same surname, with no other forenames than Gnaeus and Lucius. They gave an interesting twist to this practice by sometimes having successive members of the family known by the same forename and sometimes varying the two – for instance we know that each of the first three Ahenobarbi was a Lucius, each of the second three was a Gnaeus, after which Lucius alternated with Gnaeus. It seems to me relevant to say something about a number of members of the family, since this will suggest that Nero's vices were inherited from each of them, while at the same time degenerating from their virtues.

2. Let me go back quite a long way to Nero's great-great-great-grandfather, Gnaeus Domitius. While tribune of the people he deprived the Priestly College of its power to fill vacancies in the priesthood, and awarded it to the people; he hated the College for not having appointed him to succeed his father. As Consul he subdued the Allobroges[2] and the Arverni, and then rode through the province on an elephant with an escort of soldiers, as though he were celebrating a triumph. Licinius Crassus, the orator, remarked: 'Should his bronze beard really surprise us? After all, he has an iron face and a heart of lead.'

Gnaeus's son and namesake, while praetor, summoned Julius Caesar before the Senate, at the close of his consulship, to be examined on the charge of having defied the auspices and the laws. Afterwards, when Consul, he tried to remove Caesar from the command in Gaul, and had himself named as his successor by his own party. Then the Civil War broke out and he was soon taken prisoner by Caesar at Corfinium, but set free; whereupon he went to Massilia and supported the city fathers during the difficult days of their siege. However, he abruptly deserted them; and fell a year later in the battle of Pharsalus. This Gnaeus was rather an indecisive man, though he had a ferocious temper. Once, in a fit of desperate panic, he attempted suicide by poison, but the prospect of death so terrified him that he changed his mind and vomited up the dose – the family physician knew him well enough to have made it a mild one, which earned the wise fellow his freedom. When Pompey raised the question of how neutrals should be treated, Gnaeus was the only man who wanted them classified as enemies.

3. Gnaeus left one son,[3] without any doubt the best member of the family. Although he had taken no part in Caesar's assassination, he was condemned to die as a conspirator, under the Pedian Law, and subsequently threw in his lot with his relatives Cassius and Brutus. After their deaths he continued to command, and even to enlarge, the Pompeian fleet, of which he had been

---

1. Lake Regillus, against the Latins (*c.* 499–6 B.C.).

2. An error; his father had done this.
3. Lucius Domitius Ahenobarbus.

made commander, and would not surrender it to
Antony until his associates had been everywhere
routed; and then did so as though he were granting
an immense favour. Of all those sentenced under the
Pedian Law he alone was granted repatriation and,
once home again, held all the highest offices of state
in succession. When civil war broke out once more he
joined Antony's staff, and was later offered the supreme
command by those who found Cleopatra an embarrassment; but a sudden illness made him wary of
accepting it, although he never gave a definite refusal.
Instead, he transferred his allegiance to Augustus; and
died a few days afterwards. Antony, however, said
openly that his real motive in changing sides was to
be with Servilia Nais, his mistress.

4. His son, the Domitius[4] who became well known
later on from being nominated in Augustus's will as
the purchaser of his household and possessions, had
been a famous charioteer in his youth, and gained
triumphal decorations for his part in the German campaign; but was notorious for his arrogance, extravagance, and cruelty. While holding the office of aedile,
he ordered Lucius Plancus, then Censor, to make way
for him in the street. As praetor and again as Consul,
he made Roman knights and married women act in
stage pantomimes. The cruelty of the wild-animal
hunts presented by him in the Circus and elsewhere
at Rome, and of a gladiatorial contest, obliged
Augustus – whose private warnings he had disregarded
– to issue a cautionary edict.

5. His son by Antonia the Elder[5] became Nero's
father; and was a wholly despicable character. As a
young man he served in the East on Gaius's staff, but
forfeited his friendship by killing one of his own
freedmen for refusing to drink as much as he was told.
Yet even then he behaved no better. Once, driving
through a village on the Appian Way, he whipped up
his horses and deliberately ran over and killed a boy;
and when a knight criticized him rather freely in the
Forum he gouged out one of his eyes there and then.
He was also remarkably dishonest: cheating his
bankers of payment for goods he had bought and, while
praetor, even swindling victorious charioteers of their
prize money. His sister Domitia Lepida openly teased
him about this; and when the managers of the teams
complained he decreed that *in future* all prizes must
be paid on the spot. Just before Tiberius died he was
charged with treason, adultery, and incest with his

sister; however, Gaius's accession saved him and he
died of dropsy at Pyrgi, first formally acknowledging
the paternity of Nero, his son by Germanicus's
daughter Agrippina the Younger.

6. Nero was born at Antium on 15 December A.D.
37, nine months after Tiberius's death. The sun was
rising and its earliest rays touched the newly-born boy
almost before he could be laid on the ground. Nero's
horoscope at once occasioned many ominous predictions; and a significant comment was made by his
father in reply to the congratulations of his friends:
namely, that any child born to himself and Agrippina
was bound to have a detestable nature and become a
public danger. Another promise of ill-luck occurred on
the day of his purification: when Agrippina asked her
brother Gaius to give the boy whatever name he
pleased, he glanced at his uncle Claudius (later
Emperor, and Nero's adoptive father) and said with a
grin: 'I name him Claudius.' Since Claudius was then
the butt of the Court, Agrippina was not amused, and
ignored the suggestion.

At the age of three Nero lost his father and inherited
one-third of the estate; but Gaius, who was also named
in the will, not only took everything, but banished
Agrippina. Nero therefore grew up in very poor circumstances under the care of his aunt Domitia Lepida,
who chose a dancer and a barber to be his tutors. However, when Claudius became Emperor, Nero had his
inheritance restored to him, and a legacy from his uncle
by marriage, Passienus Crispus, left him well off. His
mother's recall from banishment allowed him to enjoy
once more the benefits of her powerful influence; and
it transpired later that Claudius's wife Messalina, realizing that Nero would become a rival to her son Britannicus, had sent assassins to strangle him during his
siesta. They were driven away in terror, people said,
by a snake which suddenly darted from beneath Nero's
pillow; but this was a mere surmise based on the discovery of a sloughed snake-skin in his bed near the pillow. Agrippina persuaded him to have this skin set in
a golden bracelet, which he wore for a long time on
his right arm. Later he threw it away because it reminded
him too vividly of her; but when his situation grew
desperate, hunted for it in vain.

7. While still a young half-grown boy, he gave an
exceptionally good performance in the Troy Game at
the Circus and earned loud applause. When he reached
the age of ten, Claudius adopted him and appointed
Annaeus Seneca, who was already a senator, as his
tutor. On the following night, the story goes, Seneca

---

4. Again Lucius.   5. Gnaeus.

dreamed that his pupil was really Gaius; and, indeed, Nero soon made sense of the dream by giving signs of a naturally cruel heart. Since Britannicus continued to call him 'Ahenobarbus' even after his adoption, he revenged himself by trying to convince Claudius that Britannicus was a supposititious child; and also testified in public against his aunt Domitia Lepida, just to please his mother who was doing everything possible to get her convicted.

Nero celebrated his maiden speech in the Forum by giving largesse to the people and a bounty to the troops, and leading a ceremonial march past of the Guards, shield in hand. Afterwards, in the Senate, he made a speech of thanks to Claudius. While Claudius was Consul, Nero pleaded two cases in his hearing: one in Latin on behalf of the people of Bononia, the other in Greek on behalf of the Rhodians and Trojans. He first appeared on the tribunal as City Prefect during the Latin Festival; eminent lawyers gave him a number of important cases to try, instead of the dull and trivial ones that normally come up on such occasions – although Claudius had expressly forbidden this. Next, Nero married Octavia; and held Games and a wild-beast hunt in the Circus, by way of wishing Claudius good health.

8. He had reached the age of seventeen when Claudius's death occurred, and presented himself to the Palace Guard that day in the late afternoon – ugly omens throughout the day having ruled out an earlier appearance. After being acclaimed Emperor on the Palace steps, he was taken in a litter to the Guards' Camp, where he briefly addressed the troops. He was then taken to the Senate House, where he remained until nightfall, refusing only one of the many high honours voted him, namely the title 'Father of the Country', and this because of his youth.

9. Nero started off with a parade of filial dutifulness: giving Claudius a lavish funeral, at which he delivered the oration in person, and finally deifying him. He also exalted the memory of his father Domitius, and turned over all his public and private affairs to Agrippina's management. On the day of his accession the password he gave to the colonel on duty was 'The Best of Mothers'; and she and he often rode out together through the streets in her litter. Nero founded a colony at Antium consisting of Guards veterans, augmented by a group of the richest retired centurions, whom he forced to move there; and also built them a harbour, at great expense.

10. As a further guarantee of his virtuous intentions,

he promised to model his rule on the principles laid down by Augustus, and never missed an opportunity of being generous or merciful, or of showing how affable he was. He lowered, if he could not abolish, some of the heavier taxes; and reduced by three-quarters the fee for denouncing evasions of the Papian Law.[6] Moreover, he presented the commons with forty gold pieces each; settled annual salaries on distinguished but impoverished senators – to the amount of 5,000 gold pieces in some cases – and granted the Guards cohorts a free monthly issue of grain. If asked to sign the usual execution order for a felon, he would sigh: 'Ah, how I wish that I had never learned to write!' He seldom forgot a face, and would greet men of whatever rank by name without a moment's hesitation. Once, when the Senate passed a vote of thanks to him, he answered: 'Wait until I deserve them!' He allowed even the commons to watch him taking exercise on the Campus Martius, and often gave public declamations. Also, he recited his own poems, both at home and in the Theatre: a performance which so delighted everyone that a Thanksgiving was voted him, as though he had won a great victory, and the passages he had chosen were printed in letters of gold on plaques dedicated to Capitoline Jupiter.

11. He gave an immense variety of entertainments – coming-of-age parties, chariot races in the Circus, stage plays, a gladiatorial show – persuading even old men of consular rank, and old ladies, too, to attend the coming-of-age parties. He reserved seats for the knights at the Circus, as he had done in the Theatre; and actually raced four-camel chariots! At the Great Festival, as he called the series of plays devoted to the eternity of the Empire, parts were taken by men and women of both Orders; and one well-known knight rode an elephant down a sloping tight-rope. When he staged *The Fire*, a Roman play by Afranius, the actors were allowed to keep the valuable furnishings they rescued from the burning house. Throughout the Festival all kinds of gifts were scattered to the people – 1,000 assorted birds daily, and quantities of food parcels; besides vouchers for grain, clothes, gold, silver, precious stones, pearls, paintings, slaves, transport animals, and even trained wild beasts – and finally for ships, blocks of city apartments, and farms.

12. Nero watched from the top of the proscenium. The gladiatorial show took place in a wooden theatre,

6. The Lex Papia Poppaea which brought sanctions against celibacy.

UNUSUAL SPECTACLES

119 (opposite, top). *Foreign goods came to Rome in trade, taxation or as war booty. Among those who benefited from the latter two were the Roman populace, who on occasion received lavish presents and were regularly entertained by displays of strange animals: Palmyrene nobles riding elaborately harnessed horses and camels. Palmyrene relief, second century* A.D. *(Cleveland Museum of Art.)*

120 (opposite, below). *Some theatrical displays required complicated engineering, which was catered for by Roman stage design. The story of Daedalus and Icarus, who hoped to escape from imprisonment by constructing wings, was the subject of one such display. Roman painting showing Daedalus and Icarus, who is about to fall into the sea* (upper right). *(London, British Museum.)*

121 (below). *The Minotaur, who had a bull's head and a human body, was the product of the union between Pasiphaë, disguised as a cow, and a bull. The Minotaur devoured seven Athenian boys and seven girls every year, and was killed by the Athenian hero Theseus. Theseus killing the Minotaur, bronze group, first century* B.C. *(Berlin East, Staatliche Museen.)*

near the Campus Martius, which had been built in less than a year; but no one was allowed to be killed during these combats, not even criminals. He did, however, make 400 senators and 600 knights, some of them rich and respectable, do battle in the arena; and some had to fight wild beasts and perform various duties about the ring. He staged a naval engagement on an artificial lake of salt water which had sea-monsters swimming in it; also Pyrrhic performances[7] by certain young Greeks, to whom he presented certificates of Roman citizenship when their show ended. At one stage of the *Minotaur* ballet an actor, disguised as a bull, actually

7. Originally war-dances; later extended to other kinds.

mounted another who played Pasiphaë and occupied the hindquarters of a hollow wooden heifer – or that, at least, was the audience's impression. In the *Daedalus and Icarus* ballet, the actor who played Icarus, while attempting his first flight, fell beside Nero's couch and spattered him with blood.

Nero rarely presided at shows of this sort, but would recline in the closed imperial box and watch through a small window; later, however, he opened the box. He inaugurated the Neronia, a festival of competitions in music, gymnastics, and horsemanship, modelled on the Greek ones and held every five years; and simultaneously opened his Baths and Gymnasium, and provided free oil for knights and senators. Ex-Consuls, drawn by lot, presided over the Neronia, and occupied the praetors' seats. Then Nero descended to the orchestra where the senators sat, to accept the wreath for Latin oratory and verse, which had been reserved for him by the unanimous vote of all the distinguished competitors. The judges also awarded him the wreath for a lyre solo, but he bowed reverently to them, and said: 'Pray lay it on the ground before Augustus's statue!' At an athletic competition held in the Enclosure, oxen were sacrificed on a lavish scale; that was when he shaved his chin for the first time, put the hair in a gold box studded with valuable pearls and dedicated it to Capitoline Jupiter. He had invited the Vestal Virgins to watch the athletics, explaining that the priestesses of Ceres[8] at Olympia were accorded the same privilege.

13. The welcome given Tiridates when he visited Rome deserves inclusion in the list of Nero's spectacles. Tiridates was the Armenian king whom he had lured to Rome with wonderful promises. Cloudy weather prevented Tiridates from being displayed to the people on the day fixed by imperial edict; however, Nero brought him out as soon as possible afterwards. The Guards cohorts were drawn up in full armour around the temples of the Forum, while Nero occupied his curule chair on the Rostrum, wearing triumphal dress and surrounded by military insignia and standards. Tiridates had to walk up a ramp and then prostrate himself in supplication; whereupon Nero stretched out his hand, drew him to his feet, kissed him, and took the turban from his head, replacing it with a diadem. When Tiridates's supplication had been translated into Latin and publicly recited by an interpreter of praetorian rank, he was taken to the Theatre (where he made a further supplication) and offered a

8. Demeter.

seat on Nero's right. The people then hailed Nero as Imperator and, after dedicating a laurel-wreath in the Capitol, he closed the double doors of the Temple of Janus, as a sign that all war was at an end.

14. The first of Nero's four consulships lasted for two months, the third for four, the second and the last for six. He let a year elapse between the first and second, and between the third and fourth; but not between the second and third.

15. When he judged a case he preferred to defer his judgement until the following day, and then give it after consideration in writing; and ruled that, instead of a case being presented as a whole, every relevant charge should be presented separately by one side and then by the other. On withdrawing to study a problem of law, he never consulted openly with his judicial advisers in a body, but made each of them write out an opinion; then mulled over these documents in private, came to his own conclusion, and passed it off as a majority opinion.

For a long time Nero excluded the sons of freedmen from the Senate, and forbade those who had been admitted under his predecessors to hold office. If too many candidates competed, he gave them legions to command in compensation for the postponement and delay. It became his practice to appoint Consuls for a period of six months, and should a Consul die before 1 January he made no substitute appointment, to mark his disapproval of the ancient case of Caninius Rebilus's one-day consulship. He awarded triumphal regalia to men of quaestorial rank, and even to some knights, though their services had not been of a military nature. The Consuls were ordered to read certain of his speeches sent for the Senate's information, thereby going over the heads of the quaestors, whose business it should have been.

16. Nero introduced his own new style of architecture in the city: building out porches from the fronts of apartments and private houses to serve as fire-fighting platforms, and subsidizing the work himself. He also considered a scheme for extending the city wall as far as Ostia, and cutting a canal which would allow ships to sail straight up to Rome.

During his reign a great many public abuses were suppressed by the imposition of heavy penalties, and among the equally numerous novel enactments were sumptuary laws limiting private expenditure; the substitution of a simple grain distribution for public banquets; and a decree restricting the food sold in wine-shops to green vegetables and dried beans –

whereas before all kinds of snacks had been displayed.
Punishments were also inflicted on the Christians, a sect
professing a new and mischievous religious belief; and
Nero ended the licence which the charioteers had so
long enjoyed that they claimed it as a right: to wander
down the streets, swindling and robbing the populace.
He likewise expelled from the city all pantomime actors
and their hangers-on.

17. A new and effective check on forgery was discovered at this time. Every signed tablet was bored
with holes through which a cord was passed three
times. Provisions were also made that the first two
pages of every will offered for witnesses to sign should
bear only the testator's name; and that no one drafting
a will for anyone else might insert in it a legacy for him-

THE IMPERIAL CULT. *Roman emperors could be the
recipients equally of flattery and of a certain sense of religious awe on the part of their subjects. Both flattery and
awe were often expressed in comparisons between the
Emperor on the one hand and the gods, the heroes or great
men of the past on the other. Nero capitalized on this
phenomenon by comparing himself to Alexander the Great
and Apollo, the lyre-playing god of prophecy, among
others.*

122 (left). *Nero as Alexander the Great. Inlaid bronze
statuette.* (London, British Museum.)

123 (right). *Apollo with the lyre and his sacred serpent
from Delphi. Marble statue from Cyrene.* (London,
British Museum.)

self. Moreover, litigants were ordered to pay their lawyers at a fixed, reasonable rate; and no charge was to be made for seats in Court which were to be provided free of charge by the Treasury. Further, all Treasury suits were in future to come before a board of arbitration in the Forum; and every appeal from the verdict of a jury was to be addressed to the Senate.

18. Nero felt no ambition or hope to extend or enlarge the Roman Empire, and even considered withdrawing his forces from Britain; yet kept them there because such a decision might have reflected on the glory won by his adoptive father Claudius. The sole additions made during his reign to the list of provinces were the Kingdom of Pontus, ceded to him by Polemo; and that of the Cottian Alps which, on the death of Cottius, reverted to Rome.

19. Nero planned only two foreign tours: one to Alexandria, the other to Greece. A warning portent made him cancel the Alexandrian voyage, on the very day when his ship should have sailed: during his farewell round of the Temples he had sat down in the shrine of Vesta, but when he rose to leave, the hem of his robe got caught and then a temporary blindness overcame him. While in Greece he tried to have a canal cut through the Isthmus, and addressed a gathering of Praetorian Guards, urging them to undertake the task. Nero took a mattock himself and, at a trumpet blast, broke the ground and carried off the first basket of earth on his back. He had also planned an expedition to the Caspian Gates, enrolling a new legion of Italian-born recruits, all six feet tall, whom he called 'The Phalanx of Alexander the Great'.

I have separated this catalogue of Nero's less atrocious acts – some deserving no criticism, some even praiseworthy – from the others; but I must begin to list his follies and crimes.

20. Music formed part of his childhood curriculum, and he early developed a taste for it. Soon after his accession, he summoned Terpnus, the greatest lyre-player of the day, to sing to him when dinner had ended, for several nights in succession, until very late. Then, little by little, he began to study and practise himself, and conscientiously undertook all the usual exercises for strengthening and developing the voice. He would lie on his back with a slab of lead on his chest, use enemas and emetics to keep down his weight, and refrain from eating apples and every other food considered deleterious to the vocal chords. Ultimately, though his voice was feeble and husky, he was pleased enough with his progress to begin to nurse theatrical

ambitions, and would quote to his friends the Greek proverb: 'Unheard melodies are never sweet.' His first stage appearance was at Neapolis where, disregarding an earthquake which shook the theatre, he sang his piece through to the end. He often sang at Neapolis, for several consecutive days, too; and even while giving his voice a brief rest, could not stay out of sight, but after bathing went to dine in the Orchestra where he promised the crowd in Greek that, when he had downed a drink or two, he would give them something to make their ears ring. So captivated was he by the rhythmic applause of a crowd of Alexandrians from a fleet which had just put in, that he sent to Alexandria for more. He also chose some young knights, and more than 5,000 sturdy ordinary youths, whom he divided into groups to learn the Alexandrian method of applause – they were known, respectively, as 'Bees', 'Roof-tiles', and 'Bricks' – and provide it liberally whenever he sang.[9] It was easy to recognize them by their bushy hair, splendid dress, and the absence of rings on their left hands. The knights who led them earned four hundred gold pieces a performance.

21. Appearances at Rome as well meant so much to Nero that he held the Neronia again before the required five years elapsed. When the crowd clamoured to hear his heavenly voice, he answered that he would perform in the Palace gardens later if anyone wanted to hear him; but when the Guards on duty seconded the appeal, he delightedly agreed to oblige them. He wasted no time in getting his name entered on the list of competing lyre-players, and dropped his ticket into the urn with the others. The Guards prefects carried his lyre as he went up to play in his turn and a group of colonels and close friends accompanied him. After taking his place and finishing his preliminary oration, he made Cluvius Rufus, an ex-Consul, announce the title of the song. It was *Niobe*; and he sang on until two hours before dusk. Then he postponed the rest of the contest to the following year, which would give him an opportunity to sing oftener. But since a year was a long time to wait, he continued to make frequent appearances. He toyed with the idea of playing opposite professional actors in public shows staged by magistrates; because one of the praetors had offered him 10,000 gold pieces if he would consent. And he did actually sing in tragedies, taking the parts of heroes and gods, sometimes even of heroines and goddesses, wear-

---

9. The Bees made a loud humming noise. The Roof-tiles clapped with their hollowed hands; the Bricks, flat-handed.

ing masks either modelled on his own face, or on the face of whatever woman he happened to be in love with at the time. Among his performances were *Canace in Childbirth, Orestes the Matricide, Oedipus Blinded,* and *Distraught Hercules.* There is a story that a young recruit on guard recognized him in the rags and fetters demanded by the part of Hercules, and dashed forward to his assistance.

22. Horses had been Nero's main interest since childhood; despite all efforts to the contrary, his chatter about the chariot races at the Circus could not be stopped. When scolded by one of his tutors for telling his fellow-pupils about a Green charioteer who got dragged by his team, Nero untruthfully explained that he had been discussing Hector's fate in the *Iliad.* At the beginning of his reign he used every day to play with model ivory chariots on a board, and came up from the country to attend all the races, even minor ones, at first in secret and then without the least embarrassment; so that there was never any doubt that he would be at Rome on that particular day. He frankly admitted that he wished the number of prizes increased, which meant that more contests were included and that they lasted until a late hour, and the faction-managers no longer thought it worth while to bring out their teams except for a full day's racing.

Very soon Nero set his heart on driving a chariot

124. CHARIOT RACING *was one of the most popular Roman entertainments. The race course – or circus – was an elongated strip of land surrounded by seats with a spina or barrier dividing it lengthwise. The spina had turning posts at either end, and was often adorned with trophies and ornaments of various kinds. Charioteers were organized into four parties, each of which had its supporters and its colour, the colours being green, blue, white, and red. The parties and their supporters were known as factions. The relief shows eight teams, two for each faction, as well as attendant staff, the spina with its decorations, and spectators. (Foligno, Museum.)*

himself, and to display himself more frequently, and after a preliminary trial in the Palace gardens before an audience of slaves and loungers, made a public appearance at the Circus; on this occasion one of his freedmen replaced the magistrate who dropped the napkin as the starting signal.

However, these incursions into the arts at Rome did not satisfy him, and he headed for Greece, as I mentioned above. His main reason was that the cities which regularly sponsored musical contests had adopted the practice of sending him every available prize for lyre-playing; he always accepted these with great pleasure, giving the delegates the earliest audience of the day and invitations to private dinners. Some of them would beg Nero to sing when the meal was over, and applaud his performance to the echo, which made him announce: 'The Greeks alone are worthy of my efforts; they really listen to music.' So he sailed off hastily and, as soon as he arrived at Cassiope, gave his first song recital before the altar of Jupiter Cassius; after which he went the round of all the contests.

23. For this purpose, he ordered those contests which normally took place only at intervals to be held during his visit, even if it meant repeating them; and broke tradition at Olympia by introducing a musical competition into the athletic games. When Helius, his freedman, reminded him that he was urgently needed at Rome, he would not be distracted by official business, but answered: 'Yes, you have made yourself quite plain. I am aware that you want me to go home; you will do far better, however, if you encourage me to stay until I have proved myself worthy of Nero.'

No one was allowed to leave the theatre during his recitals, however pressing the reason. We read of women in the audience giving birth, and of men being so bored with listening and applauding that they furtively dropped down from the wall at the rear, since the gates were kept barred, or shammed dead and were carried away for burial. Nero's stage fright and general nervousness when he took part in the competitions, his jealousy of rivals, and his awe of the judges, can scarcely be believed. Though usually gracious and charming to other competitors, whom he treated as equals, he abused them behind their backs, and sometimes insulted them to their faces; and if any were particularly good singers, he would bribe them not to do themselves justice. Before every performance he would address the judges with the utmost deference: saying that he had done what he could, and that the issue was now in Fortune's hands; but that since they were men of judgement and experience, they would know how to eliminate the factor of chance. When they told him not to worry he felt a little better, but still anxious; and mistook the silence and embarrassment of some for alienation and disfavour, admitting that he suspected every one of them.

24. During the competitions he strictly observed the rules, never daring to clear his throat and even using his arm to wipe the sweat from his brow.[10] Once, while

acting in a tragedy, he dropped his sceptre and quickly recovered it, but was terrified of disqualification. The accompanist, however – who played a flute and made the necessary dumbshow to illustrate the words – swore that the slip had passed unnoticed, because the audience were listening with such rapt attention; so he took heart again. Nero insisted on announcing his own victories; which emboldened him to enter the competition for heralds. To destroy every trace of previous winners in these contests he ordered all their statues and busts to be taken down, dragged away with hooks, and hurled into public lavatories. On several occasions he took part in the chariot racing, and at Olympia drove a ten-horse team, a novelty for which he had censured King Mithridates in one of his own poems. He fell from the chariot and had to be helped in again; but, though he failed to stay the course and retired before the finish, the judges nevertheless awarded him the prize. On the eve of his departure, he presented the whole province with its freedom and conferred Roman citizenship as well as large cash rewards on the judges. It was during the Isthmian Games at Corinth that he stood in the middle of the stadium and personally announced these benefits.

25. Returning to Italy, Nero disembarked at Neapolis, where he had made his debut as a singer, and ordered part of the city wall to be razed – which is the Greek custom whenever the victor in any of the Sacred Games comes home. He repeated the same performance at Antium, at Albanum, and finally at Rome. For his processional entry into Rome he chose the chariot which Augustus had used in his triumph in a former age; and wore a Greek mantle spangled with gold stars over a purple robe. The Olympic wreath was on his head, the Pythian wreath in his right hand, the others were carried before him, with placards explaining where and against whom he had won them, what songs he had sung, and in what plays he had acted. Nero's chariot was followed by his claque, who behaved like a triumphal escort and shouted that they were the 'Augustus men' celebrating his triumph. The procession passed through the Circus (he had the entrance arch pulled down to allow more room), then by way of the Velabrum and the Forum to the Palatine Hill and the Temple of Apollo. Victims were sacrificed in his honour all along the route, which was sprinkled from time to time with perfume, and the populace showered him with birds, ribbons, and sweetmeats. He hung the wreaths above the couches in his sleeping quarters, and set up several statues of himself playing

10. Handkerchiefs were not allowed.

the lyre. He also had a coin struck with the same device. After this, it never occurred to him that he ought to refrain from singing, or even sing a little less; but he saved his voice by addressing the troops only in written orders, or in speeches delivered by someone else; and would attend no entertainment or official business unless he had a voice-trainer standing by, telling him when to spare his vocal chords, and when to protect his mouth with a handkerchief. Whether he offered people his friendship, or plainly indicated his dislike for them, often depended on how generously or how feebly they had applauded.

26. It might have been possible to excuse his insolent, lustful, extravagant, greedy or cruel early practices (which were furtive and increased only gradually), by saying that boys will be boys; yet at the same time, this was clearly the true Nero, not merely Nero in his adolescence. As soon as night fell he would snatch a cap or a wig and make a round of the taverns, or prowl the streets in search of mischief – and not always innocent mischief either, because one of his games was to attack men on their way home from dinner, stab them if they offered resistance, and then drop their bodies down the sewers. He would also break into shops and rob them, afterwards opening a market at the Palace with the stolen goods, dividing them up into lots, auctioning them himself, and squandering the proceeds. During these escapades he often risked being blinded or killed – once he was beaten almost to death by a senator whose wife he had molested, which taught him never to go out after dark unless an escort of colonels was following him at a distance unobserved. He would even secretly visit the Theatre by day, in a sedan chair, and watch the quarrels among the pantomime actors, cheering them on from the top of the proscenium; then, when they came to blows and fought it out with stones and broken benches, he joined in by throwing things on the heads of the crowd. On one occasion he fractured a praetor's skull.

27. Gradually Nero's vices gained the upper hand: he no longer tried to laugh them off, or hide or deny them, but openly broke into more serious crime. His feasts now lasted from noon till midnight, with an occasional break for diving into a warm bath or, if it were summer, into snow-cooled water. Sometimes he would drain the artificial lake in the Campus Martius, or the other in the Circus, and hold public dinner parties there, including prostitutes and dancing-girls from all over the city among his guests. Whenever he floated down the Tiber to Ostia, or cruised past the Gulf of Baiae, he had a row of temporary brothels erected along the shore, where married women at stalls, pretending to be innkeepers, solicited him from every side to come ashore. He also forced his friends to provide him with dinners; one of them spent 40,000 gold pieces on a turban party, and another even more on a rose banquet.

28. Not satisfied with seducing free-born boys and married women, Nero raped the Vestal Virgin Rubria. He nearly contrived to marry the freedwoman Acte, by persuading some friends of consular rank to swear falsely that she came of royal stock. Having tried to turn the boy Sporus into a girl by castration, he went through a wedding ceremony with him – dowry, bridal veil and all – took him to his Palace with a great crowd in attendance, and treated him as a wife. A rather amusing joke is still going the rounds: the world would have been a happier place had Nero's father Domitius married that sort of wife. He dressed Sporus in the fine clothes normally worn by an Empress and took him in his own litter not only to every Greek assize and fair, but actually through the Street of the Sigillaria at Rome, kissing him amorously now and then.

The lecherous passion he felt for his mother, Agrippina, was notorious; but her enemies would not let him consummate it, fearing that, if he did, she would become even more powerful and ruthless than hitherto. So he found a new mistress who was said to be her spitting image; some say that he did, in fact, commit incest with Agrippina every time they rode in the same litter – the stains on his clothes when he emerged proved it.

29. Nero practised every kind of obscenity, and after defiling almost every part of his body finally invented a novel game: he was released from a cage dressed in the skins of wild animals, and attacked the private parts of men and women who stood bound to stakes. After working up sufficient excitement by this means, he was dispatched – shall we say? – by his freedman Doryphorus. Doryphorus now married him – just as he himself had married Sporus – and on the wedding night he imitated the screams and moans of a girl being deflowered. According to my informants he was convinced that nobody could remain chaste or pure in any part of his body, but that most people concealed their secret vices; hence, if anyone confessed to obscene practices, Nero forgave him all his other crimes.

30. He believed that fortunes were made to be squandered, and whoever could account for every penny he spent seemed to him a stingy miser. 'True

NERO'S GOLDEN HOUSE. *The main part of the Golden House was designed around a central axis, this being a fashionable layout at the time.*
125 (above). *Painting from Pompeii showing palaces built on a central axis.* (Naples, Museum.)
126 (left). *Coin of Nero showing the Golden House with Nero's statue in the entrance hall.*
127 (opposite). *The circular dining room of the Golden House, which had a revolving dome, in imitation of the movement of the stars. The room was thus a symbol of the cosmos, and the Emperor who found himself in it was placed, metaphorically, at the centre of the cosmos as its ruler.*

gentlemen', he said, 'always throw their money about.' He professed admiration and praise for his uncle Gaius, merely because he had run through the vast fortune which Tiberius had left him; and never thought twice, himself, about giving away or wasting money. Believe it or not, he spent 8,000 gold pieces a day on King Tiridates, and made him a parting gift of more than a million. He presented Menecrates the lyre-player and Spiculus the gladiator with houses and estates worthy of men who had celebrated triumphs, and showed equal generosity to the monkey-faced moneylender Paneros, whom he later buried in almost royal style. Nero never wore the same clothes twice; he would stake 4,000 gold pieces on each pip of the winning throw at dice; and when he went fishing used a golden net strung with purple and scarlet thread. He seldom travelled, it is said, with a train of less than 1,000 carriages; the mules were shod with silver, the muleteers wore wool from Canusium, and he was escorted by Mazacian horsemen,[11] and outriders with jingling bracelets and medallions.

11. From Numidia (N. Africa).

31. His wastefulness showed most of all in the architectural projects. He built a palace, stretching from the Palatine to the Esquiline, which he called 'The Passageway'; and when it burned down soon afterwards, rebuilt it under the new name of 'The Golden House'. The following details will give some notion of its size and magnificence. The entrance-hall was large enough to contain a huge statue of himself, 120 feet high; and the pillared arcade ran for a whole mile. An enormous pool, like a sea, was surrounded by buildings made to resemble cities, and by a landscape garden consisting of ploughed fields, vineyards, pastures, and woodlands – where every variety of domestic and wild animal roamed about. Parts of the house were overlaid with gold and studded with precious stones and mother-of-pearl. All the dining-rooms had ceilings of fretted ivory, the panels of which could slide back and let a rain of flowers, or of perfume from hidden sprinklers, shower upon his guests. The main dining-room was circular, and its roof revolved, day and night, in time with the sky. Sea water, or sulphur water, was always on tap in the baths. When the palace had been

decorated throughout in this lavish style, Nero dedicated it, and condescended to remark: 'Good, now I
can at last begin to live like a human being!'

He also had men at work on a covered bath surrounded by colonnades and stretching from Misenum
to Lake Avernus; all the hot springs in the Baiae district would be canalized to feed it. Another project
would have connected Lake Avernus with Ostia by a
ship canal 160 miles long, and broad enough for two
quinqueremes to pass. Prisoners from every part of the
Empire were ordered to be transported to Italy for
employment on this task, even those convicted of capital crimes receiving no other punishment but this.

Nero's confidence in the resources of the Empire
was not the only cause of his furious spending; he had
also been suddenly excited by tales of a great hidden
treasure, vouched for by a Roman knight who swore
that the hoard brought by Queen Dido to Carthage
centuries before, when she fled from Tyre, still lay un-
touched in certain huge African caves and could easily
be retrieved.

32. When this hope failed to materialize, Nero
found himself destitute – and his financial difficulties
were such that he could not lay hands on enough money
even for the soldiers' pay or the veterans' benefits; and
therefore resorted to robbery and blackmail.

First he made a law that if a freedman died who had
taken the name of a family connected with his own,
and could not show adequate reason, five-sixths of the
estate, not merely one half, should be forfeited to the
Privy Purse. Next, he seized the estates of those who
had shown ingratitude to their Emperor;[12] and fined
the lawyers responsible for writing and dictating such
wills. Moreover, any man whose words or deeds
offered the least handle to an informer was charged
with treason. He recalled the presents he had given to
Greek cities in acknowledgement of prizes won at
musical or athletic contests. On one market-day he sent
an agent to sell a few ounces of the amethystine and
Tyrian purple dyes which he had forbidden to be used,
and then closed the business of dealers who had bought
them. It is said that he once noticed a lady wearing this
illegal colour at one of his recitals, pointed her out to
his servants and had her dragged off – whereupon she
was stripped not only of her robe but of her entire property. His invariable formula, when he appointed a
magistrate, was: 'You know my needs! Let us see to
it that nobody is left with anything.' Finally he robbed

numerous temples of their treasures and melted down
the gold and silver images, among them the Household-gods of Rome – which Galba, however, had recast
soon afterwards.

33. Claudius was the first victim of his murderous
career: because, though Nero may not have been actually responsible for the poisoning of his adoptive father,
he knew all about it, as he later admitted by apprecia-
tively quoting a Greek proverb which calls mushrooms
(by which Claudius met his death) 'the food of the
gods'. And he did his utmost to insult Claudius's
memory, accusing him either of stupidity or of cruelty.
It was a favourite joke of his that Claudius could no
longer 'play the fool on earth', lengthening the initial
syllable of *morari* 'to linger on', so that it meant 'to play
the fool'. Nero annulled many of Claudius's decrees
and edicts, on the ground that he had been a doddering
old idiot; and enclosed the place where he had been
cremated with nothing better than a low rubble
wall.

He tried to poison Britannicus, being not merely
jealous of his voice, which was far more musical than
his own, but afraid that the common people might be
less attached to Claudius's adopted son than to his real
one. The drug came from an expert poisoner named
Locusta, and when its action was not so rapid as he
expected – the effect was violently laxative – he called
for her, complaining that she had given him medicine
instead of poison, and flogged her with his own hands.
Locusta explained that she had reduced the dose to
make the crime less obvious. 'So you think I am afraid
of the Julian law,' he said. Then he led Locusta into
his bedroom and stood over her while she concocted
the fastest-working poison that she knew. This he administered to a kid, but when it took five hours to die
he made her boil down the brew again and again. At
last he tried it on a pig, which died on the spot; and
that night at dinner had what remained poured into
Britannicus's cup. Britannicus dropped dead at the
very first taste, but Nero lyingly assured the guests that
the poor boy had 'long been subject to these epileptic
seizures'. Britannicus was buried hastily and without
ceremony on the following day during a heavy shower
of rain, and Nero rewarded Locusta for her services
with a free pardon and extensive country estates – and
actually supplied her with students.

34. The over-watchful, over-critical eye that Agrippina kept on whatever Nero said or did proved more
than he could stand. He first tried to embarrass her by
frequent threats to abdicate and go into retirement in

12. i.e., by not leaving him enough.

Rhodes. Then, having deprived her of all honour and power, and even of her Roman and German bodyguard, he refused to have her living with him and expelled her from his Palace; after which he did everything possible to annoy her, sending people to pester her with lawsuits while she stayed in Rome, and when she took refuge on her riverside estate, making them constantly drive or sail past the windows, disturbing her with jeers and cat-calls. In the end her threats and violent behaviour terrified him into deciding that she must die. He tried to poison her three times, but she

his scheme. On discovering that everything had gone wrong and she had escaped by swimming, when Lucius Agerinus, her freedman, entered joyfully to report that she was safe and sound, Nero, in desperation, ordered one of his men to drop a dagger surreptitiously beside Agerinus, whom he arrested at once on a charge of having been hired to murder the Emperor. After this he arranged for Agrippina to be killed, and made it seem as if she had sent Agerinus to assassinate him but committed suicide on hearing that the plot had miscarried. Other more gruesome details are supplied by reliable

had always taken the antidote in advance; so he rigged up a machine in the ceiling of her bedroom which would dislodge the panels and drop them on her while she slept. However, one of the people involved in the plot gave the secret away. Then he had a collapsible boat designed which would either sink or have its cabin fall in on top of her. Under pretence of a reconciliation, he sent the most friendly note inviting her to celebrate the Feast of Minerva with him at Baiae, and on her arrival made one of his captains stage an ostensibly accidental collision with the galley in which she had sailed. Then he protracted the feast until a late hour, and when at last she said, 'I really must get back to Bauli,' offered her his collapsible boat instead of the damaged galley. Nero was in a very happy mood as he led Agrippina down to the quay, and even kissed her breasts before she stepped aboard. He sat up all night, on tenterhooks of anxiety, waiting for the outcome of

128. NERO AND POPPAEA *as the sun god and the goddess Fortune on a coin of Nero.* (Hirmer.)

authorities: it appears that Nero rushed off to examine Agrippina's corpse, handling her limbs and, between drinks to satisfy his thirst, discussing their good and bad points. Though encouraged by the congratulations which poured in from the Army, the Senate and the People, he was never either then or thereafter able to free his conscience from the guilt of this crime. He often admitted that he was hounded by his mother's ghost and that the Furies were pursuing him with whips and burning torches; and set Persian magicians at work to conjure up the ghost and entreat its forgiveness. During his tour of Greece he came to Athens, where the Eleusinian Mysteries were being held, but dared not participate when a herald ordered all impious and criminal persons present to withdraw before the ceremonies began.

Having disposed of his mother, Nero proceeded to murder his aunt.[13] He found her confined to bed with severe constipation. The old lady stroked his downy beard affectionately – he was already full-grown – murmuring: 'Whenever you celebrate your coming-of-age and present me with this, I shall die happy.' Nero turned to his courtiers and said laughingly: 'In that case I must shave at once.' Then he ordered the doctors to give her a laxative of fatal strength, seized her property before she was quite dead, and tore up the will so that nothing should escape him.

35. Besides Octavia, he took two more wives – first Poppaea Sabina, a quaestor's daughter, at that time married to a knight, and Statilia Messalina, great-great-great-grand-daughter of Taurus who had twice been Consul and won a triumph. To marry Statilia he was obliged to murder her husband Atticus Vestinus, a Consul. Life with Octavia had soon bored him, and when his friends criticized his treatment of her, he retorted: 'Just being an Emperor's wife[14] ought surely to be enough to make her happy.' He tried unsuccessfully to strangle her on several occasions, but finally pronounced that she was barren, and divorced her. This act made him so unpopular and caused so great a scandal that he banished Octavia and later had her executed on a charge of adultery. Her innocence was maintained by the witnesses called by him to testify against her even under torture; so he bribed his old tutor Anicetus[15] to confess (falsely) that he had tricked her into infidelity. Though he doted on Poppaea, whom he married twelve days after this divorce, he kicked her to death while she was pregnant and ill, because she complained that he came home late from the races. Poppaea had borne him a daughter, Claudia Augusta, who died in infancy.

There was no family relationship which Nero did not criminally abuse. When Claudius's daughter Antonia refused to take Poppaea's place, he had her executed on a charge of attempted rebellion; and destroyed every other member of his family, including relatives by marriage, in the same way. He committed an indecent assault on young Aulus Plautius and then put him to death, remarking: 'Now Mother may come and

kiss my successor'; he explained that Agrippina had been in love with Aulus and induced him to make a bid for the throne. There was also his step-son, Rufrius Crispinus, Poppaea's child by her former husband. Nero had the boy's own slaves drown him on a fishing expedition simply because he was said to have played at being a general and an emperor. He banished Tuscus, the son of his foster-mother and now Prefect of Egypt, for daring to use the baths which he had built in preparation for the imperial visit to Alexandria. When his tutor Seneca repeatedly asked leave to retire, and offered to surrender all his estates, Nero swore most solemnly that Seneca had no cause to suspect him, since he would rather die than harm him; but he drove

13. Domitia Lepida.
14. Literally, 'possessing the insignia of wifehood'.
15. Anicetus, the freedman who had designed the collapsible boat, was now commanding the fleet at Misenum.

PHILOSOPHERS *were sought after as advisers and advo-*
cates in personal and religious as well as in political mat-
ters, for their education and their disciplined lifestyle was
thought to endow them both with wisdom and with impar-
tiality. At the same time, however, unvarnished free speak-
ing was not invariably welcomed in high quarters.
129 (opposite). *Zeno, the founder of the Stoic school of*
philosophy, of which Seneca, Nero's tutor and adviser, was
a member. (Naples, Museum.)
130 (above). *The philosopher's simple and rugged appear-*
ance served, ideally, as an outward sign of a well-ordered
soul. (Painting from Pompeii. Naples, Museum.)

Seneca to commit suicide nevertheless. He promised
Burrus, the Guards' commander, a cough mixture, but
sent poison instead; also poisoning the food and drink
of the rich old freedmen who had originally arranged
for him to be adopted as Claudius's heir, and had subsequently been his counsellors.

36. Nero was no less cruel to strangers than to
members of his family. A comet,[16] popularly supposed
to herald the death of some person of outstanding importance, appeared several nights running. His astrologer Balbillus observed that monarchs usually avoided
portents of this kind by executing their most prominent
subjects and thus directing the wrath of heaven elsewhere; so Nero resolved on a wholesale massacre of
the nobility. What fortified him in this decision, and
seemed to justify it, was that he had discovered two
plots against his life. The earlier and more important
one of the two was Piso's conspiracy in Rome; the
other, detected at Beneventum, had been headed by
Vinicius. When brought up for trial the conspirators
were loaded with three sets of chains. Some, while
admitting their guilt, made it seem like a favour when
they claimed that by destroying a man so thoroughly
steeped in evil as Nero, they would have been doing
him the greatest possible service. All children of the
condemned men were banished from Rome, and then
starved to death or poisoned.

37. After this, no considerations of selection or
moderation restrained Nero from murdering anyone
he pleased, on whatever pretext. Here are a few instances only: Salvidienus Orfitus was charged with
leasing three shops, which formed part of his house,
close to the Forum, as offices for the representatives
of certain allied states; and a blind lawyer, Cassius
Longinus, with keeping a mask of Gaius Cassius, one
of Julius Caesar's murderers, attached to the family-
tree; and Thrasea Paetus for looking like a cross old
schoolmaster. Those whom he ordered to commit suicide were never given more than an hour's grace. To
insure against delays he made doctors 'take care' of any
who were found still alive – which, in Nero's vocabulary, meant opening their veins. He was eager, it is said,
to get hold of a certain Egyptian – a sort of ogre who
would eat raw flesh and practically anything else he was
given – and watch him tear live men to pieces and then
devour them. These 'successes', as Nero called them,
went to his head and he boasted that no previous
sovereign had ever realized the extent of his power.

16. One is recorded in A.D. 60; the other in A.D. 64.

Often he hinted broadly that it was not his intention to spare the remaining senators, but would one day wipe out the entire Senatorial Order, and let knights and freedmen govern the provinces and command the armies, instead. He certainly gave no senator a kiss when he set out on a journey or returned from one, and never bothered to answer the Senate's greetings. In his announcement of the Isthmus Canal project, to a huge crowd, he loudly voiced the hope that it might benefit himself and the Roman people, but made no mention of the Senate.

38. Nero showed no greater mercy to the common folk, or to the very walls of Rome. Once, in the course of a general conversation, someone quoted the line:

> When I am dead, may fire consume the earth,

but Nero said that the first part of the line should read: 'While I yet live,' and soon converted this fancy into fact. Pretending to be disgusted by the drab old buildings and narrow, winding streets of Rome, he brazenly set fire to the city; and though a group of ex-Consuls caught his attendants, armed with tar and blazing torches, trespassing on their property, they dared not interfere. He also coveted the sites of several granaries, solidly built in stone, near the Golden House; having knocked down their walls with siege-engines, he set the interiors ablaze. This terror lasted for six days and seven nights, causing many people to take shelter in monuments and tombs. Nero's men destroyed not only a vast number of apartment blocks, but mansions which had belonged to famous generals and were still decorated with their triumphal trophies; temples, too, vowed and dedicated by the kings, and others during the Punic and Gallic wars – in fact, every ancient monument of historical interest that had hitherto survived. Nero watched the conflagration from the Tower of Maecenas, enraptured by what he called 'the beauty of the flames'; then put on his tragedian's costume and sang *The Sack of Ilium* from beginning to end. He offered to remove corpses and rubble free of charge, but allowed nobody to search among the ruins even of his own mansion; he wanted to collect as much loot and spoils as possible himself. Then he opened a Fire Relief Fund and insisted on contributions, which bled the provincials white and practically beggared all private citizens.

39. Fate made certain unexpected additions to the disasters and scandals of Nero's reign. In a single autumn 30,000 deaths from plague were registered at the Temple of Libitina. There was a British disaster, when two important garrison-towns were taken by storm,[17] and huge numbers of Romans and allies massacred. And there was a disgraceful defeat in the East, where the legions in Armenia were sent beneath the yoke, and we almost lost Syria.

It was strange how amazingly tolerant Nero seemed to be of the insults that everyone cast at him, in the form of jokes and lampoons. Here are a few examples of verses, in Greek or Latin, posted on city walls or current orally:

> Alcmaeon, Orestes, and Nero are brothers,
> Why? Because all of them murdered their mothers.
>
> *

> Count the numerical values
>   Of the letters in Nero's name,
> And in 'murdered his own mother':
>   You will find their sum is the same.[18]
>
> *

> Aeneas the Trojan hero
>   Carried off his aged father;
> His remote descendant Nero
>   Likewise carried off his mother:
> Heroes worthy of each other.
>
> *

> Though Nero may pluck the chords of a lyre,
>   And the Parthian King the string of a bow,
> He who chants to the lyre with heavenly fire
>   Is Apollo as much as his far-darting foe.
>
> *

> The Palace is spreading and swallowing Rome!
> Let us all flee to Veii and make it our home.
> Yet the Palace is growing so damnably fast
> That it threatens to gobble up Veii at last.

He never tried to trace the authors and, when an informer handed the Senate a short list of their names, gave instructions that they should be let off lightly. Once, as he crossed a street, Isidorus the Cynic loudly taunted him with: 'In your song about Nauplius you make good use of ancient ills, but in all practical matters you make ill use of modern goods.' Again, the comedian Datus, acting in an Atellan farce, illustrated the first line of the song 'Goodbye Father, goodbye Mother' with gestures of drinking and swimming – Claudius had been poisoned, Agrippina nearly drowned – and the last line, 'Hell guides your feet ...' with a wave of his hand towards the senators whom

---

17. Camulodunum and Verulamium.
18. Numerals were expressed by letters; and in Greek the letters of Nero's name, when converted into numerals, had the aggregate value of 1005; and so had the letters of 'murdered his own mother'.

Nero planned to massacre. He may have been impervious to insults of this sort or he may merely have pretended not to care, for fear of encouraging others to be equally witty; at any rate, he did no more than banish Datus and Isidorus.

40. At last, after nearly fourteen years of Nero's misrule, the earth rid herself of him. The first move was made by the Gauls under Julius Vindex, the governor of one of their provinces.

Nero's astrologers had told him that he would one day be removed from the throne, and were given the famous reply:

A simple craft will keep a man from want.

This referred doubtless to his lyre-playing which, although it might be only a pastime for an emperor, would have to support him if he were reduced to earning a livelihood. Some astrologers forecast that, if forced to leave Rome, he would find another throne in the east; one or two even particularized that of Jerusalem. Others assured him that he would recoup all his losses, a prediction on which he based high hopes; for when he seemed to have lost the provinces of Britain and Armenia, but managed to regain them both, he assumed that the disasters foretold had already taken place. Then the Oracle at Delphi warned him to beware the seventy-third year, and assuming that this referred to his own seventy-third year, not Galba's, he looked forward cheerfully to a ripe old age and an unbroken run of good luck; so much so that when he lost some very valuable objects in a shipwreck, he hastened to tell his friends that the fish would fetch them back to him.

Nero heard of the Gallic revolt on the anniversary of his mother's murder. He was in Neapolis at the time and took the news so phlegmatically that people diagnosed satisfaction, on his part, at finding a good excuse to strip such provinces clean, in accordance with the rules of war. Going straight to the gymnasium, he was soon engrossed in watching the athletic contests, and when a far more serious dispatch reached him at dinner time, still showed no sign of disturbance beyond a threat to punish the rebels. In fact, for eight days he wrote no orders and issued no special announcements; apparently trying to ignore the whole affair.

41. At last a series of insulting edicts signed by Vindex must have made some impression on him: in a letter to the Senate he urged them to avenge himself and Rome, but pleaded an infected throat as an excuse for not appearing at the Senate House in person. Only two taunts went home: a suggestion that he was a bad lyre-player, and an insulting reference to him as 'Ahenobarbus', rather than Nero Caesar. Yet he told the Senate that he intended to renounce his adoptive name, which was now being mocked, and resume that of his family; as for his lyre-playing, he replied that he could hardly deserve Vindex's taunt (which proved the other accusations just as false) after his long and painstaking cultivation of the art; and asked a number of people from time to time whether they knew of any better performer than himself. When further urgent despatches reached Antium in quick succession he hurried back to Rome in a state of terror. On the way, however, he happened to notice a group of monumental sculpture which represented a beaten Gaul being dragged along, by the hair, by a mounted Roman; this lucky sign sent him into a transport of joy, and he lifted his hands in gratitude to Heaven. When he arrived in the city, he neglected to address either the Senate or the people; instead, he summoned the leading citizens to his Palace where, after a brief discussion of the Gallic situation, he devoted the remainder of the session to demonstrating a completely new type of water-organ, and explaining the mechanical complexities of several different models. He even remarked that he would have them installed in the Theatre 'if Vindex has no objection'.

42. But when news arrived of Galba's Spanish revolt he fainted dead away and remained mute and insensible for a long while. Coming to himself, he tore his clothes and beat his forehead, crying that all was now over. His old nurse tried to console him by pointing out that many princes in the past had experienced similar setbacks; but Nero insisted that to lose the supreme power while still alive was something that had never happened to anyone else before. Yet he made not the slightest attempt to alter his lazy and extravagant life. On the contrary, he celebrated whatever good news came in from the provinces with the most lavish banquets imaginable, and composed comic songs about the leaders of the revolt, which he set to bawdy tunes and sang with appropriate gestures; these have since become popular favourites. Then he stole into the audience room of the Theatre, and sent a message to an actor who was being loudly applauded at the time, that he should not take advantage of the Emperor's absence from the stage on business of state, by pushing himself forward.

43. At the first news of revolt Nero is said to have formed several appalling, though characteristic, schemes for dealing with the situation. Thus, he intended to depose all army commanders and provincial

governors, and execute them on a charge that they were all involved in a single conspiracy; and to dispatch all exiles everywhere, for fear they might join the rebels; and all Gallic residents at Rome, because they might be implicated in the rising. He further considered giving the army free permission to pillage Gaul; poisoning the entire Senate at a banquet; and setting fire to the city again, but first letting wild beasts loose in the streets to hinder the citizens from saving themselves. However, he had to abandon these schemes, not because he scrupled to carry them out, but because he realized their impracticability in view of the military campaign soon to be forced on him. So he dismissed the Consuls from office before their term ended, and in their place took over the consulship himself without a colleague, declaring: 'It is fated: only a Consul can subdue Gaul.' But one day, after assuming the consular insignia, he left the dining room after a banquet with his arms around two friends' shoulders, and remarked that when he reached Gaul he would at once step unarmed in front of the embattled enemy, and weep and weep. This would soften their hearts and win them back to loyalty; and on the next day he would stroll among his joyful troops singing paeans of victory, which he really ought to be composing now.

44. In his military preparations he was mainly concerned with finding enough wagons to carry his stage equipment and arranging for the concubines who would accompany him to have male haircuts and be issued with Amazonian shields and axes. When this was settled, Nero called the Roman populace to arms; but no eligible recruit came forward, so he forcibly enlisted a number of slaves, choosing the best from each household and refusing exemption even to stewards or secretaries. All classes had to contribute a part of their incomes, and every tenant of a private house or flat was told that he owed a year's rent to his personal treasury. Nero insisted on being paid in none but newly-minted coins, refined silver, or pure gold; hence many people would not contribute anything, protesting that he would do much better if he reclaimed the fees from his informers.

45. He aggravated popular resentment by profiteering in grain, which was priced too high. And as it happened, word went around, during the general shortage of food, that a ship from Alexandria had just unloaded a cargo of sand for the imperial wrestlers.

Nero was now so universally loathed that no bad enough abuse could be found for him. Someone tied a tress of hair to the head of one of his statues, with

DREAMS. *The interpretation of dreams was an elaborate science in antiquity, because dreams were considered by many people to contain prognostications of the future. Such dreams did not have to be unusual: they could be anchored in everyday life. Nero's dreams of his death were of this type.*
131 (above). *The tomb was thought to be the dwelling place of the departed, and cinerary urns and sarcophagi were accordingly often made in the form of a house. Farewell of a married couple at the tomb, on a Roman cinerary urn (see Ill. 37). (Copenhagen, Ny Carlsberg.)*
132 (opposite). *Nations, the provinces of the Roman Empire and cities were regularly depicted as women, as personifications. Roman relief of cities in Asia Minor, A.D. 30. (Naples Museum.)*

a note attached in Greek: 'This is a real contest for once, and you are going to lose!' A sack was draped around the neck of another statue, with a similar note reading: 'I have done what I could, but you deserve the sack.'[19] Insults were scrawled on columns about

19. The sack in which parricides were thrown into the Tiber.

his crowing having aroused even the cocks – for *Galli* means both 'cocks' and Gauls – and several people played the same trick, pretending to have trouble with their slaves at night, and shouting out: 'Vengeance is coming!' – a reference to Vindex's name.

46. The implications of auspices, of omens old and new, and of his own dreams, began to terrify Nero. In the past he had never known what it was to dream, but after killing his mother he dreamed that he was steering a ship and that someone tore the tiller from his hands. Next, his wife Octavia pulled him down into thick darkness, where hordes of winged ants swarmed over him. Then, the statues of the nations, which had been dedicated in the Theatre of Pompey, began to hem him in and prevent him from getting away; while his favourite Asturian horse turned into an ape, or all except the head, which whinnied a tune. Finally, the doors of the Mausoleum opened by themselves and a voice from inside called: 'Enter, Nero!'

On 1 January the Household-gods, which had just been decorated, tumbled to the ground during pre-parations for the New Year sacrifice, and as Nero was taking the auspices Sporus gave him a ring engraved with the rape of Proserpine. Then a great crowd gathered to pay their annual vows to Nero, but the keys of the Capitol were mislaid. Again, while his speech against Vindex was being read in the Senate, a passage running: '. . . the criminals will soon incur the punishment, and die the death which they so thoroughly deserve,' was hailed on all sides with cries of: 'Augustus, you will do it!' People also noticed that Nero, at his latest public appearance, sang the part of Oedipus in Exile and ended with the line:

Wife, mother, father, do my death compel!

47. When a dispatch bringing the news that the other armies, too, had revolted was brought him at dinner, he tore it up, pushed over the table, and sent smashing to the ground two of his 'Homeric' drinking cups – so called because they were engraved with scenes from Homer. He made Locusta give him some poison, which he put in a golden box; then crossed to

the Servilian Gardens, where he tried to persuade the Guards officers to flee with him – his most faithful freedmen had gone ahead to equip a fleet at Ostia. Some answered evasively, others flatly refused. One even shouted out the Virgilian tag: 'Is it so terrible a thing to die?'

Nero turned over a number of plans in his mind. For example, he might throw himself on the mercy of the Parthians, or of Galba; or appear pathetically on the Rostra, dressed in black, to beg the people's pardon for his sins – they might at least make him prefect of Egypt, he thought, if they could not find it in their hearts to forgive him altogether. A speech to this effect was later found among the papers in his desk, and the usual view is that only fear of being torn to pieces before he reached the Forum prevented him from delivering it.

Nero suspended his deliberations until the following day, but woke at midnight to find that his bodyguard had deserted him. He leaped out of bed and summoned his friends. When they did not appear he went with a few members of his staff to their rooms. But all the doors were closed and nobody answered. He returned to his room. By now even the caretakers had absconded with the bed linen and the box of poison. He at once shouted for Spiculus the gladiator or any other trained executioner, to put an end to him. No one came. 'What? Have I then neither friends nor enemies left?' he cried, and dashed out of the Palace. Apparently he intended to hurl himself into the Tiber.

48. Changing his mind once more, however, he said that all he wanted was some secluded spot where he could hide and collect himself. Phaon, an imperial freedman, suggested his own suburban villa, four miles away, between the Nomentan and the Salarian Ways. Nero was in his tunic and barefooted; but he simply pulled on a faded cloak and hat, took horse and trotted off, holding a handkerchief over his face. Four servants went with him, including Sporus. Suddenly an earth-tremor was felt and lightning flashed in their eyes, which terrified Nero. Then, from the near-by camp soldiers began shouting about the defeat which Galba would inflict on him. He heard one man exclaim as they passed: 'Those people are in pursuit of the Emperor,' and another: 'What's the latest news of him in town?' Then Nero's horse took fright at the smell of a dead body lying by the roadside; which made him expose his face. He was immediately recognized and saluted by a Guards veteran. They reached a lane leading to Phaon's villa and, abandoning their horses, followed

a path which ran through bushes and a briar patch and a plantation of reeds to the rear wall of the house. Because the going was difficult Nero made them spread a cloak for him to walk on. When begged by Phaon to lie low for a while in a gravel pit, he answered: 'No, I refuse to go underground before I die.' While the servants made a secret entrance into the house he scooped up some water in his hands from a neighbour-ing pool and drank it, saying: 'This is Nero's own special brew.' Then he pulled out all the thorns from his ragged cloak and crawled into the villa by way of the tunnel. In the first room he came to, he sank down on a couch with a poor mattress over which an old cape had been thrown and, although hungry, refused some coarse bread that was offered him; but confessed him-self still thirsty and sipped a little warmish water.

49. Finally, when his companions unanimously in-sisted on his trying to escape from the degrading fate threatening him, he ordered them to dig a grave at once, of the right size, and then collect any pieces of marble that they could find and fetch wood and water for the disposal of the corpse. As they bustled about obediently he muttered through his tears: 'Dead! And so great an artist!'

While he hesitated, a runner brought him a letter from Phaon. Nero tore it from the man's hands and read that, having been declared a public enemy by the Senate, he would be punished 'in ancient style' when arrested. He asked what 'ancient style' meant, and learned that the executioners stripped their victim naked, thrust his head into a wooden fork, and then flogged him to death with rods. In terror he snatched up the two daggers which he had brought along and tried their points; but threw them down again, protest-ing that the fatal hour had not yet come. Then he begged Sporus to weep and mourn for him, but also begged one of the other three to set him an example by committing suicide first. He kept moaning about his cowardice, and muttering: 'How ugly and vulgar my life has become!' And then in Greek: 'This certainly is no credit to Nero, no credit at all,' and: 'Come, pull yourself together!' By this time the troop of cavalry who had orders to take him alive were coming up the road. Nero gasped:

Hark to the sound I hear! It is hooves of galloping horses.

Then, with the help of his secretary, Epaphroditus, he stabbed himself in the throat and was already half dead when a centurion entered, pretending to have rushed to his rescue, and staunched the wound with his cloak.

Nero muttered: 'Too late! But, ah, what fidelity!' He died, with eyes glazed and bulging from their sockets, a sight which horrified everybody present. He had made his companions promise, whatever happened, not to let his head be cut off, but to arrange in some way that he should be buried all in one piece. Galba's freedman Icelus, who had been imprisoned when the first news came of the revolt and was now at liberty again, granted this indulgence.

50. They laid Nero on his pyre, dressed in the gold-embroidered white robes which he had worn on 1 January. The funeral cost 2,000 gold pieces. Ecloge and Alexandria, his old nurses, helped Acte, his mistress, to carry the remains to the Pincian Hill, which can be seen from the Campus Martius. His coffin, of white porphyry, stands there in the family tomb of the Domitii, enclosed by a balustrade of stone from Thasos, and with an altar of Luna marble standing over it.

51. Physical characteristics of Nero:
 Height: average.
 Body: pustular and malodorous.
 Hair: light blond.
 Features: pretty, rather than handsome.
 Eyes: blue and rather weak.
 Neck: squat.
 Belly: protuberant.
 Legs: spindling.

His health was good: for all his extravagant indulgence he had only three illnesses in fourteen years, and none of them serious enough to stop him from drinking wine or breaking any other regular habit. He was entirely shameless in the style of his appearance and dress but always had his hair set in rows of curls and, when he visited Greece, let it grow long and hang down his back. He often gave audiences in an unbelted silk dressing-gown and slippers, with a scarf round his neck.

52. As a boy Nero read most of the usual humanities subjects except philosophy which, Agrippina warned him, was no proper study for a future ruler. His tutor Seneca hid the works of the early rhetoricians from him, intending to be admired himself as long as possible. So Nero turned his hand to poetry, and would dash off verses enthusiastically, without any effort. It is often claimed that he published other people's work as his own; but notebooks and papers have come into my possession, which contain some of Nero's best-known poems in his own handwriting. Many erasures and cancellations, as well as words substituted above the lines, prove that he was neither copying nor dictating, and are written just as people write when they are thinking and composing. Nero also took more than an amateur's interest in painting and sculpture.

53. His dominant characteristics were his thirst for popularity and his jealousy of men who caught the public eye by any means whatsoever. Because he had won so many stage victories, most people expected him to take part in athletic contests at the next Olympiad. For he practised wrestling all the time, and everywhere in Greece had watched the gymnastic competitions like the judges, squatting on the ground in the stadium, and if any pair of competitors worked away from the centre of the ring, would push them back himself. Because of his singing he had been compared to Phoebus Apollo and because of his chariot-riding to the Sun-God; now, apparently, he planned to become a Hercules, for

THE SYRIAN GODDESS. *Atargatis or Ishtar is mentioned in the Old Testament and was worshipped throughout the Middle East as Divine Mistress and Mother.*
133. *Atargatis enthroned with the city goddess of Palmyra on a Palmyrene relief, first century* A.D. (Damascus, National Museum.)

THE MYSTERIOUS EAST. *In the imagination of many Romans of the Western Mediterranean, the Eastern provinces of the Empire and the countries beyond them were a world of untold riches and strange religious cults. Here, unlike in the West, the influence of Greece and Rome never amounted to more than a thin veneer.*

134 (above). *The gods Aglibol (moon), Baalshamin (sky) and Malakbel (sun) face their worshippers. Relief from Palmyra, first century* A.D. *(Paris, Louvre.)*

135 (opposite). *Silver face mask attached to a helmet of iron, from Emesa. First century* A.D. *(Damascus, National Museum.)*

according to one story he had a lion so carefully trained that he could safely face it naked before the entire amphitheatre; and then either kill it with his club or else strangle it.

54. Just before the end Nero took a public oath that if he managed to keep his throne he would celebrate the victory with a music festival, performing successively on water-organ, flute, and bagpipes; and when the last day came would dance the role of Turnus in Virgil's *Aeneid*. He was supposed to have killed the actor Paris because he considered him a serious professional rival.

55. Nero's unreasonable craving for immortal fame made him change a number of well-known names of things and places in his own favour. The month of April, for instance, became Neroneus; and Rome was on the point of being renamed 'Neropolis'.

56. He despised all religious cults except that of the Syrian Goddess,[20] and showed, one day, that he had changed his mind even about her, by urinating on the divine image. He had come, instead, to rest a superstitious belief – the only one, as a matter of fact, to which he ever remained faithful – in the statuette of a girl sent him by an anonymous commoner as a charm against conspiracies. It so happened that a conspiracy came to light immediately afterwards; so he began to worship the girl as though she were a powerful goddess, and sacrificed to her three times a day, expecting people to believe that she gave him knowledge of the future. He did inspect some entrails once, a few months before his death, but they contained no omen at all favourable to him.

57. Nero died at the age of thirty-one, on the anniversary of Octavia's murder. In the widespread general rejoicing, citizens ran through the streets wearing caps of liberty. But there were people who used to lay spring and summer flowers on his grave for a long time, and had statues made of him, wearing his fringed toga, which they put up on the Rostra; they even continued to circulate his edicts, pretending he was still alive and would soon return to confound his enemies. What is more, King Vologaesus of Parthia, on sending ambassadors to ratify his alliance with Rome, particularly requested the Senate to honour Nero's memory. In fact, twenty years later, when I was a young man, a mysterious individual came forward claiming to be Nero; and so magical was the sound of his name in the Parthians' ears that they supported him to the best of their ability, and only handed him over with great reluctance.

20. Atargatis.

VII
GALBA

With Nero the line of the Caesars became extinct. Among the many prophetic indications of this event two were outstanding. As Livia, years before, was returning to her home near Veii immediately after marrying Augustus,[1] an eagle flew by and dropped into her lap a white pullet which it had just pounced upon.

1. 38 B.C.

PUBLIC WORKS
136 (opposite). *The theatre of Merida, one of the most important cities of Roman Spain.*

GALBA
137 (above). *Coin from Rome.* (Hirmer.)

Noticing a laurel twig in its beak she decided to keep the pullet for breeding and to plant the twig. Soon the pullet raised such a brood of chickens that the house is still known as 'The Poultry'; moreover the twig took root and grew so luxuriously that the Caesars always plucked laurels from it to wear at their triumphs. It also became an imperial custom to cut new slips and plant these close by. Remarkably enough, the death of each Emperor was anticipated by the premonitory wilting of his laurel; and in the last year of Nero's reign not only did every tree wither at the root, but the whole flock of poultry died. And, as if that were insufficient warning, a thunderbolt presently struck the Temple of the Caesars, decapitated all the statues at a stroke and dashed Augustus's sceptre from his hands.

2. Galba succeeded Nero. Though not directly related to the Julians, he came from a very great and ancient aristocratic house, and used to amplify the inscriptions on his own statues with the statement that Quintus Catulus Capitolinus was his great-grand-father; and when he became Emperor he even had a tablet set up in the Palace forecourt, tracing his ancestry back to Jupiter on the male, and to Pasiphaë, Minos's wife, on the female side.

3. It would be a long story to reproduce this pedigree here in all its glory; but I shall touch briefly on Galba's immediate family. Why the surname 'Galba' was first assumed by a Sulpicius, and where it originated, must remain moot points. One suggestion is that after a tediously protracted siege of some Spanish town the Sulpicius in question set fire to it, using torches smeared with resin (*galbanum*). Another is that he resorted to *galbeum*, a kind of poultice, during a long illness. Others are that he was very fat, the Gallic word for which is *galba*; or that, on the contrary, he was very slender – like the *galba*, a creature which breeds in oak trees. The Sulpicii acquired lustre during the consul-

ship of Servius Galba, described as the most eloquent speaker of his time, and preserve a tradition that, while governing Spain, he massacred 30,000 Lusitanians – an act which provoked the war with Viriatus. Servius Galba's grandson, enraged when Julius Caesar, whose lieutenant he had been in Gaul, passed him over for the consulship, joined the assassins Brutus and Cassius, and was subsequently sentenced to death under the Pedian Law.[2] The Emperor Galba's father and grandfather were descended from this personage. The grandfather had a far higher reputation as a scholar than as a statesman, never rising above the rank of praetor but publishing a monumental, and not negligible, historical work. The father, however, won a consulship; and although so squat as to be almost a hunchback, and a poor speaker into the bargain, he proved an indefatigable pleader. He married, first Mummia Achaica, grand-daughter of Catulus and great-granddaughter of the Lucius Mummius who sacked Corinth; and then Livia Ocellina, a rich and beautiful woman, whose affections are said to have originally been stirred by his rank, but afterwards even more by his frankness – in reply to her persistent advances he stripped to the waist, in private, and revealed his hump as a proof that he wished to hide nothing from her. Achaica bore him two sons: Gaius and Servius. Gaius, the elder, left Rome owing to financial embarrassment; and, because Tiberius crossed him off the list of governors when he became due for a province, committed suicide.

4. On 24 December 3 B.C., while Marcus Valerius Messala and Gnaeus Lentulus were Consuls, Servius Galba, the Emperor-to-be, was born in a hillside country house by the road which links Tarracina with Fundi. To please his stepmother Livia Ocellina, who had adopted him, he took the name Livius, the surname Ocella, and the forename Lucius, until becoming Emperor. According to tradition, when he was a boy and called with some of his contemporaries to pay his respects to Augustus, the Emperor pinched his cheek, saying in Greek: 'You too will taste a little of my power, child'; and Tiberius, hearing that he would be Emperor when an old man, grunted: 'Very well, let him live; the news does not concern me in the least.' One day, as Galba's grandfather was invoking sacrificial lightning, an eagle suddenly snatched the victim's intestines out of his hands and carried them off to an oak-tree laden with acorns. A bystander suggested that this sign portended great honour for the family. 'Yes,

yes, perhaps so,' the old man agreed, smiling, 'on the day that a mule foals.' When Galba later launched his rebellion, what encouraged him most was the news that a mule had, in fact, foaled. Although everyone else considered this a disastrous omen, Galba remembered the sacrifice and his grandfather's saying, and interpreted it in precisely the opposite sense.

By the time he reached adult years, he had already dreamed that the Goddess Fortune visited him to announce that she was tired of waiting outside his door and would he please let her in quickly or she would be fair game for the next passer-by. He awoke, opened the door of the hall and found beside the threshold a bronze image of the Goddess, almost two feet tall. This he carried lovingly to Tusculum, his summer home, and consecrated it in a room of the house; worshipping it from that time onwards with monthly sacrifices and an annual vigil.

Even as a young man he faithfully observed the national custom, already ancient and obsolescent, which survived only in his own household, of summoning his slaves twice a day in a body to wish him goodmorning and good-night, one after the other.

5. Galba applied himself to liberal studies with care, and was particularly skilled in law. He took marriage seriously but, on losing his wife Lepida and the two sons she had borne him, remained single for the rest of his life. Nobody could interest him in a second match, not even Agrippina the Younger who, when her husband Domitius died, made such shameless advances to him – though he had not yet become a widower – that his mother-in-law gave her a public reprimand, going so far as to slap her in front of a whole bevy of married women.

Galba always behaved most graciously to Livia Augusta, who showed him considerable favour while she lived, and then left him half a million gold pieces,

2. See Nero 3.

TOWNS. *The foundation or refoundation of towns was initially the chief vehicle of bringing the Roman way of life to a newly conquered province. But the countryside was often as yet only partially pacified and the towns were accordingly in need of defence.*
138 (top). *Roman walls of Tarragona on Iberian foundations.*
139 (below). *Roman mosaic showing a town wall with tower and gate.* (Pamplona, Museo de Navara.)

the largest bequest of all. But, because the amount was expressed in figures, not words, Tiberius, as her executor, reduced it to a mere 5,000; and Galba never handled even that modest sum.

6. He won his first public appointment while still under age. As praetor in charge of the Floral Games he introduced the spectacular novelty of tightrope-walking elephants. Then he governed the province of Aquitania for nearly a year, and next held a consulship for six months. It so happened that Galba succeeded Nero's father, Gnaeus Domitius, and preceded Salvius Otho, father of Otho – a foreshadowing of the time when he should reign between these two Consuls' sons. At Gaius's orders Galba replaced Gaetulicus as commander in Upper Germany. The day after taking up his command he put a stop to applause at a religious festival, by posting a notice to the effect that 'hands will be kept inside cloaks on all occasions'. Very soon the following doggerel went the rounds:

> Soldier, soldier, on parade,
> You should learn the soldier's trade,
> Galba's now commanding us –
> Galba, not Gaetulicus!

Galba came down just as severely on requests for leave. By gruelling hard work he toughened old campaigners as well as raw recruits, and sharply checked a barbarian raid into Gaul. Altogether, he and his army made so favourable an impression when Gaius arrived that they won more praise and prize money than any of the other numerous troops assembled from all the provinces. Galba scored a personal success by doubling for twenty miles, beside the Emperor's chariot, while continuing to direct manoeuvres, shield in hand.

7. Although strongly urged to take advantage of the opportunity after Gaius's murder, Galba held back, thus earning Claudius's heartfelt gratitude. Claudius, indeed, considered Galba so close a friend that, when a slight indisposition overtook him, the British expedition was postponed on his account. Later, Galba became proconsul in Africa for two years, holding a special appointment[3] with instructions to suppress the disturbance caused there by domestic rivalries and a native revolt. He executed his commission somewhat ruthlessly, it is true, but showed attention to justice even in trivial matters. Discovering, for instance, that while rations were short during a foray, a certain

3. i.e., chosen *extra sortem*, without the drawing of lots.
4. i.e., Nearer Spain (from its capital Tarraco).

THE ROMANS IN SPAIN, *as elsewhere, made their presence felt by constructing, or encouraging others to construct, a series of major public works.*
140 (opposite). *The bridge of Alcantara near Caceres, built from funds supplied by a group of Iberian nobles.*

legionary had sold a peck of surplus wheat for a gold piece, he gave orders that no one should feed the fellow when his stores were exhausted; and so he starved to death. At a court of inquiry into the ownership of a transport animal, Galba found the evidence on both sides and the pleadings unsatisfactory and, since the truth seemed to be anybody's guess, gave orders: 'Lead the beast blindfold to its usual trough and let it drink. Then uncover its eyes and watch to whom it goes of its own accord. That man will be the owner.'

8. For these achievements in Africa and his previous successes in Germany, Galba won triumphal decorations and a triple priesthood, and was elected both to the Board of the Fifteen, and to the Titian brotherhood and priesthood of Augustus. But from then onwards, until the middle years of Nero's reign, he lived almost exclusively in retirement, never going anywhere, even for a country drive, without the escort of a second carriage containing 10,000 gold pieces. At last, while living at Fundi, he was offered the governorship of Tarraconensian Spain;[4] where, soon after his arrival, as he sacrificed in a temple, the incense-carrying acolyte went white-haired before his eyes – a sign read by some as portending a change of rulers and the succession of a young Emperor by an old one. And presently, when a thunderbolt struck a lake in Cantabria, twelve axes, unmistakable emblems of high authority, were recovered from it.

9. He ruled Tarraconensian Spain for eight years in a varying and inconsistent manner, beginning with great enthusiasm and energy, and even going a little too far in his punishment of crime. He sentenced a dishonest money-changer to have both hands cut off and nailed to the counter; and crucified a man who had poisoned his ward to inherit the property. When this murderer begged for justice, protesting that he was a Roman citizen, Galba recognized his status and ironically consoled him with: 'Let this citizen hang higher than the rest, and have his cross whitewashed.' As time wore on, however, he grew lazy and inactive; but this

was done purposely to deny Nero any pretext for disciplining him. In his own words: 'Nobody can be forced to give an account of doing nothing.'

Galba was holding assizes at New Carthage when news reached him of the revolt in the Gallic provinces. It came in the form of an appeal for help sent by the Roman Governor of Aquitania, which was followed by another from Gaius Julius Vindex asking, would he make himself the liberator and leader of humanity? He accepted the suggestion, half hopefully, half fearfully, but without much delay, having accidentally come across Nero's secret orders (sent to his agents) for his

own assassination; and took heart from certain very favourable signs and portents, especially the predictions of a nobly-born girl which (according to Jupiter's priest at Clunia) matched the prophecies spoken in a trance by another girl two centuries before – the priest had just found a record of these in the inner shrine of the Temple, following directions given him in a dream. The gist of these prophecies was that the lord and master of the world would some day arise in Spain.

10. Accordingly, Galba took his place on the tribunal, as though going about the business of freeing slaves, but before him were ranged statues and pictures

Emperor and Empire

*From its inception, the Roman Empire was an absolute monarchy: as
the lawyer Ulpian expressed it in the late second century* A.D.: '*The
decision of the Emperor has the force of law.' But in outward appearance, this absolute monarchy expressed itself in the traditions and the
religious and constitutional forms of the Roman Republic. The magistracies and priesthoods of the Republic continued in imperial times
to be filled with Roman notables, and, at times, by notables from the
provinces of the Empire, but the authority and executive power which
these offices had once carried now belonged to the Emperor alone.*

Suetonius's Twelve Caesars *covers the period during which this
transformation from Republic to Empire took place, and his narrative
is crowded with references, direct or implied, to the tensions and con-
flicts which it caused. For the ideal Emperor, as visualized by many
aristocratic Romans of the first century* A.D., *had little semblance to
the reality. Ideally, the Emperor would be an eminent citizen among
other eminent citizens, that is, especially the senators of the city of
Rome; he would be deferred to by them, but also he would consult them
on matters of state. In some way, the constitutional processes of the
Republic would survive, it was hoped, in more than mere form.*

*This was an unrealistic hope, for it was rooted in the ancient history
of Rome and its immediate vicinity at a time when Rome was no longer
the sole or exclusive point of reference in matters of politics and power.
While the aristocrats of Rome reconciled themselves as best they could
to the facts of empire and absolute monarchy, the Empire itself, its
provinces, which now ringed the Mediterranean in a continuous chain,
prospered. Therefore the position of the Emperor came to depend less
on the loyalty and support of the aristocrats of Rome, and more on
the loyalty and support of the people of the provinces, and of the army.
This was one of the aspects of the transformation of a small Italian
state, the Roman Republic, into a large power.*

*In the last decades of the Republic, the Roman army was still re-
cruited from among the peasants of Italy, while subject or allied rulers
would at times send auxiliary forces. This changed during the first century* A.D.: *Roman soldiers were now recruited throughout the Empire.
What held them together was the discipline of army life, which was
the same everywhere[3]. While the senators and aristocrats of Rome
might debate to what extent they could pay respect and homage to an
absolute ruler, the choices of a soldier in this matter were simple: they
comprised only rebellion or unreserved personal loyalty to the Emperor
(cf. Augustus 25).*

1. Roman silver platter: the goddess Roma ▶

2. Roman military camp, Masada, Israel

3. Tombstone of a Roman soldier,
first century A.D.

4. Roman road in Greece

5. Roman canal at Seleucia

6. The Gemma Augustea. *Top:* Augustus, enthroned with the goddess Roma, receives Tiberius, who approaches on a triumphal chariot. *Bottom:* soldiers, with conquered enemies, erect a trophy

7. Alexander the Great and Darius in the battle of Issus; mosaic from Pompeii   8 (*overleaf*). Hadrian's Wall

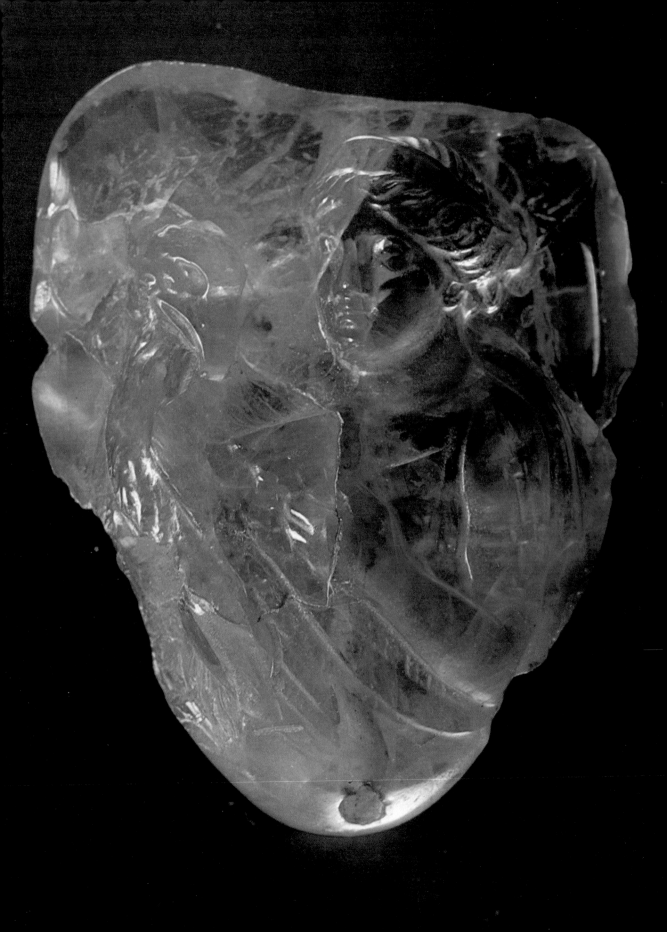

Such loyalty came to be reinforced by institutional uniformity. The Roman Empire accommodated much regional diversity, but in matters of defence and civilian organization[5] it imposed its own patterns. On a far-flung network of paved roads[4], armies, tax-collectors and administrators travelled from one end of the Empire to the other. An equally far-flung network of military installations served to defend the Empire against foreign powers and to forestall and if need be crush unrest or rebellion within the frontiers of the Empire[2 and 8]. Such was the price of internal and external peace. It was a heavy price, of which people were not unaware, for the course and the consequences of warfare were depicted on many Roman monuments with surprising accuracy and realism[6].

But this was not the only perspective within which war and violent conflict within the Empire and on its frontiers could be absorbed and understood. Successful warfare could also serve to exalt the individual general – principally the Emperor, in whose name all wars were fought; in such a perspective, the Emperor was at times viewed as a living exemplar of the heroes of the past[7], and war was idealized, both in itself and as a means of achieving peace. This perspective, and the interpretation of the role of the Emperor in the light of it became increasingly prevalent during the imperial period.

For the subjects of the Empire in the provinces were largely indifferent to the ancient values of the Roman Republic, to those ideals of free speech and free political activity among equals which had conspired to bring about the civil wars of the late Republic. What mattered instead to the subjects of the Empire was the peace which was the outcome of Roman warfare and autocracy, of the government of one man, the Emperor. Many Roman subjects were therefore content to live and express themselves within the framework which was allowed by Roman imperial propaganda, without finding it restricting or compromising, and this reflected on the forms which the propaganda took. The gods of imperial Rome were worshipped in many a provincial shrine; the Emperor's almost divine person was honoured in countless inscriptions, scattered throughout the territories of the Empire, and the figure of Roma, personification of the city of Rome[1], became a concept whereby to unite the diverse peoples who made up the population of the Empire.

◀ 9. Venus with the imperial eagle; sapphire gem
(reproduced larger than actual size)

of Nero's prominent victims. A young nobleman, recalled from exile in the near-by Balearic Islands for this occasion, stood near while Galba deplored the present state of the times. Galba was at once hailed as Imperator, and accepted the honour; announcing that he was now the representative of the Roman Senate and People. He closed the courts, and began raising legions and auxiliaries from the local population to increase his existing command of one legion, two squadrons of cavalry, and three infantry cohorts. Next, he chose the most intelligent and oldest noblemen available as members of a kind of senate, to which matters of State importance could be referred. He also picked certain young knights, instead of ordinary troops, to guard his sleeping quarters, and although these ranked as volunteers they still wore the gold rings proper to their condition. Then he called, by proclamation, upon the whole provincial population to join his movement both individually and corporatively, and aid the common cause to the best of their ability. At about this time a ring of ancient design was discovered in the fortifications of the city that he had chosen as his headquarters; the engraved gem represented Victory raising a trophy. Soon afterwards an Alexandrian ship drifted into Dertosa, loaded with arms, but neither helmsman, crew, nor passengers were found aboard her – which left no doubt in anyone's mind that this must be a just and righteous war, favoured by the gods.

Suddenly, however, without the least warning, Galba's enterprise nearly collapsed. As he approached the station where one of his cavalry squadrons was quartered, the men felt ashamed of their defection and tried to go back on it; Galba kept them at their posts only by a great effort. Again, he was nearly murdered on his way to the baths: he had to pass down a narrow corridor lined by a company of slaves whom an imperial freedman had presented to him – with treachery in view. But while they plucked up their courage by urging one another 'not to miss the opportunity', someone took the trouble to ask: 'What opportunity?' Later they confessed under torture.

11. Galba's grave embarrassments were increased by the death of Vindex, which almost turned him to despair and suicide. Presently, however, messengers arrived from Rome with the news that Nero, too, was dead, and that the citizens had all sworn obedience to himself; so he dropped the title of Governor and assumed that of Caesar. He now wore an imperial cloak, with a dagger hanging from his neck in front of his chest and did not put on a toga again until he had

THE RELIGION OF THE COUNTRYSIDE. *In the countryside, Roman cults, as well as pre-Roman cults in Roman guise, survived down to the Christian period.*

141 (above). *Health (Salus; see Ill. 52) Umeritana (inscribed): a medicinal spring has been personified in the Roman manner. The nymph of the spring reclines with her urn at the top of this silver plate. The water flows into a rocky opening, where a young man pours it into a container. A devotee is offering incense on an altar (upper right edge) and another pours a libation (centre left). A patient is being given water from the spring to drink (lower right), and more water is being poured into a barrel ready to be transported elsewhere. (From Otanes near Santander. Private collection.)*

142 (opposite, top). *The Romano-British divinity of the medicinal springs at Bath, from the temple of Sulis Minerva. (Bath, Museum.)*

143 (opposite, below). *Relief dedicated to the springs and nymphs. In the foreground reclines a river god; the three Graces are on the left, and on the right two nymphs abduct Hylas, the friend of Hercules. In the background are Hercules and Mercury, looking for Hylas. Second century A.D. (Rome, Capitoline Museum.)*

accounted for those plotting against him: Nymphidius Sabinus, Commander of the Praetorian Guard, and then Fonteius Capito and Clodius Macer, who commanded respectively in Germany and Africa.

12. Stories of Galba's two characteristics, cruelty and greed, preceded him; he was said to have punished townships that had been slow to receive him by levying severer taxes and even dismantling their fortifications; to have executed not only officers and imperial agents, but their wives and children too; and, when the people of Tarraco offered him a golden crown from the ancient Temple of Jupiter, described as weighing 15 lb, to have melted this down and made them supply the three ounces needed to tip the scales at the advertised weight. Galba more than confirmed this reputation on his entry into Rome. He sent back to rowing duty some sailors whom Nero had turned into marines;[5] and when they stubbornly insisted on their right to the Imperial Eagle and standards, ordered his cavalry to charge them; then had every tenth man cut down. Galba also disbanded the German Guard, who had served previous emperors and proved loyal in many critical tests; repatriating them without a bounty on the grounds that they had shown excessive devotion to Gnaeus Dolabella by camping close to his estate. Other anecdotes to his discredit, possibly true, possibly false, went the rounds: when an especially lavish dinner was set before him he had groaned aloud; when presented by his chief steward with a summarized account, he had rewarded his scrupulous labours with a bowlful of beans; and, delighted by Canus's performance on the flute, he had drawn five denarii from his purse with his own hand and pressed them on him.

13. Galba's accession was not entirely popular, as became obvious at the first theatrical show he attended. This was an Atellan farce, in which occurred the well-known song 'Here comes Onesimus, down from the farm . . .' The whole audience took up the chorus with fervour, repeating that particular line over and over again.

14. Thus his power and prestige were far greater while he was assuming control of the Empire than afterwards; though affording ample proof of his capacity to rule, he won less praise for his good acts than blame for his mistakes. Three officials, nicknamed his tutors, lived with him in the Palace and never left his side. These were the greedy Titus Vinius, one of his former officers in Spain; the intolerably arrogant

and stupid Cornelius Laco, a former judge's assessor and now Commander of the Guard; and his own freedman Icelus who, having recently acquired the surname of Marcianus and the right to wear a gold ring, now had his eye on the highest appointment available to a man of his rank, namely Laco's. Galba let himself be so continuously guided by these experts in different kinds of vice that he was far less consistent in his behaviour – at one time meaner and more bitter, at another more wasteful and indulgent – than an elected leader, at his time of life, had any right to be.

He sentenced senators and knights to death without trial on the scantiest evidence, and seldom granted applications for Roman citizenship. Nor would he concede the prerogatives which could, in law, be enjoyed by every father of three children, except to an occasional claimant; and then for a fixed and limited period only. When the judges recommended the formation of a sixth judicial division, Galba was not content simply to turn this down, but cancelled the privilege, which Claudius had allowed them, of being excused court duties in the winter months and New Year.

15. It was generally believed that he intended to restrict all official appointments, both for nights and senators, to two-year periods, and choose only men who either did not want them or could be counted on to refuse. He annulled all Nero's awards, letting the beneficiaries keep no more than a tenth part, enlisting the help of fifty knights to ensure that his order was obeyed, and ruling that if any actor or other performer had sold one of Nero's gifts, spent the money, and was unable to refund it, the missing sum must be recovered from the buyers. Yet there was nothing which he did not permit his friends and freedmen to sell at a price or give away as a favour – immunity from taxes, an innocent party sentenced here, a culprit excused there. Moreover, when a popular demand arose for the punishment of Halotus and Tigellinus, the vilest of all Nero's assistants, Galba not only protected their lives but gave Halotus an important post as his agent, and even published an imperial edict charging the people with undeserved hostility towards Tigellinus.

16. Thus he outraged almost all classes at Rome; but the most virulent hatred of him was to be found in the Army. Though a larger bonus than usual had been promised soldiers who had pledged their swords to Galba before his arrival in the city, he would not honour this commitment, but announced: 'It is my custom to levy troops, not to buy them.' This remark infuriated the troops everywhere; and he earned the

5. i.e., regular members of the armed forces.

Guards' particular suspicion and resentment by his dismissal of a number of them suspected of being in Nymphidius's pay. The loudest grumbling came from camps in Upper Germany, where the men claimed that they had not been rewarded for their services against the Gauls and Vindex. These, the first Roman troops bold enough to withhold their allegiance, refused on 1 January to take any oath except in the name of the Senate; informing the Guards, by messenger, that they were thoroughly at odds with this Spanish-appointed Emperor, and would the Guards please choose one who would be acceptable to the Army as a whole?

17. Galba heard about this message and, thinking that he was being criticized for his childlessness rather than his senility, singled out from the crowd at one of his morning receptions a handsome and well-bred young man, Piso Frugi Licinianus, to whom he had already shown great favour, and appointed him perpetual heir to his name and property. Calling him 'my son', he led Piso into the Guards' camp, and there formally and publicly adopted him – without, however, mentioning the word 'bounty', and thus giving Otho an excellent opportunity for his *coup d'état* five days later.

18. A rapid succession of signs, from the beginning of his reign, had been portending Galba's end in accurate detail. During his march on Rome people were being slaughtered right and left all along his route whenever he passed through a town; and once an ill-timed axe blow made a frenzied ox break its harness and charge Galba's chariot, rearing up and drenching him with blood. Then, as he climbed out, one of his scouts, pushed by the mob, nearly wounded him with a spear. When Galba first entered the city, and again when he came into the Palace, an earthquake shock was felt, and a sound arose as of bulls bellowing. Clearer presages followed. Galba had set aside from his treasures a pearl-mounted collar and certain other jewels, which were to decorate the Goddess Fortune's shrine at Tusculum. But, impulsively deciding that they were too good for her, he consecrated them to Capitoline Venus instead. The very next night Fortune complained to him in a dream that she had been robbed of a gift intended for herself, and threatened to take back what she herself had already given him. At dawn, Galba hurried in terror towards Tusculum to expiate the fault revealed by his dream, having sent men ahead to prepare sacrifices; but when he arrived, found only warm ashes on the altar and an old black-cloaked fellow offering incense in a glass bowl, and wine in an earthen-

ware cup. It was noticed, too, that while he was sacrificing on 1 January his garland fell off, and that the sacred chickens flew away when he went to read the auspices. Again, before Galba addressed the troops on the subject of the adoption, his attendants forgot to set a camp chair on the tribunal; and in the Senate House his curule seat was discovered to be facing the wrong way.

19. When attending morning sacrifice before the victim was killed, Galba was now repeatedly warned by a soothsayer to expect danger – murderers were about. Soon afterwards news came that Otho had seized the Guards' Camp. Though urged to hurry there in person, because his rank and presence could carry the day, Galba stayed where he was, bent on rallying to his standard the legionaries scattered throughout the city. He did, indeed, put on a linen corselet, but remarked that it would afford small protection against so many swords. Meanwhile, some of his supporters rashly assured him that the affair was over and the rebels suppressed – their troops were on the way to surrender and offer their congratulations, ready to obey all his orders. Galba went forward to meet them in the utmost confidence. When a soldier claimed with pride to have killed Otho, he snapped: 'On whose authority?' and hurried on to the Forum. There a party of cavalrymen, clattering through the city streets and dispersing the mob, caught sight of him from a distance. These were his appointed assassins. They reined in for a moment, then charged at him; his followers abandoned him, and he was butchered.

20. Just before his death Galba is said to have shouted out: 'What is all this, comrades? I am yours, you are mine!' and gone so far as to promise the bounty; but, according to the more usual account, he realized the soldiers' intention, bared his neck and encouraged them to do their duty and kill him. Oddly enough, no one present made any attempt at rescue, and all who were summoned to rally around him turned a deaf ear. A single company of Germans alone rushed to his assistance because he had once treated them with kindness while they were convalescents; not knowing the city well, however, they took a wrong turning, and arrived too late.

Galba was murdered beside the Curtian pool, and left lying just as he fell. A private soldier returning from the grain issue set down his load and decapitated Galba's body. He could not carry the head by the hair – for there was none – but stuffed it in his cloak; and presently brought it to Otho with his thumb thrust into the mouth. Otho handed the trophy to a crowd of serv-

ants and camp-boys, who stuck it on a spear and carried it scornfully round the camp chanting at intervals:

> Galba, Galba, Cupid Galba,
> Please enjoy your vigour still!

Apparently Galba had enraged them by quoting Homer to someone who congratulated him on his robust appearance:

> So far my vigour undiminished is.

A freedman of Patrobius Neronianus bought the head for 100 gold pieces, but only to hurl it to the ground where Patrobius had been murdered at Galba's orders. In the end his steward Argivus consigned it, with the trunk, to the tomb in Galba's private gardens which lay beside the Aurelian Way.

21. The following is a physical account of Servius Sulpicius Galba:

Height: medium.

Hair: none.

Eyes: blue.

Nose: hooked.

Hands and feet: twisted by gout, which made him unable to unroll or even hold a parchment scroll or wear shoes.

Body: badly ruptured on the right side, requiring a truss for support.

He was a heavy eater, in winter always breakfasting before daylight; and with a habit, at dinner, of passing on the leavings, which had accumulated in front of him, to his attendants. A homosexual invert, he showed a preference for mature and very sturdy men. It is said

THE CURTIAN POOL *was perhaps named after Marcus Curtius. In 360 B.C., a chasm opened in the Roman Forum; Marcus Curtius concluded that the gods of the underworld desired a sacrifice, and threw himself, fully armed and mounted on his horse, into the gap, which closed after him.*

144. *Relief of the first century* B.C. (Rome, Conservatori.)

that when Icelus, one of his old-time bed-fellows, brought the news of Nero's death, Galba openly showered him with kisses and begged him to get ready and have intercourse with him without delay.

22. Galba died at the age of seventy-two, before he had reigned seven months. The Senate, as soon as it was allowed to do so, voted that a column decorated with ships' beaks should be set up in the Forum to accommodate his statue and mark the spot where he had fallen. Vespasian, however, subsequently vetoed this decree; he was convinced that Galba had sent agents from Spain to Judaea with orders for his assassination.

VIII
OTHO

The seat of Otho's ancient and distinguished family was the city of Ferentium; they could trace their origins back to an Etruscan royal house. His grandfather, Marcus Salvius Otho, the son of a Roman knight and a girl of humble birth – she may not even have been free-born – owed his place in the Senate, where he never rose above praetor's rank, to the influence of Livia in whose home he was brought up. His son, Lucius Otho, was of a distinguished family on his mother's side, with many impressive connections, and was generally supposed to be a bastard of Tiberius,

OTHO

147 (below). *Coin from Rome.* (Glasgow, Hunterian Museum.)

STREET LIFE. *In ancient Rome, as in Mediterranean towns today, a large part of daily life and work took place in public places. Workshops opened directly onto the street and goods were displayed to passers-by.*
145 and 146 (opposite and left). *Cutler's workshop and shop counter. Funerary altar.* (Rome, Vatican.)

to whom the boy was very dear and bore a close resemblance. This Lucius had the reputation of being a strict disciplinarian, whether during his magistracies at Rome or his proconsulship in Africa, or when on special military missions. In Illyricum he went so far as to carry out the execution of those soldiers who, repenting of having been led by their officers to join Camillus's rebellion killed them and they were put to death in his presence in front of his headquarters; though he knew well enough that the Emperor Claudius himself had rewarded these same men with promotion for the act. Lucius Otho's deed may have increased his reputation, yet it certainly put him out of favour at Court until soon afterwards, by extorting information from a group of slaves, he contrived to uncover a plot against the Emperor's life. Thereupon the Senate paid Lucius the unique honour of setting up his statue in the Palace; and Claudius, in raising him to patrician rank, is said to have panegyrized him as 'one whose loyalty I can hardly dare hope that my children will emulate'. Albia Terentia, his nobly-born wife, bore him two sons: the elder named Lucius Titianus, and the younger Marcus Otho, like his grandfather; also a daughter, who was betrothed almost before she was marriageable to Germanicus's son Drusus.

2. Otho, the Emperor-to-be, was born on 25 April A.D. 32 while Arruntius Camillus and Domitius Ahenobarbus were Consuls. His early wildness earned him many a beating from his father; he is said to have been in the habit of wandering about the city at night and seizing and tossing in a blanket any drunk or disabled person who crossed his path. After his father's death he pretended a passion for an influential freedwoman at Court, though she was almost on her last legs; with her help he insinuated himself into the position of Nero's leading favourite. This may have happened naturally enough, since Nero and Otho were birds of a feather, yet it has quite often been suggested that their relationship was decidedly unnatural. Be that as it may, Otho grew so powerful that he did not think twice before bringing one of his own protégés, a former Consul found guilty of extortion, back into the Senate House, and there thanking the senators in anticipation for the pardon that they were to grant him, having accepted an immense bribe.

3. As Nero's confidant he had a finger in all his schemes and secrets, and on the day chosen by the Emperor for murdering his own mother, threw everyone off the scent by inviting them both to an exceptionally elegant banquet. Otho was asked to become the protector of Poppaea Sabina – who had been taken by Nero from her husband to be his mistress – and they went through a form of marriage together. However, he not only enjoyed Poppaea, but conceived so deep a passion for her that he would not tolerate even Nero as a rival; we have every reason to believe the story of his rebuffing, first, the messengers sent by Nero to fetch Poppaea, and then Nero himself, who was left on the wrong side of the bedroom door, alternately threatening and pleading for the lady and claiming the return of his trust. Fear of scandal alone kept Nero from doing more than annul the marriage and banish Otho to Lusitania as its Governor. So the following lampoon went the rounds:

> 'Otho in exile?' '*Yes and no;*
> *That is, we do not call it so.*'
> 'And may we ask the reason why?'
> '*They charged him with adultery.*'
> 'But could they prove it?' '*No and yes:*
> *It was his wife he dared caress.*'

Otho, who held the rank of quaestor, governed Lusitania for ten years with considerable moderation and restraint.

4. Yet he seized the earliest opportunity of revenging himself on Nero, by joining Galba as soon as he heard of the revolt; but the political atmosphere was so uncertain that he did not underrate his own chances of sovereignty. Seleucus, an astronomer who encouraged these ambitions, had already foretold that Otho would outlive Nero, and now arrived unexpectedly with the further prediction that he would soon also become Emperor. After this Otho missed no chance of flattering or showing favour to anyone. When he entertained Galba at dinner, for instance, he gave a gold piece to every man of the praetorian cohort on guard, and did everything possible to put all the soldiers in his debt in one way or another. Once a friend of Otho's laid claim to part of a neighbour's estate, and asked him to act as arbitrator; Otho bought the disputed piece of land himself and presented it to him. As a result of such measures, no one at Rome questioned his fitness to wear the imperial purple, and it was openly said that he alone was worthy to succeed to the Empire.

5. Galba's adoption of Piso came as a shock to Otho, who had hoped from day to day to secure this good fortune himself. Resentment and a massive accumulation of debts now prompted him to revolt. His one

chance of survival, Otho frankly admitted, lay in becoming Emperor. He added: 'I might as well fall to some enemy in battle as to my creditors in the Forum.' The 10,000 gold pieces, paid him for a stewardship by one of the Emperor's slaves, served to finance the undertaking. To begin with he confided in five of his personal guards, each of whom co-opted two others; they were paid 100 gold pieces a head and promised fifty more. These fifteen men recruited a certain number of assistants, but not many, since Otho counted on mass support as soon as he had raised the standard of revolt.

6. His first plan was to occupy the Guards' camp immediately after Piso's adoption, and to capture Galba during dinner at the Palace. But he abandoned this because the same cohort happened to be on guard duty as when Gaius had been assassinated, and again when Nero had been left to his fate; he felt reluctant to deal their reputation for loyalty a further blow. Unfavourable omens, and Seleucus's warnings, had taken up the time that had elapsed since then. However, on the day that was then fixed, Otho posted his fellow-conspirators in the Forum at the gilt milestone near the Temple of Saturn while he entered the Palace to greet Galba (who embraced him in the usual way) and attended his sacrifice. The priests had finished their report on the omens of the victim, when a freedman arrived with the message: 'The architects are here.' This was the agreed signal. Otho excused himself to the Emperor, saying that he had arranged to view a house that was for sale; then slipped out of the Palace by a back door and hurried to the rendezvous. (Another account makes him plead a chill, and leave his excuses with the Emperor's attendants, in case anyone should miss him.) At all events he hastily got into a closed sedan-chair of the sort used by women, and headed for the Camp, but jumped out and began to run when the bearers' pace flagged. As he paused to lace a shoe, his companions hoisted him on their shoulders and acclaimed him Emperor. The street crowds joined the procession as eagerly as if they were sworn accomplices, and Otho reached his headquarters to the sound of cheers and the flash of drawn swords. He then dispatched agents to murder Galba and Piso and, avoiding all promises, told the troops merely that he would welcome whatever powers they might give him, but claim no others.

7. Towards evening Otho delivered a brief speech to the Senate claiming to have been picked up in the street and compelled to accept the imperial power, but promising to respect the general will. Then he proceeded to the Palace, where he received fulsome congratulations and flattery from all present, making no protest even when the crowd called him Nero. Indeed, he undoubtedly allowed some of Nero's condemned busts and statues to be replaced, and reinstated procurators and freedmen of his whom Galba had dismissed; and the first decree of the new reign was a grant of half a million gold pieces for the completion of the Golden House.

Otho is said to have been haunted that night by Galba's ghost in a terrible nightmare; the servants who ran in when he screamed for help found him lying on the bedroom floor. After this he did everything in his power to placate the ghost; but next day, while he was taking the auspices, a hurricane sprang up and caused him a bad tumble – which made him mutter repeatedly: 'Playing the long pipes is hardly my trade.'[1]

8. Meanwhile, the armies in Germany took an oath of loyalty to Vitellius. Otho heard of this and persuaded the Senate to send a deputation, urging them to keep quiet, since an Emperor had already been appointed. But he also wrote Vitellius a personal letter: an invitation to become his father-in-law and share the Empire with him. Vitellius, however, had already sent troops forward to march on Rome under their generals, and it had become clear that war was inevitable. Then, one night, the Guards gave such unequivocal proof of their faithfulness to Otho that it almost involved a massacre of the Senate. A detachment of marines had been ordered to fetch some arms from the Praetorian Camp and take them aboard their vessels. They were carrying out their instructions at dusk when the Guards, suspecting treachery on the part of the Senate, rushed to the Palace in a leaderless mob and demanded that every Senator should die. Having driven away or murdered the senior officers who tried to stop them, they burst into the banqueting-hall, dripping with blood. 'Where is the Emperor?' they shouted; but as soon as they saw him they calmed down.

Otho set out on his campaign with great vigour, and indeed with too great haste, which prevented him from paying sufficient attention to the omens. The sacred shields had not yet been returned[2] – traditionally a bad sign – and this was the day when the worshippers of the Goddess Cybele began their annual wailings and

---

1. Proverbial of undertaking an enterprise beyond one's capacity.
2. To the Temple of Mars, after an annual procession. This was a period when it was believed unlucky to undertake any enterprise.

lamentation.[3] Besides, the auspices were most unfavourable: at a sacrifice offered to Father Dis the victim's intestines had a healthy look – exactly what
they should not have had on such an occasion. Otho's
departure was, moreover, delayed by a flooding of the
Tiber; and at the twentieth milestone he found the
road blocked by the ruins of collapsed buildings.

9. Vitellius's forces being badly off for supplies and
having little room for manoeuvre, no one doubted that
Otho should have protracted the war, yet he rashly
staked his fortunes on an immediate victory. Perhaps
he suffered from nervousness and hoped to end the war
before Vitellius himself arrived; perhaps he could not
curb the offensive spirit of his troops. But when it came
to the point he remained behind at Brixellum and kept
clear of the fighting. Although his army won three
lesser engagements – in the Alps, at Placentia, and at
a place called 'Castor's' – they were tricked into a final
and decisive defeat near Betriacum. There had been
talk of a conference, but Otho's troops, led out under
the expectation that they were going to discuss peace-
terms, and already fraternizing with the enemy, found
themselves unexpectedly committed to battle.

Otho immediately decided on suicide. It is more
probable that his conscience prevented him from continuing to hazard lives and property in a bid for
sovereignty than that he believed his men had become
demoralized and incapable of success; fresh troops
stood in reserve for a counter-offensive and reinforcements were on their way from Dalmatia, Pannonia, and
Moesia. What is more, his defeated army were by no
means too shattered to face further perils, and anxious
to redeem their reputation, even without such assistance.

10. My own father, Suetonius Laetus, a colonel,
served with the Thirteenth Legion in this campaign.
He often said afterwards that Otho had so deeply
abhorred the thought of civil war while still a private
citizen that he would shudder if the fates of Brutus and
Cassius were mentioned at a banquet. And that he
would not have moved against Galba to begin with, unless in the hope of a bloodless victory. Otho had now
ceased to care what happened to himself, my father
added, because of the deep impression made on him
by the soldier who arrived at Brixellum to report that
the army had been defeated. When the garrison called
him a liar and a cowardly deserter, the man fell on his

3. 24 March.

FOREIGN CULTS *were introduced in Rome both at the*
initiative of Romans themselves, and by strangers who
lived in Rome and brought the religion of their homeland
with them.
148 (above). *The cult of Cybele, the Great Mother, was*
formally introduced in Rome in 204 B.C. (see Ill. 64),
during a period of crisis at the end of the second Punic
War. During her festival in spring, the devotees of the
goddess celebrated her union with her lover Attis, and then
mourned his death. Throne of Cybele, carried on a bier
by her eunuch priests. (Cambridge, Fitzwilliam
Museum.)
149 (opposite). *The cult of Isis from Egypt found no*
official patronage, but was none the less very widely
spread. Isis on an elephant chariot. Pompeii, shop of the
draper Verecundus. (See Ill. 36.)

sword at Otho's feet. At this sight Otho, my father reported, cried out that he would never again risk the lives of such gallant men, who had deserved so well. Embracing his brother, his nephew, and his friends, he dismissed them with orders to consult their own safety. Then he retired and wrote two letters: of consolation to his sister, and to Nero's widow, Statilia Messalina, whom he had meant to marry – at the same time begging her to bury him and preserve his memory. He next burned all his private correspondence to avoid incriminating anyone if it fell into Vitellius's hands, and distributed among the staff whatever loose cash he had with him.

11. After thus making his final preparations for suicide Otho heard a disturbance outside, and was told that the men who had begun to drift away from camp were being arrested and detained as deserters. He forbade his officers to award anyone any punishment, and saying: 'Let us add one extra night to life,' went to bed, but left his door open until a late hour, in case anyone wished to speak with him. After drinking a glass of cold water and testing the points of two daggers, he put one of them under his pillow, closed the door and slept soundly. He awoke at dawn and promptly stabbed himself with a single stroke below the left breast. His attendants heard him groan and rushed in; at first he could not decide whether to conceal or reveal the wound, which proved fatal. They buried him at once,

as he had ordered them to do. His age was thirty-seven; and he died in the ninety-fifth day of his reign.

12. Otho, who did not look or behave like a very courageous man, was of medium height, bow-legged, and with splay feet; but almost as fastidious about appearances as a woman. His entire body had been depilated, and a toupee covered his practically bald head, so well made and fitted that no one suspected its existence. He shaved every day, and since boyhood had always used a poultice of moist bread to prevent the growth of his beard. He used publicly to celebrate the rites of Isis, wearing the approved linen smock.

In view of these habits, the sensation caused by Otho's end was, I am inclined to think, largely due to its contrast with the life he had led. Soldiers who were present kissed the dead man's hands and feet, weeping bitterly and praising him as the bravest man they had ever known and the best Emperor imaginable; and afterwards they committed suicide themselves close to his funeral pyre. Stories are also current of men who were not there having killed one another in an access of grief when the news of his death reached them. Thus many who had hated Otho very fiercely while he was alive loaded him with praises when he was dead; and he was even commonly believed to have killed Galba with the object not so much of becoming Emperor as of restoring the country's system of government and liberty.

IX
VITELLIUS

Vitellius's family may have been an old and noble one; or it may have been new, and of undistinguished and even mean extraction. Both views are held, and either might reasonably be discounted as due to the flatterers and assailants of the Emperor, were it not that these origins had been hotly argued about many years previously.

Writing a book addressed to Quintus Vitellius, one of Augustus's quaestors, Quintus Elogius described the family as follows:

> You Vitellii are descended from Faunus, king of the Aborigines, and Vitellia, who was widely worshipped as a goddess. At one time, you ruled over the whole of Latium, but later the surviving members of the family moved from Sabine territory to Rome, where they became patricians. Traces of that origin have long remained in the name of the Vitellian Way, which runs from the Janiculum to the sea, as well as in a colony of the same name, which once asked the Senate's permission to defend itself against the Aequiculi, with troops raised from their own family. Later, at the time of the Samnite war, when an army was dispatched to Apulia, a group of Vitellii established themselves at Nuceria; but eventually their descendants went back to resume senatorial privileges at Rome.

The popular story, on the other hand, was that the family had been founded by a freedman; Cassius Sev-erus and others added that he was a shoemaker, whose son made a comfortable living as a dealer in confiscated property and an informer, before marrying a common prostitute, the daughter of a baker named Antiochus, and fathering on her a Roman knight. This disputed question may be left open.

2. At all events, whether he was of ancient stock or of parents and forefathers who inspired shame, this Publius Vitellius of Nuceria was certainly a knight, and steward to Augustus. He passed on his family name to four sons who attained distinction, and possessed different forenames: Aulus, Quintus, Publius, and

VITELLIUS
151. *Coin from Rome.* (Glasgow, Hunterian Museum.)

THE SACRED WAY, *passing through the Roman Forum and then ascending to the Capitoline Hill was the route taken by triumphal processions. It was lined with public buildings and shops.*
150 (opposite). *The Sacred Way facing towards the arch of Titus (far right); on the left, steps to the temple of Antonius and Faustina; on the right, foundations of the temple of Caesar.*

AN ITALIAN HILLTOWN. *While many families which played a major role in Roman politics had been settled in the city of Rome for generations, others had come recently from neighbouring towns and even from further afield.*

152. *Italian walled town with orchards and country houses outside the walls.* (Avezzano, Museo Torlonia.)

Lucius. Aulus, an epicure famous for his magnificent banquets, died during his consulship, as partner to Nero's father Domitius. Quintus, the second brother, was degraded in a purge of undesirable senators proposed by Tiberius. Publius, the third, was an aide-de-camp to Germanicus, whose murderer,[1] Gnaeus Piso, he arrested and brought to justice. He attained the praetorship, but was himself arrested as an accomplice of Sejanus's conspiracy.[2] When handed over to the custody of his own brother, Aulus, he cut his wrists with a penknife; yet allowed them to be bandaged up, not through any fear of death, but because his friends begged him to stay with them. Later, he fell ill and died in prison. Lucius, the youngest son, became first Consul, and then Governor of Syria[3] where, with masterly diplomacy, he induced King Artabanus of Parthia to attend a conference and even do obeisance to the legionary Eagles. Afterwards, Lucius shared two further regular consulships with the Emperor Claudius, held the office of Censor, and took full charge of the Empire while Claudius was away on the British expedition. Lucius's integrity and industry were outstanding; the only blot on his fame being a scandalous infatuation for a certain freedwoman, whose spittle he would actually mix with honey and use, not just secretly or rarely, but every day, quite openly, as a lotion for his neck and throat. A skilful flatterer, he instituted the practice of worshipping Gaius as a god; and on his return from Syria, never dared enter the imperial presence without uncovering his head, averting his gaze, and finally prostrating himself. Since Claudius, Gaius's successor, was ruled by his wives and freedmen, Lucius, who lost no chance of advancement, begged Messalina to grant him the tremendous privilege of removing her shoes; whereupon he would nurse the right shoe between his toga and his tunic, and occasionally take it out to kiss it. He placed golden images of Claudius's secretaries Narcissus and Pallas among his Household-gods; and the 'May you do this very often!' joke in congratulation of Claudius at the Saecular Games is attributed to him.

3. Lucius died of paralysis on the day after he had been accused of high treason;[4] but lived to see his two sons by Sextilia – a very reputable woman of distinguished family – achieve the consulship in a single year; the younger following for its last six months. The Senate awarded him a public funeral and a statue on the Rostra inscribed: 'Steadfast in loyalty to the Emperor'.

Lucius's son Aulus Vitellius, the Emperor-to-be, was born on 24 September A.D. 14, or perhaps on 7

---

1. Or rather, alleged murderer.   2. A.D. 31.   3. A.D. 35.

4. A.D. 51, by a senator named Junius Lupus.

September, while Drusus the Younger and Norbanus Flaccus were Consuls. The boy's horoscope, announced by the astrologers, so horrified his parents that Lucius always did everything in his power to prevent him from winning a provincial governorship; and when he was sent to the legions and subsequently proclaimed Emperor, his mother gave him up for lost. Vitellius had spent his boyhood and adolescence on Capreae, among Tiberius's male prostitutes. There he won the nickname 'Spintria',[5] which clung to him throughout his life; by surrendering his chastity, the story goes, he secured his father's first advancement to public office.

4. Vitellius who, as he grew up, was notorious for every sort of vice, became a fixture at Court. Gaius admired his skill in chariot-driving; Claudius, his skill at dice; Nero not only appreciated these talents, but was indebted to him for one particular service. At the festival celebrated in his own honour, Nero was always anxious to compete in the lyre-playing contest, but never dared do so without express invitation; so he used to leave the theatre, while all its occupants clamoured for him enthusiastically, and disappear until Vitellius, as President of the Games, came in pursuit and, on behalf of the audience, persuaded him to reconsider his decision.

5. Since he was thus the favourite of three emperors, Vitellius won public offices and important priesthoods, and later served as Governor of Africa and Curator of Public Works. His reputation and energies, however, varied with the employment given him. Though exceptionally honest during the two-year administration of Africa, where he temporarily acted for his brother (who succeeded him), Vitellius's behaviour while in office at Rome was by no means so commendable: he used to pilfer offerings and ornaments from the temples or provide substitutes, replacing gold and silver with brass and tin.

6. He married Petronia, a consul's daughter who, in her will, made their one-eyed son, Petronianus, her heir, though stipulating that Vitellius must renounce paternal rights. To this he consented; but his subsequent story – that Petronianus, having shown parricidal leanings, had been overcome by feelings of guilt and drunk the poison with which he had intended to orphan himself – won little credence; most people believed simply that Vitellius had done away with the boy. Next, he married Galeria Fundana, whose father

5. Sexual invert.

was a praetor; she bore him one daughter, and a son who had so bad a stammer that he could hardly force out a word.

7. Galba's appointment of Vitellius to the governorship of Lower Germany was a surprising one; it has been suggested that Titus Vinius arranged it. This Vinius, a man of great influence, was well-disposed towards Vitellius because they were fellow-supporters of the 'Blues' in the Circus. Yet since Galba had openly stated that a glutton was the sort of rival whom he feared least, and that he expected Vitellius to cram his belly with the fruits of the province, the appointment must have been made in contempt, not approval. When Vitellius was about to start, he was so short of funds for his travelling expenses, and in such low water generally – this is common knowledge – that he rented an attic for his wife and children at Rome, let his own house for the remainder of the year and, to finance the journey, actually pawned a pearl from an ear-ring in his mother's ear. The only means by which he could shake off the huge crowd of creditors who were continuously waylaying him – these included the people of Sinuessa and Formiae whose public funds he had embezzled – was to scare them with false accusations. Thus he pressed an action for assault against a freedman who had dunned him once too often, claiming to have been struck and kicked, and wringing from him damages to the amount of 500 gold pieces.

The army's dislike of Galba having now reached a stage little short of mutiny, they welcomed Vitellius with open arms, as a gift from the gods. After all, here was the son of a man who had held three consulships; in the prime of life, too, and of an easy, generous disposition. Vitellius's conduct on the march further enhanced their good opinion of him. He would greet even private soldiers with an embrace, and at wayside inns behaved most affably towards the muleteers and such like whom he met in the morning, inquiring whether they had yet breakfasted, and then belching loudly to prove that he had done so himself.

8. Immediately he came into the camp he granted every favour asked of him, and actually of his own accord cancelled the black marks of men who were in disgrace, the legal actions against those who were awaiting trial in mourning, and the penalties of people who had been convicted. Consequently, before a month had passed, a group of soldiers suddenly crowded into his bedroom, saluted him as Emperor and, late though the hour was, carried him around the larger villages without even giving him time to dress.

CONCORD AND LOYALTY, *traditional virtues of Roman public life, were conspicuous by their absence in* A.D. *69, the 'year of the four Emperors,' but were none the less advertised on the coinage.*
153 (left). *Concord: reverse of a coin of Vitellius from Rome.* (Glasgow, Hunterian Museum.)
154 (right). *Loyalty: coin from Upper Germany. The obverse reads 'loyalty of the soldiers', with clasped hands, and the reverse has 'concord of the Praetorian Guards' with the image of personified Concord.* (London, British Museum.)

9. As soon as news reached Germany of Galba's murder, Vitellius put his affairs there in order, splitting the army into two divisions, one of which stayed under his own leadership. He sent the other against Otho, and it was at once granted a lucky augury: an eagle, swooping down from the right hand, hovered over the standards, and flew slowly ahead of the advancing columns. However, when he marched off with the second division, several equestrian statues raised in his honour collapsed because the horses' legs were weakly made; also, the laurel wreath which he had so ceremoniously bound on his head fell into a stream, and a few days later while he was presiding over a court at Vienna, in Gaul, a rooster perched first on his shoulder, then on his hand. These presages were confirmed by future events, for he proved unable to support the weight of power won for him by his generals.

In the first flush of congratulation someone presented Vitellius with a drawn sword, taken from a temple of Mars, which had once been Julius Caesar's, and this he carried in his hand. During his absence a stove set fire to the dining-room at Headquarters; but when this apparently unlucky portent caused general concern and alarm he told the troops: 'Courage, my men! Light is given us.' That was the only speech he made them. The army in Upper Germany had previously pledged its loyalty to the Senate, in place of Galba, and now came out in his favour. Vitellius then eagerly accepted the surname Germanicus, which everyone pressed on him, but hesitated to accept the title Augustus, and permanently rejected the surname Caesar.

EQUESTRIAN STATUES. *The erection of statues, equestrian or other, was a common means of honouring public figures. The image of a mounted Emperor conveyed the notion of victory, and the collapse of such a statue was therefore a particularly ill-starred omen.*
155 (opposite). *Equestrian statues in the Forum of Pompeii, painting from Pompeii.* (Naples, Museum.)

EATING. *The increasing affluence of the city of Rome during the imperial period helped to create a taste for exotic foods among its inhabitants. But even some relatively simple dishes, for which the main ingredients could be procured in Italy, required imported spices and condiments.*
156, 157, 158, 159. *Pictures from a Roman larder: eels, partridges, a rabbit, a pomegranate, an apple, mushrooms, and thrushes.* (From Herculaneum. Naples, Museum.)

10. The news of the victory at Betriacum, and of Otho's suicide, reached Vitellius before he had left Gaul. At once he disbanded all Guards battalions in Rome by a comprehensive decree, accusing them of a disgraceful lapse in discipline: they must surrender their arms to the commanding officers. He gave further orders for the pursuit and punishment of 120 Guards known to have demanded a bounty from Otho in respect of services rendered at Galba's assassination. These irreproachably correct acts raised the hope that Vitellius would make an admirable Emperor, but the rest of his behaviour was in keeping, rather, with the natural character he had shown in the past, and fell far short of imperial standards. At the outset of his march, for instance, he had himself carried through the main streets of the cities on his route, in triumphal fashion; crossed rivers in elaborately decorated barges wreathed in garlands of many kinds; and always kept a lavish supply of delicacies available. He let discipline go by the board among his household and soldiers, and would joke about the excesses and depredations committed by his men; not content with being feasted everywhere at public expense, they amused themselves by freeing slaves at random and then beating, whipping, wounding, and even murdering whoever tried to restrain them. When he reached the recent battlefield, where the stench of unburied corpses caused some consternation, Vitellius cheered his companions with the brazen remark: 'Only one thing smells sweeter to me than a dead enemy, and that is a dead fellow-citizen.' Nevertheless, he took a good swig of neat wine to counteract the stink and generously passed the flagon around. Equally arrogant and offensive was his remark when he came across Otho's simple headstone: 'Well, he deserved this type of mausoleum.' Having sent the dagger with which Otho had killed himself to the Temple of Mars at Colonia Agrippinensis, he staged an all-night debauch on the heights of the Apennines.

11. At last, amid fanfares of trumpets, Vitellius entered Rome in general's uniform and surrounded by standards and banners. His staff also wore military cloaks, and his soldiers carried drawn swords. Paying less and less attention to all laws, human or divine, Vitellius next assumed the office of Chief Priest, and chose to do so on the anniversary of the Allia defeat.[6] On the same occasion he announced the elections for ten years ahead, and appointed himself Consul for life. Then he dispelled any doubt as to which of the Caesars was to be his model by sacrificing to Nero's ghost and, at the subsequent banquet, while a popular flutist was performing, called for something from 'the Master's Book' as an encore. When the flutist obliged with one of these compositions, Vitellius jumped up delightedly and led the applause.

12. This was how his reign began. Later, he based many important political decisions on what the lowest performers in the theatre or arena told him, and relied particularly on the advice of his freedman Asiaticus. Asiaticus had been Vitellius's slave and boy love, but soon grew tired of this role and ran away. After a while he was discovered selling cheap drinks[7] at Puteoli, and

put in chains until Vitellius ordered his release and made him his favourite again. However, Asiaticus behaved so insolently, and so thievishly as well, that Vitellius became irritated and sold him to an itinerant trainer of gladiators; but impulsively bought him back when he was just about to take part in the final match of a gladiatorial contest. When sent to govern Lower Germany, Vitellius freed Asiaticus, and on his first day as Emperor presented him with the gold ring of knighthood; although that very morning he had rejected a popular demand for this award, with the emphatic statement that Asiaticus's appointment would disgrace the Order.

13. Vitellius's ruling vices were extravagance and cruelty. He banqueted three and often four times a day, namely morning, noon, afternoon, and evening – the last meal being mainly a drinking bout – and survived the ordeal well enough by taking frequent emetics. What made things worse was that he used to invite himself out to such meals at the houses of a number of different people on one and the same day; and these never cost his various hosts less than 4,000 gold pieces each. The most notorious feast of the series was given him by his brother on his entry into Rome; 2,000 magnificent fish and 7,000 game birds are said to have been

6. *c.* 390 B.C.; a day of evil omen.
7. *Posca*, sour wine or vinegar mixed with water.

served. Yet even this hardly compares in luxuriousness with a single tremendously large dish which Vitellius dedicated to the Goddess Minerva and named 'Shield of Minerva the Protectress of the City'. The recipe called for pike-livers, pheasant-brains, peacock-brains, flamingo-tongues, and lamprey-milt; and all these ingredients, collected in every corner of the Empire from the Parthian frontier to the Spanish Strait, were brought to Rome by naval captains and triremes. Vitellius paid no attention to time or decency in satisfying his remarkable appetite. While a sacrifice was in progress, he thought nothing of snatching lumps of meat or cake off the altar, almost out of the sacred fire, and bolting them down; and on his travels would devour cuts of meat fetched smoking hot from wayside cookshops, and even yesterday's half-eaten scraps.

14. His cruelty was such that he would kill or torture anyone at all on the slightest pretext – not excluding noblemen who had been his fellow-students or friends, and whom he lured to Court by promises of a share in the rule of the Empire. One of them, with fever on him, asked for a glass of cold water; Vitellius brought it with his own hands, but added poison. As for all the money-lenders, tax-collectors and dealers who had ever dunned him, or demanded payment for a debt at Rome or a duty incurred on a journey,[8] it is doubtful whether he showed mercy in a single instance. When one of these men paid a courtesy call at the Palace, Vitellius sent him off to be executed, but a moment later countermanded the order. The courtiers praised this clemency, but Vitellius explained that he merely wished to give himself a treat by having the man killed before his eyes. Two sons came to plead for their father's life; he had all three of them dispatched together. A knight who was being marched away to his death called out: 'You are my heir!' Vitellius granted a stay of execution until the will had been produced; then, finding himself named as joint-heir with the knight's freedman, ordered master and man to die together. He executed some members of the general public for disparaging the 'Blues', on the suspicion that such criticism was directed against him, in the hope of a revolution. He particularly disliked lampoonists and astrologers, and made away at once with any who came up before him, without hearing their defences. This resentment dated from when an edict of his, forbidding any astrologers to remain in Italy after

1 October, had been capped with a counter-edict:

Decreed by all astrologers
In blessing on our State:
Vitellius will be no more
On the appointed date.

According to some accounts, a prophet of the Chatti, a woman whom Vitellius credited with oracular powers, had promised him a long and secure reign if he outlived his mother; so when she fell sick, he had her starved to death. Another version of the story is that his mother, grown weary of the present and apprehensive of the future, begged him for a supply of poison; a request which he was not slow to grant.

15. In the eighth month of Vitellius's reign the Moesian and Pannonian legions repudiated him and swore allegiance to Vespasian, distant though he was; those in Syria and Judaea did the same, and took their oaths to him in person. To keep the goodwill of his remaining troops, Vitellius embarked on a course of limitless public and private generosity. He opened a recruiting campaign in the city and promised volunteers immediate discharge after victory, with the full rights and privileges of regular service. When his enemies pressed him hard by land and sea, he sent against them on one front the troops who had fought at Betriacum, under their original officers, and put his brother in command of a fleet manned by recruits and gladiators. Since, however, he was beaten or betrayed on every side, he bargained with Flavius Sabinus, Vespasian's brother, to keep his life and a million gold pieces. Later, from the Palace steps, Vitellius announced his decision to the assembled soldiers, explaining that the imperial power had, after all, been forced upon him against his will. When an uproar of protest greeted this speech, he postponed a decision; but next day went in mourning to the Rostra and tearfully read his oration out again from a scroll. Once more the soldiers and the city crowds shouted 'Stand fast!' and outdid one another in their expressions of loyalty. Suddenly taking heart, Vitellius drove Sabinus and his Flavian relatives into the Capitol, set fire to the Temple of Jupiter Best and Greatest, and killed them. He watched the battle and the fire while banqueting in the mansion which had belonged to the Emperor Tiberius; but was soon overcome by remorse and put the blame on someone else. He next called an assembly and forced all present to bear witness that peace was now his sole objective. Then, drawing his dagger, he tried in turn

8. *Portorium*, the tax on imports and exports.

to make the Consul, the praetors, the quaestors, and the remaining senators accept it. When all refused, he went to lay it up in the Temple of Concord. However, they called him back by shouting: 'No, you yourself are Concord!' So back he came, saying: 'Very well, I will keep the dagger and adopt the surname Concordia.'

16. Vitellius also persuaded the Senate to send envoys, accompanied by the Vestal Virgins, to arrange an armistice, or at least to gain time for consultations. But on the following day, while he was waiting for a reply, a scout arrived with news that enemy detachments were close at hand. Stowing himself furtively into a sedan-chair, and accompanied by only two companions, his pastry-cook and chef, he hurried to his father's house on the Aventine. He had planned an escape from there into Campania. But a faint and doubtful rumour of peace tempted him back to the Palace, which he found deserted, and when his companions drifted away, he strapped on a money-belt full of gold pieces and hid in the janitor's quarters, tethering a dog outside and jamming a bed and mattress against the door.

17. The vanguard of the advancing army had now burst into the Palace, and, without opposition, began looting, as was to be expected. They hauled Vitellius from his hiding-place and, not recognizing him, asked who he was and whether he knew the Emperor's whereabouts. Vitellius gave some lying answer, but was soon identified; so he begged to be placed in safe custody, even if that meant prison, because he had something to say concerning the welfare of Vespasian. Instead, his hands were tied behind him, a noose was fastened round his neck, and amid cheers and abuse the soldiers dragged him, half-naked, with his clothes in tatters, along the Sacred Way to the Forum. They pulled his head back by the hair, as is done with criminals, and stuck a sword-point under the chin, to force him to expose his face and not lower it. Dung and filth were hurled at him, also such epithets as 'Fire-raiser' and 'Glutton', and his bodily defects were mocked. In fact, Vitellius was unusually tall, with an alcoholic flush at most times, a huge paunch and a somewhat crippled thigh, from being run into by a four-horse chariot – the Emperor Gaius had been driving at the time. The soldiers put him through the torture of the little cuts before finally killing him near the Stairs of Mourning. Then they dragged his body to the Tiber with a hook and threw it in.

18. Vitellius died at the age of fifty-six; his brother and his son perished with him. The omen of the rooster at Vienna (noted above) had been interpreted as meaning that a Gaul would kill him – *gallus* is both a 'cock' and a 'Gaul'. This proved correct: the enemy general who brought him down was one Antonius Primus, a native of Tolosa, and his boyhood nickname had been Becco ('rooster's beak').

X
VESPASIAN

The family of the Flavians at last brought stable government to the Empire; they had found it drifting uneasily through the usurpations and deaths of three successive emperors. They were admittedly an obscure family, none of whose members had ever enjoyed high office. Yet there is no cause to be ashamed of their record, though it is generally admitted that Domitian's cruelty and greed justified his assassination.

Titus Flavius Petro, a citizen of Reate, who fought for Pompey in the Civil War as a centurion, or perhaps a volunteer reservist, made his way back there from the battlefield of Pharsalus; secured an honourable discharge, with a full pardon, and took up tax-collecting. Although his son Sabinus is said either to have been a leading-centurion, or to have resigned command of a cohort on grounds of ill-health, the truth is that he did not experience military service but became a customs supervisor in Asia, where cities honoured him with statues, which remained in existence, inscribed: 'To an Honest Tax-gatherer'. He later turned banker among the Helvetii, and there died, leaving a wife, Vespasia Polla, and two sons, Sabinus and Vespasian. Sabinus, the elder, attained the rank of City Prefect at Rome; Vespasian became Emperor. Vespasia Polla belonged to a good family from Nursia. Vespasius Pollio, her father, had three times held a colonelcy and been Camp Prefect; her brother entered the Senate as a praetor. Moreover, on a hilltop some six miles along the road to Spoletium, stands the village of Vespasiae, where a great many tombs testify to the family's antiquity and local renown. As for the popular account of their origins – that the Emperor's great-grandfather had been a contractor for the Umbrian labourers who cross the Po every summer to help the Sabines with their harvest, and that he married and settled in Reate – my own careful researches have turned up no evidence to substantiate this.

2. Vespasian was born on 17 November A.D. 9 in the hamlet of Falacrina, just beyond Reate, during the consulship of Quintus Sulpicius Camerinus and Gaius Poppaeus Sabinus, and five years before the death of Augustus. His paternal grandmother, Tertulla, brought him up on her estate at Cosa; and as Emperor he would often revisit the house, which he kept exactly

VESPASIAN
160 (opposite). *Portrait head of Vespasian from Ostia.* (Rome, Terme Museum.)
161 (right). *Roman coin minted in Spain.* (Glasgow, Hunterian Museum.)

as it had always been, in an attempt to preserve his childhood memories intact. On feast days and holy days, he made a practice of drinking from a little silver cup which had once belonged to his grandmother, so dear was her memory to him.

For years he postponed his candidature for the broad purple stripe of senatorial rank, already earned by his brother, and in the end it was his mother who drove him to take this step; not by pleading with him or commanding him by parental authority, but by constant sarcastic use of the phrase 'your brother's footman'.[1]

Vespasian served as a colonel in Thrace, and when quaestorships were being assigned by lot, drew that of Crete and Cyrenaica. His first attempt to win an aedileship came to nothing; at the second he scraped through in only the sixth place; however, as soon as he stood for the praetorship, he obtained it at the first time of asking, among those who were at the head of the list. The Senate then being at odds with Gaius, Vespasian, in order to miss no chance of winning his favour, proposed that special Games should be held to celebrate the Emperor's German victory. He also proposed that, as an additional punishment, the conspirators[2] should be denied public burial; and, during a full session of

TAXATION AND TRANSPORT. Collecting taxes with which to pay its armies and ensuring an adequate circulation of goods were fundamental tasks of Roman government. Throughout the imperial period, the Roman economy remained essentially rooted in the countryside, and agriculture was the main source of revenue. The countryside also provided the majority of people with almost all the necessities of life.

162 (above). _Tax-gathering on a relief from Trier._ (Trier, Landesmuseum.)
163 (opposite). _A boat carrying barrels of wine being towed upstream._ (Avignon, Musée Calvet.)

the House, acknowledged the Emperor's graciousness in having invited him to dine at the Palace.

3. Meanwhile, Vespasian had married Flavia Domitilla, the ex-mistress of Statilius Capella, an African knight from Sabrata. Her father, Flavius Liberalis, a humble quaestor's clerk from Ferentium, had appeared before a board of arbitration and established her claim to the full Roman citizenship, in place of only a Latin one. Vespasian had three children by Flavia, namely Titus, Domitian, and Domitilla; but Domitilla died before he held a magistracy, and so did Flavia herself; he then took up again with Caenis, his former mistress and one of Antonia's freedwomen and secretaries, who

1. There is no modern English equivalent for the Latin _anteambulo_: meaning a client who goes in front of his important patron to clear the way.
2. Marcus Aemilius Lepidus and Gnaeus Cornelius Lentulus Gaetulicus.

remained his wife in all but name even when he became Emperor.

4. On Claudius's accession, Vespasian was indebted to Narcissus for the command of a legion in Germany; and proceeded to Britain, where he fought thirty battles, subjugated two warlike tribes, and captured more than twenty towns, besides the entire Isle of Vectis. In these campaigns he served at times under Aulus Plautius, the commander of consular rank, and at times directly under Claudius, earning triumphal decorations; and soon afterwards held a couple of priesthoods, as well as a consulship for the last two months of the year. While waiting for a proconsular appointment, however, he lived in retirement: for fear of Agrippina the Younger's still powerful influence over Nero, and of the animosity which she continued to feel towards any friend of Narcissus even after his death.

In the distribution of provinces Vespasian drew Africa, where his rule was characterized by great justice and dignity, except on a single occasion when the people of Hadrumetum rioted and pelted him with turnips. It is known that he came back no richer than he went, because his credit was so nearly exhausted that, in order to keep up his position, he had to mortgage all his estates to his brother and go into the mule-trade; which gave him the nickname 'Mule Driver'. Vespasian is also said to have earned a severe reprimand after getting a young man raised to senatorial rank, against his father's wishes, for a fee of 2,000 gold pieces.

He toured Greece in Nero's retinue but offended him deeply, by either leaving the room during his song recitals, or staying and falling asleep. In consequence he not only lost the imperial favour but was dismissed from Court, and fled to a small out-of-the-way township, where he hid in terror of his life until finally offered a province with the command of an army.

An ancient superstition was current in the East, that out of Judaea at this time would come the rulers of the world. This prediction, as the event later proved, referred to a Roman Emperor; but the rebellious Jews, who read it as referring to themselves, murdered their Governor, routed the Governor of Syria when he came down to restore order, and captured an Eagle. To crush this uprising the Romans needed a strong army under an energetic commander, who could be trusted not to abuse his considerable powers. The choice fell on Vespasian. He had given signal proof of energy and nothing, it seemed, need be feared from a man of such modest antecedents. Two legions, with eight cavalry squadrons and ten auxiliary cohorts, were therefore dispatched to join the forces already in Judaea; and Vespasian took his elder son, Titus, to serve on his staff. No sooner had they reached Judaea than he impressed the neighbouring provinces by his prompt tightening up of discipline and his audacious conduct in battle after battle. During the assault on one enemy fortress he was wounded on the knee by a stone and caught several arrows on his shield.

5. When Nero and Galba were both dead and Vitellius was disputing the purple with Otho, Vespasian began to remember his imperial ambitions, which had originally been raised by the following omens. An ancient oak-tree, sacred to Mars, growing on the Flavian estate near Rome, put out a shoot for each of the three occasions when his mother was brought to bed; and these clearly had a bearing on each child's future. The first slim shoot withered quickly: and the eldest child, a girl, died within the year. The second shoot was long and healthy, promising good luck; but the third seemed more like a tree than a branch. Sabinus, the father, is said to have been greatly impressed by an inspection of a victim's entrails, and to have congratulated his mother on having a grandson who would become Emperor. She roared with laughter and said: 'Fancy your going soft in the head before your old mother!'

Later, during Vespasian's aedileship, the Emperor Gaius, furious because Vespasian had not kept the streets clean, as was his duty, ordered some soldiers to load him with mud; they obeyed by stuffing into the fold of his senatorial gown as much as it could hold – an omen interpreted to mean that one day the soil of Italy would be neglected and trampled upon as the result of civil war, but that Vespasian would protect it and, so to speak, take it into his embrace.

Then a stray dog picked up a human hand at the cross-roads, which it brought into the room where Vespasian was breakfasting and dropped under the table; a hand being the emblem of power. On another occasion a plough-ox shook off its yoke, burst into Vespasian's dining room, scattered the servants, and fell at his feet, where it lowered its neck as if suddenly exhausted. A cypress-tree was also uprooted and hurled to the ground on his grandfather's farm, though there had been no gale to account for the accident; yet by the next day it had taken root again and was greener and stronger than ever.

In Greece, Vespasian dreamed that he and his family would begin to prosper from the moment when Nero lost a tooth; and on the following day, while he was in the imperial quarters, a dentist entered and showed him one of Nero's teeth which he had just extracted.

In Judaea, Vespasian consulted the oracle of the God of Carmel and was given a promise that he would never be disappointed in what he planned or desired, however lofty his ambitions. Also, a distinguished Jewish prisoner of Vespasian's, Josephus by name, insisted that he would soon be released by the very man who had now put him in fetters, and who would then be Emperor. Reports of further omens came from Rome; Nero, it seemed, had been warned in a dream shortly before his death to take the sacred chariot of Jupiter Best and Greatest from its shrine to the Circus, calling at Vespasian's house as he went. Soon after this, while Galba was on his way to the elections which gave him a second consulship, a statue of Julius Caesar turned of its own accord to face east; and at Betriacum, when the battle was about to begin, two eagles fought in full view of both armies, but a third appeared from the rising sun and drove off the victor.

6. Still Vespasian made no move, although his adherents were very ready and indeed impatient to press his claims to the Empire; until he was suddenly stirred to action by the fortuitous support of a distant group of soldiers whom he did not even know: 2,000 men belonging to the three legions in Moesia that were reinforcing Otho. They had marched forward as far as Aquileia, despite the news of Otho's defeat and suicide which reached them on the way, and there taken advantage of a breakdown of discipline to plunder at pleasure. Then, fearing what the reckoning might be on their return, they hit on the idea of choosing and setting up their own Emperor. They felt they were in no way inferior to the troops in Spain who had appointed Galba; and the Guards who had appointed Otho; and the troops in Germany who had appointed Vitellius. So they went through the whole list of provincial governors of consular rank at the time, rejecting each name in turn for this reason or that, until in the end they unanimously chose Vespasian – on the strong recommendation of some Third Legion men who had been sent to Moesia from Syria just prior to Nero's death – and marking all their standards with his name. Though they were temporarily recalled to their allegiance at this point, and the plan was thus checked, the news of their decision leaked out. Tiberius Alexander, the prefect in Egypt, thereupon became the first to make his legions take the oath to Vespasian; this was 1 July, later celebrated as Accession Day, and on 11 July the army in Judaea swore allegiance to Vespasian in person.

Three things helped him greatly. First, the copy of a letter (possibly forged) in which Otho begged him most earnestly to avenge his death and come to the aid of the Empire. Second, a persistent rumour that Vitellius had planned, after his victory, to re-station the

TOWN AND COUNTRY: THE EFFECTS OF ROMAN-
IZATION. *Centralized government and a centralized
power structure had the effect that, in Rome and other
cities, fashions changed and became more elaborate and
sophisticated in the course of the first century* A.D. *In the
countrysides of the Empire, on the other hand, the age-
old patterns of living continued almost unchanged.*
164 (below). *Roman lady with a hairstyle of the Flavian
period.* (Rome, Capitoline Museum.)
165 (right). *Woman drawing wine from a vat.
Sepulchral stone.* (Merida, Museum.)
166 (below, right). *Person weaving. Funerary stele.*
(Burgos, Museum.)

*VESPASIAN was a realist and a sound judge of men, quali-
ties which emerge clearly in the matter-of-fact tone of his
official portraits. His realism did not, however, prevent
some of the messianic expectations which were in the air
during his lifetime from focusing on him.*
*167. The sun-god and Vespasian juxtaposed on the obverse
and reverse side of a coin. Solar imagery was regularly
used to exalt rulers of the ancient world. (Hirmer.)*

legions, transferring those in Germany to the Orient,
a much softer option. Lastly, the support of Licinius
Mucianus, one of the provincial governors,[3] who, swal-
lowing his jealous hostility towards Vespasian which
he had long made no effort to hide, promised him the
army in Syria; and the support of Vologaesus, King
of the Parthians, who promised him 40,000 archers.

7. So Vespasian began a new civil war: having sent
generals and troops ahead to Italy, he crossed over in
the meantime to Alexandria, so as to be able to control
the keys to Egypt. There he dismissed all his entourage
and entered the Temple of Serapis, alone, to consult
the auspices and discover how long his reign would last.

3. He was governor of Syria.

After many propitiatory sacrifices he turned to go, but
was granted a vision of his freedman Basilides handing
him the customary sacred branches, garlands, and
bread – although he was well aware that no one had
admitted Basilides, who had, furthermore, for a long
time been nearly crippled by rheumatism and was,
moreover, far away. Almost at once dispatches from
Italy brought the news of Vitellius's defeat at Cremona,
and his assassination at Rome.

Vespasian, still rather bewildered in his new role of
Emperor, felt a certain lack of authority and impres-
siveness; yet both these attributes were granted him.
As he sat on the Tribunal, two labourers, one blind,
the other lame, approached together, begging to be
healed. Apparently the god Serapis had promised them
in a dream that if Vespasian would consent to spit in
the blind man's eyes, and touch the lame man's leg with
his heel, both would be made well. Vespasian had so
little faith in his curative powers that he showed great
reluctance in doing as he was asked; but his friends
persuaded him to try them, in the presence of a large
audience, too – and the charm worked. At the same
time, certain soothsayers were inspired to excavate a
sacred site at Tegea in Arcadia, where a hoard of very
ancient vases was discovered, all painted with a striking
likeness of Vespasian.

8. With such a mighty reputation – he had now been
decreed a triumph over the Jews – Vespasian, on his

return to Rome, added eight more consulships to the one he had already earned.[4] He also assumed the office of Censor, and throughout his reign made it his principal business first to shore up the State, which was virtually in a state of prostration and collapse, and then to proceed to its artistic embellishment. The troops, conceited owing to their victory, or distressed and humiliated by defeat, had been indulging in all sorts of wild excesses; and internal dissension could be noted in the provinces and free cities, as well as in certain of the client kingdoms. This led Vespasian to discharge or punish a large number of Vitellius's men and, so far from showing them any special favour, he was slow in paying them even the rewards to which they were entitled. He missed no opportunity of tightening discipline: when a young man, reeking of perfume, came to thank him for a commission he had asked for and obtained, Vespasian turned his head away in disgust and cancelled the order, saying crushingly: 'I should not have minded so much if it had been garlic.' When the marine fire brigade, detachments of which had to be constantly on the move between Ostia or Puteoli and Rome, applied for a special shoe allowance, Vespasian not only turned down the application, but instructed them in future to march barefoot; which has been their practice ever since.

He reduced the free communities of Achaea, Lycia, Rhodes, Byzantium, and Samos, and the kingdoms of Trachian Cilicia and Commagene, to provincial status. He garrisoned Cappadocia as a precaution against the frequent barbarian raids, and appointed a Governor of consular rank instead of a mere knight.

In Rome, which had been made unsightly by fires and collapsed buildings, Vespasian authorized anyone who pleased to take over the vacant sites, and build on them if the original owners failed to come forward. He personally inaugurated the restoration of the burned Capitol by collecting the first basketful of rubble and carrying it away on his shoulders; and undertook to replace the 3,000 bronze tablets which had been lost in the fire, hunting high and low for copies of the inscriptions engraved on them. Those ancient, beautifully phrased records of senatorial decrees and ordinances of the Assembly dealt with such matters as alliances, treaties, and the privileges granted to individuals, and dated back almost to the foundation of Rome.

9. He also started work on several new buildings:

a temple of Peace near the Forum, a temple to Claudius the God on the Caelian Hill, begun by Agrippina but almost completely destroyed by Nero; and the Colosseum, or Flavian Amphitheatre, in the centre of the city, on discovering that this had been a favourite project of Augustus's.

He reformed the Senatorial and Equestrian Orders, weakened by frequent murders and longstanding neglect; replacing undesirable members with the most eligible Italian and provincial candidates available; and, to define clearly the difference between these Orders as one of status rather than of privilege, he pronounced the following judgement in a dispute between a senator and a knight: 'No abuse must be offered a senator: it may only be returned when given.'

10. Vespasian found a huge waiting list of lawsuits: old ones left undecided because of interruptions in regular court proceedings, and new ones due to the recent state of emergency. So he drew lots for a board of commissioners to settle war compensation claims and make emergency decisions in the Centumviral Court, thus greatly reducing the number of cases. Most of the litigants would otherwise have been dead by the time they were summoned to appear.

11. Since nothing at all had been done to counteract the debauched and reckless style of living then in fashion, Vespasian induced the Senate to decree that any woman who had taken another person's slave as a lover should lose her freedom; and that nobody lending money to a minor should be entitled to collect the debt, even if his father had died.

12. In all other matters he was from first to last modest and lenient, and more inclined to parade, than to cast a veil over, his humble origins. Indeed, when certain persons tried to connect his ancestors with the founders of Reate, and with one of Hercules' comrades whose tomb is still to be seen on the Salarian Way, he burst into a roar of laughter. He had anything but a craving for outward show; on the day of his triumph the painful crawl of the procession so wearied him that he said frankly: 'What an old fool I was to demand a triumph, as though I owed this honour to my ancestors or had ever made it one of my own ambitions! It serves me right!' Moreover, he neither claimed the tribunician power nor adopted the title 'Father of the Country' until very late in his life; and even before the civil war was over, discontinued the practice of having everyone who attended his morning audiences searched for concealed weapons.

13. Vespasian showed great patience if his friends

4. Every year from A.D. 70 to A.D. 79, except A.D. 78.

took liberties with him in conversation, or lawyers made innuendos in their speeches, or philosophers treated him impertinently; and great restraint in his dealings with Licinius Mucianus, a notoriously immoral fellow who traded on his past services, by treating him disrespectfully. Thus, he complained only once about Mucianus, and then in private to a common acquaintance, his concluding words being: 'But personally, I am content to be a male.' When Salvius Liberalis was defending a rich client he earned commendation from Vespasian by daring to ask: 'Does the Emperor really care whether Hipparchus is, or is not, worth a million gold pieces?' And when Demetrius the Cynic, who had been banished from Rome, happened to meet Vespasian's travelling party, yet made no move to rise or salute him, and barked out some rude remark or other, Vespasian merely commented: 'Good dog!'[5]

14. Not being the sort of man to bear grudges or pay off old scores, he arranged a splendid match for the daughter of his former enemy Vitellius, even providing her dowry and trousseau. And when Vespasian had been dismissed from Nero's Court, and cried in terror: 'But what shall I do? Where on earth shall I go?' one of the ushers answered: 'Oh, go to Plagueville!'[6] and pushed him out of the Palace. He now came to beg for forgiveness, and Vespasian did no more than show him the door with an equally short and almost identically framed goodbye.

5. 'Cynic' is derived from the Greek word *kuon*, dog.
6. The Latin is *Morbia*: there was no such place.

THE COLOSSEUM *was begun by Vespasian, dedicated by Titus in* A.D. *80 and completed under Domitian. Its site was shrewdly chosen: it was centrally and conveniently situated, and it had been occupied by the artificial lake of Nero's Golden House. A site set aside for the personal enjoyment of an Emperor was thus made available for the people of Rome. In later years, the Colosseum became a lasting symbol of Rome's greatness –*

While stands the Colosseum, Rome shall stand,
When falls the Colosseum, Rome shall fall,
And when Rome falls – the World.

168 (top). *View of the Colosseum.*
169 (bottom). *Model showing the interior, with stairway of one of the seventy-six entrances and vaulted corridors, which supported the seating.*

So far was he from being impelled by suspicion or fear to bring about anyone's death that, warned by his friends against Mettius Pompusianus, who was believed to have an imperial horoscope, he saddled him with a debt of gratitude by making him Consul.

15. My researches show that no innocent party was ever punished during Vespasian's reign except behind his back or while he was absent from Rome, unless by deliberate defiance of his wishes or by misinforming him about the facts in the case. Towards Helvidius Priscus who, on his return from Syria, was the only man to greet him by the private name of 'Vespasian', and who, throughout his praetorship, omitted all courteous mention of him from official orders, he showed no anger until he felt himself virtually reduced to the ranks by Priscus's insufferable rudeness. Thereupon Vespasian banished him and presently gave orders for his execution. Nevertheless, he still attached great importance to saving his life by any possible means, and dispatched messengers to stop the executioners; and he would have saved him, had it not been for a mistaken report that Priscus had already been executed. Vespasian never rejoiced in anyone's death, and would often weep when convicted criminals were forced to pay the extreme penalty.

16. His one serious failing was avarice. Not content with restoring the duties remitted by Galba he levied new and heavier ones; increased, and sometimes doubled, the tribute due from the provinces; and openly engaged in business dealings which would have disgraced even a private citizen – such as cornering the stocks of certain commodities and then putting them back on the market at inflated prices. He thought nothing of exacting fees from candidates for public office, or of selling pardons to the innocent and guilty alike; and is said to have deliberately raised his greediest procurators to positions in which they could fatten their purses satisfactorily before he came down hard on them for extortion. They were, at any rate, nicknamed his sponges – he put them in to soak, only to squeeze them dry later.

Some claim that greed was in Vespasian's very bones – an accusation once thrown at him by an old slave of his, a cattleman. When Vespasian became Emperor the slave begged to be freed but, finding that he was expected to buy the privilege, complained: 'So the fox has changed his fur, but not his nature!' Still, the more credible view is that the emptiness alike of the Treasury and the Privy Purse forced Vespasian to raise money by plunderings and robbery; he himself had confirmed this by declaring at his accession that 400,000,000 gold pieces were needed to put the country on its feet again. Certainly he spent his income to the best possible advantage, however questionable its sources.

17. Vespasian behaved most generously to all classes: granting subventions to senators who did not possess the property qualifications of their rank; securing impoverished ex-Consuls an annual pension of 5,000 gold pieces; rebuilding on a grander scale than before the many cities throughout the Empire which had been burned or destroyed by earthquakes; and proving himself a devoted patron of the arts and sciences.

18. He first paid teachers of Latin and Greek rhetoric a regular annual salary of 1,000 gold pieces from the Privy Purse; he also awarded magnificent prizes and lavish rewards to leading poets, and to artists as well, notably the restorers of the Venus of Cos[7] and the Colossus.[8] An engineer offered to haul some huge columns up to the Capitol at moderate expense by a simple mechanical contrivance, but Vespasian declined his services: 'I must always ensure,' he said, 'that the working classes earn enough money to buy themselves food.' Nevertheless, he paid the engineer a very handsome fee.

19. When the Theatre of Marcellus opened again after Vespasian had built its new stage, he revived the former musical performances and presented Apelles the tragic actor with 4,000 gold pieces; Terpnus and Diodorus the lyre-players, with 2,000 each; and several others with 1,000. His lowest cash awards were 400. But he also distributed several gold crowns. Moreover, he ordered a great number of formal dinners on a lavish scale, to encourage the victualling trade. On 23 December, the Saturnalian Festival, he gave special gifts to his male dinner guests, and did the same for women on 1 March.[9] But even this generosity could not rid him of his reputation for stinginess. Thus the people of Alexandria continued to call him 'Cybiosactes' ('a dealer in small cubes of fish'), after one of the meanest of all their kings. And when he died, the famous actor Favor,[10] who wore his funeral mask in the procession and gave the customary imitations of his

gestures and words, shouted to the imperial agents 'How much will all this cost?' 'A hundred thousand,' they answered. 'Then I'll take a thousand down, and you can just pitch me into the Tiber.'

20. Vespasian was square-bodied, with strong, well-proportioned limbs, but always wore a strained expression on his face; so that once, when he asked a well-known wit: 'Why not make a joke about me?' the answer came: 'I will, when you have finished relieving yourself.' He enjoyed perfect health and took no medical precautions for preserving it, except to have his throat and body massaged regularly in the ball-alley, and to fast one whole day every month.

21. Here follows a general description of his habits. After becoming Emperor he would rise early, before daylight even, to deal with his private correspondence and official reports. Next, he would admit his friends and receive their greetings while he put on his shoes and dressed himself. Having attended to any business that had come up he would first take a drive and then return to bed for a nap – with one of the several mistresses whom he had engaged after Caenis's death. Finally, he took a bath and went to dinner, where he would be in such a cheerful mood that members of his household usually chose this time to ask favours of him.

22. Indeed Vespasian, not only at dinner but at other times as well, was nearly always just as good-natured, cracking frequent jokes; and, though he had a low and scurrilous form of humour and often used obscene expressions, some of his witty sayings are still remembered. Taken to task by Mestrius Florus, an ex-Consul, for vulgarly saying *plostra* instead of *plaustra* (waggons), he greeted him the following day as 'Flaurus'. Once a woman declared that she was desperately in love with him, and he took her to bed with him. 'How shall I enter that item in your expense ledger?' asked his accountant later, on learning that she had got 4,000 gold pieces out of him; and Vespasian replied, 'just put it down to "passion for Vespasian".'

23. With his knack of apt quotation from the Greek classics, he once described a very tall man whose genitals were grotesquely over-developed as:

Striding along with a lance which casts a preposterous shadow.[11]

And when, to avoid paying death duties into the Privy Purse, a very rich freedman named Cerylus changed

---

7. Consecrated in the new Temple of Peace; apparently a copy of Praxiteles' Venus of Cos.

8. The colossal statue of Nero (whose head was replaced by the Sun's). It was afterwards moved by Hadrian to the north of the Flavian Amphitheatre (Colosseum).

9. The Matronalia.

10. A leading mime (*archimimus*).

11. Homer's *Iliad*.

his name to Laches and announced that he had been
born free, Vespasian quoted:

O, Laches, when your life is o'er,
Cerylus you will be once more.[12]

Most of his humour, however, centred on the disreput-
able ways he made money; he always tried to make
them sound less offensive by passing them off as jokes.
One of his favourite servants applied for a stewardship
on behalf of a man whose brother he claimed to be.
'Wait,' Vespasian told him, and had the candidate
brought in for a private interview. 'How much
commission would you have paid my servant?' he
asked. The man mentioned a sum. 'You may pay it
directly to me,' said Vespasian, giving him the stewardship without delay. When the servant brought the matter up again, Vespasian's advice was: 'Go and find
another brother. The one you mistook for your own
turns out to be mine!'

Once, on a journey, his muleteer dismounted and
began shoeing the mules; Vespasian suspected a ruse
to hold him up, to give a man involved in a lawsuit a
chance to approach him. Vespasian made the muleteer
tell him just what his shoeing fee would be; and insisted
on being paid half. Titus complained of the tax which
Vespasian had imposed on the contents of the city uri-
nals. Vespasian handed him a coin which had been part
of the first day's proceeds: 'Does it smell bad?' he
asked. And when Titus said 'No,' he went on: 'Yet it
comes from urine.' When a deputation from the Senate
reported that a huge and expensive statue had been
voted him at public expense, Vespasian held out his
open hand, with: 'The pedestal is waiting.'

Nothing could stop this flow of humour, even the
fear of imminent death. Among the many portents of
his end was a yawning crevice in Augustus's Mausoleum. 'That will be for Junia Calvina,' he said, 'she is
one of his descendants.' And at the fatal sight of a comet
he cried: 'Look at that long hair! The King of Parthia
must be going to die.' His death-bed joke was: 'Dear
me! I must be turning into a god.'

24. During his ninth consulship Vespasian visited
Campania, and caught a slight fever. He hurried back
to Rome, then went on to Cutiliae and his summer
retreat near Reate, where he made things worse by
bathing in cold water and getting a stomach chill. Yet
he carried on with his imperial duties as usual, and even
received deputations at his bedside; until he almost
fainted after a sudden violent bout of diarrhoea,
struggled to rise, muttering that an Emperor ought to
die on his feet, and collapsed in the arms of the attendants who went to his rescue. This was 23 June A.D. 79
and he had lived sixty-nine years, seven months, and
seven days.

25. All accounts agree on Vespasian's supreme confidence in his horoscopes and those of his family. Despite frequent plots to murder him, he dared tell the
Senate that either his sons would succeed him or no
one would. He is said to have dreamed about a pair
of scales hanging in the vestibule of the Palace: Claudius and his adopted son Nero, in one pan, were exactly
balanced against himself, Titus and Domitian in the
other. And this proved an accurate prophecy, since the
families were destined to rule for the same number of
years and an equal length of time.

12. From Menander.

XI
TITUS

AFTERWARDS DEIFIED

Titus, surnamed like his father,[1] had such winning ways – perhaps inborn, perhaps cultivated subsequently, or conferred on him by fortune – that he became an object of universal love and adoration. Nor was this an easy task, because it happened only after his accession: both as a private citizen and later under his father's rule, Titus had been not only criticized but loathed. He was born on 30 December A.D. 41, the

1. Vespasian.

TITUS
170 (opposite). *The arch of Titus erected posthumously in his honour.* (Rome.)
171 (above). *Coin from Rome.* (London, British Museum.)

memorable year of Gaius's assassination, in a small, dingy, slum bedroom close to the Septizonium.[2] The house, which is still standing, is open to the public.

2. He grew up at Court with Britannicus, sharing his teachers and following the same curriculum. The story goes that when one day Claudius's freedman Narcissus called in a physiognomist to examine Britannicus's features and prophesy his future, he was told most emphatically that Britannicus would never succeed his father, whereas Titus (who happened to be present) would achieve that distinction. The two boys were such close friends that when Britannicus drank his fatal dose of poison, Titus, who was reclining at the same table, is said to have tasted it as well and to have been dangerously ill for a long time. He did not forget what had happened, but later set up two statues of Britannicus: a golden one to be installed in the Palace, and an ivory equestrian one which is still carried in the Circus procession, and which he personally followed around the ring at its dedication.

3. When Titus came of age, the beauty and talents that had distinguished him as a child grew even more remarkable. Though not tall, he was both graceful and dignified, both muscular and handsome, except for a certain paunchiness. He had a phenomenal memory, and displayed a natural aptitude alike for almost all the arts of war and peace; handled arms and rode a horse with great skill; could compose speeches and verses in Greek or Latin with equal ease, and actually extemporized them on occasion. He was something of a musician, too: sang pleasantly, and had mastered the harp. It often amused him to compete with his secretaries at shorthand dictation, or so I have heard; and he claimed that he could imitate any handwriting in

2. Some seven-storey building; but not the famous structure of that name, which was much later.

existence and might have been the most celebrated forger of all time.

4. Titus's reputation while an active and efficient colonel in Germany and Britain is attested by the numerous inscribed statues and busts found in both countries. After completing his military service he pleaded in the Roman Forum as a barrister; but in

hopes were soon confirmed,[3] and he was left to complete the conquest of Judaea. In the final assault on Jerusalem Titus managed to kill twelve of the garrison with successive arrows; and the city was captured on his daughter's birthday. Titus's prowess inspired such deep admiration in the troops that they hailed him as

3. i.e., by the accession of Vespasian to the throne.

order to make a reputation, not because he meant to make a career of it. The father of his first wife, Arrecina Tertulla, was only a Roman knight but commanded the Guards. When she died, Titus married the very well-connected Marcia Furnilla, whom he divorced after she had borne him a daughter. When his quaestorship at Rome ended, he went to command one of his father's legions in Judaea, and there captured the strongly fortified cities of Tarichaeae and Gamala. In the course of the fighting he had a horse killed under him, but mounted another belonging to a comrade who fell at his side.

5. Titus was presently sent to congratulate Galba on his accession, and attracted attention wherever he went because of a general belief that he had been sent for so that the Emperor could adopt him. Seeing, however, that the Empire was again in a state of confusion, Titus turned back to visit the oracle of Venus at Paphos to consult it about his voyage, and there heard his own prospects of wearing the purple mentioned again. His

THE JUDAEAN WAR. *In* A.D. 66, *sacrifices for the safety of the Roman Emperor in the temple of Jerusalem were brought to an end as being an infringement of the worship of one God – but oppressive Roman government also played its role in provoking this act of rebellion. The Roman reconquest followed; Jerusalem fell in* A.D. 70, *and in 73 the last survivors of the revolt committed suicide in the fortress of Masada.*

172 (above, left). *Coin of the Jewish revolt.* (London, British Museum.)

173 (above, right). *Coin of Titus, 'Judaea conquered': prisoner and mourning woman under a palm tree.* (London, British Museum.)

174 (opposite, top). *In* A.D. 71, *Titus celebrated his triumph over Judaea: the triumphal chariot of Titus, from his Arch.* (Rome.)

175 (opposite, below). *The spoils of Jerusalem, showing the seven-branched candlestick from the Temple preceded by a placard identifying it for the spectators.* (Arch of Titus, Rome.)

Imperator and, on several occasions, when he seemed on the point of relinquishing his command, urged him on with prayers and even threats either to stay or to let them all go with him. Such passionate devotion aroused a suspicion that he planned to revolt from his father and make himself king in the East, especially since he had worn a diadem while attending the consecration of the Apis bull at Memphis on his way to Alexandria; this accorded with ancient ritual, but gave rise to unfavourable interpretations. Because of these, Titus sailed for Italy at once in a naval transport, touching at Rhegium and Puteoli. Hurrying on to Rome, he exploded all the false rumours by greeting Vespasian, who had not been expecting him, with the simple words: 'Here I am, Father, here I am!'

6. He now became his father's colleague, almost his guardian; sharing in the Judaean triumph, in the Censorship, in the exercise of tribunician power, and in seven consulships. He bore most of the burdens of government and, in his father's name, dealt with official correspondence, drafted edicts, and even took over the quaestor's task of reading the imperial speeches to the Senate. Titus also assumed command of the Guards, a post which had always before been entrusted to a knight, and in which he behaved somewhat high-handedly and tyrannically. If anyone aroused his suspicion, Guards detachments would be sent into theatre or camp to demand the man's punishment as if by the agreement of everyone present; and he would then be executed without delay. Titus disposed of Aulus Caecina, an ex-Consul, by inviting him to dinner and having him stabbed almost before he had left the dining room; yet here he was impelled by a critical situation – the manuscript of a speech which Caecina intended for the troops had fallen into his hands. Actions of this sort, although an insurance against the future, made Titus so deeply disliked at the time that perhaps no more unwelcome claimant to the supreme power has ever won it.

7. He was believed to be profligate as well as cruel, because of the riotous parties which he kept going with his more extravagant friends far into the night; and immoral, too, because he owned a troop of inverts and eunuchs, and nursed a notorious passion for Queen Berenice, to whom he had allegedly promised marriage. He also had a reputation for greed, since it was well known that he was not averse to using influence to settle his father's cases in favour of the highest bidder. It was even thought and prophesied quite openly

that he would prove to be a second Nero. However, this pessimistic view stood him in good stead: so soon as everyone realized that here was no monster of vice but an exceptionally noble character, public opinion had no fault to find with him.

His dinner parties, far from being extravagant, were very pleasant occasions, and the friends he chose were retained in office by his successors as key men in their own service and in national affairs. He sent Queen Berenice away from Rome, which was painful for both of them; and broke off relations with some of his favourite boys – though they danced well enough to make a name for themselves on the stage, he never attended their public performances.

He never took anything away from any citizen, but showed the greatest respect for private property, and would not even accept the gifts that were permissible and customary. Nor had any of his predecessors ever displayed such generosity. At the dedication of his Amphitheatre[4] and the Baths, which had been hastily built beside it, Titus provided a most lavish gladiatorial show; he also staged a sea-fight on the old artificial lake,[5] and when the water had been let out, used the basin for further gladiatorial contests and a wild-beast hunt, 5,000 beasts of different sorts dying in a single day.

8. Titus was naturally kind-hearted, and though no Emperor, following Tiberius's example, had ever consented to ratify individual concessions granted by his predecessor, unless they themselves had conferred the same privileges on the same individuals, Titus did not wait to be asked but signed a general edict confirming all such concessions whatsoever. He also had a rule never to dismiss any petitioner without leaving him some hope that his request would be favourably considered. Even when warned by his staff how impossible it would be to make good such promises, Titus maintained that no one ought to go away disappointed from an audience with the Emperor. One evening at dinner, realizing that he had done nobody any favour throughout the entire day, he spoke these memorable words: 'My friends, I have wasted a day.'

He took such pains to humour his subjects that, on one occasion, before a gladiatorial show, he promised to forgo his own preferences and let the audience choose what they liked best; and kept his word by refusing no request and encouraging everyone to tell him what each wanted. Yet he openly acknowledged

4. The Flavian Amphitheatre (Colosseum).   5. The Naumachia.

his partisanship of the Thracian gladiators, and would gesture and argue vociferously with the crowd on this subject, though never losing either his dignity or his sense of justice. So as to miss no occasion whatever of courting popularity sometimes he would use the new public baths, in company with the common people.

Titus's reign was marked by a series of dreadful catastrophes – an eruption of Mount Vesuvius in Campania,[6] a fire at Rome which burned for three days and nights, and one of the worst outbreaks of plague that had ever been known. Throughout this assortment of disasters, he showed far more than an Emperor's concern: it resembled the deep love of a father for his children, which he conveyed not only in a series of comforting edicts but by helping the victims to the utmost extent of his purse. He set up a board of ex-consuls, chosen by lot, to relieve distress in Campania, and devoted the property of those who had died in the eruption and left no heirs to a fund for rebuilding the stricken cities. His only comment on the fire at Rome was: 'This has ruined me!' He stripped his own country mansions of their decorations, distributed these among the public buildings and temples, and appointed a body of knights to see that his orders were promptly carried out. Titus attempted to cure the plague and limit its ravages by every imaginable means, human as well as divine – resorting to all sorts of sacrifices and medical remedies.

One of the worst features of Roman life at the time was the licence long enjoyed by informers and their managers. Titus had these well whipped, clubbed, and then taken to the amphitheatre[7] and paraded in the arena; where some were put up for auction as slaves and the remainder deported to the most forbidding islands. In further discouragement of any who, at any future time, might venture on similar practices, he allowed nobody to be tried for the same offence under more than one law, and limited the period during which inquiries could be made into the status of dead people.

9. He had promised before his accession to accept the office of Chief Priest as a safeguard against committing any crime, and kept his word. Thereafter he was never directly or indirectly responsible for a murder; and, although often given abundant excuse for revenge,

swore that he would rather die than take life. Titus dismissed with a caution two patricians convicted of aspiring to the Empire; he told them that this was a gift of Destiny and they would be well advised to renounce their hopes. He also promised them whatever else they wanted, and hastily sent messengers to reassure the mother of one of the pair, who lived some distance away, that her son was safe. Then he invited them to dine among his friends; and, the next day, to sit close by him during the gladiatorial show, where he asked them to take and inspect the blades of the contestants' swords brought for him to look at. Finally, the story goes, he consulted the horoscopes of both men and warned them what dangers threatened, but at some future date and from another person – quite correctly, as events proved.

Titus's brother Domitian took part in endless conspiracies against him, stirred up disaffection in the armed forces almost openly, and toyed with the notion of fleeing to them. Yet Titus had not the heart to execute Domitian, dismiss him from Court, or even treat him less honourably than before. Instead, he continued to repeat, as on the first day of his reign: 'Remember that you are my partner and chosen successor'; and often took Domitian aside, begging him tearfully to return the affection he offered.

10. Death, however, intervened; which was a far greater loss to the world than to Titus himself. At the close of the Games he wept publicly; and then set off for Sabine territory in a gloomy mood because a victim had escaped when he was about to sacrifice it, and because thunder had sounded from a clear sky. He collapsed with fever at the first posting station, and on his way from the place in a litter, is said to have drawn back the curtains, gazed up at the sky, and complained bitterly that life was being undeservedly taken from him – since only a single sin lay on his conscience. What that was he did not reveal, and it was difficult to guess what he meant, and he did not disclose it at the time; the enigmatic remark has been taken as referring to incest with Domitian's wife, Domitia, but she herself solemnly denied the allegation. Had the charge been true she would surely never have made any such denial but boasted of it – as she did of all her other misdeeds.

11. Titus died at the age of forty-one, in the same country house where Vespasian had also died. It was 1 September A.D. 81, and he had reigned two years, two months, and twenty days. When the news spread, the entire population went into mourning as though

---

6. The eruption that destroyed Pompeii, Herculaneum, Stabiae, and Oplontis.
7. The Flavian Amphitheatre (Colosseum).

ON THE WINGS OF AN EAGLE. *While at life's end ordinary mortals entered the world of the dead, the divinized Emperor joined the gods.*

176 (left). *The dead Titus is carried to the gods by an eagle. Relief in the vault of the Arch.*

177 (below). *Body lying in state with mourners.* (Rome, Tomb of the Haterii.)

they had suffered a personal loss. Senators hurried to the House without waiting for an official summons, and before the doors had been opened, and then when they were open, began speaking of him, now that he was dead, with greater thankfulness and praise than they had ever used while he was alive and among them.

XII
DOMITIAN

On 24 October A.D. 51, a month before his father,[1] as Consul-elect, was due to take office, Domitian was born in Pomegranate Street, which formed part of the sixth district of Rome. Later, he converted his birthplace into the Temple of the Flavians. He is said to have spent a poverty-stricken and rather degraded youth: without even any silver on the family table. At all events, it is an established fact that Clodius Pollio,

1. Vespasian.

DOMITIAN
178 (opposite). *Cuirassed statue of Domitian.* (Rome, Vatican.)
179 (above). *Coin from Rome.* (Glasgow, Hunterian Museum.)

an ex-praetor and the target of Nero's satire *The One-eyed Man*, used to show his guests a letter in Domitian's handwriting, which he had kept, promising to go to bed with him. It is also often insisted that Domitian was sexually abused by his eventual successor, the Emperor Nerva.

During the war against Vitellius, Domitian, with his uncle Sabinus and part of the forces under him, fled to the Capitol; but when the enemy burst in and set the temple on fire, Domitian concealed himself all night in the caretaker's quarters and, at daybreak, disguised as a devotee of Isis, took refuge among the priests of that rather questionable order. Presently he managed to escape with a single companion across the Tiber, where the mother of one of his fellow-students hid him so cleverly that she outwitted the agents who had followed in his tracks. Emerging when his side was victorious, Domitian was hailed as 'Caesar' and accepted an appointment as City Praetor with consular powers – but in name only, because he left all judicial decisions to his next colleague. However, the lawlessness with which he exploited his autocratic position clearly showed what might be expected of him later. I shall not discuss this subject in any detail; suffice it to say that Domitian had affairs with many married women, and took off Domitia Longina and married her, although she was the wife of Aelius Lamia; and that once, when he had distributed more than twenty appointments at home and abroad in the course of a single day, Vespasian murmured: 'I wonder he did not name my successor while he was about it!'

2. To acquire power and rank that would compare favourably with his brother Titus's, Domitian planned a quite unnecessary expedition into Gaul and Germany, from which his father's friends managed to dissuade him. He earned a reprimand for this and was made to feel more conscious of his youth and unimpor-

tance by having to live with his father. Whenever Vespasian and Titus now appeared seated in their official chairs, he had to be content with following behind in a litter; and, while taking part in their Judaean triumph, rode on a white horse.[2] Of the six consulships enjoyed by Domitian before becoming Emperor, only one was a regular one,[3] and that came his way because Titus had stood down in his favour.

Domitian pretended to be extremely modest, and though he displayed a novel devotion to poetry, which he would read aloud in public, his enthusiasm was matched by a later neglect and contempt of the art. However, he did everything possible to get sent against the Alani when a request for auxiliary troops, commanded by one of Vespasian's sons, arrived from Vologaesus, King of the Parthians. And he subsequently tried by bribes and promises to coax similar requests from other Oriental kings.

At Vespasian's death Domitian toyed for a while with the idea of offering his troops twice as large a bounty as Titus had given them; and stated bluntly that his father's will must have been tampered with, since it originally assigned him a half-share in the Empire. He never once stopped plotting, secretly or openly, against his brother. When Titus fell suddenly and dangerously ill, Domitian told the attendants to leave him for dead before he had actually breathed his last; and afterwards granted him no recognition at all, beyond approving his deification. In fact, he often slighted Titus's memory by the use of ambiguous terms in speeches and edicts.

3. At the beginning of his reign Domitian would spend hours alone every day doing nothing but catch flies and stabbing them with a needle-sharp pen. Once, on being asked whether anyone was closeted with the Emperor, Vibius Crispus answered wittily: 'No, not even a fly.' Then he awarded his wife Domitia the title of Augusta. She had presented Domitian with a daughter during his second consulship and, in the following year, with a son. But he divorced her because she had fallen in love with Paris, the actor. This separation, however, proved to be more than Domitian could bear; and he very soon took her back, claiming that such was the people's wish. For a while he governed in an uneven fashion: that is to say, his vices were at first balanced by his virtues. Later, he transformed his

virtues into vices too – for I am inclined to believe that this was contrary to his original character; it was lack of funds that made him greedy, and fear of assassination that made him cruel.

4. Domitian presented many extravagant entertainments in the Colosseum and the Circus. Besides the usual two-horse chariot races he staged a couple of battles, one for infantry, the other for cavalry; a sea-fight in the amphitheatre;[4] wild-beast hunts; gladiatorial shows by torchlight in which women as well as men took part. Nor did he ever forget the Games given by the quaestors, which he had revived; and allowed the people to demand a combat between two pairs of gladiators from his own troop, whom he would bring on last in their gorgeous Court livery. Throughout every gladiatorial show Domitian would chat, sometimes in very serious tones, with a little boy who had a grotesquely small head and always stood at his feet dressed in red. Once he was heard to ask the child: 'Can you guess why, on the last appointment day, I made Mettius Rufus Prefect of Egypt?' A lake was dug at his orders close to the Tiber, surrounded with seats, and used for almost full-scale naval battles, which he watched even in heavy rain.

He also held Saecular Games, fixing their date by Augustus's old reckoning, and ignoring Claudius's more recent celebration of them; and for the Circus racing, which formed part of the festivities, reduced the number of laps from seven to five, so that 100 races could be run off in the day. In honour of Capitoline Jupiter he founded a threefold festival of music, horsemanship, and gymnastics, to be held every five years, and awarded far more prizes than is customary nowadays. The festival included Latin and Greek public-speaking contests, competitions for choral singing to the lyre and lyre-playing alone, besides the usual solo singing to lyre accompaniment; he even instituted foot races for girls in the Stadium. When presiding at these functions he wore buskins, a purple robe in the Greek fashion, and a gold crown engraved with the images of Jupiter, Juno, and Minerva; and at his side sat the Priest of Capitoline Jupiter and the Priest of the Deified Flavians, wearing the same costume as he did, except that their crowns were decorated with his likeness as well. Domitian also celebrated the annual five-day festival of Minerva[5] at his Alban villa, and founded in her honour a college of priests, whose task it was to supply officers, chosen by lot, for producing lavish

2. The usual mount for a young prince on such occasions.

3. i.e., as one of the *consules ordinarii* who gave their name to the year.

4. The Flavian Amphitheatre (Colosseum).   5. The Quinquatria.

wild-beast hunts and stage plays, and sponsoring competitions in rhetoric and poetry.

On three occasions Domitian distributed a popular bounty of three gold pieces a head; and once, to celebrate the Feast of the Seven Hills, gave a splendid banquet, at which large hampers of food were distributed to senators and knights, and smaller ones to the populace; taking the inaugural bite himself. The day after, he scattered all kinds of gifts to be scrambled for, but since most of these fell in the seats occupied by the public, had 500 tokens thrown into those reserved for senators, and another 500 into those reserved for knights.

5. He restored a great many important buildings that were now gutted ruins, including the Capitol which had just been burned down again,[6] but allowed no names to be inscribed on them, except his own – not even the original builder's. He also raised a temple to Jupiter the Guardian on the Capitoline Hill, the Forum of Nerva (as it is now called), the Flavian Temple, a stadium, a concert hall, and the artificial lake for sea battles[7] – its stones later served to rebuild the two sides of the Great Circus which had been damaged by fire.

6. Some of Domitian's campaigns were unprovoked, others necessary. The war against the Chatti was uncalled for; but not so that against the Sarmatians, who had massacred a legion and killed its commander.[8] And when the Dacians defeated first the ex-Consul Oppius Sabinus, and then the Commander

THE MARTIAL IMAGE, which many Roman Emperors sought to convey, while displeasing to urban Romans, was rooted in realities. Military defeat was the most serious threat to an Emperor's staying in power, and throughout the history of the Empire, the threat was an almost constant one.

180. The Emperor Domitian sets out from Rome: he is led forward by Minerva, his guardian goddess, and Mars the god of war, both wearing helmets. The goddess Roma, dressed as an Amazon, holds the Emperor's arm and follows behind. The Genius of the Senate and the Genius of the Roman People wave farewell. Cancelleria relief. (Rome, Vatican.)

of the Guards Cornelius Fuscus,[9] Domitian led two punitive expeditions in person. After several indecisive engagements he celebrated a double triumph over the Chatti and Dacians; but did not insist on recognition for his Sarmatian campaign, contenting himself with the offer of a laurel crown to Capitoline Jupiter.

Only an amazing stroke of luck checked the rebellion of Lucius Antonius, commander in Upper Germany, during Domitian's absence; the Rhine thawed in the very hour of battle, preventing Antonius's barbarian allies from crossing the ice to join him, and the troops who remained loyal were able to disarm the rebels. Even before news of this success arrived, Domitian had wind of it from portents: on the very day of battle, a

6. A.D. 80.   7. The Naumachia.   8. A.D. 70.

9. A.D. 85 and 86.

huge eagle embraced his statue at Rome with its wings, screeching triumphantly; and a little later, rumours of Antonius's death came so thick and fast that a number of people claimed to have seen his head being carried into Rome.

7. Domitian made a number of social innovations: cancelled the public grain issue, restored the custom of holding formal dinners, added two new teams of chariot drivers, the Golds and the Purples, to the existing four in the Circus and forbade actors to appear on the public stage, though still allowing them to perform in private. Castration was now strictly prohibited, and the price of eunuchs remaining in slave-dealers' hands officially controlled. One year, when a bumper vintage followed a poor grain harvest, Domitian concluded that the cornlands were being neglected in favour of the vineyards. He therefore issued an edict that forbade the further planting of vines in Italy, and ordered the acreage in the provinces to be reduced by at least half, if it could not be got rid of altogether; yet took no steps to implement this edict. He divided some of the more important Court appointments between freedmen and knights. Another of his edicts forbade any two legions to share a camp, or any individual soldier to deposit at headquarters a sum in excess of ten gold pieces; because the large amount of soldiers' savings laid up in the joint winter headquarters of the two legions on the Rhine had provided Lucius Antonius with the necessary funds for launching his rebellion. Domitian also raised the legionaries' pay by one quarter, from nine to twelve gold pieces a year.

8. He was most conscientious in dispensing justice, and convened many extraordinary legal sessions on the tribunal in the Forum; annulling every decision of the Centumviral Court which seemed to him unduly influenced, and continually warning the Board of Arbitration not to grant any fraudulent claims for freedom. It was his ruling that if a juryman were proved to have taken bribes, all his colleagues must be penalized as well as himself. He personally urged the tribunes of the people to charge a corrupt aedile with extortion, and to petition the Senate for a special jury in the case; and kept such a tight hold on the city magistrates and provincial governors that the general standard of honesty and justice rose to an unprecedented high level – you need only observe how many such personages have been charged with every kind of corruption since his time!

As part of his campaign for improving public morals, Domitian made sure that the appropriation by the general public of seats reserved for knights was no longer condoned; and came down heavily on authors who published lampoons on distinguished men and women. He expelled one ex-quaestor from the Senate for being over-fond of acting and dancing; forbade women of notoriously bad character the right to use litters or to benefit from inheritances and legacies; struck a knight from the jury-roll because he had divorced his wife on a charge of adultery and then taken her back again; and sentenced many members of both Orders under the Scantinian Law.[10] Taking a far more serious view than his father and brother had done of unchastity among the Vestals, he began by sentencing offenders to execution, and afterwards resorted to the traditional form of punishment. Thus, though he allowed the Oculata sisters, and Varronilla, to choose how they should die, and sent their lovers into exile, he later ordered Cornelia, a Chief-Vestal – acquitted at her first trial, but re-arrested much later and convicted – to be buried alive, and had her lovers clubbed to death in the Comitium. The only exception he made was in the case of an ex-praetor, who was permitted to go into banishment after confessing his guilt, for the interrogation of witnesses under torture had failed to establish the truth of the crime with which he was charged. As a lesson that the sanctity of the gods must be protected against thoughtless abuse, Domitian made his soldiers tear down a tomb built for the son of one of his own freedmen from stones intended for the Temple of Capitoline Jupiter, and fling its contents of bones and ashes into the sea.

9. While still young, Domitian hated the idea of bloodshed; and once, in his father's absence, remembered Virgil's line:

Before an impious people took to eating slaughtered
bullocks...

and drafted an edict forbidding the sacrifice of oxen. No one thought of him as in the least greedy or mean either before, or for some years after, his accession – in fact, he gave conspicuous signs of self-restraint and even of generosity, treating all his friends with great consideration and always insisting that, above all, they should do nothing mean; refused to accept bequests from married men with children, and cancelled a clause in Rustius Caepio's will which required the heir to find an annual sum of money for distribution among newly-appointed senators.

10. Against unnatural practices.

Moreover, if suits against debtors to the Public Treasury had been pending for more than five years, he quashed them and permitted a renewal of proceedings only within the same twelvemonth, and ruled that if the prosecutor should then lose his case, he must go into exile. Although the Clodian Law restricted the private business activities of quaestors' scribes, Domitian now pardoned such of them as had broken it; and allowed former owners, as if by right of possession, the stretches of land which had been left unoccupied in one place or another after the assignment of plots to veterans. He checked and severely penalized informers who had brought false accusations for the benefit of the imperial treasury. A saying attributed to him runs: 'An Emperor who does not punish informers encourages them.'

10. His leniency and self-restraint were not, however, destined to continue long, and the cruel streak in him became apparent – rather before his avaricious traits. He executed one beardless boy, in distinctly poor health, merely because he happened to be a pupil of the actor Paris,[11] and closely resembled him in his style of acting and appearance. Then Hermogenes of Tarsus died because of some allusions that he had introduced into a historical work; and the slaves who acted as his copyists were crucified. A chance remark by one citizen, to the effect that a Thracian gladiator might be 'a match for his Gallic opponent, but not for the patron of the Games', was enough to have him dragged from his seat and – with a placard tied around his neck reading: 'A Thracian supporter[12] who spoke disloyally' – torn to pieces by dogs in the arena.

Domitian put many senators to death, among them a group of ex-Consuls, three of whom, Civica Cerealis, Acilius Glabrio, and Salvidienus Orfitus, he accused of conspiracy; Cerealis was executed while governing Asia; Glabrio while already in exile. Others were executed on the most trivial charges. Aelius Lamia lost his life as a result of some suspicious but old and harmless witticisms at Domitian's expense: he had been robbed of his wife by Domitian, and when someone later praised his voice remarked drily: 'I have given up sex and gone into training!'; and then, encouraged by Titus to marry again, asked: 'What! You are not wanting a wife, too, are you?' Salvius Cocceianus died because he continued to celebrate the birthday of the Emperor Otho, his paternal uncle; and Mettius Pompusianus, because his birth was said to have been attended by imperial portents, and because he always carried with him a parchment map of the world and a collection of speeches by kings and generals extracted from Livy – and because he had named two of his slaves 'Mago' and 'Hannibal'! Sallustius Lucullus, Governor of Britain, had equally offended Domitian by allowing a new type of lance to be called 'the Lucullan'; so had Junius Rusticus, by publishing eulogies of Thrasea Paetus and Helvidius Priscus in which he described them as saintly characters – an incident which led Domitian to banish all philosophers from Italy; and Helvidius the Younger by his farce about Paris and Oenone, which seemed a reflection on Domitian's divorce; and Domitian's own cousin, Flavius Sabinus, by being mistakenly announced by the election day herald as Imperator, instead of Consul.

After his victory in the civil war, Domitian grew even more cruel. He hit on a novel form of investigation, scorching his prisoners' genitals to make them divulge the whereabouts of other rebels still in hiding; and cut off the hands of many more. It is a fact that only two leaders of the revolt – a colonel of senatorial rank and a centurion – earned his pardon; which they did by the simple expedient of proving themselves to have been so disgustingly immoral that they could have exerted no influence at all over either their commander[13] or the troops.

11. Domitian was not merely cruel, but cunning and sudden into the bargain. He summoned a Palace steward to his bedroom, invited him to join him on his couch, made him feel perfectly secure and happy, condescended to share a dinner with him – yet had him crucified on the following day! He was as gracious, or more than usually gracious, to the ex-Consul Arrecinus Clemens, a friend and agent, just before his death-sentence, and invited him out for a drive. As they happened to pass the man who had informed on Arrecinus, Domitian asked: 'Shall we listen to that rascally slave tomorrow?' And the abuse he inflicted on his subjects' patience was all the more offensive because he prefaced all his most savage sentences with the same speech about mercy; indeed, this lenient preamble soon became a recognized sign that something dreadful was on the way. Having brought a group of men before the Senate on a treason charge, he announced that this must be a test of his popularity with the House; and

11. *Pantomimus.*

12. A *Parmularius*, armed with a shield, i.e., a Thracian – an insulting description of a Roman citizen.

13. Lucius Antonius Saturninus.

thus easily got them condemned to 'old-style execution'.[14] However, he then seems to have become appalled by the cruelty involved, because he vetoed the sentence, in order to make himself less unpopular. His exact words are interesting: 'Gentlemen of the Senate, I know that you will not readily grant me what I ask, but let me beg one favour of you, because of your love for me: pray allow these men to choose the manner of their deaths! That will be easier on your eyes; and the world will know that I took part in the meeting of the House.'

12. The new building programme, added to his entertainments and the rise in army pay, exhausted Domitian's resources; so he decided to reduce expenditure by cutting down the military establishment. But, then realizing that this would expose his frontiers to barbarian attack, without appreciably easing the financial situation, he resorted unhesitatingly to every form of extortion. Any charge, brought by any accuser – to have spoken or acted in prejudice of the Emperor's welfare was enough – might result in the confiscation of a man's property, even if he were already dead. A single claim that someone had been heard, before his death, to name the Emperor as his heir, even though he were in no way connected with him, was sufficient pretext for taking over the estate. Domitian's agents collected the tax on Jews[15] with a peculiar lack of

14. The condemned man was stripped, had his head fastened to a wooden fork, and was flogged to death. See Nero 49.

15. The tax had been imposed by Vespasian after the destruction of the Temple of Jerusalem in A.D. 70.

KISSING THE HAND *was a sign of veneration as to divine beings. This divine status and the veneration it entailed could be claimed by an Emperor by directly approximating himself to a god, or by making a divine being his special companion or guardian. Domitian's guardian was Minerva.*

181 (left). *Minerva standing on a ship's prow brandishes a javelin; her sacred bird, the owl, sits at her feet. Coin of Domitian.* (Glasgow, Hunterian Museum.)

182 (above). *Statue of Minerva in the guise of Victory, period of Domitian.* (Ostia.)

183 (opposite). *Theseus, slayer of the Minotaur (see Ill. 121), has his hands kissed by the children whose lives he saved. Painting from Pompeii.* (Naples, Museum.)

mercy; and took proceedings not only against those who kept their Jewish origins a secret in order to avoid the tax, but against those who lived as Jews without professing Judaism.[16] As a boy, I remember once attending a crowded court where the imperial agent had a ninety-year-old man inspected to establish whether or not he had been circumcised.

From his earliest years Domitian was far from affable, indeed consistently discourteous and presumptuous in word and deed. When Caenis, his father's mistress, returned from Istria and, as usual, offered him her cheek to kiss, he held out his hand instead. He objected when his nephew-by-marriage dressed his servants in white – Domitian's own servants wore white livery – and quoted at him Homer's line:

> Too many rulers are a dangerous thing.

13. On his accession Domitian did not scruple to boast to the Senate of having himself conferred the imperial power on Vespasian and Titus – they had now merely returned it to him! He also spoke of his action in taking Domitia back, after the divorce, as 'a recall to my divine bed'; and on the day of his public banquet delighted to hear the crowd in the amphitheatre shout: 'Long live our Lord and Lady!' At the competition of Capitoline Jupiter, when unanimously implored by the audience to pardon Palfurius Sura, whom he had expelled from the Senate some time previously but who had nevertheless won the prize for public speaking, Domitian would not reply and sent a public crier to silence them. Just as arrogantly he began a letter, which his agents were to circulate, with the words: 'Our Lord and God instructs you to do this!' and 'Lord and God' became his regular title both in writing and conversation. Images dedicated to Domitian in the Capitol had to be of either gold or silver, and of a certain weight; and he raised so many and such enormous arcades and arches, decorated with chariots and triumphal insignia, in various city districts, that someone scribbled 'arci', meaning 'arches' on one of them – but used Greek characters, and so spelled out the Greek word for 'Enough!' He held seventeen consulships, which was a record. Only the seven middle ones formed a series, but all were virtually nominal: he relinquished most of them after a few days, and every one of them before 1 May. Having adopted the surname 'Germanicus'

after his two triumphs he renamed September and October, the months of his accession and birth, respectively, 'Germanicus' and 'Domitianus'.

14. All this made him everywhere hated and feared. Finally, his friends and favourite freedmen conspired to murder him, with the connivance of his wife.[17] Astrological predictions had long since warned him in what year and day he would die; they even specified the hour and manner. Vespasian once teased him openly at dinner for refusing a dish of mushrooms, saying that it would be more in keeping with his destiny to be afraid of swords. As a result, Domitian was such a prey to fear and anxiety that the least sign of danger unnerved him. The real reason for his reprieving the vineyards, which he had ordered to be rooted up, is said to have been the publication of this stanza:

> You may tear up my roots, goat,
> But what good will that do?
> I shall still have some wine left
> For sacrificing you.

Though he loved honours of all kinds, this same anxiety made him veto a Senatorial decree that, whenever he held the consulship, a group of knights should be picked by lot to walk, dressed in purple-striped robes and armed with lances, among the lictors and attendants who preceded him.

As the critical day drew near his nervousness increased. The gallery where he took his daily exercise was now lined with plaques of highly-polished moonstone, which reflected everything that happened behind his back; and no imperial audiences were granted to prisoners unless Domitian were alone with them, and actually had tight hold of their fetters. To remind his staff that even the best of intentions could never justify a freedman's complicity in a master's murder, he executed his secretary[18] Epaphroditus, who had reputedly helped Nero to commit suicide after everyone else had deserted him.

15. Finally he executed, suddenly and on some trivial pretext, his own cousin, Flavius Clemens, just before the completion of a consulship; though Clemens was a man of despicable idleness, and Domitian had previously named Flavius's two small sons as his heirs and changed their names to Vespasian and Domitian.

So much lightning had fallen during the past eight months that Domitian cried out: 'Now let him strike whomever he pleases!' The Temple of Capitoline

---

16. These 'Judaizers', or 'sympathizers', loose adherents of Judaism, are sometimes (wrongly) believed to have called themselves 'God-fearers'.

17. Domitia Longina.   18. *A libellis*.

Jupiter, the Temple of the Flavians, the Palace, even Domitian's own bedroom were all struck; and a hurricane wrenched the inscription plate from the base of a triumphal statue of his and hurled it into a near-by tomb. The tree which had been blown down but had then taken root again, while Vespasian was still a private citizen, now collapsed a second time. Throughout his reign Domitian had made a practice of commending each new year to the care of the Goddess Fortune at Praeneste, and every year she had granted him the same favourable omen; but this year the omen was a dreadful one, portending bloodshed. Domitian also dreamed that Minerva, whom he worshipped with superstitious reverence, emerged from her shrine to tell him that she had been disarmed by Jupiter and could no longer protect him. What disturbed him most, however, was a prediction by the astrologer Ascletario, and its sequel. This man, when charged, made no secret of having revealed the future, which he had foreseen by his magical arts. Domitian at once asked whether he could prophesy the manner of his own end, and upon Ascletario's replying that he would very soon be torn to pieces by dogs, had him executed on the spot, and gave orders for his funeral rites to be conducted with the greatest care, as a further proof that astrology was a fake. But while the funeral was in progress a sudden gale scattered the pyre and dogs mangled the half-burned corpse. Latinus, the comic actor,[19] who happened to witness this incident as he passed by, mentioned it at dinner when he brought Domitian the day's gossip.

16. On the day before Domitian's assassination someone brought him a present of apples. 'Serve them tomorrow,' he told the servants, adding: '– if only I am spared to eat them.' Then, turning to his companions he remarked: 'There will be blood on the Moon as she enters Aquarius, and a deed will be done for everyone to talk about throughout the entire world.' With the approach of midnight Domitian became so terrified that he jumped out of bed; and at dawn condemned to death a soothsayer from Germany who was charged with having said that the lightning portended a change of government. Domitian then scratched a festering wart on his forehead and made it bleed, muttering: 'I hope this is all the blood required.' Presently he asked for the time. As had been prearranged, his freedmen answered untruthfully: 'The sixth hour,' because they knew it was the fifth he feared. Convinced that the

danger had passed, Domitian went off quickly and happily to take a bath; whereupon his head valet, Parthenius, changed his intention by delivering the news that a man had called on very urgent and important business, and would not be put off. So Domitian dismissed his attendants and hurried to his bedroom – where he was killed.

17. Virtually all that has come to light about either the plot or the assassination is that his niece Domitilla's steward, Stephanus, had been accused of embezzlement, and that while the conspirators were debating when and how it would be better to murder Domitian, in his bath or at dinner, Stephanus offered them his advice and his services. Then, to divert suspicion, he feigned an arm injury and went around for several days with his arm wrapped in woollen bandages – in which a dagger was concealed. Finally he pretended that he had discovered a plot, and was for that reason granted an audience: whereupon, as the amazed Domitian perused a document he had handed him, Stephanus stabbed him in the groin. The wounded Emperor put up a fight, but succumbed to seven further stabs, his assailants being a subaltern named Clodianus, Parthenius's freedman Maximus, Satur a head-chamberlain, and one of the imperial gladiators. The boy who was, as usual, attending to the Household-gods in the bedroom, witnessed the murder and later provided these additional details. On receiving the first blow, Domitian bade the boy hand him the dagger which was kept under his pillow and then call the servants; the dagger, however, proved to have no blade, and all the doors were locked. Meanwhile Domitian grappled with Stephanus and bore him to the ground, where they struggled for a long time, while Domitian attempted to seize the dagger and to claw out his assailant's eyes with his lacerated fingers.

He died at the age of forty-four, on 18 September A.D. 96, in the fifteenth year of his reign. The body was carried away on a common litter by the public undertakers, as though he were a pauper; and cremated by his old nurse Phyllis in her garden outside the city on the Latin Way. She secretly took the ashes to the Temple of the Flavians and mixed them with those of his niece Julia, who had also been one of her charges.

18. Domitian had a ruddy complexion; large, rather weak eyes; and a modest expression. He was tall and well-made, except for his feet which had hammer-toes. Later, he lost his hair and developed a paunch; and, as a result of protracted illness, his legs grew spindling. He took as a personal insult any reference, joking or

19. Mime.

otherwise, to bald men, being extremely sensitive about his own baldness; yet in his manual *Care of the Hair*, which he published with a dedication to a friend, he wrote by way of mutual consolation:

Cannot you see that I, too, have a tall and beautiful person?

and added to this Homeric quotation the following prose comment:

Yet my hair will go the same way, and I am resigned to having an old man's head before my time. How pleasant it is to have good looks, yet how quickly that stage passes!

19. Domitian hated to exert himself. While in Rome he hardly ever went for a walk, and during campaigns and travels seldom rode a horse, but almost always used a litter. Weapons did not interest him, though he was an exceptionally keen archer. Many people have seen him shooting hundreds of wild animals of various kinds on his Alban estate, and sometimes deliberately bringing down a quarry with two successive arrows so dexterously placed in the head as to resemble horns. Occasionally he would tell a slave to post himself at a distance and hold out his right hand, with the fingers spread; then shot arrows between his fingers with such accuracy that the man was not harmed.

20. Although, at the beginning of his reign, he went to a great deal of trouble and expense in restocking the burned-out libraries, hunting everywhere for lost volumes, and sending scribes to Alexandria to transcribe and emend them, this did not mean that he was a student himself. No longer bothering with either history or poetry, or taking pains to acquire even the rudiments of a style, he now read nothing but Tiberius's note-books and official memoirs, and let secretaries polish his own correspondence, speeches and edicts. Still, Domitian had a lively turn of phrase, and some of his remarks are well worth recording. Once he said: 'Ah, to be as good-looking as Maecius thinks he is!' and on another occasion compared a friend's red hair, which was turning white, to 'mead spilt on snow'.

AFRICA. Suetonius was born in Hippo Regius in North Africa. During the period he describes, North Africa was fully integrated into the Roman Empire.

184 (above). The Medracen, a Numidian royal tomb, probably of the first century B.C. Numidia became a Roman province under Augustus.

185 (opposite). The Forum of Hippo Regius, where an inscription in honour of Suetonius has been discovered.

21. He also claimed that the lot of all Emperors is necessarily wretched, since only their assassination can convince the public that the conspiracies against their lives are real. His chief relaxation, at all hours, even on working days and in the mornings, was to throw dice. He used to bathe before noon, and then eat such an enormous lunch that a Matian apple[20] and a small pitcher of wine generally contented him at dinner. His many large banquets were never prolonged past sunset, or allowed to develop into drinking bouts; and he spent the rest of the day, until it was time to retire, strolling by himself in seclusion.

22. Domitian was extremely lustful, and called his constant sexual activities 'bed-wrestling', as though it were a sport. Some say that he preferred to depilate his concubines himself, and would go swimming with the commonest prostitutes. He had been offered the hand of his brother's daughter[21] while she was still a young girl, but persistently refused to marry her on account of his infatuation for Domitia. Later, however, when his niece took another husband, he seduced her, though Titus was still alive; and after both her father and husband were dead, demonstrated his love for her so openly and ardently that she became pregnant by

20. Named after Gaius Matius (Calvena), a friend of Caesar, Cicero and Augustus.
21. Julia the daughter of Titus.

him and died as the result of an abortion which he forced on her.

23. Though the general public greeted the news of Domitian's fate with indifference, it deeply grieved the troops, who at once began to speak of Domitian the God – they would have avenged him had anyone given them a lead, and indeed achieved this later on when they insisted that his assassins should be brought to justice. The senators, on the other hand, were delighted, and thronged to denounce the dead Domitian in the House with bitter and insulting cries. Then, sending for ladders, they had his votive shields and statues hurled down before their eyes and dashed to the ground; and ended by decreeing that all inscriptions referring to him must be effaced, and all records of his reign obliterated.

A few months before the murder a raven perched on the Capitol and croaked out the words: 'All will be well!' – a portent which some wag explained in the following verse:

> There was a raven, strange to tell,
>   Perched upon Jove's own gable, whence
> He tried to tell us 'All is well!' –
>   But had to use the future tense.[22]

Domitian himself is said to have dreamed that a golden hump sprouted from his back, interpreting this as a sure sign that the Empire would be richer and happier when he had gone; and soon the wisdom and restraint of his successors proved him right.

22. The raven was supposed to say 'Cras, cras' – 'tomorrow, tomorrow' – and medieval painters therefore adopted it as an emblem of hope.

186. THE ROMAN EMPIRE AT WORK. *Aerial view of Roman Timgad, founded in* A.D. *100. The streets in the foreground laid out on a chessboard plan belong to the first period of building.*

GENEALOGICAL TABLES
OF THE JULIAN AND FLAVIAN HOUSES

THE JULIAN HOUSE

C. Julius Caesar = Marcia

JULIUS CAESAR = Cornelia   M. Atius Balbus = Julia

Mucia = Pompey = Julia   C. Octavius = Atia

Sextus Pompeius   Scribonia = AUGUSTUS = Livia = Ti. Claudius Nero   Octavia = Antony

M. Agrippa = Julia = TIBERIUS = Vipsania   Drusus sen. = Antonia

Gaius Caesar   Lucius Caesar   Agrippina the elder = Germanicus   Agrippa Postumus   Drusus jun. = Julia Livilla* the elder   Germanicus = Agrippina the elder   CLAUDIUS = Messalina

Ti. Gemellus

Octavia   NERO   Britannicus

Nero Caesar   Drusus Caesar   GAIUS (Caligula)   Agrippina the younger = Cn. Domitius Ahenobarbus (later = CLAUDIUS)   Drusilla   Julia Livilla the younger

NERO

*Julia Livilla the elder was subsequently betrothed
to Lucius Aelius Sejanus, praetorian prefect.

THE FLAVIAN HOUSE

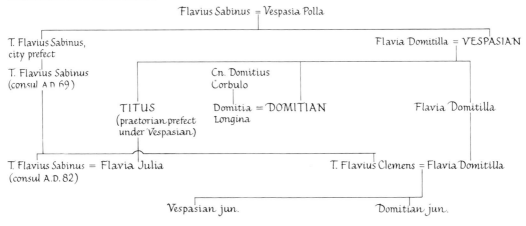

Flavius Sabinus = Vespasia Polla

T. Flavius Sabinus, city prefect   Flavia Domitilla = VESPASIAN

T. Flavius Sabinus (consul A.D. 69)

Cn. Domitius Corbulo

TITUS (praetorian prefect under Vespasian)   Domitia Longina = DOMITIAN   Flavia Domitilla

T. Flavius Sabinus = Flavia Julia (consul A.D. 82)   T. Flavius Clemens = Flavia Domitilla

Vespasian jun.   Domitian jun.

DATES OF THE TWELVE CAESARS

JULIUS CAESAR *dictator*   49–44 B.C.

and the following Emperors:

JULIO-CLAUDIAN DYNASTY

AUGUSTUS (assumed that name in 27 B.C.)   31 B.C.–A.D. 14

TIBERIUS   A.D. 14–37

GAIUS (Caligula)   37–41

CLAUDIUS   41–54

NERO   54–68

CIVIL WARS

GALBA   68–69

OTHO   69

VITELLIUS   69

FLAVIAN DYNASTY

VESPASIAN   69–79

TITUS   79–81

DOMITIAN   81–96

(The 'adoptive' Emperors, who followed, were Nerva, 96–98,
Trajan, 98–117,
and Hadrian, 117–138.)

KEY TO TERMS

AEDILES. Roman officials ranking above quaestors and below praetors. There were two branches of the aedilate, curule and plebeian, but by this time the functions of both related to little more than the care of the city of Rome.

AGENTS, IMPERIAL. This term is used here for the 'procurators' of the Emperor (see KNIGHTS), whom he employed to staff certain departments under his control, to manage his property and to handle the national finances in the provinces and armies for which he was directly responsible. (Other procurators served as governors of certain minor provinces.)

ASSEMBLY (*comitia*). Still officially the sovereign elective and legislative body, though almost powerless under the Emperors.

ATELLAN FARCES. A native Italian form of comedy, employing stock characters; it was named after Atella (near Aversa) in Campania.

AUGURS. The official Roman diviners; one of the four great Orders of Priesthood.

AUSPICES. Certain types of divination – particularly from birds – officially practised at elections, inaugurations of office, and entrances into a province, as well as in the conduct of wars. A general operating under the supreme command of another was subject to his auspices.

AUXILIARIES. Building on a Republican tradition, Augustus recruited a permanent auxiliary army (i.e. supplementary to the legions) of infantry and cavalry. The auxiliaries were officered by Roman citizens but were not citizens themselves, though from the time of Claudius, and perhaps earlier, they received citizenship on discharge.

BASILICA. A multi-purpose public meeting-hall such as regularly adjoined the Fora of towns in the western part of the Roman Empire.

BIREME. A ship with two banks of oars, one above the other.

CENSORS. Officials originally appointed every four (then, every five) years to draw up and maintain the list of citizens, and from the fourth century B.C. entrusted with the re-

vision of the list of senators as well. The last appointments outside the imperial family date from Augustus, who also assumed censorial powers himself. Claudius had himself made censor, and Domitian assumed the office for life.

CENTUMVIRAL COURT. Special civil court at Rome; or, more correctly, a panel numbering 105 persons during the Republic and 180 in the Empire, from which the members of the court were chosen.

CENTURIONS. The chief professional officers of the Roman army. There were about sixty in a legion, commanding between 100 and 1,000 men each and engaged in staff duties. Centurions were divided into a number of different grades, of which *primipilus* was the highest.

CHIEF PRIEST. The Pontifex Maximus was head of the Pontifices, the most important of the four great Orders of Priesthood; and he was thus the head of the entire state clergy. From 12 B.C. onwards successive Emperors held the office.

CLIENT KINGS. The rulers of states which although autonomous and (for the most part) outside the imperial frontiers formed part of the imperial system. In accordance with the ancient Roman institution of *clientela*, they were clients of the Emperor, and he was their *patronus*.

COHORT. A unit of the Roman army. There were ten cohorts in a legion, each divided into six centuries; and the Praetorian Guard and city troops and fire brigade were also divided into cohorts. So were auxiliary infantry units; and there were some mixed auxiliary units of infantry and cavalry combined.

COLONEL. This is the translation used here for *tribunus militum*, the title of senior officers of legions and metropolitan and auxiliary troops, partly of senatorial and partly of equestrian origin.

COLONY. Roman colonies (and *municipia*) were towns of which the inhabitants were Roman citizens, whereas in Latin colonies only the local officials possessed Roman citizenship.

COMITIUM. The chief place of political assembly in Republican Rome, north of the Forum. It was limited by Caesar to a small space.

CONSULS. The supreme elected civil and military officials of Rome, originally two in number, holding office for one year. Emperors accepted the office for themselves at intervals; and replacements during the year now became frequent, so as to spread the honour as widely as possible.

COUNCIL, IMPERIAL (*consilium principis*). A body of counsellors summoned by the Emperors (at first on an unofficial basis, serving for a period of six months) as a kind of Privy Council, to prepare business for the Senate, advise on administrative questions, and act as assessors in judicial inquiries.

CURRENCY. 4 *asses*= 1 *sestertius*. 4 *sestertii*= 1 *denarius*. 25 *denarii*= 1 *aureus*. The *as* was a copper coin, the *sestertius* and its half the *dupondius* were brass; these were token denominations. The *denarius* was of silver, and the *aureus* gold. Suetonius uses various sorts of reckoning, but in this translation sums of money are presented in gold pieces (*aurei*). The 'talent' was Greek.

DENARIUS. See CURRENCY.

DICTATOR. Originally a temporary, extraordinary, supreme office for an emergency, restricted to six months. Sulla assumed the power for an indefinite period but resigned it, and Caesar, after three renewals, assumed it permanently at the end of his life. After his death the dictatorship was abolished.

EQUESTRIAN ORDER. See KNIGHTS.

FETIALS. An ancient order of priestly officials who conducted rituals concerning international relationships, e.g., treaties and declarations.

FORUM. The chief public square of a town, surrounded by temples, halls and other buildings. At Rome, there was the ancient Forum Romanum, near which Caesar, Augustus, Domitian and Trajan created supplementary Fora bearing their names. The Forum begun by Domitian was known as the Forum of Nerva, or Transitorium.

FREEDMEN. Former slaves. A freed slave still owed deference and service to his former master (as client to patron), but his son, although supposed to maintain the family tie, became a full citizen.

GLADIATORS. Types mentioned here include 'Thracians' (who carried a curved scimitar and a small square or round shield, and wore two greaves), 'men-at-arms' (heavily armoured *hoplomachi*, successors of the 'Samnites', and *murmillones*, successors of the 'Gauls', who wore a representation of a fish, *mermylos*, in their helmets), and 'net and trident' fighters (the lightly clad *retiarii*, from *rete*, a net, in which they tried to ensnare their opponents).

GOVERNORS. The governors of provinces, of consular or praetorian rank, included the proconsuls of senatorial provinces and the *legati pro praetore of imperial provinces*. Governors of knightly (equestrian) status were the prefect of Egypt and the procurators of certain minor provinces including Judaea (of which the governor, however, was at first designated prefect).

GUARD. The Emperors had two personal bodyguards, one of Germans and the other the Praetorian Guard (q.v.), to which 'Guard' generally refers.

GUILDS or Corporations (*collegia*). Clubs composed of men practising the same trade or craft; they were often burial clubs in origin, and included other philanthropic activities, but their principal purposes were social.

IMPERATOR. (1) A general title for Roman commanders. (2) The title by which they were saluted after a victory. (3) The title which Emperors employed as a prefix (*praenomen*) to indicate their imperial position. Augustus, Nero (late in his reign) and Otho adopted this practice, and Vespasian definitively incorporated the *praenomen* into the imperial titulature.

KINGS. In the earliest stages of Roman history there were kings at Rome, before the establishment of the Republic which probably took place shortly before 500 B.C. The kings of imperial date referred to by Suetonius are mostly client kings (q.v.) of Rome, with the exception of the King of Parthia, beyond the eastern frontier, who was independent.

KNIGHTS (*equites*, the equestrian order). The order next in importance to the Senate, with a minimum property qualification of 400,000 *sestertii* (4,000 gold pieces). In the later Republic, it included large landowners, with interests similar to those of senators, and financiers, whose interests clashed with those of senators in the provinces. Augustus reformed the order which henceforward provided the occupants of many administrative posts.

LEGION. The principal unit of the Roman army, comprising 5,000 infantry and 120 cavalry; auxiliary troops, too, were often united under the same command during military operations.

LIBURNIAN (*liburna, liburnica*). A light and fast warship invented by the Illyrian Liburni and taken over for the imperial fleet.

MARINES (*classiarii*). Together with the lower grade of sailors, they manned the imperial fleet; most were freedmen. They were expected to serve for twenty-six years, a year longer than the auxiliaries.

MASTER OF THE HORSE. In the Republic, an official nominated by a dictator to represent him either on the field of battle or at Rome.

MEN-AT-ARMS. See GLADIATORS.

MIME (*fabula riciniata*). Semi-dramatic solo dances, in which the performers used gesture, voice and feature in their imitations. In imperial times the mime and pantomime (q.v.) enjoyed enormous popularity.

NET-AND-TRIDENT FIGHTERS. See GLADIATORS.

OVATION. A lesser triumph (q.v.).

PANTOMIME. The very popular, sophisticated ballets of the *pantomimi*, who danced traditional themes in dumb-show, with music and chorus. First seen at Rome under Augustus.

PATRICIANS. An inner circle of the most ancient aristocratic families. Fourteen patrician clans (*gentes*), comprising thirty families, still survived at the beginning of the imperial epoch.

PLEBEIANS. The general body of Roman citizens, as opposed to the patricians.

PRAETORIAN GUARD. The imperial bodyguard organized by Augustus in nine cohorts, 1,000 strong. In the reign of Tiberius, Sejanus concentrated them in a single camp (A.D. 23). Gaius added three cohorts, Vitellius added four more (employing legionaries from Germany as his praetorians), Vespasian reverted to the Augustan total, and Domitian (?) added one cohort.

PRAETORS. The state officials next in importance to the consuls; the most important was the city praetor (*praetor urbanus*). In the earlier imperial period there were usually twelve praetors; it was Tiberius's practice to nominate four of them.

PREFECT. The Prefect of the Camp was the legionary camp commandant, an ex-centurion with administrative duties. See also GOVERNOR.

PRIESTS. The four principal priestly colleges were the *Pontifices* (to whom the term 'priest' generally refers), the augurs (q.v.), the Board of Fifteen (for religious ceremonies), and the Fetials (q.v.). See also CHIEF PRIEST.

PRIVY PURSE. The term used here for the *fiscus*, or imperial (as opposed to public) treasury. The nature and origin of this institution is disputed, and it is suspected that Suetonius's references are inexact and anachronistic.

PROCURATOR. See AGENTS, GOVERNORS.

QUAESTORS. The lowest office of state in the senator's official career, ranking below the aedilate and tribunate (q.v.). From the time of Augustus onward there were twenty quaestors, many of them attached as finance officers and assistants to the governors of senatorial provinces.

QUINQUEREME. The standard warship in the fleets of the Hellenistic states and the Roman Republic, still used, in a less important capacity, in the imperial fleet. Probably groups of five oarsmen pulled a single large oar.

SATURNALIA. Festival of Saturn in December, from which Christmas originated.

SENATE. Still the chief (technically advisory) council of the state, though severely limited in power by the Emperors, under whom, however, it developed far-reaching judicial functions. Augustus fixed membership at 600 and minimum property qualification at 1 million *sestertii* (10,000 gold pieces). The Senate was automatically recruited from quaestors (q.v.).

SESTERTIUS. See CURRENCY.

'THRACIANS'. See GLADIATORS.

TREASURY, PUBLIC (*aerarium Saturni*). Still the state treasury at Rome, although the Privy Purse (q.v.) and military treasury (*aerarium militare*) also now played a leading part in financial activity and policy.

TRIBUNES OF THE PEOPLE. A step in the senatorial career (for plebeians) corresponding with the aedilate (q.v.). Nero further restricted the powers of both. The ancient 'democratic' powers of the tribunate had long since vanished: but see TRIBUNICIAN POWER.

TRIBUNICIAN POWER. Augustus, followed by his successors, selected this (divorced from office) as the most distinctive prerogative of the Emperor (who numbered his regnal years by it). This was largely because of the antique, revered, long since obsolete, 'democratic' powers of the tribunes of the people (q.v.), empowering them to 'protect' the citizenry by intercession and veto. Emperors found the power useful, too, as a legal basis for the introduction of measures in the Senate. They also arranged for it to be conferred on their principal collaborators and, before long, on heirs within the imperial family.

TRIREME. The principal warship of the Roman fleet. Its arrangement is much disputed; probably three men rowed their individual oars through one port, sitting on a single bench.

TRIUMPH. The traditional procession of a victorious Roman to the temple of Jupiter Best and Greatest on the Capitoline Hill. Under the Empire, triumphs soon became a monopoly of the Emperor and his family, but victorious generals (and others) could be granted 'triumphal' ornaments.

TRIUMVIRS. The First Triumvirate (60 B.C.) was an informal compact between Pompey, Crassus and Caesar; the Second (43 B.C.) was an official, quasi-dictatorial, commission conferred upon Antony, Octavian (the future Augustus) and Lepidus.

TROY GAME (*Lusus Troiae*). Military and sporting exercises carried out by Roman boys destined for official careers. This institution was revived by Augustus and led by his grandsons Gaius and Lucius as Princes of Youth (*principes iuventutis*).

VESTAL VIRGINS. Normally six in number, they served the goddess Vesta in her temple beside the Forum, residing near by. They served, in historical times, for thirty years, during which they had to remain virgin. They received numerous privileges, and the Chief Vestal Virgin was a greatly revered figure.

SOME BOOKS ABOUT SUETONIUS

E. CIZEK, *Structure et idéologie dans les vies des douze Césars de Suétone*, Les Belles Lettres, Paris, 1977

G. D'ANNA, *Le idee letterarie di Svetonio*, La Nuova Italia, Florence, 1954

F. DELLA CORTE, *Svetonio: eques Romanus*, 2nd ed., La Nuova Italia, Florence, 1967

M. GRANT, *The Ancient Historians*, Weidenfeld and Nicolson, London, and Scribners, New York, 1970

M. GRANT, *The Twelve Caesars*, Weidenfeld and Nicolson, London, and Scribners, New York, 1975

C. GRASSI, *Svetonio*, 1972

H. GUGEL, *Studien zur biographischen Technik Suetons*, Wiener Studien Beiheft 7, Vienna, 1977

W. STEIDLE, *Sueton und die antike Biographie*, Zetemata 1, Beck, Munich, 1951

D. R. STUART, *Epochs of Greek and Roman Biography*, University of California, Berkeley, 1928 (reprint 1967)

G. B. TOWNEND in T. A. Dorey (ed.), *Latin Biography*, Routledge and Kegan Paul, London, 1967

P. VENINI, *Sulla tecnica compositiva Svetoniana*, 1975

INDEX
OF PERSONAL NAMES AND PEOPLES

Except for members of the imperial family, whose best-known name is generally given,
Romans are mostly designated here by the name of their family (*gens*).*
Page numbers in *italic* refer to illustrations.

*The following (ancient) abbreviations are used for Roman first
names (*praenomina*): A.: Aulus; Ap.: Appius; C. Gaius; Cn.:
Gnaeus; Dec.: Decimus; L. Lucius; M.: Marcus; Man.: Manius;
P.: Publius; Q.: Quintus; Sex.: Sextus; T.: Titus; Ti.: Tiberius.

ACKNOWLEDGEMENTS

COLOUR ESSAY ILLUSTRATIONS

NATURE AND THE GODS (between pages 56 and 57): 1 and 5. Museo del Terme, Rome (photo: Scala); 2. Staatliche Museen, Berlin (East) (photo: Museum); 3. Museo Nazionale, Naples (photo: M. Henig, Oxford); 4. (photo: J. C. Allen, Lincoln); 6 and 7. Museo Nazionale, Naples (photo: Scala); 8. Kunsthistorisches Museum, Vienna (photo: © Photo Meyer, Vienna); 9. Museum, Tripoli (photo: Scala); 10. Museo Nazionale, Naples (photo: Leonard von Matt, Buochs).

TOWNS (between pages 104 and 105): 1 and 3. (photo: Metropolitan Museum, New York, Rogers Fund 1903); 2, 7, 8 and 9. (photo: Werner Forman Archive, London); 4 and 5. Museo Nazionale, Naples (photo: Scala); 6. Museo Arqueológico, Barcelona (photo: MAS); 10. (photo: Roger Wood, London).

LIVING AND THE FAMILY (between pages 152 and 153): 1 and 5. (photo: The Metropolitan Museum of Art, New York, Rogers Fund, 1903); 2. Staatliche Museen, Berlin (East) (photo: Museum); 3. (photo: J. C. Allen, Lincoln); 4. (photo: Werner Forman Archive, London); 6 and 8. Courtesy of the Trustees of the British Museum (photo: Museum): 7. (photo: V. Sharp, Oxford); 9. Museo Nazionale, Naples (photo: Scala).

EMPEROR AND EMPIRE (between pages 216 and 217): 1. Antikenmuseum, Staatliche Museen, Berlin (West) (photo: Ingrid Geske); 2, 4 and 5. (photo: J. C. Allen, Lincoln); 3. Colchester and Essex Museum (photo: Museum); 6. Kunsthistorisches Museum, Vienna (photo: © Photo Meyer, Vienna); 7. Museo Nazionale, Naples (photo: Scala); 8. (photo: Jon Wyand): 9. Fitzwilliam Museum, Cambridge (photo: Museum).

BLACK AND WHITE ILLUSTRATIONS

Alinari, Mansell Collection: 6–8, 26, 48, 81, 85, 90, 98, 129, 152, 175, 177; Anderson, Mansell Collection: 21, 96; Musée des Antiquités Nationales, St-Germain-en-Laye: 12, 20; Archives Photographiques, Paris/S.P.A.D.E.M.: 71; Ashmolean Museum, Oxford: 32, 110; Bath City Council: 142; Courtesy of the Trustees of the British Museum: 13, 17, 25, 33, 45, 46, 60, 62, 93, 99, 106, 118, 120, 123, 127, 153, 154, 171–3; Musée Calvert, Avignon: 163; Gerald Cinamon, London: 137; Cleveland Museum of Art, Purchase from the J. H. Wade Fund: 119; Damascus National Museum: 134, 135; Durham University: 109; Musée Fénaille, Rodez: 78: Fitzwilliam Museum, Cambridge: 148, 179; Werner Forman Archive, London: 185; Fototeca Unione, Rome: 9, 14, 15; German Archaeological Institute, Rome: 1–4, 16, 18, 19, 23, 24, 27, 30, 31, 35–8, 40, 43, 47, 49, 55–9, 61, 64–8, 72, 82, 84, 86, 91, 92, 94–6, 100, 104, 105, 111, 112, 117, 124, 125, 130, 132, 143, 144, 146, 149, 155–60, 164, 168, 169, 174, 178, 180, 183; Photographie Giraudon, Paris: 50, 51, 70; Martin Henning, Oxford: 182; Hirmer Fotoarchiv, Munich: 22, 28, 87, 88, 114–16, 128, 129, 136, 167; Hunterian Museum, Glasgow: 147, 161, 181; S. F. James, Dorset: 34; A. F. Kersting, London: 39; H. Koppermann, Munich: 63; Landesmuseum, Trier: 10, 75, 163; Musée du Louvre, Paris: 5, 52, 79: W. MacDonald, Massachusetts: 41; MAS, Barcelona: 138–41, 165, 166; Mittelrheinisches Landesmuseum, Mainz: 73, 74, 76; Nationalmusset, Copenhagen: 29; Ny Carlsberg Glyptotek, Copenhagen: 11, 54, 131; Photo Ofalec: 184, 186; Réunion des Musées Nationaux, Paris: 42, 44, 80, 134; Rheinisches Landesmuseum, Bonn: 69, 77; Society of London Antiquaries: 108; Staatliche Museen, Berlin (East): 89, 121; Staatliche Museen, Berlin (West): 101, 113; Victor Thomke, Bingen: 53.